Burglary Blues

A Lexie Sarcone/Michael Riley
Romantic Suspense Novel

Elisa Archer

This is a work of fiction. Names, characters, places, events, and other concepts are the product of the author's imagination or are used fictitiously. Any resemblance to actual persons, living or dead, places, establishments, events, and locations is entirely coincidental.

A Modus Operandi imprint

ISBN: 1942710003
ISBN-13: 978-1-942710-00-4

For my muse

OTHER BOOKS IN THE LEXIE SARCONE SERIES:

Burglary Blues

Break-ins and Bouquets

Compromised Position

Deadly Liaisons

Undercover Engagement

ONE

"Alessandra Sarcone?"

My eyes shot up at the sound of my name, the ridiculously long, ethnic sounding moniker that my parents had stuck me with as a tribute to my father's grandmother. We were Americans. Somewhere down the line, I had an Italian heritage, complete with dark brown hair and olive skin. But I didn't speak Italian. I didn't even know the proper way to pronounce half the desserts or cheeses when I was ordering in a restaurant. But just like a bad cliché, I became one of the city's finest.

Movies and television shows portrayed those with my heritage as either gangsters or coppers, and I knew a fair share of each. So maybe the stereotype wasn't entirely inaccurate. Thankfully, no one in my immediate family was named Carmine or Guido. Then again, who knew what my distant relatives back in the old country called themselves. I snorted at the insane rambling that played through my head. It was something that happened when I was nervous, and since my transfer from vice, I was nothing but a walking, talking bundle of nerves. I was still feeling out my new co-workers. A few of my fellow officers were also recent transfers to the division, but it didn't make me feel any better. As it was, the lieutenant in charge of roll call this morning didn't even know my name.

"It's Lexie, sir," I corrected, blushing.

My transfer to burglary division had come after a harrowing experience that placed me in the crosshairs of some Jack the Ripper wannabe. And after assisting the female homicide lieutenant in nailing the asshole to the wall, my undercover vice days were behind me. However, being a brunette with a decent rack and shapely figure had immediately made the male brass at the precinct believe that I was incapable of anything other than being a decoy hooker, and admittedly, a lot of johns had been fooled by the bright red lipstick and thick eyeliner.

"Whatever, Sarcone. I was just making sure you were here," Lieutenant Peterson muttered as he continued through roll call, passing out ride along assignments.

As I waited to figure out who my partner was going to be for today's tour, a detective I had never seen before entered the room. My eyes immediately roamed over his body. He had broad shoulders, a narrow waist, and under the fitted navy shirt he wore was the outline of washboard abs. Glancing at his face, I found piercing blue eyes, a strong jaw with a day's worth of stubble, and short dark brown, nearly black, hair. It was longer than a crew cut. Frankly, it was just long enough to give a girl something to tug on. Shaking off my thoughts, which were traveling into the gutter, I blew out a slow, calming breath.

It had been two years since I'd been intimately

involved with anyone. My last boyfriend had decided he was too macho to date a cop, and once I was accepted into the police academy, he had been accepted into some blonde bimbo's bed. I hoped she gave him the clap. Anyway, I had better things to focus on besides men, except parading around street corners in skimpy skirts and barely there tops had attracted plenty of men. Thankfully, the vast majority were seedy or sleazy enough to make me cringe and stick to being celibate. However, that was how things had been when I was working vice. This was burglary. And the detective who just entered roll call was a tall glass of water, and I ached to get wet.

Stop it, Sarcone, my internal voice snapped.

The detective turned away from us, speaking to the lieutenant. The two men seemed to be in a heated debate, and based on rank alone, the detective probably should have shown a bit more respect. However, Lieutenant Peterson flipped through the roll call sheet, handing it over. A few seconds later, an agreement was reached.

"Are you sure?" the lieutenant asked, and Detective Strong, Dark, and Ruggedly Handsome nodded. "Okay. But these are the newest additions to the division, so don't come crying to me when they screw up your investigation." The lieutenant looked up, surveying the room of bored uniformed officers seated in front of him. "Hawking, Kemper, and Sarcone, follow Detective Riley. You're not patrolling today, so he'll brief you on what you will be doing."

Ducking my head to try to hide my embarrassment due to my brief, x-rated thoughts, I followed the other two officers out of the room. No one said a word as we went up the stairs and into one of the squad rooms. A couple of first grade detectives were sipping lattes and studying case files. I didn't know any of them by name, and I glanced at the gold nameplates on their desks, trying to familiarize myself. The empty desk boasted the nameplate Detective Michael Riley. That must be the man that freed me from the tedium of patrolling today.

The other two desks were occupied by Detectives Jack Lieberman and Samantha Preston. Lieberman was known by his reputation for being a hardnosed, no-nonsense cop. And Preston was the only female first grade burglary detective. She and Lieberman barely glanced up from the paperwork as our posse entered the room.

"I'm glad you brought us some gofers, Michael," Detective Lieberman whispered to Riley, just loud enough that I heard the comment. Great, we were going to be doing the legwork for the detectives or perhaps updating their files.

"You said we needed help," Riley remarked, "so I brought us help. The lieutenant gave them each a gold star for eagerness. So I'm sure they'll be up for any challenge we can throw at them." Riley noticed my gaze and winked. If only I could disappear.

"Okay, here's the deal, people," Lieberman said, standing up and looking at the group assembled. "There have been a string of B&Es around this neighborhood, and until we figure out who's responsible, we gotta go knock on some doors, ask some questions, and be a pain in everyone's ass. Since most of us have better things to do, like investigate the liquor store and gas station robberies that occurred two nights ago, we're going to have you go knock on some doors. It's called canvassing. Maybe you heard about it in the academy."

Officer Hawking, the oldest of the three of us, nodded his head. He had served in the military and knew it was important to be respectful to a superior.

Officer Kemper was smart enough to follow his buddy's example, but I always had a slight attitude problem. And since the three of us had been cops for at least two years prior to joining burglary division, there was no need for Lieberman to treat us like rookies.

"Canvassing?" I asked, hiding my smirk. "But don't you think we might need some gear for that? Maybe a couple of paintbrushes and some acrylics?" I turned to the two uniformed officers. "Unless you guys rather work with oils or watercolors."

Hawking remained stone-faced, and Kemper snorted. At least someone was amused. But the room immediately went silent, and the temperature dropped ten degrees when Lieberman took a step toward me.

"Oh, you're being funny. You think you're a funny girl?" Lieberman looked annoyed. "Do you think it's funny that hardworking people have been coming home from third shift and finding their apartments cleaned out?"

"No, sir," I muttered, hating that he had just put me in my place. One of these days, I would stop being such a wiseass.

"Then get to work," he ordered.

He pointed to the open manila folder on top of his desk. It contained the addresses of the buildings that had been burglarized, so the three of us wrote down the information and marched out of the room after being properly dismissed.

~*~

This neighborhood had become a hotbed for crime. A few automobiles had been jacked, but the number of thefts wasn't substantial enough to warrant our investigation. The real problem was the home invasions. One of the neighborhood gangs was initiating new members into their crew, and the going price of admission was jewelry, electronics, and cash. Weapons, particularly handguns, were all the rage. And the vast majority of items stolen fell into one of those four categories.

The problem was no one knew who was behind it. And the neighbors that had been home at the time were either asleep or pretended to be. It was likely they didn't want to get roped into police or court proceedings. And I couldn't blame them. Gangs were scary. Drive-bys were commonplace, and payback was indeed a bitch. These innocent, hardworking people weren't crooks or part of the criminal lifestyle, but by speaking out, they feared they'd jeopardize themselves or their families. Then again, there were a few helpful citizens that would say or do just about anything for the attention, so it was a tossup to determine if no information or too much information was more cumbersome to the investigation.

After a final interview at our current location, I went down the steps, glancing at the top corners of the interior hallways, but I didn't find a single security camera in sight. Why couldn't we get lucky?

"How'd you guys do?" I asked, sidling up to Hawking and Kemper.

"I got spit on," Hawking complained as we met outside the second building we had canvassed. "I tried to ask a simple question, and this old woman spat on me."

"She must not be a fan of the uniform," Kemper snorted. "There was this smokin' hot chick in 2B that couldn't take her hands off of me. I think she watched that stripper movie one too many times because she kept asking if I was wearing a thong."

"Are you?" I teased, and Kemper sashayed his hips and rubbed his palms down his chest.

"Did you learn nothing from joking around this morning?" Hawking inquired as we went back to the patrol car. "Lieberman was furious. I thought he was going to crap his pants since no one ever mouths off to him like that. You need to watch it, unless you want to get demoted to meter maid."

"We aren't rookies," I defended. "For the past year, I've been trying to sell my ass to half the city and arresting the men who planned to take me up on that offer. I transferred to burglary in the hopes of getting some respect, but apparently that's a pipe dream." The three of us got into the car and went to the last location listed on the sheet. "You've both been in burglary a bit longer than I have. What can you tell me about the detectives?"

"Lieberman is a hard ass. He thinks he's the only real cop in the entire precinct. He's a bit of a narcissistic blowhard if you ask me. Most of us ignore him, even the other detectives. Um, Preston is quiet and serious. She'll get the work done, but you won't see her sitting at a desk once the case is closed. As soon as her shift's over, she's out of there. A couple of uniforms have a pool going on whether or not she has a secret family and kids or if the reason for her fast getaways has to do with a certain ex-lover," Kemper said.

"What ex-lover?" It was unsubstantiated gossip, but it was a fun distraction.

"Rumor has it she used to be hot and heavy with Riley. They worked a bunch of stakeouts together," Hawking said. "But as far as I'm concerned, it's all just hearsay."

"C'mon, man, late nights in a car with nothing else to do," Kemper said before mimicking seventies porn music. “Bow chicka wow-wow.”

“Remind me not to spend any late nights in a car with you, Kemper,” I added.

“Trust me, I’m too hot for you to handle, Sarcone.” He flipped down the vanity mirror and winked. “But for whatever the reason, it seems like she tries to distance herself from Riley.”

“Does Detective Riley avoid her too?” There was no point in inquiring, but the topic had piqued my interest. Plus, this was only friendly conversation.

“Not that I’ve noticed,” Hawking said, narrowing his eyes at me through the rearview mirror. “Does someone have a crush?”

“No. Not in the least,” I said vehemently.

The two of them exchanged a glance and teased me mercilessly for the rest of the ride. It was a relief when we got out of the car to canvass the final building for today’s tour. To save time, we were splitting up again. It was a routine check with the neighbors. We were here to ask a couple of questions and continue on our way. There really wasn’t a need to have back-up, and splitting up saved time.

As I stepped onto the third floor landing, I heard a commotion coming from the end of the hallway. A man and woman were screaming, but their words were garbled. Assuming it was a run-of-the-mill argument, I resisted the urge to radio for assistance, instead waiting to see if the commotion would die down naturally. A few seconds later, the voices quieted.

Returning to my task, I knocked on the first door to the right. It was apartment 307, the scene of last night’s break-in. According to the police report, a television, Blu-ray player, laptop, and two tablets were stolen from inside. The apartment owner hadn’t been home at the time of the robbery. He had been picking up an extra shift at work. I knocked again, but there was no answer.

"Sir, this is the police. Open up," I called through the thick door.

All at once, the door at the end of the hallway swung open, and a man wearing a dark hoodie bolted from the apartment. He flew past me before I even had time to process what was happening. He had a backpack shoved over his shoulder, and as he sprinted past me, a jewelry box fell out of the bag.

"Stop," I yelled. "Police. Freeze." The suspect continued to flee, and I clicked the radio, requesting back-up, as I darted after him. As I raced down the two flights of steps, Kemper came down the stairs from the floor above to assist. "Evidence is on the third floor," I called up to him. "Grab it. We need to establish chain of custody."

The suspect burst through the front door and ran to the left. I sprinted after him, gaining as we went down the next street. He was approaching a crosswalk, and just when I was close enough to take him down, an unmarked cruiser rolled to a stop in front of him. The suspect collided with the car and fell backward, his bag of loot spilling onto the ground.

"Officer Sarcone," Detective Riley greeted as he handcuffed the perpetrator, "I believe you called for back-up."

"Uh-huh." Inhaling ragged gasps, I put my hands on my head and forced my lungs to fill completely.

"Good job." Riley pushed the handcuffed guy into the back of the car, just as Kemper and Hawking came up behind me. "Did you secure the area?" he asked them.

"Yes, another unit is at the apartment," Hawking responded. He had put the jewelry box inside an evidence bag. "I think he dropped this."

"He did," I said firmly.

"Okay." Riley took the bag. "Sarcone, let's take a ride."

TWO

Riley pulled the cruiser to a stop underneath an overpass and turned off the engine. The thief was still handcuffed in the back, but that fact didn't seem to matter. His attention was focused on the food carts and trucks parked in front of us.

"Sarcone, it's lunchtime. Why don't you go get us a few hot dogs?"

"Um...okay," I said, confused by his casual comments and lackadaisical attitude when we had a perp handcuffed in the back of the car.

Before I could say another word or ask a question, Riley turned around and spoke to our suspect. "What do you want, Frank?"

"Turkey dog with kraut and mustard and make sure they hold the relish," the suspect replied. "The last time I said no relish, they gave me extra relish."

"What the hell?" I shifted my confused look back to Riley.

"Don't worry about it," Frank the Suspect said from the back seat. "Mikey and I go way back. So far back in fact, that it's his turn to buy lunch."

"So you're a frequent flyer or a C.I. or something?" The confusion was apparent on my face, and Riley hid his laughter in a phony cough.

"Not exactly." The suspect leaned forward, and a second later, he pulled his hands free from behind his back. The handcuffs hung ineffectually from his left wrist, and he offered his hand. "I'm Frank Devereaux, the one stop shop for all your undercover needs."

"Just get us some lunch, Sarcone," Riley sighed, unhooking the other bracelet from Frank's wrist. "This guy will toot his own horn all day if you keep asking him questions." He pulled a twenty from his pocket and held it out. "Whatever you want is on me."

True, I thought wistfully as I climbed out of the car and headed for the hot dog stand. Although answers might have been more practical than fetching lunch or fantasizing about one of the detectives.

By the time I made it back to the car with a sack of hot dogs and fries, Riley and Frank were in the midst of a heated discussion. I ate in silence as I listened to Frank and Michael talk about last night's baseball game. Neither mentioned a word about the current case or why an undercover cop had broken into an apartment in the building we were canvassing or had fled the scene. None of it sat right with me, but I was just a gofer. Plus, I was positive the only reason Riley let me ride with him was so I could go get the hot dogs.

"Okay, the coast is clear," Riley announced after Frank finished eating his lunch. "Just watch yourself out there. If we arrest you again, we're going to have to make it look real and book you. Today, you were lucky that Sarcone didn't cuff you before I arrived, or someone would have spotted you on the street and expected to see you in lockup."

"Sure, sure," Frank said as he opened the car door. "I'll catch you guys later." And he disappeared down the street.

"So, Alessandra," Riley said, turning to face me, "tell me about yourself."

"It's Lexie. Sarcone. Your personal assistant assigned to retrieve lunch. Whatever." I was annoyed for being made a fool, particularly by some hotshot detective who despite his jackass demeanor was still too attractive for his own good. "I transferred from vice. And before you make some smartass joke about that, just know that I've heard them all already."

He smirked. "I wouldn't dream of it." He grabbed a fry out of the bag and nibbled it. Then he wiped his mouth. "Hey, you've got something right there." He leaned in and ran his thumb across my bottom lip. Instantly, my heart fluttered, and I stared out the windshield, afraid he would notice my blush. He pulled his hand away. "Ketchup," he announced. "Apparently there was a fatality involving a tomato."

"Cute."

"Yes, you are. That's why they had you working vice, isn't it?"

I looked at him and shrugged. Did he just give me a compliment? Or was that flirting? I had been out of the game so long I didn't remember what a guy making a move looked like. Obviously, I was out of my mind if I even thought someone like him would have any interest in me.

"I'm sorry about today. Lieberman likes to play ops close to the vest. Frank has infiltrated a local gang we believe is responsible for the recent home invasions. The apartment he ransacked was a plant, so he could get into the gang's good graces. It's all good. The back-up unit who responded to your call is aware of the situation. So," his eyes penetrated through my soul,

"I'm sure no one will hold today against you. After all, you were just doing your job. And you did it incredibly well. Too well, in fact."

"That's me. Always striving for a job well done." *What a stupid thing to say*, I criticized. Obviously, being around Riley had turned my normally competent self into a bumbling idiot.

"I enjoy a well done job." His voice sounded sultry.

Stop thinking these things. There is no double meaning. He's just trying to be polite because he thinks you're a complete moron. And being polite is what you do when you're around stupid people so they don't feel quite so stupid.

"Um, okay," I mumbled. He was still staring, and I wondered if I was completely covered in ketchup. "Shouldn't we get back to the station? Don't I need to fill out a report or something?"

"I guess we should get back, so you can get to it." He put the car in gear and pulled into traffic. "So why'd you become a cop? It seems to me someone as pretty as you could have done something else. Lawyer, doctor, artist, model. Whatever." He smiled. "I don't think anyone could deny you anything."

I snickered. "Yeah, I had plenty of options. It was either this or work in my parents' luggage shop. And frankly, I hate luggage. This makes more sense. The work we do is important. Growing up, my family didn't always live in the best neighborhoods. A lot of neighbors and friends were targeted by some of the crime families. The neighborhood shops had to pay protection to organized crime. Occasionally, someone would just vanish. It wasn't a good situation."

"Where'd you grow up?"

"On the southside, before it was gentrified. Organized crime was on the way out, but a few of the established families hung on as long as they could.

Not to be a bad joke, but you know how things go in the Italian neighborhoods."

"I hear it's like that now in Little Moscow and parts of Chinatown. OCU has its hands full. Damn, you must be one tough lady."

I shrugged. "Not really. It was just how things were. My parents moved out of the neighborhood when I started high school, and we left that world behind."

"Not all of it. Something stuck."

"Maybe." I fell silent, contemplating how my life might have gone differently if I hadn't always been driven to right the wrongs I had seen as a kid.

He nodded a few times. "Is that why you left vice for burglary?"

"No. I never wanted to work vice. Being female and a cop already comes with enough objectification, but those perverts take it to an entirely different level. Plus, shit got real when I was on the job. Do you remember that serial killer that we put away a few months ago? I worked with homicide on making that bust. They sent me out as bait. After that, I needed a change." I chuckled. "It's funny though because that was the only case I ever worked that really seemed to matter. The rest of them were just demeaning. So a transfer was in order, but it also came with a lot of snickers behind my back. A lot of guys around the precinct talk. At this point, I don't even hear the sexist remarks and harassment anymore. I think it's because I've dealt with much worse."

"You shouldn't let them get away with it," Riley protested. "If someone's being a dick, you should report him."

"Yeah, and we both know how that's likely to turn out." We remained quiet for a few minutes, and then I asked, "So Detective Riley, how long have you been on the job?"

"It's Michael." He dazzled me with a bright smile. "If we're going to be working together, we should be on a first name basis. And I've been doing this for six years. It's our family business. My dad was a cop, his dad, and his dad. Both of my brothers are cops. It wasn't a decision so much as a way of life." He stopped for a traffic light. "Anyway, getting back to business for a sec, if Frank had been an actual perp, you would have made a fantastic collar today. I feel responsible for ruining it, especially since you're still struggling to make a name for yourself in this division. So would you be willing to stick around and help out the current team on the apartment heists, or did you have your heart set on picking up new cases every day from the lieutenant during roll call? I can't promise that this will be as exciting as stopping a serial killer, but it might be better than walking the beat."

"I guess I can help out." I wanted to appear smooth, even though I was practically jumping at the opportunity. This was a big case. It could help with a promotion since I had been considering the detective's exam, and it would mean enjoying some eye candy.

"Great." He gave me a friendly smile as he parked in the back lot at the precinct. "I'm happy to be the first to welcome you to the team."

He walked around the car and extended his hand. We shook, and goosebumps erupted on my skin at the slight jolt from his touch. I really must be hard pressed for a guy to be reacting like this.

"Thanks, Detect...Michael."

He slung an arm around my shoulders in a friendly manner and escorted me inside to share the news with the other two detectives.

~*~

Despite the fact that I had been invited to work the investigation with the detectives, Lieberman and Preston kept me at arms' length. I was an officer, only on the job for a little over two years, and unless someone needed me to take my clothes off and try to solicit sex, they saw no practical use for me. Michael was the only exception. He took me along with him on calls and let me spitball ideas about means, motive, and opportunity.

As it was, the break-ins still hadn't stopped. Four handguns and two hunting rifles had been stolen, along with estimated cash and property worth twenty-two thousand dollars. With a dozen burglarized apartments, the value of stolen items was rapidly increasing. Additional cruisers were sent to patrol the area at night, but until the gang initiation was over, the crime spree was likely to continue.

The detectives were attempting to split their time between the larger thefts and the home invasions, but there were only so many hours in the day. Kemper, Hawking, and I were still assisting by performing the grunt work and following up with the victims. I had been taking copious amounts of notes and sharing the intel with the three detectives.

Lieberman always appeared bored, and Preston barely even glanced in my direction as she read through her case files and clicked on the keyboard. Michael was the only one who actually seemed to care what progress was being made. Then again, from the whispers and looks, it was obvious that he was in charge of keeping Kemper, Hawking, and me in line, so maybe that's why he cared so much.

It was getting late, and Preston had just escaped from her desk, making a beeline for the exit. I spotted

Kemper across the room, and he looked pointedly at her retreating back. Ignoring his intended message, I typed the last few words from my notepad into the word processing program and saved my file on the computer.

"Why do you do that?" Riley asked, rolling his chair next to mine.

"It makes life easier. Everything is just one click away," I said in my best infomercial voice. "This way, if I need to reference my notes, I can hit control plus f, type in a key phrase, and voila."

I reached for the keyboard to demonstrate, and our fingertips touched. Again, I felt the same electric intensity I did the day we first met. Riley must have felt it too because he ran his pointer finger up the back of my hand, from my fingernail to my wrist, sending wonderful tingles throughout my body.

"Sorry," his voice sounded hoarse, but I probably imagined it. "Can you print a few copies of your notes out? I like to keep things organized in the file folders. It's easier for briefings and reviewing the intel when everything's in one place."

"Sure, no problem." I hit print and waited for the ancient community printer in the corner of the room to fire up. When it started whirring, I went to collect the pages. "Here ya go. I made three copies. Is that sufficient?"

"It's excellent." He smiled. "And with that, I'm calling it a night." He stuffed the sheets into the case file and locked it inside his top desk drawer. Then he slipped into his jacket, pulling the hem free from his holster. "Would you like to grab a drink?" My mouth must have dropped because he quickly added, "A bunch of us are going across the street to the bar."

"Oh, um," I must have resembled a deer in headlights because Michael was clearly amused by my expression, "I have other plans."

"A date?"

"Excuse me?"

"Do you have a date?"

"No. Nothing like that." I shook my head. And he chuckled. "Not that dating is a bad thing. I just don't. I mean...I'm not dating anyone." Sighing dramatically, I laughed at my own idiocy. "It's been a while since I've been on a date." *Shut up now*, my mind screamed.

"Someone should definitely rectify that very unjust situation." He stood up from the chair. "Have a good night, Lexie. If you change your mind, feel free to meet us across the street."

"Thanks. Good night, Michael."

After he was gone, I sat back in the chair, read through my notes, highlighted a few points of interest and interviews that had to be conducted in the morning, and went in search of the evidence folder. After making sure I had everything completed and filed for the night, I shut down the computer and swiveled in my chair. Kemper was on his way out too.

"Are you going to get your drink on tonight?" he asked. "I heard Riley is buying a round for everyone. Half of shift will be hanging out. It's a great way to get to know your fellow officers." He waggled his eyebrows at me.

"Not tonight."

"You rarely come out with us. Is it because you can't hold your liquor?"

"I can hold my liquor just fine. But we have an early morning, and I want to be sharp," I insisted.

"I bet you're a lot more fun when you're tipsy." His lips curved into a devious smirk, and he snatched my purse off the desk. I had been in the process of emptying my pockets and putting the necessities like my cell phone and shield inside when he took my bag.

"I'm not giving this back until you agree to one drink."

"Kemper," I growled, lunging for my purse, but he held it over my head, "give it back."

"One drink." He cocked his head to the side questioningly. "Okay?"

"Fine."

He looked smug and victorious, practically letting out a cheer. "Great. Let's go." He hooked his fingers around my elbow and dragged me toward the stairs, still holding my purse.

On our way out of the precinct, we encountered Riley on his way back inside. The detective's gaze shifted from Kemper to me. I shook my head, embarrassed by the way I was being dragged to the bar.

"Lexie," Riley asked, "is everything okay?"

"Yeah. What are you doing? Didn't you just leave? Did we get a call?" I asked, hoping for an excuse to get out of drinks with Kemper.

"No, nothing like that. I just thought of something and wanted to run a check before I forget." His gaze went back to Kemper, sizing up the other man. "Where are you two going?"

"To get drinks, man." Kemper smiled and offered a fist-bump to Riley. "I had to take this little lady's purse hostage to get her to agree to one drink. Can you believe that?"

"Maybe I would have tried that if I was channeling my twelve year old self," Riley retorted, and I snickered. Kemper didn't catch on, which made me laugh even harder. "I also don't think any woman likes to be called little lady."

"Whatever. Lexie doesn't mind, right?" He bumped against my shoulder. "We'll see you over there, Mike," Kemper called as Riley continued up the steps.

THREE

The bar was crowded. It appeared that every officer and detective that just got off shift had gone for a drink. It was a cop bar, and aside from the uniformed officers' girlfriends and a few badge bunnies, the only civilians inside worked there. Kemper ordered two beers as we took a seat at the corner of the bar.

"Are you enjoying being Riley's pet project?" he asked, taking a long pull from the bottle.

"I'm not his pet project."

"Well, it's not like Hawking and I have gotten to ride along with him. We've been inside, running background checks, examining surveillance feeds, and processing evidence. You actually get to go outside and see the light of day."

"It's because I came close to making an arrest the day we were canvassing the building. It just as easily could have been you."

"I doubt that." He took a deep breath. "Look, I'm not trying to sound sexist here, but don't you think it's possible that Riley thinks you're hot and that's why he's letting you hang around with him?"

"For god's sakes." I rolled my eyes. "You're such a prick." I climbed off the stool and slammed the beer down. "Because there's no way in hell that it has anything to do with my level of competence, right?" I glared at him. "Not that it's any of your business, but I've worked some big cases in vice. Hell, I even helped homicide get a killer off the streets. So until you have a few commendations in your file, I suggest you shut your fucking mouth."

"Whoa," he held up his hands in surrender, "easy. I just wanted you to be careful. Mr. Hotshot Detective might expect some favors in return for showing you the ropes. That's all I was trying to say." He glanced around and lowered his voice conspiratorially. "Word is that's how Preston got to be a first grade detective."

I scoffed at his pathetic argument. "That's unsubstantiated gossip. It has no bearing on any of this. And I think you ought to mind your own business." I stormed toward the door. "And if you take my purse again, I'll shoot you."

~*~

Returning home from a long day, I trudged up the steps to my apartment, unlocked the door, and slammed it shut. I was pissed. And the small voice inside my head couldn't help but wonder if there was any truth to Kemper's warning. Maybe the only reason Riley humored me was for what he hoped to get in return. It happened in a lot of professions, and I didn't know him well enough to know what kind of guy he was outside of the job. Depending on how true the rumors were concerning him and Preston, bedding his co-workers could just be part of his repertoire.

Searching for my cell phone, I wanted to call my best friend, Emma, and ask for some much needed advice and female perspective, but I couldn't find my phone. Dammit. It must still be on my desk at work. At the moment, I despised Kemper for sullying my self-confidence, ruining my otherwise quiet evening, and making me leave my phone at the station.

"Fuck," I growled, feeling the need to burn off some aggression through the use of expletives. Stomping into my room, I changed into workout clothes and pounded out a few miles on the treadmill. After that, I took a soothing shower and crawled into bed, forcing myself not to think about anything related to the job or my abilities.

Eventually, I drifted into an uneasy sleep. Less than an hour later, I woke up full of self-doubt. What if Kemper was right and Riley was only using me? And the scarier thought was that maybe I liked Riley a little too much to care. As a rule, I despised women that allowed some handsome asshole to sweet talk her into doing anything, all while treating her like crap. In truth, I'd been that woman before, and I promised myself I would never be like that again.

However, having a one night stand or a fuck buddy didn't equate to a relationship. But could I be one of those girls who had a fling and didn't care? I'd never been one of them before, but Emma had encouraged me to casually date or have a random one night stand, particularly after the unfortunate circumstances surrounding the break-up with my ex. But I was never wired that way, and after working vice, I'd seen too much to ever seriously entertain the thought of picking up a stranger at a bar. But a casual romp with Detective Ruggedly Handsome wouldn't be dangerous. It's not like he was a serial killer or sexual predator. At least, I hoped not.

Working myself into a tizzy over the what ifs, I opened the drawer in my nightstand, looking for my e-reader. It blinked on, flashed the charge button, and immediately powered itself off. Nothing was working tonight.

I rolled over, beat my pillow into a preferable shape, and twisted and turned for another twenty minutes. No matter how much I tried to force my thoughts away from Michael and work, somehow they found a way to circle back. Coming up with another idea, I pulled a box from the bottom of my drawer and opened it. Even if I shouldn't consider sleeping with the real Michael Riley, there was nothing in this world preventing me from fantasizing about him. And the imaginary version wouldn't compromise my job or standards. It might actually be the best of both worlds. Unfortunately, that didn't exactly work out either.

The constant pounding at my door dragged me from bed. It was two a.m., not that I was asleep. After another failed plan and more twisting and turning, I spent the last hour beating myself up for acting like such an idiot, and my intended distraction turned into another epic fail. The batteries in BOB were dead, leaving me frustrated and even more annoyed. BOB was my battery operated boyfriend, and after the way I had been turning to mush around Riley and seriously considering violating my own moral code, I thought I might need to take the edge off in order to gain some clarity. Obviously, that was an ill-conceived notion since I was destined to be frustrated and annoyed.

Grabbing my robe, I tied it around my waist and went into the living room. After a quick peek through the peephole, I glanced around my living room, making sure nothing embarrassing was in view before opening the door.

"Hey, Lexie," Riley leaned heavily against my

doorjamb, “I thought you could use this.” He reeked of tequila and was clearly drunk. He held up my cell phone but seemed to forget what to do with it and put it back in his pocket. “God, you have such pretty eyes.”

“Thanks.” Was I dreaming? “So do you,” I responded, pulling my robe tighter around my waist. “How much did you have to drink? Did you drive here?”

“Just a little bit. And no, I took a cab.” He shook his head, focusing again on the reason he was outside my front door, and fished my cell phone out of his pocket, this time handing it to me. “You left this at work. ‘Cuz if you didn’t, I wouldn’t have found your address stored in the phone’s memory and wouldn’t have known where you lived. I guess I could have just called to tell you you left your phone instead of showing up. But I didn’t know your number. Do you have a landline? That would have made this easier. I should have looked in your personnel file. Damn.” Apparently drunk Riley had a tendency to ramble incoherently.

“You came all this way just to bring me my phone?”

“Uh-huh,” he gave me a huge, lopsided smile, “okay, good night.” He staggered backward, away from my apartment.

“Michael,” I called, stepping into the hallway and grabbing his arm, “come inside. You should sober up a little before you go. The last thing you need to do is wander the streets. What would Lieberman think if he has to bail you out of the drunk tank in the morning?”

“He’d probably just think I’m a lot of fun.” Michael smirked and teetered. “But hanging around for a bit doesn’t sound like such a bad idea.” He let me lead him inside my apartment and onto the couch. “You’ve got a lovely place.” He was staring wide-eyed at the room. “I used to have a place kinda like this, except the walls were beige and the couch was brown."

"How about I make you some coffee?" I poured the water and put a dark roast cup into the machine to brew. A minute later, I carefully put the mug on the table in front of him. "Drink some coffee, Detective."

"Michael," he insisted. He picked up the cup and took a long sip before putting it down. "Did I interrupt anything?" He looked around the room, searching for something or someone. When he didn't spot whatever he hoped to find, his gaze settled on me. His fingers found the sleeve of my robe, and he played absently with the material.

"Not at all. I was having problems falling asleep," I admitted.

"Insnowmia?" He scrunched his face together, realizing the word didn't come out correctly. "Snommnia."

"Insomnia?"

"That's it." He pointed a finger at me and smiled.

"Drink some more coffee," I insisted, debating if my worries warranted a conversation.

"But then I won't be able to sleep either," he complained, shaking his head to clear the cobwebs. "So what's keeping you up?"

"Kemper said I'm getting special treatment at the station because I'm a girl."

"Kemper's a douche. You're smart and have an excellent record." He drained the mug and put it back on the table. I scooped it up to brew another cup while Michael sunk deeper into the couch cushions and put his feet on my coffee table. "And you're beautiful."

"See, stupid comments like that undermine everything else you just said." Leaning against the kitchen counter, I rubbed my face. "You're not supposed to let that play a role in determining my ability to do the job. Is that why you let me shadow you at work?"

"I let you ride with me because you seem to have a knack for taking care of what needs to be done. The fact that you're easy on the eyes is just a bonus."

"Stop saying things like that. It's not like I'm drop dead gorgeous. I'm average. The only thing I can say about my looks is that, with enough makeup, I make a convincing prostitute. And frankly, I'm not sure that's a good thing."

"Well, I think I could be a damn good gigolo." He shifted sideways on the couch to look at me. "And I know I'm attractive and have no problem using that to my advantage." His arrogance was starting to make him a bit less attractive.

"It's different, and you know it." I brought the refilled mug back to the sofa and handed it to him. "When women use their looks, ugly rumors start to circulate. Haven't you heard the things they say about Preston?"

An angry fire burned behind his eyes. "They aren't rumors when they're true." He took another long sip of coffee, calming as if the hot liquid had somehow put out the blaze. "But you've used your looks for the job. In fact, it was required in order to do the job. That's precisely how you were able to assist homicide, so stop being so self-deprecating. Insecurity won't lead to a detective's shield."

Stifling my yawn, I studied his relaxed posture. He appeared slightly more sober than when he arrived. "Tell me the truth. Why did you come here tonight?"

"To return your phone." He looked apologetic. "I should get going." I didn't particularly believe him. After all, there was no reason why he couldn't have stuck it inside my desk drawer for the morning, but before I could call him out on it, he spoke again. "Unless," his eyes traveled up my silk robe, from the belt around my waist to my breasts and upward, stopping at my lips and eventually settling on my eyes, "you want to do something else."

My breath caught in my throat. My lips were dry, and my tongue immediately moistened them. Riley was drunk. Was he taking advantage, or was I? And wouldn't that just undermine my entire argument and make the torturous hours I'd spent thinking about this a total waste of my time?

"Like what?" I asked, studying his blue eyes, his perfectly formed grapefruit red lips, and wanting nothing more than to run my hands along his shoulders, his torso, and downward.

He scooted closer, so close I felt his warm breath against my neck as he gently nibbled on my earlobe. I tilted my head to the side to give him better access, and his lips moved to my throat. Finding my pulse point, he sucked gently, and a slight moan escaped my lips. The stubble on his cheek brushed against my chin as he pulled back and then placed his lips over mine.

He tasted of coffee and tequila. His tongue gently urged my lips apart and slipped into my mouth. I heard a faint groan coming from the back of his throat, and he eased us down against the couch cushion. I panicked, my heart beating faster in my chest. Did I want this? Yes. Should I want this? Probably not.

"Lexie," he whispered, breaking the kiss, "we shouldn't be doing this. I'm sorry."

"No, we shouldn't," I agreed, scooting out from underneath him. Glancing down, I saw my hands had a mind of their own and had unbuttoned his shirt and were working on his belt buckle. "Sorry," I replied, swallowing, "I wasn't thinking. It's been a long day. I guess I just wanted something to take my mind off of it."

His eyes studied his partially unhooked belt for a moment. Then his gaze slowly traveled up my arms and back to my lips. "Then let's not think about anything for the next few minutes." He grasped my face in his hands and kissed me again, encouraged by my actions. "I like a girl who knows exactly what she wants." His eyes burned with lust, and the look caused my stomach to flip. Even though we had done nothing but kiss a little, I could feel the heat beginning to pool between my legs. "For the record, this has nothing to do with our dynamic at work. But I'll stop if you tell me to."

His words set off warning bells in my brain. "Did you plan this?"

"No." He looked sincere, at least sincere enough for my revved up libido, and I tangled myself around him. "Just give me a second to catch up," he remarked playfully. His eyes turned devilish, and he tugged on my robe's belt. It immediately came undone, almost as quickly as I was, and the silk fell to the sides. "Better than what I expected," he said appreciatively, leaning down to place a trail of kisses across my neck and collar.

Thankfully, I was wearing a pair of lace trimmed panties and a cami. It wasn't the sexiest lingerie, but it was preferable to the ratty t-shirt and shorts I slept in the night before.

I moaned as his hand caressed my left breast, and he suckled the right through the material. My nipples were taut, and I arched into him, wanting him to remove the cloth barrier that was in our way.

"Michael." My voice was ragged, filled with desire and need.

He stopped momentarily, and I sat up. He pulled my top over my head and found my lips once more.

Our tongues did battle as I tugged his unbuttoned shirt down to his elbows, and he released the grasp he had on my face long enough to let it drop onto the couch behind us.

"Now where was I?" he asked, his eyes dancing in the dim light.

He pushed me back on the couch and alternated between nipping and licking along my cleavage, my breasts, and my nipples. I squirmed underneath him, being overtaken by desire and wanting to feel him inside of me, wanting the release I hadn't had in far too long. While my body screamed out yes, worrisome thoughts were coursing through my mind.

When he gently bit the skin covering my ribs, I jerked upright from the sudden jolt of pain that caught me off guard, and he smirked evilly.

"Oh yeah? Turnabout is fair play," I purred, deciding I wanted to make sure he felt the same torturous, writhing, ready-to-explode need that he had caused me.

Pushing him backward, I straddled his lap, sensitive and aware of the rough denim against the barely there cotton of my panties. My hips rocked automatically, wanting to ease the burning desire that had been building since the day we met. He let out a groan at the sudden pressure, as his erection rubbed against my opening. If only we didn't have the few layers of material blocking our ability to join together. *Oh shit*, rational thought suddenly flickered on inside my brain.

"Do you have a condom?" I asked. My thinking was starting to clear, and I wasn't sure what I wanted him to say.

"Fuck. I just used the last one." He rubbed his eyes, sobering from the alcohol and our making out. "I wasn't planning on...this. Don't you have any in your apartment?"

"Newsflash, even though I worked vice, I don't entertain men frequently. I've been having a dry spell lately," I snapped, my mind reeling from his previous statement. *He just used the last one.*

His hand left my ass and circled around to my thigh. His thumb brushed against the sopping wet cotton at my crotch. "I think the dry spell's over." He grinned. "And I'm sure, between the two of us, we can come up with some solution in the meantime."

A single digit slipped underneath the fabric of my panties and brushed against my lower lips, causing a delightful shiver, but his words triggered something in my brain. Suddenly, the entire situation felt wrong.

"Stop." I pressed my palms into my eyes in order to think without seeing the need behind those ice blue eyes of his. This shouldn't be happening, particularly after the argument I had with Kemper. "I can't do this."

"Oh-kay." Riley was completely confused. "What can't you do?"

"Have sex. Mess around. Whatever it is that we're about to do. We can't. I can't." I extricated myself from his lap on shaky legs. "Are you sober enough to get home?"

"Lexie," he reached for me, but I stepped backward, "I'm sorry if I came on to you. It's late, and I'm drunk. I didn't mean to offend you." He shook off his confusion, adjusted himself slightly, put his shirt back on, and went to the door. "I'll see you tomorrow."

"Michael," I began, not sure if I wanted to grill him, apologize for changing my mind, or berate him for letting things escalate.

"Don't worry. It never happened."

FOUR

The next day at work was awkward. At least, I felt awkward. Riley was slightly hungover, so he splurged on two drink carriers of lattes and a dozen donuts for our team. Kemper tried to be apologetic, and the cold shoulder I had been giving him thawed since the last twelve hours had practically demonstrated his point. I hated that he was right. I never should have let things escalate with Michael. I wouldn't fall for the nice guy routine or those amazing blue eyes again.

"Lexie," Riley called from his desk across the bullpen, "can you print another copy of your notes from Tuesday?"

"Sure." I didn't look at him. I was too embarrassed, and I hoped that he didn't remember anything due to the tequila haze. "Do you need anything else, Detective?"

"No." He grabbed the papers off the printer and turned his back on me. "I'm meeting with Frank to see what progress he's made," Riley said to Lieberman. "Do you have any messages that need relaying?"

Lieberman shook his head, but before Riley could leave, Preston handed him a note. “Pass that on to Frank,” she said. “He’ll understand.”

“Sure, no problem.” Riley tucked it into his shirt pocket and glanced at Hawking and Kemper. “Do one of you want to tag along?”

“Absolutely,” Kemper said, jumping to his feet. Riley threw a glance in my direction. “Sorry, Sarcone, but I’d hate for anyone to think I’ve been playing favorites.”

“Not a problem.”

I forced my face into a fake smile and busied myself with processing the evidence found at the site of the home invasions. But it stung to know that Kemper had been right. Michael Riley was nothing more than an arrogant son of a bitch. And now he was showing his true colors. Luckily, he hadn’t taken all of my dignity away with his cocky personality and good looks. That bastard. And I thought he might have actually been a good guy. Throwing myself into work was the only way I was going to make it through the day.

“Hey, Hawking, I could use another set of eyes to proof the compiled manifest.”

“You got it,” he said, sliding his chair over to my desk.

With Riley and Kemper gone, Hawking and I managed to get a lot of work done. It was easier to work when there weren’t any distractions nearby. Based on a few comments we received from victims and witnesses, the gang responsible for this string of burglaries was run by William “Big Bill” Thompson. He was just a punk kid who’d outgrown his britches. Hawking went down to records to grab his file, and I ran a background and searched for his known associates.

After taping the information to the whiteboard that stood in the corner of the room, we began hanging mug shots of the suspected gang initiates underneath. By the time I turned around to ask Lieberman a question, he and Preston were gone.

"Wow, they left us without any adult supervision," I remarked, tossing a smile at Hawking. "Quick, search their drawers, I bet one of them keeps a stockpile of candy."

"You're crazy, Lex," Hawking replied, returning the grin. "So," he leaned back to assess our work, "we have strong leads on a few of our suspects based upon the limited angles we've pulled from nearby surveillance feeds and from a few eyewitness accounts. Not bad, considering sixteen places have been burglarized in the last five weeks." He shook his head, annoyed at the slow progress we'd been making.

"Hey, you and I haven't been helping out that long. We're just doing our jobs. Plus, investigations are slow going unless you catch the perp red-handed or have irrefutable proof, and no one's been that willing to cooperate with us. But if it'll make you feel better, just blame the detectives. Riley's probably dicking around somewhere with Kemper."

"Trouble in paradise?" Hawking asked, checking to make sure we were still alone. "Because I never expected Riley to invite one of us to go along with him this afternoon. Who knew he had become so buddy-buddy with Kemper all of a sudden? Last night, they almost came to blows at the bar."

"Really?"

"It looked that way to me." He shrugged. "For a sec, I thought it might have had something to do with you."

"I wasn't even there at the time. I ducked out after Kemper pissed me off. I think he just has a tendency to rub people the wrong way."

"He's like a puppy that shits the carpet. You want to smack him with a newspaper, but he runs away before he can get punished. At least he did last night. A couple of guys from homicide dragged Riley away, and Kemper took off after that. I guess they must have made up for Kemper to volunteer to go with him today."

"Yeah, I guess. Or Riley doesn't play favorites. He announced that right before he and Kemper went skipping off into the sunset." I didn't hide the bitterness from my voice, but Hawking found it amusing and laughed.

"So everything's just smooth sailing, except it appears that the dream team of detectives have no clue how to put a stop to these home invasions."

"Whatever. The detectives have their own way of doing things. They are sort of our unofficial bosses or commanding officers since you like all that military jargon," I teased. "But they should know what they're doing. We don't. And despite what I just said, Riley seems perfectly capable of doing his job. And that's all there is to it. We're co-workers. Nothing more." I rolled my eyes. "Last night, Kemper was making a few comments that the only reason I get to ride with Riley is because I'm female. I guess Michael must have heard the conversation and wanted to put a stop to the allegations before they continued."

"Sure. That makes sense."

"Yeah." My mind flashed to the feel of Michael's mouth on my neck, and I turned away before Hawking could notice my lie. "So should we go have a talk with some of these suspects or interview the victims again?"

"No," Lieberman snarled from the doorway, striding into the room like he owned the place. He was the oldest man on the team, in his forties, and he was in charge. He assessed the board. "Good work. Riley's on his way back with additional intel, and Preston's been at the crime lab, talking to the forensic teams. The two of you will update our information as it comes in. And I'll take it from there."

"Yes, sir," Hawking and I replied simultaneously.

"Don't be cute," Lieberman snapped as if we planned to choreograph our response.

"No, sir," we said again, and I thought Lieberman was going to have an aneurysm. Instead, he stormed out of the room, barking at an officer he passed to get eyes on Big Bill.

"Do you think he'll demote us to traffic?" I whispered to Hawking, who sighed dramatically and went to get a new dry erase marker.

Hawking and I spent the rest of the night doing precisely what Lieberman told us to do. It was a pain in the ass, and by the time it was all said and done, I was ready to call it quits. Maybe I'd ask Lieutenant Peterson, the man in charge of burglary division, if I could go back to patrolling. Life made more sense on the streets. You walk a beat. You respond to calls, deal with crimes in progress, and you do the paperwork. Easy peasy. And I wouldn't have to see Michael every day.

While we were working, Riley and Kemper returned from their outing. Riley didn't say a word as he updated the board and his notes to reflect the progress Frank had made on infiltrating the gangs. And Kemper played with the copy machine, spending a good twenty minutes trying to figure out how to load paper into the tray. Thankfully, he was smart enough not to ask for my help.

"Big Bill's been arrested," Preston declared, hanging up her desk phone. "A couple of unis pulled him over on a routine stop, spotted some hot merchandise inside his vehicle, and arrested him. He's in the interrogation room." She shifted her gaze around the room. "Hawking, have you ever sat in on an interrogation?"

"No, ma'am," he replied.

"Great, you're about to. Follow me. And don't say a word. This is a learning experience, got it?"

"Yes, ma'am."

"And if you call me ma'am again, I'll have you cleaning the women's locker room with your personal toothbrush, understand?" She smiled sweetly at him, and I decided that Detective Samantha Preston was my new role model. It didn't matter if she had a string of torrid affairs; she was one badass chick.

"You two can call it a night," Lieberman said to Kemper and me. "Big Bill will be begging for counsel within the next ten minutes, and his attorney won't be here until the morning. Tonight's a wash." He jerked his head at the door. "Take off."

Kemper didn't need to be told twice and was out the door before I even shut down my computer. On my way out, I passed the observation room that was connected to the interrogation room. On the other side of the two-way mirror, Preston was asking Big Bill questions while Hawking meticulously jotted down his responses. I stepped into the room to watch for a minute. I'd been inside an interrogation room before, but I had never observed one being conducted like this.

The audio equipment was turned off, but it appeared that Big Bill was cooperating. Was it possible Lieberman's prediction was wrong? If Big Bill was cooperating, that probably meant there'd be a chance we'd be called in to work a double. Perhaps I should hang around a bit longer just to make sure. I didn't want to drive all the way home, just to have to turn around and come back.

"Lexie?" Riley asked, confused why I was standing in observation and staring at the interrogation. "Are you taking notes?"

"No. Hawking is though." I jerked my chin at the glass, but Riley didn't seem to care.

"Can we talk?"

"I don't have anything to say, Detective."

"Michael. My name is Michael." He stepped in front of me, blocking my view of the interrogation. "What's going on with you?"

"Nothing. I was told to go home. If this is a breach of protocol or something, I'll leave now." I moved toward the door, but Michael grabbed my arm, pulling me against his chest. "Let go."

"Not until you tell me what the hell happened last night."

"What do you remember?" I asked, hoping he'd have a vague recollection.

"Everything. I'm not a blackout drunk or an alcoholic," he snapped. "You were afraid that I was using you. And I said we should stop, but you practically had your hands down my pants at that point. So I thought you were into it. You acted like you were. So what happened?"

"I take it you aren't used to being rejected." I shook my head, pulling away from him. "You're not as hot as you think you are. In fact, you're kind of a jerk."

"Oh, so you're pissed because I took Kemper to meet with Frank instead of you." He focused on my eyes. "Correct me if I'm wrong, but didn't you tell me that Kemper thought you were being favored because you're so damn fine?"

"I said it was because I was female."

"Yes, a damn fine female." He smirked, hoping it

would force some of my anger to dissipate.

"Stop. Just stop," I insisted. "I'm tired and annoyed, and I feel like such a fool for acting the way I did."

"You can make it up to me," Riley offered, a teasing tone in his voice. "I'm not opposed to letting you treat me to a slice or a sandwich or something. After all, it's dinnertime, and I'm starving."

"I'm not taking you out to dinner. If anything, you should be offering to buy me dinner." As soon as the words left my mouth I realized that had been his plan. Michael Riley was a world-class manipulator. Just another negative quality to add to his list of attributes, right above gorgeous eyes and sexy abs.

"Okay, I hope you have a hankering for Chinese takeout, but we're eating it at your place. And that point is non-negotiable."

"Michael," I protested, but he ignored me, leading the way out of the observation room and out of the precinct.

The bastard was smart enough to know that I wouldn't make a scene at work, and I figured he must have picked up on that fact after the purse incident with Kemper last night. Making a mental note to murder Kemper when I got the chance, I decided to play nice in order to get this meal over with as quickly as possible. Then maybe things could return to normal.

We split up. Michael insisted he'd pick up dinner and meet me at my place. I drove home, changed out of the stiff police uniform, and tried on half a dozen outfits. What in the world was I thinking? Why was I so worried about impressing him? He'd seen me half naked the night before. And he was a jerk today at work.

Growling at my own stupidity, I pulled on a

sweatshirt and jeans, ran a brush through my hair, and forced myself to leave the bathroom before I could do something else stupid, like put on makeup or curl my hair. This was not a date. I didn't know what the hell it was, but it most definitely was not a date.

In order to further ensure that there were no other date-like qualities to the evening, I dug through the kitchen drawers for some plastic utensils, grabbed a Corona from my fridge, popped the top, and drank out of the bottle. No glass. No manners. Nothing. If Riley wanted a beer, he could help himself. Then I settled onto the couch and waited for him. A few minutes later, I heard a knock.

"It's open," I called, not even bothering to get off the couch.

"You're a cop. You should know better than to leave your door unlocked," Riley scolded, carrying a plastic bag that smelled of Asian spices. He cocked an eyebrow at my appearance. "You look comfortable."

"What can I say? I wasn't in the mood to have any dinner guests."

"Seriously, Lexie, you need to chill." He put the bag down on the coffee table and pulled out a couple of cartons. "I'm not your enemy."

"I know." I bit my lip and leaned forward. My stomach growled, and I glanced at the cartons. "I get bitchy when I'm hungry."

"Noted." He smirked and named the various options.

I grabbed a container of egg drop soup and nestled against the corner of the couch, pulling my legs up and sitting sideways in order to face him. We ate our soup in silence before moving on to the main course.

"Do you want my eggroll?" I asked, holding out the fried object.

"Is that a peace offering?"

"Sure. But for the record, I despise eggrolls. Now if it were a cream cheese wanton or a crab Rangoon, then that would really mean something." I smiled, letting him take the offered snack. "Why did you really come over last night?"

"To return your phone." He bit into the eggroll to buy time. "And because I wanted to see you. You wouldn't join me for drinks last night, but I ran into you going to the bar with Kemper. You said you weren't seeing anyone, but he was carrying your purse. I am a detective. I do notice these things." He shrugged, burying his chopsticks into the carton of orange chicken. "He left the bar early last night, and I wondered if he came to see you."

"That's none of your business. But for the record, I'm not into Kemper."

"You seemed pretty into me last night until you freaked." He went back to eating, not looking in my direction. "Care to explain that one?"

"We work together. The department frowns upon personal relationships. Lieberman would send me back to vice in a heartbeat. And frankly, I barely know you. Last night, I considered making a mistake, but I came to my senses." I shook my head. "I'm sorry if I led you on. But you said we shouldn't be doing that. You said it last night when you were practically on top of me. And you were right. Plus, you just used your last condom. I would think someone like you would buy them in bulk to prevent that from happening."

"Someone like me? You don't know anything about my sexual history, and you haven't even bothered to ask. That's not fair."

"I think it is."

"No." He shook his head. "You can't say that until you get to know me." His blue eyes shone with determination. "I like orange chicken and hot and sour soup. My place is too messy for any houseguests, and I made an ass out of myself today by taking that putz with me instead of you." He put the carton on the table and scooted closer. "What more do you need to know?" I stared into my carton, hoping to come up with a witty response. "I'm also a wonderful kisser and a great lay."

"Can Detective Preston vouch for that?" My eyes shot up, and I saw the answer on his face. "Y'know what," I climbed off the couch to get another beer, "don't answer that. We can be friends. But that's it. No benefits."

"Are you sure about that?" He came up behind me and put his hands on my waist, pulling me backward against his chest. "We have amazing chemistry." He buried his nose in my hair, inhaling deeply, and his lips brushed lightly against the back of my neck.

"I worked vice for two years with the sleaziest men in the city drooling all over me. I'm not looking for a physical relationship with anyone right now."

"Okay." He released his grasp and stepped away from me. "I can do friends, but you'll see that you're wrong. I'm not a bad guy. I guess I'll just have to prove it." He paused for a second, and then asked, "So since we're friends, can I have a beer?"

"Help yourself."

FIVE

By the next morning, everything was back to normal. Or at least, I thought it was. Big Bill was negotiating some type of deal. His lawyer and someone from the district attorney's office were hashing out the details. From the constant in and out that was taking place inside the interview room, it was apparent whatever Big Bill wanted to share was something big. Who knew his nickname would be so apt.

Lieberman didn't like it, and he paced the squad room, throwing nervous glances down the hallway and bitching quietly to himself. Preston's eyes never left the corridor as she watched the ADA talk on his phone. Riley, unlike the other two detectives, was behind his desk, clicking away at the keyboard.

"Okay, what's going on?" Kemper finally asked. He had the biggest mouth of all and couldn't stand to be in the dark. "What did Big Bill say?"

"He hasn't officially said anything yet," Lieberman replied, surprising us by answering. "But unofficially, his crew's been stealing the stuff in order to avoid a turf war with another rival gang."

"Why would they do that?" Hawking asked. The story made little sense.

Lieberman shrugged. "Big Bill and his pathetic gang are tiny. So they figured they'd pay their dues to the V7Ts in exchange for protection. Frank Devereaux, our inside man, says that Alfonso Sigfried is hocking drugs in exchange for stolen items instead of cash. He knows how narcotics operates. If we see a cash exchange, we'll snatch them up for possession with intent to distribute. So the V7Ts got smart. Instead of taking cash as payment, they'll take jewelry, guns, or fancy electronics."

"It's a classic barter system," Preston added.

"What the hell does that have to do with Big Bill and his gang?" Kemper asked.

Lieberman gave the curious officer a patient look. "It seems some of the junkies weren't in the mood to barter, and Big Bill thinking he was big shit decided to take advantage. Sigfried caught some of Bill's guys dealing in their neighborhood and is forcing them to pay retribution. Whatever dope they sold, he's making them pay back with stolen merchandise."

"Before this case, I never heard of the V7Ts," Riley piped up from behind his desk. "And they aren't in the databases. Are we certain Big Bill isn't full of shit? He knows he needs to serve up some valuable intel or else he's going down for the crime spree and the drugs."

"If his intel's sound, he gets a deal. And if it isn't, we throw the book at him. It's as simple as that," Lieberman said, dropping into a chair. "I just hate waiting for these legal eagles to come to a decision. It's holding us back from doing actual police work."

The ADA poked his head into the room. "Hey, Jack, we need to talk."

Lieberman immediately went down the hallway with the ADA. I shook off my confusion. I didn't know anyone was capable of making Lieberman scurry. Apparently I learned something new today. Deciding that was an accomplishment in and of itself, I went to the coffeemaker and brewed a fresh pot, needing the caffeine pick-me-up.

Preston joined me at the pot, refilling her mug. "We ought to keep you around, Sarcone. You make great coffee."

"Thanks," I said, wondering why she was being so friendly. Did I step into the *Twilight Zone*? "Did you need something?"

"Actually," she looked a little sheepish, "I'm compiling as much information as I can on the V7Ts in case Bill's story pans out, and I would really appreciate it if someone could go through the records room and sift through some of the older case files. Like Riley said, there's very little about the gangs in the databases. And even though a lot is computerized, every once in a while a file is corrupted or something gets missed. I like to be thorough. And it's easier when we have hard copies in hand to review."

"No problem." I smiled, concealing my dread over this new assignment. "I'll see what I can find."

Taking my coffee cup, I went upstairs to records, signed in, and began the arduous task of searching for anything that might be relevant. The good news was the V7Ts were a new gang that only recently came into existence in the last year and a half. They were led by a man named Alfonso Sigfried. Scanning for additional information that pertained to him, I determined that he had a mile long rap sheet. He'd spent a decade behind bars for selling drugs, and he was suspected of running a prostitution ring. Idly, I wondered if I'd ever encountered him or his working girls when I was in vice.

After copying the relevant files, I returned downstairs, placed the files on the corner of Preston's desk, and glanced around the room. The only person remaining was Kemper.

"Where'd everyone go?" I asked.

"Preston and Riley went out on a call. Lieberman's in the interrogation room with Big Bill and the lawyers. And Hawking wasn't feeling good, so he went home early," Kemper replied.

"Okay," I bit my lip, thinking, "I'm going to stop by vice and see if they have any additional information that might be useful. I came across a few interesting facts about Alfonso Sigfried and the V7Ts while I was perfecting my filing skills. So if Preston gets back before I do, tell her where I am."

"All righty." Kemper tossed a look in my direction. "Hey, Lexie, about the other night at the bar, I wasn't trying to say you were incompetent or anything."

"No sweat."

"Really? You've barely spoken to me since that night. I was afraid you were holding a grudge."

"I've had more important things to worry about. But if you really want to make it up to me, don't do it again." I returned to the stairwell and went down the steps to vice.

Entering my old stomping grounds was a bit anticlimactic. I expected to see a few familiar faces or hear someone call out my name, but neither of those things happened. Knocking on the lieutenant's door, I waited to gain admittance and asked if he knew anything about the rumors that the V7Ts were involved in prostitution. He looked through a few files, but nothing substantial surfaced.

Passing the question off to the closest detective, I waited again for answers. Still, none came. After almost two hours of non-responses, I went back up the stairs to burglary division. Letting out a sigh at the self-imposed tedium, I returned to my desk. This time, I was all alone. Even Kemper was gone.

Perhaps Lieberman was still inside the interrogation room with Big Bill and the lawyers. Deciding I should go check since I had been given no other instructions, I headed down the hallway and entered the observation room. My heart stopped, and my mouth dropped. From what I could tell, Big Bill had been shot. The man was slumped over the table in the interrogation room, and blood was dripping down the sides and onto the floor. Where were my fellow police officers? Where were the attorneys? Why wasn't anyone responding to this?

Radioing for assistance, I burst through the door to check his pulse. Suspects weren't supposed to die in police custody, particularly from a gunshot wound inside a locked interrogation room. Something didn't sit right, and I searched for a pulse but didn't feel one. My radio squawked a response, officers and paramedics were on the way. Until they arrived, I was to secure the area. This was a police station. Help was fifty feet down the hall and would be here in a moment.

"Remove your gun and radio, real slow," a voice said, and I practically jumped out of my skin.

A scrawny guy wearing a dark hoodie that obscured his face was pressed against the rear wall. He was standing in the only blind spot inside the room, obscured from being seen through the two-way mirror in the adjoining observation room and far enough to the side so entering officers wouldn't notice him either. He must have snuck in to perform the hit and got trapped when the door closed.

"Sir," I used the calm authoritarian voice we were

taught in the academy, even though I was scared to death, "I need you to lower your weapon."

"Do what I say," he snapped. Footsteps sounded outside the room. "Now."

"I can't do that." I unclipped my radio in a show of good faith and let it fall to the ground. Then I reached for my gun, pulling the strap free and letting my fingers run across the handle. "Just relax. Why don't you tell me who you are and what happened here?"

"Bitch, don't move. Tell them to stay back."

"Stay back," I repeated, glancing at the stunned police officers in the doorway. Several had their weapons drawn, but they didn't have a clear shot. "We have a situation here."

The group split up. A few radioed in the code while the others tried to determine the best angle to take out the shooter. Too bad he wasn't cooperating with their efforts. He remained pressed against the wall, protected from the armed officers in the adjacent room and the hallway. Even though my colleagues were only a few feet away, I was alone. It was just the shooter, a dead Big Bill, and me.

He leveled his gun at my face, and I bit my lip. I didn't want to die. The fear and adrenaline were coursing through my veins, and I tried to recall my training. Help was five feet away. I needed to control the situation while they devised a solid plan.

"What do you want?" I asked, attempting to distract and negotiate. "You're inside a police station. Getting out of this alive might be tricky. You have to help yourself here. Lower your weapon."

He didn't fidget or show fear. He kept the barrel of his gun trained on me as he contemplated my words. "Come here."

I didn't move.

"I will kill you if you don't listen," he said. My hand

tightened around my gun. And he dropped his gaze to my side. “Don’t do that.”

“Okay.” I raised my hands a little higher, still keeping the tips of my fingers against the handle.

“Don’t try that shit. Lower your hands. Lower. Down at your sides.” Swallowing, I let my hand drop away from my holster. “Now get your ass over here. I won’t say it again.”

Hand-to-hand combat was mandatory training, so moving in closer might increase my chances of subduing him or distracting him long enough for one of my fellow officers to take him down. It was my best bet and my only choice. He had a gun, and he wouldn’t take no for an answer.

I stepped slowly toward him, and he reached for my belt, yanking at my holstered weapon. He pulled it free from the leather, and I spun, elbowing him in the face. My gun crashed to the floor and skittered underneath the table.

He shoved me and fired a shot. The bullet whizzed past my head, deafening me in one ear and striking the cinderblock wall. The discharge in the enclosed space echoed and boomed, causing a dozen police officers to race inside. Weapons were drawn, but the shooter grabbed my arm and aimed his gun at my forehead. He ducked behind me as best he could, making sure to keep me between him and his impending death.

“Get me out of here,” he snarled.

“There’s nowhere to go,” someone said from behind me.

He stared into my eyes, looking as panicked and vicious as a cornered animal. “I’ll make sure you die before I do if you don’t get me the hell out of here,” he growled, low enough that only I could hear him. His trigger finger itched and flexed, and I believed he’d do it. "Do what I say, and don't try anything else."

I complied, and he spun me around to face the room of officers. Yanking on my braid, he pulled me flush against his body. The barrel of his weapon pressed into the side of my neck, and I bit my lip to keep from crying out as the hot metal burned my skin due to its recent discharge.

"Everyone keep cool," I said, mustering more calm than I thought I possessed. I didn't struggle as he edged along the wall, toward the exit. He rounded the doorway, keeping his back against the wall and slamming my side into the doorknob as we turned. I hissed in pain, and for a second, I thought a couple of the officers were going to open fire. "Just keep cool," I said as he led us a few steps down the corridor, forcing the responding officers to reluctantly make a hole.

The tension was thick. Radio calls were being made, and I heard someone mention that Emergency Services was on the way. Lieberman skittered to the edge of the squad room with Riley by his side. I didn't know where they came from, but I was relieved to see some familiar faces. Another call went out over the radio, announcing a lockdown at the precinct due to the hostage situation.

Somehow, the fact that this was a hostage situation and I was the hostage had eluded me. But the thought sent a ball of dread into the pit of my stomach. I felt dizzy and inhaled a deep breath. I was going to die. The gunman already killed one man. Surely, he wouldn't hesitate to kill me once he realized he wasn't going to make it out of this alive.

"Move it," the gunman growled, yanking me backward at a faster rate. I stumbled, and he swore, pulling me so tight against him, I could feel the cell phone in his pocket pressing into my skin.

"There's nowhere left to go," someone said from

behind us. "You're not stepping foot outside of this police station."

"Then neither will she." He turned completely sideways, pressing his back into the wall and keeping me in front of him. He'd been edging toward the exit, but with the latest announcement, he was afraid that someone would try to take him from behind. The angles hadn't been great before, but I imagined they must be worse now.

Why the hell did I ever step foot inside that interrogation room? Why did I think working for burglary division would be safer? A sob escaped my lips, and I swallowed it back down. I needed to hold it together. This was the job. I knew the risks, even if I never imagined something like this would happen.

"Lexie," Riley's voice cut through the radio squawks and whispers, "you're going to be okay. Trust me. Everything's just fine. Look at me." I locked onto his blue eyes, seeing an inferno erupting in their deep pools. He stepped out of the squad room and into the hallway. The other officers sought protection from doorways and furniture, but Michael was out in the open, completely exposed to the lunatic with the gun.

"Don't speak to her," my captor hissed.

"Listen, buddy, you have three seconds to do the right thing and let the lady go," Riley replied, and I shuddered, frantically searching for ESU's laser sight. "Lexie, look at me," Riley begged. Even if my captor didn't know what was about to happen, I did. "Keep your eyes on me. I'm right here. I'm not going anywhere. You're going to be fine. Nothing's going to happen to you. I won't let it."

"Bullshit." The guy hauled me backward another few feet, deciding to make a break for the entrance and may the consequences be damned.

"Two," Riley whispered. His eyes were on mine,

and he looked determined. “One.”

The force of the impact propelled my captor forward, knocking us both to the ground. He landed on top of me, and I screamed. It wasn’t professional, but I couldn’t stop it. The cops swarmed, pushing the assailant off of me, confiscating his weapon, and even going so far as to cuff him, even though he was more than likely dead.

Michael raced to me, kneeling on the ground and pulling me into his arms. He held me close and whispered soothing words in my ear. When I calmed slightly, he asked, “Are you okay?” His focus kept shifting between what was happening with the shooter and with me. “Sarcone, look at me. Let me see those pretty eyes of yours.”

He grasped my face in his hands, quickly assessing my head and neck for any injuries. No matter how hard I tried, I couldn’t stop my body from trembling. It was the adrenaline surge and the shock of what just happened.

“He killed Big Bill,” I managed through my gasps. “He was in the interrogation room when I went inside. I didn’t see him. He was hiding in the blind spot next to the glass.”

“Easy. It’s okay. You’re okay.” He hoisted me to my feet. But the world spun, and I clung to his strong arms which were around me again, hugging me tightly to his chest. “You did good. It’s over now. You’re safe.”

“Give her some room to breathe,” Preston said, tugging one of Michael’s arms loose. “Apparently the newest member to our division has to make sure this place runs smoothly. Where the hell was Lieberman and the officer assigned to keep watch over the suspect? Who the hell let this jackass into the precinct in the first place?” She jerked her head at what remained of the assailant, and my eyes followed the movement.

Seeing the pool of dark red blood, the pieces of skull and brain matter, and the look of sheer shock on what was left of my captor's face, a strong wave of nausea bubbled inside of me, and I ran into the nearest bathroom. I wretched until my body couldn't take it anymore, and I collapsed, my cheek dropping against the cold porcelain toilet seat. Randomly, I considered the number of germs that must be on it. Luckily, there was nothing left in my stomach to expel, or else that thought might have made me sick.

Michael followed me into the bathroom and knelt next to me, pressing a cold, damp cloth to the back of my neck. He stroked my back and made sure my hair didn't fall in front of my face. He didn't say anything. He just stayed to make sure I was okay.

"This is the ladies' room, Michael," Preston said from behind. "So unless you're planning to cut something off, I'll take it from here."

"Sam," Michael growled, but she made a tsk sound. "Fine." He leaned closer. "I'll be right outside if you need me."

I nodded, and he left.

"It's okay, Sarcone," Preston said. She knelt in the spot Michael had just vacated, pulled my hair out of my face, and rubbed my back just like he did. "We all react like this the first time something traumatic happens. At least you made it into the bathroom rather than vomiting all over our DB." She smiled, attempting to crack a joke. "Come on, let's get you cleaned up. Once you go back out there, a few detectives are standing by to take your statement and ask a dozen questions. You're entitled to have your union rep present if you want, but they aren't looking to blame you for anything. They just want to know what happened. You weren't at fault. In fact, you're the only one in this whole goddamn place who was even paying attention today. If it hadn't been for you, that creep would have snuck out, and who knows who else he might have killed."

"Who was he?" I asked.

"We're working on it. I'm sure Riley's tasked half the department and everyone in homicide to do some digging. We'll get to the bottom of this." She narrowed her eyes, seeing the burn on my neck. "Does anything hurt? Do you need medical attention?"

"I'm okay. Honestly, I just want to go home."

She laughed. "The sooner we get off this disgusting bathroom floor, the sooner you can go home."

SIX

I remained at my desk, sipping a soda and jittery as hell. I'd written my statement and recounted the event a dozen times. From the intelligence that had been collected so far, the shooter, Stryker King, ran with Alfonso Sigfried's crew. Sigfried must have suspected that Big Bill was going to rat on him and sent a shooter to take care of the problem. It was ballsy to send someone into a police station to kill a guy, and clearly, King was stupid enough to think he could shoot his way out.

Det. Michael Riley had been hovering since the shooting, and now that I was finally free to call it a night, he drove me home. Despite the fact my car was parked out back, I wasn't sure how focused I'd be on the road. And after what happened, my body was numb and buzzing at the same time. That was probably a bad sign.

"Michael," I swallowed, "is any of this real?"

He parked outside my apartment building and studied my eyes. "It's just the shock of today. You'll feel better in the morning. All you need is a stiff drink and a good night's sleep."

"I can't feel anything."

He lifted my hand in his and pressed my palm against my chest. "Do you feel your heart beating?"

"I guess, but it seems disconnected somehow."

He frowned but didn't say anything else. Instead, he came around to my side of the car, opened the door, and took my hand. My fingers still held a slight tremble, and I didn't know if that was from his touch or the earlier ordeal. He took my keys, unlocked my apartment door, and stepped inside.

"I'll make you a drink. Where do you keep the booze?"

"I don't think I can stomach that right now. But help yourself." I pointed at one of the cabinets and went into the bedroom. "Can I ask you a favor?"

"Anything."

"I want to take a shower. But will you stay for a little while? I don't want to be alone."

"Sure. I'll be right here." He poured some bourbon into a glass, took a seat on my couch, and flipped on the television.

After the horrors of the day washed down the drain, I dried my hair and went into the living room. Michael was watching a baseball game, but from the way his jaw muscles clenched and his fingers drummed a beat against the side of the glass, I knew he wasn't seeing what was happening on the screen.

"Thanks for staying," I said, taking a seat next to him. I blinked a few times, resisting the urge to run my hands through his hair. The only thing I wanted at this moment was to feel his arms around me again.

"Are you feeling better?" He turned off the TV and brushed his fingers against the burn on my neck. "Does that sting? Do you want some ice or aloe or something?"

Grasping his hand in mine, I brought his fingers to my lips, kissing each of them and then his palm. He ran his free hand through my hair but didn't move closer. "I want to know that I'm still alive. I want to feel alive."

"Lexie," he began, but I moved closer.

"All I can think about is how it could have ended in the blink of an eye. If Emergency Services had been an inch off, I'd be on that floor too."

"They're professional shooters, trained for long-distance tactical resolutions. You were safe."

I flashed to the look on his face before the shot was fired. "He could have killed me at any time. I might not have even made it out of the interrogation room."

"Lex, you're safe." Michael pulled his hand from my grasp and hugged me. "It's normal to be rattled after a trauma occurs. The department has a shrink on the payroll. Maybe you should think about talking to him."

"I don't want to talk to him. I just want to feel something in order to know I'm still here. That I'm still me." The incident today had made me brave. And the surge of adrenaline and hormones coupled with the fear had left me wanting companionship. "I want you, Michael."

"No, you don't." But he didn't pull away. "That's just what happens after a shooting. Trust me, all the guys at the precinct will tell you how we end up with raging hard-ons after a close call. It's just the natural physiological response. You're not thinking clearly."

"I don't care." I placed open-mouthed kisses on his neck, sucking gently. "Please, I need you."

"No. I'm not having sex with you. We're just friends, no benefits, remember? I won't take advantage. You're vulnerable right now."

"I am not vulnerable," I snapped. "I just want it to stop. When I close my eyes all I see is his gun in my face, and when there's nothing but silence, I hear that shot ring out and the wet sound of the bullet piercing his skull." I shuddered again, and Michael lifted me onto his lap.

"When you put it that way, I'll lend a hand. But that's it. And only if you're sure."

I locked onto his lips, and our tongues found a rhythmic caress. He unzipped my jeans and slipped a hand inside, teasing my opening and occasionally brushing against my clit.

"Oh, god." I wanted so much more than for him to finger me to completion. "Let me show you some gratitude. We're still wearing too many articles of clothing for this to be mutually fun."

"Oh, I'm having loads of fun. But this is about you." His eyes were clouded with desire. I stood up, shimmying out of my pants and tossing my top away. He licked his lips. "God, Lexie, take it easy. It's bad enough the noises you're making have gotten me this fucking hard. I'm trying to be a gentleman here, but you're making that impossible."

His hips bucked as I began trailing kisses down his neck, along the cords to his shoulder, back to his pectoral muscles. I ripped open his shirt and shoved it off of him. My mouth lavished his chest as my fingers deftly traced the deep crevices outlining his abdominal muscles. He was in amazing shape. He wasn't bulky like a bodybuilder. He was trim and lean, but his muscles were well pronounced and ended in a deep V at the waistband of his jeans. I playfully bit his nipple, and his hips jerked again. His restrained cock twitched upward, straining against the denim. My fingers found their way to his belt, and I undid the button of his jeans, slowly tugging on the zipper.

"This can't be comfortable," I said, pulling it all the way down and reaching inside to set his imprisoned manhood free. He grabbed my hand, knowing he shouldn't let this continue. "Please, Michael."

"Don't make this harder than it is." He winked at the play on words. "I don't want you to regret anything that happens between us."

"I won't," I insisted, but he shook his head, knowing I'd say anything at the moment to distract myself from the fear that the shooting had caused.

He picked me up off his lap and carefully zipped his jeans. From what I could tell, he probably made the guys in the locker room envious. The thought of that heavy, heated flesh had me salivating.

"Sorry, babe, but the rest is staying on, or we'll end up doing something that you'll regret." Pushing me back into a horizontal position, he removed my panties and pressed his palm against my center. "You're so wet." He sounded amazed. Carefully, he slipped a finger inside, and I let out an exhale at the pleasurable invasion. "And you're insanely tight."

He pumped that single digit inside of me a couple more times before pulling out and popping it into his mouth to taste my juices. The sight made me even hotter. He stroked my clit in tight circles, and my hips bucked wildly. He held my thighs down and began placing kisses along my stomach, heading south at an achingly slow pace when both of our phones rang.

The sudden intrusion caused me to jump into a seated position. Reaching for my cell phone, I saw it was the precinct. He grabbed his phone off the coffee table and shook his head.

"Duty calls," he muttered, standing up and reaching for his belongings as I attempted a level of modesty and quickly reached for my underwear. He met my eyes. "Hopefully, they've made some progress on what happened this afternoon." I nodded, still breathless. "This was fun. Perhaps next time, it will be even more fun." Before I could slip back into my panties, he leaned down and kissed me hard on the mouth and pushed two fingers deep inside my aching sex.

"Michael," my fingers clamped around his wrist, "we don't have time. We have to go back to work."

"Trust me. I know my way around the female body. This won't take long." His lips found mine, and he thrust his tongue into my mouth, mimicking the pattern of his fingers. He created a frenzied rhythm until my muffled cries were joined by my inner walls clenching around his fingers. He slowed his pace until the aftershocks from my orgasm subsided. He pulled back from the kiss and removed his fingers, leaving an emptiness inside of me. He pressed his lips to my forehead as I took a deep breath, my heart rate slowly returning to normal. "I promised I'd ease your suffering. Hopefully, that helped, but remember, this isn't exactly my A-game since we're just friends. No benefits." He winked and grabbed his shirt and buttoned it as I remained in a gelatinous state on the couch. "You should stay home tonight. Call in and tell them you're taking the night off."

"No. I want to know what happened."

"You need to get some sleep. And I need to know you're somewhere safe. But if you insist on going to work in the morning, call me, and I'll pick you up since your car is still at the station."

After Michael left, I crawled into bed and slept for almost twelve hours. When I woke up, it was noon and my clock radio was playing a pop song. It must have been on for the last five hours, but it wasn't enough to wake me. Briefly, I wondered if I sustained hearing damage, but that didn't seem likely. The truth was I was exhausted – emotionally and physically drained.

Oh my god, did I really beg Michael to have sex with me last night? I hid my face in my hands and tried to justify the insanity that had overtaken my life. What had I been thinking? We'd just gotten back on an even keel too. Crap.

Pulling myself out of bed, I trudged into the kitchen to make some coffee. I was starving, and just as I was searching the refrigerator for something to eat, a knock sounded at the door. Opening it, I was surprised to find Michael holding a paper sack from one of the nearby burger joints.

"Hey," he looked unsure of himself, a look I hadn't seen the cocky detective exhibit before, "how are you?"

"Embarrassed." I gestured for him to come inside. "I'm really sorry about last night." I laughed. "And I'm starting to sound like a broken record."

"There's no reason to be embarrassed or to apologize. Yesterday was crazy. It was just a fluke. I get it. We don't need to talk about it. Your nymphomaniac side is one secret I promise to protect." He smiled, and I slapped his arm, blushing. "When you didn't call this morning, I got worried. I also happened to remember how lacking your fridge and pantry were and thought you could use something to eat." He put the bag on the table, an amused glint developed in his eyes as I rifled through the contents, unwrapped the burger, and took a huge bite. "Obviously, I was right."

"It was bound to happen at some point," I teased. "Is Lieberman pissed I didn't show up this morning?"

"No. I covered and told him you called and said you'd be a little late. The people investigating yesterday's incident have a few more questions. So

whenever you're ready, I'll drive you to work."
"Thanks."

~*~

When we arrived at the precinct, I was ushered into an office and had to recount again what happened yesterday. Now that I had time to process, the investigator wanted to make sure that my story didn't change and that I didn't leave anything out. I didn't. After that, I returned to the squad room.

Preston smiled in my direction. "You look better today, Sarcone. Is everything okay?"

"Yeah, I just had to go through another recount of yesterday's events. By now, I'm feeling pretty desensitized to the whole thing."

"That's good," Lieberman interjected, "because I need to have a word with you." I followed him into the lieutenant's vacant office, and he closed the door behind us. "What were you doing checking in on the interrogation?"

"I was looking for Detective Preston and happened to pass by." Did Lieberman think I was telling internal affairs he was at fault? Was he at fault?

"I'm glad you did. We wouldn't have the leads we do if we didn't discover Stryker King inside. Even though Big Bill can no longer testify, the DA believes Bill's last few statements are still admissible in court because it was basically a deathbed confession. Burglary's going after Alfonso Sigfried, and the gangs unit is keeping tabs on his followers. Everything that happened yesterday is the break we've been waiting for on the home invasion spree. So good job, Sarcone. There might just be a permanent place for you here." The way he said those words made me think he wanted to ensure my loyalty to him, but I didn't say anything. I simply thanked him and returned to the squad room.

SEVEN

For the next few days, all I did was research. Kemper, Hawking, and I were tasked with cataloging files and ensuring that the gangs unit and burglary division were both up to speed on what was happening with the V7Ts. Being stuck behind a desk was boring, but I welcomed it. Plus, the more time I spent inside the precinct, the more comfortable I became. Immediately following my encounter with Stryker King, I would jump or cringe every time I heard a door or drawer slam. But things were returning to normal, and I was starting to feel safe again.

The burglary detectives were busy. Not only were they keeping tabs and questioning the V7Ts, but they were responding to the normal calls that came in on a daily basis. Michael and I had barely glimpsed one another in four days, and I was doing my best not to take it personally. We were friends. Friends didn't have to see each other every day or talk all the time, even my girl friends and I didn't do that.

Friday night, I returned home from work, made dinner, and decided to go to bed early. From the long hours and tedium of being behind a desk, I was tired. Maybe I was still a bit shell-shocked. The last few evenings I'd woken in a cold sweat from a nightmare. It was normal, but I hoped tonight I'd get a good night's sleep without any interruptions or horror-filled dreams.

This time, when I woke up, it was to the sound of incessant ringing. By the time I found my phone, the noise had stopped, but the caller left a message. The precinct was swamped, and all available officers were required to report for duty.

I arrived almost an hour later. The voicemail message had said to come in, and given that it was the middle of the night, an hour seemed like a reasonable timeframe. I was slightly giddy at the prospect of seeing Michael. Since this wasn't a normal shift, there was a chance we might get to work together, but I was unsure how I would react to being in such close proximity to him after what transpired in my apartment. Honestly, I was beginning to wonder if any of it was even real. Could I have dreamt the entire thing?

"Lexie," Kemper said, "we've got reports of a hold-up at Tenth and Albemarle. The detectives are on scene, but there have been two more calls, one at an apartment that we canvassed in relation to the home invasions and the other took place two floors above. Until Lieberman's dream team can tear themselves away from the hold-up, they want us lowly officers to maintain the two other crime scenes."

"Great," I muttered unenthusiastically.

"Let's get going. I need back-up to ride along," Kemper insisted, and I followed him from the building and out to the black and white cruiser he was assigned. "What were you doing when you got the call? You look way too awake for four a.m."

"I might have been dreaming. I'm not entirely sure. But the wide awake thing tends to happen when the super fails to fix the hot water in your shower," I pointed out.

Kemper drove through nonexistent traffic, and we made it to the scene in ten minutes. A few cruisers were out front, and as we went upstairs, I offered to take the seventh floor if he kept watch outside the fifth floor apartment. The responding officers were in charge of taking statements and talking to the victims, the neighbors, and making sure no evidence grew legs and walked away. I was there to keep all the nosy looky-loos away.

Leaning against the wall, I fielded some radio chatter concerning the scene, the victims, suspects, and what was allegedly stolen. It was grunt work, but most police work tended to be. My mind wandered, and my eyes threatened to close. I shifted my weight onto my other leg and crossed my arms, hoping not to fall asleep.

"Does anyone have a twenty on Riley?" Lieberman asked over the radio.

Apparently Michael hadn't arrived at work yet. Although since it was a Friday night, or Saturday morning at this point, Riley might have been slightly inebriated. He tended to go out for drinks after shift. Maybe he went home to sober up or had other matters to take care of. He might have been on a date. My stomach clenched, and I recognized that feeling as a pang of jealousy. How stupid was that? I listened for a response to confirm Riley's location, but no one had any idea where he was.

After spending the next thirty minutes keeping

watch outside one of the two tossed apartments, a man in a dark blue jumpsuit approached. He smiled and tugged on the lanyard around his neck, pulling it free from the coveralls.

"Officer Sarcone?" he asked.

"That would be me. How can I help you, sir?"

"I'm with the crime lab. The responding officer requested I print the place." He showed me his identification and badge. "May I begin?"

I radioed for verification before letting the crime scene investigator into the apartment. He started working, and we chitchatted for a time as he spread black powder and placed tape over the fingerprints.

"I heard the owner is at the station for questioning. She came home to find some stranger in her apartment. Thankfully, no one got hurt," I said.

"The amount of burglaries lately has been insane. From the scuttlebutt I've heard, it's some new gang's initiation method. Granted, I'm thankful they're not randomly popping people. But still," he shook his head, "shouldn't America's youth have better things to do with their time, like playing gory zombie-killing video games and smoking pot behind the school gym? At least that's what we did as kids."

I giggled. "And yet you still became a police officer."

"Crime tech," he clarified. "Completely different. I can be a video game loving dork, and as long as I lay off the illegal substances, the department seems happy with my work."

"Nice."

He was just shutting his briefcase, having properly labeled the samples after tagging and numbering everything, when Detective Preston arrived. She nodded to the tech as he packed up his belongings and left the building.

"Sarcone, I'll take it from here. Did you notice anyone suspicious, or did anyone try to enter the apartment while you were here?" she asked.

"No, ma'am."

"Okay, go back to the station. Lieberman's adding the three burglaries from tonight as new leads and evidence against Alfonso Sigfried. By now, I'm sure Mr. Hardnose has devised a new plan of attack." She smirked, and I chuckled at her nickname for Lieberman. "And he probably needs someone there who knows how to use the copier."

"I'm on it." I turned to leave.

"Hey," she called, "Riley is back at the precinct. Make sure you tell him to pop in and see Lieberman before he tries to sneak out and avoid the briefing."

"Sure thing." I continued down the hallway to see if Kemper was ready to leave.

Once we were back inside the police station, I passed Preston's message on to Michael who simply nodded. He looked busy. His desk was covered in case files, and he was on the phone.

Quietly excusing myself, I took a seat at my desk and hoped that no one would ask me to do anything else for the rest of the night. I was tired and wanted nothing more than to go home and go back to bed. Five minutes later, Lieberman appeared, and we worked nonstop through the rest of what turned into my scheduled shift.

"Lexie, can you do me a favor?" Kemper asked. I had just finished pulling a double and wasn't in the mood to do anyone any favors.

"What is it?" I wished I could just tell him no.

"Can you copy your notes from Lieberman's debrief? Since this thing just keeps getting bigger, Hawking and I were asked to liaise between burglary and gangs."

"Here," I hit print and pointed to the community printer across the room, "help yourself. But fair warning, my notes are basically pointless. The detectives just want us to work on their paperwork and keep all the files in order. We aren't doing any actual police work, and therefore, we're not privy to most things. We'd be better off going out on our normal tours than pulling desk duty."

"Someone's in a bitch of a mood."

"It happens. Deal with it."

"Chicks," he muttered, and I glared at him.

"Are you complaining, Sarcone?" Riley asked from behind. I had no idea he was there. Not that it should matter. Ever since he left my apartment that afternoon after bringing me lunch and giving me a ride back to the precinct, he was giving me the cold shoulder. He hadn't even offered a friendly smile, let alone a single word that wasn't work related. Maybe he realized I was a tease. I'd been incredibly hot and cold toward him, but that was because we worked together. This thing, whatever it was, had turned into a huge mess, and the insanity of our jobs wasn't helping matters either. "Because I have a box of old cases that have to be assessed for similar MOs, and someone needs to get right on that."

"I'm off the clock," I growled, annoyed for being made to feel like an idiot.

"You're a cop. There is no clock." I spun in my chair and caught the slightest amused glint in his sparkling blue eyes that immediately brought a smile to my face. He looked like a little boy with a secret, and I raised a questioning eyebrow. "The box is on my desk. You should get started." He winked and sauntered away.

"Asshole," I said to his retreating back, hoping he caught the playful tone to my words. He chuckled, waving goodbye.

I pulled the chair out from under his desk and opened the file box. As promised, there was a stack of files, but there was one other item inside the box. Glancing around, I plucked the sticky note off the smaller box.

"Thought you could use a little something to brighten your day. They matched your eyes, so I couldn't resist" was scrawled on the paper that had been attached to a velvet box. Inside was a pair of earrings. I was sure I was beet red.

Glancing around, I quickly shoved the lid back on the file box and dragged it over to my desk. Once there, I carefully looked around before opening my bottom drawer, taking out my purse, and tossing the jewelry safely inside. I guess I hadn't dreamt the entire thing, after all.

Unfortunately, Michael hadn't been lying about the files. Resigned to doing actual police work, I called in Officers Kemper and Hawking to be my reinforcements, and together, the three of us managed to find two old cases that fit the descriptions of our current crime spree. At least it was a start.

When I got home from work, I called Michael to thank him for the earrings. "You shouldn't have," I said. "Plus, it's illegal to bribe a police officer."

"It wasn't a bribe."

"Yes, it was. You tricked me into doing your paperwork."

"I did not." I could hear the smile in his voice. "It was just a little something to cheer you up. You've seemed off this week, but I haven't had the chance to check in with you. Are you doing okay?"

"I'm fine. I haven't been sleeping well. Nightmares," I admitted.

"Do you want to talk about it?"

"Not really. You were there. You know what

happened."

"I also know what happened afterward." He inhaled deeply. "Not to further complicate things, but what would you say to going out sometime? I think I owe you a real date after rounding second and almost sliding into third."

"I think you did slide into third. Repeatedly." Memories of his mouth and hands flooded my mind, and I sighed.

"Is that a yes?" he asked.

"Can I think about it?"

"What's to think about?" He paused. "Haven't you gotten to know me yet? This is because we work together, isn't it?"

"That's part of it."

"So if I were just some guy you met at a bar, then you'd go out with me?"

"I don't pick up men at bars. That stopped when I left vice," I retorted, and he laughed at the joke. "It's also because I haven't dated anyone in a long time. My last boyfriend didn't like the fact that I wanted to be a cop. It was too butch of a profession for him to accept."

"That's because he was clearly an insecure prick. And I love that you're a cop. I wouldn't know you otherwise. And for the record, I'm neither insecure nor a prick."

"Let's finish this case first. And once I'm back working the beat, then you can take me out."

"I'm holding you to that." He laughed, a deep, contented sound. "And I know where you live, so don't even think about ducking me."

"Ducking? Oh, don't worry, I won't think about ducking you. But I might think about doing something else to you."

"Mmm, you're such a tease. Good night."

"I'll see you tomorrow."

EIGHT

Briefly, I saw Michael the next day, but that was pretty much it. Over the course of the next week, Michael Riley was busy. We were all busy, working on identifying and disbanding the gang responsible for the string of robberies plaguing the neighborhood. But still, I couldn't help but wonder if he was actually busy or just too busy for me. I played it cool, one of the things I wasn't sure I could do, and focused on work. I didn't go out of my way to see him, speak to him, or acknowledge anything that he said or did. This was our job, and I was sure the brass would frown upon interdepartmental romance.

Frank Devereaux, the undercover officer I had nearly arrested, entered the precinct. He looked a bit rough around the edges. His eye was black, and there were other obvious signs that he'd recently been in a fight. He went straight to Lieberman's desk and began laying out everything he knew on the gang. An hour later, we were called to the roll call room, which doubled as a conference room, for another briefing.

"The gang responsible for this spree of thefts has

doubled its membership in the last month," Lieberman began. "It's come to our attention that these little shitheads aren't our typical gangbangers. The V7Ts are run by Alfonso Sigfried. His motley crew is comprised of thirty or more members, aged sixteen to twenty years old. They've been knocking over convenience stores, liquor stores, and ransacking apartments in the hopes of hitting a big score. The bigger their score, the more impressed their leader is. What makes matters worse is what Sigfried is using to incentivize these miscreants." Lieberman's gaze landed on each of us. "He's been trading smack for money, jewelry, and other pawnable items. It's exactly what Big Bill told us, but we don't have enough hard evidence to arrest Sigfried. If Stryker King hadn't killed Big Bill inside our interrogation room, this would probably be resolved by now."

"Have we made any progress on that?" Riley asked from the corner.

"Internal affairs is still investigating how King got inside the interrogation room, but when we arrested Big Bill, word traveled fast. And it's rumored that Sigfried put a hit out on him and anyone else that snitches, so no one wants to talk to us."

"Obviously, he'd do anything to hide his drug dealing on trade," Preston piped up. She rolled her eyes. "Just when I think I've seen it all. Is it even a gang or just a hardcore dealer that beats his buyers into submission?"

Frank cleared his throat. "It's the latter, Samantha. And it's only a matter of time before he kills someone for bringing him a toaster instead of a stereo."

"Sigfried doesn't like to deal with cash. We've speculated it might be because it would make arresting him easier. If we could match the serial numbers from the cash stolen out of an apartment to what's in his pocket, it'd be game over. He might have realized some of the places that have been hit were a plant, particularly since Devereaux isn't exactly twenty years old anymore."

"I'm close enough," Frank replied. "Well, within the same decade at least."

"Regardless," Lieberman didn't enjoy being interrupted and glared in the other man's direction, "some nearby pawn shops have landed on our radar. Sometimes, Sigfried takes the stolen items there to exchange for cash, or he sends one of his guys to do it for him. So we're going to set up a sting operation. Frank's been on the inside, and he just informed me that a few of the V7Ts made a huge score the other night. One of these wannabe badasses decided that he and his buddies ought to hit an apartment on the West Side, and now they have twenty hot tablets to pass along to Sigfried. The trade hasn't gone down yet, and that's a lot of merchandise to move, so Sigfried might spread it out among different shops in order to bring in the most cash. Go ahead and share your plan with the team, Preston," Lieberman concluded.

Detective Preston skimmed through the file, striding to the front of the room to take over the briefing. She and Devereaux had been communicating during his undercover assignment and had devised a plan before presenting it to Lieberman.

"We're dividing up into teams. One detective will be assigned an officer to ride along. That way, everyone has adequate training and back-up. We'll use unmarked cars and monitor the area around a few of the pawn shops. Hopefully, we'll get lucky and spot our guy or one of his trusted minions." Preston pointed to a blown-up mug shot of Sigfried. "This is our target. Make sure you remember what he looks like. Are there any questions?" No one said a word.

"Fine, I'll take Kemper, and we'll surveil this location." She pointed to the map.

"I've got Hawking and the shop in the southeast," Lieberman said, not pleased that someone else had taken over his briefing. He liked to be in charge. Of course, that left Detective Riley with only one option.

"I guess we're partnered together," he whispered in my ear, struggling to sound resigned to this unfortunate turn of events. "I don't understand how I always end up drawing the short straw."

"Is that what you call it?" I grabbed a printout of Sigfried's photo from the table and followed Riley out the door.

"No, I actually call it the jackhammer." He smiled, crinkling his nose. "Actually, a very lovely lady called it that, and the name stuck."

"Ugh." I rolled my eyes. "You really need to work on censoring what comes out of your mouth. I didn't need to know that." I climbed inside the unmarked Mustang that the police department recently procured and fidgeted with the seatbelt. "What the hell is wrong with you? God, what the hell is wrong with me?"

Only after we pulled away from the precinct and were two blocks away did he speak. "Are you mad about something? I was just joking around."

"I'm not mad."

I stared out the window. It wasn't fair to Michael that I had trust issues when it came to men, and being made to feel like just another notch on his bedpost didn't help alleviate that issue. It made it worse. And the earrings, while thoughtful and sweet, had reminded me of so many of those johns that I arrested. Plus, we hadn't even been out on a date. It wasn't like I could have the 'where do we stand in our relationship' conversation yet. And did I want a relationship? Frankly, with men like Michael, expecting nothing more than a roll in the hay would be a much safer and more realistic expectation to have.

"You seem mad. That night after the incident in the precinct, I hated to leave, but I had to get to work. But I stopped by the next day to bring you lunch and check on you. You seemed fine after that. And we've talked on the phone a few times since, so don't tell me you're not mad because I know you. And you weren't upset about anything until a few minutes ago, so did my stupid comment really piss you off that badly? It was dumb, but don't you think you're overreacting?"

I turned and stared at him. He drove one-handed with his left hand on the wheel, making the muscles in his forearm bunch as he turned the car right, heading down another street.

"I'm not a detective, so maybe you can help me figure something out."

"Anything, babe." He shot me a smile.

"One minute, you're all over me, but then days go by where I barely see you at work. You leave me a present and we talk on the phone, but you boast about the other women you've been with. Then you ask me on a date and refuse to take no for an answer. So you want to make sure I'm hooked, but at the same time, you act like you don't want me to get the wrong idea about what this is. So what is this? Is there a reason you're acting like this?" I stopped, horrified. "Oh my god, you're in a relationship. You just want a sidepiece."

"No." He laughed. He actually laughed at me. "But when we're at work, it's important we keep it professional. And even though we haven't had a chance to go out yet, I know you'll be hooked once we do." He took his eyes off the road and looked at me. "Your ex-boyfriend screwed you over," his jaw clenched tightly, and his hand gripped the steering wheel even harder, "and that's something incredibly difficult to get past. I know it is. I've been there myself. God, I'd love to teach that guy some manners, but I'm not him. And even though we're not even dating yet, I want you to know, I haven't been with anyone since the night I showed up at your door, drunk on tequila."

"Oh, wow, now look who's having a dry spell." I couldn't help the sarcasm, and Michael took my hand in his and kissed my knuckles.

"You can trust me. I won't hurt you, Lexie. And if you give me a chance, I'll prove it."

"Just not at work."

"Let's just say I'm not everyone's favorite person, and I don't want our fun to hurt your reputation. You were afraid of what the brass would think of this, so remember, you didn't want to advertise our affiliation either."

"I know." I rubbed my eyes with my free hand. I felt neurotic. "But for the record, it has nothing to do with my reputation." I scoffed, thinking of the lewd and sexist things I'd heard a lot of men at the station whisper behind my back. "What reputation? I worked vice for god's sake. Even I know what the guys say in the locker room about me. It's not true. It's just because they're convinced police work is for boys only. That's just how this job is, sometimes. So I'm not worried about that."

"That's not what I meant." He shot me a look. "This isn't going to help my case any, particularly after you told me to censor what I say, but you should know, Preston and I used to be a thing. It's in the past, but I have no desire to rub her face in any of my new..." He faltered for a word.

"Conquests?" I icily asked.

"I don't think of you like that. I don't know how to think of you. But I do think about you." His voice sounded deep and sexy when he said that. And my mind flashed to an image of him in the shower, steam rising around his toned, naked body. *Stop*, I scolded myself. "Would you," he stuttered slightly, "like to go out on an actual date sometime sooner than we planned? Like, say tonight?"

For someone as attractive as he was, Riley lacked being suave. I guess when you are a detective who looks like that, you probably don't have to ask girls out, what with all the badge bunnies at the bars and everything. But I found the way he fumbled around the word endearing.

"Really?" I hesitated.

"C'mon, Lexie, I don't know what to do here. You obviously like me. You can't deny that. And I'm crazy about you. Give me a chance. It's the only way I'll ever be able to prove that I'm a good guy."

A truer sentiment had never been uttered, and I caved. My stomach flew into my throat as a million butterflies took flight inside of me. "Okay, but I must warn you, I don't have sex on a first date."

"Okay, we'll have sex and then go on a date." He smirked. "And before you change your mind, I promise I was only kidding."

Biting my lip, I hid my smile away. There was a one in a million chance that this wouldn't end horribly wrong. He was a bad boy. He was unbelievably sexy, a little wild, and a professional badass. This was the exact type of guy that mothers warned their daughters about, and yet, I was drawn to him, knowing he'd probably break my heart. But the small voice inside my head held out hope. Michael was kind, generous, and absolutely amazing. Things between us could be phenomenal. And despite my dislike for taking unnecessary risks, something that we were always cautioned against in the academy, Michael Riley was one risk that I couldn't just walk away from.

"So where are you taking me tonight?" I asked, finding my voice just as he parked the car near the pawn shop and we began our reconnaissance.

"It's a surprise."

"So in other words, you have no idea."

"That's the surprise." He laughed, rubbing his thumb in lazy circles on the back of my hand. "We might as well get comfortable. We'll probably be here all day." He released my hand, and I immediately missed the contact as he adjusted his seat. Then he dug through his pocket for a pen and paper and began scribbling down some words that he hid from me. "Pay attention, Officer," he jerked his chin out the windshield, "we're only here to scout this location for signs of Sigfried." He smiled but didn't look at me. "And our perp looks nothing like me."

"Ha ha." I focused out the windshield, glancing at him occasionally as he diverted his focus from the paper to the surrounding area and back again. "What are you doing?" I finally asked.

"Just some prep work for this evening." He put the list into his pocket. "And now we wait."

The only problem with sting operations was they tended to last forever. Michael and I played twenty questions back and forth for a while as he attempted to get to know me. Unfortunately, I didn't feel like I was that exciting. I told him about my family, the pets I had growing up, where I went to school, my best friend Emma, and my uncertainty about taking the detective's exam.

"You'd be great," he encouraged. He spoke about his brothers. One was a detective in Philadelphia and the other was just down the road at a nearby precinct.

They had dreams of leadership and were planning on vying for a lieutenant or captain position one day. "I don't know. I was never as driven as they are. Sometimes, I think I must have been adopted. When I was a kid, I wanted to be a painter, and then I wanted to be a race car driver. And I think before it was all said and done I had come up with the worst possibility of all."

"Which is?"

"Firefighter." He chuckled. "My dad still holds a grudge over the fire department's hockey win over the police department from fifteen years ago. To him, that idea was worse than saying I was going to become an assassin for hire, which I proudly announced when I was ten after watching the movie, *The Jackal*."

"But let me guess, you watched *Die Hard* afterward and decided to be the next John McClane which is what led to that shiny detective's shield of yours."

"Nice Bruce Willis reference," he complimented. He reached out and gently brushed a lock of my hair out of my face that had come loose from my bun. I shut my eyes as his thumb caressed my temple, my cheek, and my jaw. "You're breathtaking."

"You're not so bad yourself."

He gave me a bittersweet look. "Then give me a real chance at this." He gestured between us. I caught his sultry look. Throwing one last glance out the windshield, I scooted over in the seat and kissed him. It was electric, and I sighed into his mouth.

"You're really good at that," I whispered, slowly pulling back so we could resume performing our duties.

"Promise me, no matter what happens, you'll be fearless. There's no reason to deny yourself what you want or at least the chance to go out there and get it." He put a hand on my neck and pulled me back to him for another kiss. "For the few weeks that I've known you, I've seen you hide from what you want. You keep doing it over and over again. With me. With the idea of vying for a promotion. With the way you let people give talk shit. The only time you went for what you wanted was after that horrible day at the station."

"And you denied me." I pulled back, looking out the windshield. "I'm glad you did. You were right not to give in. And you were a gentleman for not taking advantage beyond giving me what I needed, but," I shrugged, "you still rejected me."

My insecurities were laid out on the table for him, along with my emotional baggage, but he didn't run for the hills. Instead, he leaned closer and placed a chaste kiss on my cheek.

"I'll never reject you again."

NINE

He kissed me hard, dipping his tongue into my mouth. "We shouldn't be doing this. We need to be focused on work," he insisted when we broke for air. I let out a contented sigh and leaned as close to him as I could get since the center console was in the way. My head rested against the crook of his neck, and I continued to plant soft, gentle kisses against his warmed skin.

After ten minutes of sitting in silence with my face buried in his neck, he kissed my forehead and sat up straight. Playtime was over for now. I scooted away and took a few deep breaths.

"Don't you dare tell any of the guys at the precinct about this," I threatened. "Surveillance assignments are always rumored to be full of crazy sexual escapades, but I'd prefer if everyone still believed that was only urban legend. Our making out does not need to become fodder or anecdotal to support such claims."

"Scout's honor," he promised. He met my eyes,

looking sincere and serious in his admiration. "Lexie, I think I could fall–"

"Isn't that our guy?" I asked, spotting movement near the pawn shop.

He looked outside. "Hot damn. I never thought we'd actually get eyes on Sigfried our first time out."

We watched from our position in the car as Sigfried made his way down the street and entered the pawn shop. Riley opened the car door, checking the small of his back to make sure his gun was still holstered underneath his jacket and his cuffs were concealed from passersby.

"Should I radio for back-up?" I asked.

"Yes. Call it in, and I'll see if I can catch him red-handed with some stolen items. If I need your help, I'll let you know." He opened the car door and strutted toward the shop.

Picking up the radio, I called in the request for back-up and waited. Within two minutes, Lieberman and Hawking pulled up next to us. Lieberman got out of the car, marching off in the direction of the pawn shop, but Hawking just looked at me and shrugged. We were still in uniform, and our presence would make Alfonso run. We didn't want that to happen. So we were stuck waiting inside the cars in case a radio call came through for immediate assistance. Hopefully, that wouldn't happen.

This operation was a game for detectives. We were simply on-site support. But clearly, the call for back-up had gone through dispatch because a few black and whites rolled up. They parked nearby, but the officers inside didn't get out of their vehicles either. Instead, we anxiously waited for verification of an arrest or a radio call for assistance.

The waiting was interminable. My leg bounced against the seat cushion, and I turned the volume up on my radio for fear that I would miss something. But still, we waited. A few minutes later, chatter erupted. The suspect was last seen fleeing east on foot. He was wearing a navy blue hooded jacket and jeans and was to be considered armed and dangerous. Two detectives were in pursuit.

The two patrol cars that had been waiting with us took off down the street, splitting up in order to flank the fleeing suspect from both sides. Meanwhile, Hawking and I jumped out of our vehicles and raced toward the pawn shop. Hawking was a few feet ahead, and I followed the direction he took. Four blocks later, he slowed his pace, and I practically slammed into his back.

"Where are they?" he asked. He checked his radio to make sure it was still functioning and asked for a twenty on the suspect.

"We lost him," a very frustrated Lieberman responded. "Rendezvous at the pawn shop. We're bringing the owner in."

"Copy that," Hawking replied. He looked at me. "Race you back?"

"Not on your life." I shook my head, and we headed back the way we came at a brisk pace. I turned around a few times, wondering where Riley and Lieberman were. They should be behind us, but there was no sign of either of them. "Do you think we went the wrong way?"

"No, they probably detoured down a side street or alleyway." He sighed. "I don't see how they lost the suspect or why it took so long for them to radio for assistance."

"They probably tried to box him in, so he couldn't rabbit. But I guess Sigfried noticed."

"Or the pawn shop guy alerted him to what was going down," Hawking suggested. "Ugh. Civilians are a pain in the ass." I laughed at his comment, earning myself a small smile. "On the bright side, at least we don't have to fill out an action report explaining how Alfonso Sigfried eluded us."

"We might. We were sitting outside the shop, doing nothing but twiddling our thumbs."

"Shit, that's what Lieberman's going to make it sound like." Hawking let out a growl. "How come he gets to take all the credit when things go well but when they go sideways, we take all the blame?"

"It's because he's in charge. We both need promotions."

"I'll second that."

"You'll second what?" Lieberman asked, surprising us from behind. "What the hell are you two rookies talking about?"

"Other things we could have done to assist in apprehending Sigfried," Hawking replied smoothly. "How long were you in pursuit, sir?"

"Long enough." Lieberman studied my gaze, which was focused on the alleyway he had just emerged from. "Are you looking for Riley?"

I nodded. But he didn't offer an explanation, and I didn't ask any questions. Instead, the three of us returned to the pawn shop to begin questioning the owner and maintaining the scene until a search warrant could be signed and delivered.

The shop contained a ton of electronics, everything from mp3 players to home entertainment centers. This had to be Sigfried's primary cash exchange location. As I browsed the cases, I wondered how much of the merchandise was hot. Lieberman was asking the questions, and Hawking was meticulously taking notes. I leaned against the back wall and felt something give. Furrowing my brow, I knocked against the paneling, hearing a hollow echo.

"Detective," I called, waiting for Lieberman to turn before I repeated the action, "I think there's something back there."

He spun on the owner. "Open it."

"What? She's crazy," the owner insisted. His name was John Wolfe, and he had priors for selling illegal weapons and stolen merchandise. "That's a freaking wall."

"I'm not asking you again," Lieberman said, his voice low and even. "You either open it, or I'll put your head through it. Either way, I'm gonna find out what's inside."

Hawking glanced at me. Neither of us had spent that much time alone with Lieberman, and even we didn't know if it was a joke. Mr. Wolfe swallowed audibly and slowly went around the counter where Lieberman had wedged him in. He hit a button, and the panel slid to the side, exposing a dozen handguns, a few grenades, and an assault rifle or two.

"I have no idea how those got there," Wolfe said, and Lieberman rolled his eyes.

"Mr. Wolfe, you have the right to remain silent," Lieberman began, clicking a pair of handcuffs around Wolfe's wrists, "but the more you cooperate, the more likely I am to overlook whatever else we find in your shop. I don't particularly care what you're doing. I just want Alfonso Sigfried. So I'll give you a minute to think about it. And if you don't want to cooperate, then I'm taking you in."

While the three of us waited for Wolfe to make a decision, the two patrol cars from earlier returned, and Michael climbed out of one of the cars. He said something to the guys, and they pulled away just as the second patrol car parked in front. Detective Riley and the two other officers entered the shop and took up unobtrusive positions near the door.

Michael was bleeding. There was a deep cut running from his ripped sleeve down the length of his arm, and his face was slightly battered. He looked angry.

"Are you okay?" I asked.

His eyes flicked to my face, seeing the worry there. He nodded before returning his focus to Lieberman. The other detective glanced in his direction but didn't say anything. I didn't know what transpired, but something didn't jive.

More police vehicles arrived on the scene, and Lieberman dismissed Michael and me. As we went out the door, Michael slipped the car keys into my palm and went around to the passenger's seat. Before I even started the car, he had pulled some gauze from the first aid kit inside the glove box and was holding it against his arm.

I gave him a worried look, but he played it off with a rugged smile. "I didn't want to get bloodstains on the new upholstery. The department's cars don't stay nice very long."

"What the hell happened?" I asked, wanting to do something to help or at least knock some compassion into Lieberman.

"Sigfried got away."

"But what about your arm? And your face?" I stopped at a red light and gingerly touched his cheek.

"Chain-link fence and a brick wall. I'm okay. Really." He focused out the windshield. "The light's green."

"Are you sure? You might need stitches. Should I take you to the emergency room?"

"Lexie, I'm fine. Stop being so dramatic, sweetheart. Getting banged up is just a consequence of the job." He snorted. "So is getting banged." I knew he said it in order to distract me from worrying about his injuries, and I gave him a withering glare and continued to the station.

Once we arrived, Michael disappeared inside the men's locker room to clean and bandage his wounds, and I went to my desk to start on the paperwork. My involvement in the botched apprehension and securing the pawn shop was minimal, so it didn't take long to record what needed to be reported. By the time I was finished, Michael was at his desk.

"Can I see what you wrote?" he asked, and I printed a copy and brought it to him. "Thanks." He was all business, and I let him focus while I went in search of something to keep myself busy.

An hour and a half later, Lieberman, Hawking, and the troop of responding officers returned from the pawn shop. Mr. Wolfe was arrested as an accessory and for trafficking in the sale of stolen goods. More severe charges would probably come to light in the next day or so, but it was enough to detain him at the present.

"Sarcone, I need a word," Lieberman barked, and automatically, I gulped, feeling like I'd just been called into the principal's office. Out of the corner of my eye, I saw Riley tense, the muscles in his arm bunching, and he threw an intense look at Lieberman. "Now, Sarcone."

"Yes, sir." I followed him down the corridor and into the stairwell. "What's wrong?"

"Nothing." He towered over me, stepping closer. "Nice work back at the pawn shop. You really made the owner sweat when you happened upon that hidden panel. How'd you know it was there?"

"It was luck."

"Luck, huh?" He eyed me. "If you say so." He fell silent as a pair of officers went down the steps, passing us with a respectful nod at the detective.

"What were you and Hawking doing while Riley and I were chasing down the suspect?"

"Monitoring the situation." It was true, and it sounded more professional than saying we were sitting in the car. "Why didn't you radio sooner, sir? We might have been able to circle around, preventing Sigfried from escaping."

"Did you write that in your report?"

"No." Suddenly, the questions didn't seem quite so friendly. "I can't attest to what occurred in an area where I was not present."

"Very good." He nodded. "I'm glad you have the lingo down. After that scuffle with Stryker King, internal affairs has been keeping tabs on my unit. And since you were the hostage taken, they'll probably talk to you about it. It's good to know you can remain detached and professional."

"What does any of that have to do with what happened today?" Immediately, I regretted asking the question.

"It's the same gang. Same types of people." He scooted unbearably close, completely disregarding my personal space. "Let me ask you something. Do you blame me for what happened to you the other day?"

"No."

"Do you believe I'd intentionally let a perp like Sigfried walk away?"

"No, sir."

"Then we don't have a problem here." He smiled and patted my shoulder. I found it disconcerting. "Normally, I have a feel for what my team is thinking, but you're new to this division and to my team. It's nice to know we're on the same page." He looked at his watch. "Finish your paperwork and check out at shift change. You've been working too damn hard lately."

Without another word, I did what he said. That exchange left a bad taste in my mouth. Was Lieberman really just covering his ass? Or did he think I was a rat or a troublemaker? And the more important question that I was too afraid to ask was if he did something wrong.

TEN

That strange encounter with Detective Lieberman left me baffled. The rest of my shift was nothing but a blur. When I made it home and unlocked my apartment door, I couldn't help but think of everything that had happened since being tasked to assist the detectives on the home invasion spree. A suspect was killed in custody inside a police station by a man who ran in Sigfried's crew. Then after Riley and I positively identified Sigfried, back-up arrived, but somehow the suspect managed to outrun two detectives and two patrol cars. And why was Lieberman lurking in that alley when Hawking and I were returning to the pawn shop? He and Riley must have split up, but that didn't make sense either. What the hell was going on?

A headache formed behind my eyes, and I squeezed the bridge of my nose, grabbing a pen and paper to detail the few facts I knew. This was a puzzle, and it didn't make sense. At least, it didn't make sense to me.

The knock at my door made me gasp, and I reached

for my Glock. Watching my hand tremble as it moved over the dark steel, I forced myself to relax. This case was making me jumpy. And I thought burglary would be safer than vice. Snorting at my own idiotic thought, I went to the door and checked the peephole.

"Shit." I opened the door to find Michael holding a slightly wilted bouquet of wildflowers.

"Are you allergic?" he asked, pulling the flowers away.

"No. It's not that." I reached to take them from him, and he put them behind his back, forcing me to reach around and hug him as I tried to grab them. He put his free hand against the small of my back and pulled me close as both of my arms encompassed his waist.

"Hi," he said quietly, his smile infectious.

"Hi." I lifted up onto my tiptoes and brushed my lips gently against his. "Don't hate me, but I forgot."

"You forgot that you like flowers?"

"No." I released him, taking the bouquet and leading the way into my apartment. "I didn't forget that I like flowers. I forgot that we had a date. After what happened this afternoon, I wasn't sure you'd remember either."

"I made a note." He held up the list he had scribbled earlier in the car.

"Why didn't I think to do that?" I dug through the cabinet beneath the sink for a vase.

"It seems you've been making other lists." He frowned at the information I'd been working to piece together. "What did Lieberman say to you this afternoon?"

"Nothing. He said I did a good job." I filled the vase with water and put it on the counter. "That guy gives me the creeps. I know he's the detective in charge, but the things he does just don't seem to add up."

"I'm sure everything's fine. You worry too much."

"God, look at you." I turned, focusing on the bandages peeking out from beneath his short sleeve shirt. "Where was Lieberman when that happened?"

"I don't know. We split up during the pursuit."

"That does not instill within me a vast amount of confidence in Lieberman."

"Look at you and the big words." He wrapped his arms around me and buried his face in my hair. "Are you going to let me take you out somewhere nice, or would you rather stay here and talk about work all night?"

I sighed. "Michael, will you be honest with me for a minute?"

"I've never lied to you." His brow furrowed. "What's up?" He stepped back, resting his hips against my kitchen table.

"What happened after you got out of the car to pursue Sigfried?"

He rubbed his eyes, clearly annoyed. "I followed him inside and watched him speak to the shop owner. He seemed spooked." Michael shrugged. "When he presented what I'm certain was stolen contraband, I moved in to make the arrest. He darted out a back entrance, and I pursued him for nine blocks before he jumped a fence that was blocking an alley. My arm got tangled in one of the rusted wires. I face planted against a brick wall, and a patrol car gave me a lift back while the other attempted to reroute and pursue." He exhaled. "Why do you need to know that?"

"Where was Lieberman when that went down?"

"How would I know?" Michael looked utterly confused, and I shook my head. The pounding in my skull was getting worse. "Lexie?"

"Lieberman rolled up before the radio call for

assistance came through. He said the two of you pursued the suspect."

"If that's what he said, then I'm sure that's what he did."

"Then where the hell was he when you were inside the pawn shop?"

"C'mon, you're fishing. Just drop it. Lieberman's a good cop. Did IA put you up to this? Are you reporting to them? Did they want you to ask me these things? Is that why you've been so hot and cold after declaring we were nothing more than friends? Is that why you said you'd go out with me?"

"No one put me up to anything. I'm just confused why Lieberman was acting so guarded and called me out so we could speak privately. And now you're looking at me like I'm crazy or a snitch or something."

"Look, I've had a tough day. The last thing I want to do is talk about work. When I leave the precinct, I leave that behind. Or at least I try to. It's not healthy to think about nothing but the job." He blinked and returned to my living room. "Maybe I should go, and we can reschedule for another night when you haven't forgotten that we've made plans."

"Michael, I'm sorry."

"Yeah. Me too." He left, slamming my front door behind him.

I stood in my kitchen, stunned. We weren't even dating yet, but already, the sting of rejection burned through my entire body. The empty, painful hollow began in my stomach and erupted in strangled gasps and salty tears. Less than twelve hours ago, he promised he wouldn't reject me again, but in my mind, this was rejection. And it hurt.

Giving the flowers a final glance, I plucked the bouquet from the vase, tossed them into the trashcan, poured the morning's coffee grounds on top, and slammed the lid. Yes, it was childish, but it made me feel better. Then I wiped the pathetic tears from my cheeks. I would not wallow in self-doubt or pity. This was stupid. He was being defensive for no reason, and that was not my fault.

My head hurt, but the last thing I wanted to do was stay home and think about Riley or work. So I quickly touched up my makeup, grabbed my purse, and went down the stairs to find a cab. With my cell phone in hand, I scanned my address book for a friend who might want to go out and get mildly drunk in the middle of the week. Just as the call connected with Emma, my best friend, someone cleared his throat.

"What's up, girl?" Emma asked.

"Hey, Em. I hit the wrong number. Let me call you back." I disconnected before she could say another word. "I thought you left." Michael had never seen me angry before, but he was about to. "That was what the parting words and slamming door indicated. I might not be a detective, but those clues seemed pretty obvious."

"I fucked up."

"Yeah. You fucked up." I rolled my eyes. "And I fucked up for forgetting. That doesn't mean that you can act defensive and storm out when I ask you a question."

"No, Lex," he shook his head, as if I didn't get it, "at work. I fucked up at work."

"Michael," my headache was on the cusp of full-blown migraine, "I don't care. You left. So leave. Just go." My chin trembled, and tears stung my eyes. No. I wouldn't cry. Not in front of him. Not over something this stupid.

"Hey, listen," he took a step closer, reaching for me, but I batted his hand away, "Sigfried made me. He must have spotted the badge or the gun. I don't know.

But he was antsy. He was out the back before I even had a chance to announce. I think Lieberman was waiting outside because I caught a glimpse of someone darting after him. It happened so fast, and going through the back alleys, all the paths intersect. Jack probably just branched off and ran up on a dead end. I didn't see him, but that doesn't mean he wasn't there, right?" It sounded more like a question than an explanation.

"Then why the hell didn't you just say that in the first place?" I snapped. I put my palm against the wall and covered my eyes with my hand, forcing my emotions to remain in check. "Whatever the hell your deal is, it's not my problem."

He moved against me, pinning me against the wall. His hands were gentle against my sides even as I slapped at his wrists and told him to go away.

"That's what Lieberman said happened. And I didn't want to question a fellow officer, especially one with twenty years of service." He pressed his lips to my temple, and I turned further into the wall, trying to get away from him. My heart was too fragile. I thought I could do this, but that pathetic scene upstairs was practically my undoing. "It scared me to see your suspicions written down in black and white on the table upstairs and to hear those accusations coming out of your mouth."

"I didn't accuse you of anything," I said, my resolve weakening by the second as his warm hands continued to rub up and down my ribs.

"But if I covered for Lieberman, then I'm just as blame-worthy." He swallowed, tugging on my chin until our eyes met. "There have been whispers that he left Big Bill unattended intentionally. It means nothing. People say shit all the time."

"Do you think it's true?"

"I didn't, but now, I don't know." He looked to be in utter agony. "But if your suspicions are accurate, those could be too."

"Not necessarily," I hedged, still not seeing what the problem was or why he was all over the emotional map. One emotional wreck was more than enough, and I had called dibs.

"Whoever let that asshole into the precinct to eliminate Big Bill is the same person responsible for nearly killing you. And god help him if I ever find out who that is." His hands tangled in my hair, and he pressed his forehead against mine. "It makes me sick to think that I might be covering for that man." He shuddered. "I couldn't stand in your apartment for another second, thinking I might be responsible for every horrible thing you've been through since your reassignment." He swallowed. "I called Preston just now and had her update my incident report to reflect my uncertainty over Lieberman's position during today's failed bust."

I tucked my head underneath his chin and listened to his pounding heartbeat. "You didn't have to do that. I doubt Lieberman's to blame. He's been a cop too long to do something like that. Sure, the guy gives me the creeps, but I just think he's paranoid and overreacted. Kinda like you."

"You're the only thing that matters to me outside of work. I have to keep you safe."

"That's not your job."

"Then where do I apply for the position of white knight?" Michael asked, pulling me away from his chest and seeing the hurt and betrayal on my face for the first time. "Goddammit," he swore, "I promised not to hurt you, and I screwed up again. I'm so sorry, babe."

"I feel like a yo-yo. Two minutes ago, I planned to

tell you to go to hell, but how can I after you said the things you just did? Please, stop jerking me around. I don't know that I'm strong enough or smart enough to walk away from you."

"Then don't." He met my eyes. "Do you want me to stay? Please say yes." I nodded. I grimaced at the sharp pain in my temples, my knees buckled, and his grip around my waist tightened. "Are you okay?"

"I'll be fine. It's just a migraine. I haven't eaten all day. Let's go upstairs and order a pizza."

He scooped me into his arms and carried me up the steps. "I order a mean pepperoni. Or are you a mushroom girl? Pineapple and anchovies?" He smirked, kissing my forehead. "I bet you can't get enough of the meat lover's special."

"Plain cheese," I said as he put me down so I could unlock the door. "I hope that's not too boring for you."

"It's not. It's perfect, just like you."

He nuzzled the back of my neck, and I leaned my head against his shoulder. After a few quiet moments of soothing affection, he dialed a nearby pizza delivery place while I popped a few aspirins and nestled onto the sofa. He sat next to me, placing a pillow on his lap so I could lie down. He rubbed my shoulders and back, and I closed my eyes, fearing how attached I already was.

"Don't break my heart."

He laughed. "I won't. But next time we have a date planned, don't start the evening by breaking my balls."

"Deal."

ELEVEN

I awoke the next morning to a warm body and strong arms wrapped around me. My head was on Michael's chest, and I could hear the steady, reassuring beat of his heart in my ear. What do you know? Michael Riley wasn't a heartless playboy after all. Closing my eyes, I didn't want to start a new day. The last thing I wanted was to go to work. Inside my apartment, we were safe from the stresses of the job. And in this perfect moment, my mind didn't fill in worst case scenarios that involved Michael discovering he couldn't stand me, or cheating on me, or one of us getting hurt or killed in the line of duty. Right now, everything was as close to perfect as it could be. And then the phone rang.

Michael shifted, reaching absently toward the nightstand. He grabbed the object, hitting answer without looking or thinking.

"Riley," he said, his voice thick with sleep.

"Who the hell is Riley?" I heard the shrill sound of Emma's voice. "What the hell are you doing with

Lexie's phone? Where the hell is Lexie? Have you done something with her? I'll call the police if you don't tell me where she is right now. She's a cop. They'll find you and kill you."

"Huh?" Michael opened his eyes and blinked a few times. He pulled the phone away from his ear, realizing it wasn't his. "Sorry." He handed it to me and resumed his previous position, holding me against his chest and shutting his eyes.

"Morning, Emma," I said reluctantly, knowing exactly what was about to happen.

"What's going on? Are you okay? Who was that guy that answered your phone?"

"That was Detective Riley. We work together."

"You're at work? It's six a.m. When are you supposed to get your beauty sleep?"

"If it's that early, why are you calling?"

"Because you didn't call me back last night, and I have an early shift at the hospital this morning. They don't give us a break, ever. ER nurses aren't allowed to get beauty sleep either apparently. I guess we're just supposed to make googly eyes at plastic surgeons, so they'll work on us for free."

"Emma, it's six a.m. Can we please talk about this later?"

"That depends." She sounded indignant. "Is Mr. Riley going to be answering your phone the next time I call?"

"I don't think so."

"Uh-huh." She didn't sound convinced. "You never said you were at work. And he sounds like he's half asleep."

"Goodbye, Em."

"Oh my god, did you seriously get back on the horse last night? How come you've never mentioned him before?"

"Goodbye, Em," I repeated, hitting the disconnect button. So much for my perfect tranquil moment.

"I'm a horse?" Michael murmured into my hair. "Am I a stud?"

"I don't know." I sighed and snuggled closer to him. "How did we end up in my bedroom?"

"You fell asleep on the couch. And when I carried you to bed, you insisted that I stay."

"Really? I insisted? That doesn't sound like me."

"Yeah, your friend doesn't seem to think so either." He turned to look at the clock. "I have to go home, so I can get ready for work."

"Don't leave. We didn't get to the fun part of the date yet."

He laughed. "We ate pizza. You fell asleep and then cuddled with me all night. That's a pretty amazing first date."

"Did you cop a feel?" I asked, cognizant of my bra digging into me. The stupid contraption must have been invented by a man and most definitely wasn't intended to be slept in. Then again, sleeping in my clothes wasn't comfortable either, and I was sure I'd have red indentions from my belt buckle pressed into my stomach. Either that, or Michael would since I used his body as a pillow. A very firm pillow.

"I am a gentleman." He smirked, and I rolled onto my back, so he could climb out of bed. "And gentlemen never tell."

"Jerk," I teased. He leaned down for a kiss, but I turned away, not wanting to assault him with morning breath after eating garlicky pizza. "Not until I brush my teeth."

"I'll settle for your cheek in the meantime." He gave me a quick peck. "We'll call that the goodnight kiss since I didn't get to kiss you goodnight on account of your unconscious state."

"I'm sorry. I don't entertain much. Somehow, the fact that I'm not supposed to fall asleep when I have company must have slipped my mind."

"And you said you didn't sleep with someone on a first date." He winked, heading out of the bedroom. "Liar."

"No, I said I don't have sex on a first date. And we didn't. The sleeping part, obviously, I'm totally cool with that."

"I am too." He went into the bathroom, and I climbed out of bed, ran my fingers through my hair, and went into the kitchen to brew some coffee. I found a few travel mugs and filled one for him to take.

He met me in the kitchen, gladly accepting the coffee. Then he detoured into the living room and collected his belongings off the coffee table. "So were the flowers a casualty of our fight? Or do you really hate flowers?"

"The first," I admitted, sipping my own coffee.

"Okay. I just wanted to make sure before I bring you another floral arrangement, so if flowers don't do it for you, speak up now because I'm also great at buying candy and lingerie."

"You mean after everything that happened you want a second date?"

"And a third. And a fourth. And a lot more after that." He went to my door. "We'll talk about this tonight. I'll call you."

"Won't you see me at work?"

"Yes, but I'm still going to call you."

"You might need to negotiate the phone schedule with Emma."

"What are you going to tell her about the stud?" he asked.

"That after being a total asshole and almost sabotaging the entire evening, the frog actually turned into a prince."

"Maybe you should wait until date number two before you tell her anything. That way, her first impression won't make her think you're dating another horrible jackass." He opened the door. "Next time, we'll start things the right way. I promise."

"Don't make another promise you can't keep," I warned.

"I'll see you soon." He started to pull the door closed behind him. "And just so you know, you're adorable when you're asleep."

"I'm always adorable," I replied jokingly.

"Yes, you are."

~*~

When I arrived at work, Detective Lieberman was inside the lieutenant's office, and despite the fact that the door was completely closed, I could hear angry words dissipating throughout the squad room. This wasn't good. Another man that I didn't recognize entered the office without knocking, and the conversation continued. Quickly, I volunteered to ride along with Kemper on a call that just came through dispatch.

On my way out, I noticed Riley speaking to Preston in the corner of the room. Putting two and two together, I had a feeling the reason Lieberman was getting reamed was because of the changes Riley made to his report last night. He had done that on account of me and my suspicions. Lieberman was going to be on the warpath today, and I had no intention of getting caught in the line of fire. Hopefully, Michael would duck and cover too, at least until this mess blew over.

"Earth to Lexie," Kemper said, snapping his fingers

in front of my face, "what planet are you on? Mars? Saturn? Uranus?" He laughed at the juvenile joke, and I rolled my eyes.

"I'm here. I just zoned out."

"Well, try to pay more attention. We have to perform our due diligence since it's another home invasion, and even though it's in a different neighborhood and unlikely to be connected with the V7Ts, we still need to make sure."

"Wow, look at you, taking police work seriously all of a sudden."

"I have to. Lieberman's fit to be tied. Did you see the internal affairs investigator this morning? They arrived early today with a truckload of files. They cleared Lieberman from any involvement with Big Bill's murder, but while they were looking into that, something else pinged. From the water cooler gossip, Lieberman's spending is off the charts compared to his earnings."

"That's stupid," I said, dismissing Kemper's story and wanting to focus on anything other than Lieberman. "He could have inherited money or moonlights on the side or something. It's none of our business."

"Fine. I was just telling you what I heard." He knocked on the door, and our workday began.

The elderly woman who reported the break-in couldn't tell us what was stolen or if anything was damaged. Her only complaint was that her furniture was moved. Kemper and I exchanged a look. It wasn't uncommon to get bogus calls, and this felt like one of those.

"Where was the furniture before it was moved?" I asked, playing along as Kemper walked through the rest of her apartment to make sure nothing was amiss.

"It was here but a few inches in the other

direction." She dropped into a rocker and furrowed her brow. "Maybe two inches that way." She pointed to the left.

"I see."

Kneeling down, I scooted the coffee table slightly, noticing the deep indentions in the carpet. It was obvious the furniture hadn't been moved.

"No, not that," she squawked, and I slid the table back to its original place. "The television and entertainment center." She pointed across the room. "It was centered on the wall before. Now it's not."

"So someone broke in, decided to steal your television, but changed her mind, and put it back in the wrong place?"

"That's what I think happened," the woman said, sounding ridiculously sincere given the story she just agreed to.

"Okay, how about I put it back where it was, and we'll call it a day?" I asked, realizing the only reason she called us was to move her furniture.

"That sounds fair."

Sighing, I spent the next twenty minutes adjusting the shelves on her entertainment center so the glare from the window wouldn't reflect on the screen. Kemper had taken a seat next to her on the couch and was making helpful suggestions as I went. If there wasn't a witness, I probably would have shot him.

"The next time we're tasked with moving furniture, you can do it," I said, laughing at how bizarre the job could be. Calls like this were pointless, but they always lightened my mood. Not everything had to be serious and dire. "In fact, the next time I need my furniture moved, I'll just call you."

"Hey," he protested.

"You owe me. You could have helped. That stupid entertainment center had twelve different shelves and four settings for each shelf position. We could have been finished in half the time if you didn't sit on your ass and suggest that she might like the TV a little more to the left."

"There was a glare if she sat on the couch. It needed to be moved to the left." He chuckled. "I was just doing my job to the best of my ability. Protect and serve, Sarcone. That's exactly what I was doing, protecting her television from a glare to better serve her needs."

"Well, I think you should do something to serve my needs."

"Oh yeah?" His eyes twinkled. "What needs would those be? Because I'm up for it."

"Lunch. And you're buying." I narrowed my eyes at him. "What the hell did you think I was going to ask you to do?"

He shrugged. "I don't know. But I would have been up for it or down for it. Whichever you prefer."

"Oink," I said. "Don't be a pig."

"Surely, you must be used to jokes like that after being a decoy for vice for two years."

"Yeah. But I didn't appreciate them then, and I don't appreciate them now. And with IA snooping around, you don't want a sexual harassment complaint at the moment."

"I was just joking."

"So was I." I smirked. "Lighten up, Kemper. I'm in a good mood, despite your inappropriate comments, so I'll even let you pick the place."

"Yes, milady." He smiled and parked outside a sandwich joint. "Turkey breast and Swiss?"

"Yep." I was surprised he knew my standard lunch order. "Thanks."

He opened the car door. "No problemo."

TWELVE

The rest of the day flew by with unrelated calls. Kemper and I joked around, and even though we were still tasked with assisting Lieberman and the team on the Sigfried case, we basically just performed a normal tour. It was nice to get out of the office and back on a beat. None of the robberies or break-ins were that serious. A few kids had shoplifted. Someone came home to a broken window, which was merely vandalism and not a burglary. And a store had been robbed, but the surveillance cameras had caught the guy in the act. It was an easy day, and after yesterday, I could go for a lot more easy days.

While I changed back into normal clothes, I phoned Emma to see if she wanted to meet for dinner. We hadn't seen each other since my transfer, and after the phone call this morning, I knew she must be dying for an update on my life. We were going to our usual haunt, a bar and grill situated almost equidistant between our two apartments. It was closer to the hospital than the precinct, which meant she was tasked with getting a good table and ordering a pitcher of beer and an appetizer while she waited for my arrival.

Walking inside, I immediately found her in a corner booth. A tall, blond guy with a dragon tattoo on his bicep was leaning against her side of the booth, chatting her up. Shaking my head, I went over to the table.

"Should I find somewhere else to sit?" I asked. She squealed, shoving him out of the way so she could get up and hug me. "I'll take that as a no."

"Sit your ass down. Chad's just leaving."

"But I thought...," Chad stuttered, confused why she no longer had any interest in him. "I paid for the pitcher of beer."

"And we appreciate the contribution." I poured a glass and toasted in his direction. "Better luck next time."

"Bitch," he muttered, and I brought out my badge, crinkling my nose at him.

"Officer Bitch," I corrected. He held up his hands and backed away from the table. I looked at Emma. "Poor, Chad. You need to stop tricking men into buying us beer."

"He was a douche," Emma said, twirling her ponytail around her finger. "From the moment I came in, he's been gaming me and staring at the girls. Someone needed to teach him a lesson." She sighed. "You didn't seem quite this offended when you were working vice. Back then, you despised being hit on. For a while, I thought you might consider playing for the other team."

"I wasn't that bad."

"Taking a celibacy vow for two years is pretty bad." She raised an eyebrow at me. "But that had more to do with the pinhead you dated. I swear, you should have let me castrate him. I'm a nurse. I wouldn't have killed him. I would have cauterized as I cut in order to control the bleeding."

"Em, you're killing my good mood with all this talk. Why the hell are you bringing up ancient history? Vice is old news, and my ex is ancient."

"You didn't think so the last time we went out," she picked up a cheese fry and chewed thoughtfully, "and that was less than two months ago." Her smile brightened. "In two months, little Lexie found a man. So tell me about this mysterious Mr. Riley."

"He's a detective."

"I need a bit more than that. Is he a good lay?"

"Em!" I blushed bright red. "We haven't gotten that far yet."

"Uh-huh," she narrowed her eyes as if she didn't believe me, "but you guys had a sleepover. He was there last night when you called, wasn't he?"

"Yes and no."

I proceeded to fill her in on our fight and our attempt to date. As usual, she was completely enthralled with the details of my dating life. Good or bad, Emma had been there for all of it. We'd been friends since we turned sixteen and had stayed close through high school, college, and numerous crushes and break-ups.

"So what are you waiting for?" she asked, refilling her glass with beer. "Go bang his brains out."

"I have to be sure."

"Sure that he's a good lay? Girl, you said he has great hands and a nice sized package."

"And he's a really good kisser." I blushed, smiling as I remembered our make-out session yesterday.

"Then I have a feeling he'll get you there." She turned serious, knowing I wasn't the slutty one out of our group of friends. "But this isn't about that."

I blinked, playing with the straw wrapper. "I don't want to go through another messy relationship and an even messier break-up. Plus, Michael's a player."

"And Kevin was an asshole." Emma knew not to mention my ex-boyfriend's name. I didn't like to hear it. As far as I was concerned, he didn't deserve to be called a word that wouldn't be bleeped on broadcast television. "I get it. He was your first real love. Your first real adult relationship. But you're twenty-six years old. You have your entire life ahead of you. Why can't you just have fun instead of immediately wondering if this thing with Riley is going to turn into a relationship? Casual dating is great. You screw who you want. And you go on. You don't have to worry about cheating because there is no commitment."

"I can't do it that way. I've seen and experienced too much. I could never feel safe just picking up a random guy in a bar."

"Y'know, life would be far less complicated right now if you had gone to work in your parents' store and got your masters instead of becoming a cop."

"Too late," I said.

"Fine, then I'm gonna have to meet this Michael Riley and have a friendly chat with him." She grabbed my phone before I could stop her and dialed his number.

"Em," I lunged across the table, but she turned to the side so I couldn't reach the phone, "this isn't funny. Don't do it."

"Hey, Riley," she said, and I knew he must have answered, "this is Emma. We spoke this morning. I'm still not quite clear on why you thought you should answer Lexie's phone at six a.m., but I'm willing to let that one slide if you agree to meet us. We're at McGinty's Bar and Grill. Do you know where it is?" She paused. "Great. I look forward to meeting you too."

"No. Tell me you didn't do that. Tell me it was a joke and that you reached his voicemail or called my house phone or something," I insisted as she handed back my cell phone.

"I love you. And you like this guy. So we need to see if he passes my test because I'm not going to stand by and let someone else break your heart. He needs to know what's what." She refilled my glass. "Drink, you look like you need it."

I put my face in my hands. Sometimes, I really didn't understand why we were friends.

Thirty minutes later, Michael showed up, and I wanted to sink into an invisible puddle underneath the booth. Unfortunately, my body didn't cooperate with my wishes, and Michael spotted us easily. He sauntered over to the booth, offering a dazzling smile.

"I am so sorry for what's about to happen," I said when he was within hearing distance. But he held the smile and slid into the booth beside me. "You do in fact have the right to remain silent. You should wait for counsel to arrive before saying another word."

He laughed, a deep, amused sound, pecking my cheek before extending his hand across the table. "Emma?"

"Riley," she said it like it was a foreign word as she shook his hand.

"Michael, actually," he corrected. "Michael Riley."

"Can you spell that for me?" she asked. "I'm also going to need your badge number, three references, and closest living relative."

"Here, you can have my card," Michael said, removing one from his pocket like this was a business meeting or job interview. "Will you also be needing a urine or blood sample before the end of the night?" He smirked.

“That would be lovely. We’ll just pop over to the hospital and get that taken care of,” Emma replied.

“Emma’s an ER nurse,” I said, “so you probably shouldn’t joke about that. She might just take you up on the offer.”

“It depends on how he plays his cards,” Emma said, staring like a predator preparing to pounce.

“We’ve known each other since high school, and although she appears to be a functioning adult, she clearly lacks basic social skills.” I glared at her. “And the ability to mind her own goddamn business.”

She stuck her tongue out at me, and I kicked her underneath the table.

“Ladies,” Michael said, making me feel even more idiotic than normal, “thanks for asking me to join you.” He motioned to the waitress for another pitcher of beer and leaned back in the seat. “So shall we get started with the inquisition?” He was being a good sport about this, but I wanted to push him out the door and tell him to run far and fast. If Michael didn’t leave after dealing with Emma, there was a good chance he never would.

“How many people have you slept with?” Emma asked.

“Don’t answer that,” I hissed. “I don’t want to know.”

“Fine,” Emma looked smug, “how many relationships have you been in since high school?”

“Six,” Michael replied.

“How old are you?” Emma asked, already calculating the estimated lengths of these relationships.

“Twenty-nine.”

Emma continued asking rapid-fire questions, while I buried my face in my hands, occasionally intervening if the question was too personal. None of the things she asked was any of her business. Hell, I didn't even know the answer to a lot of the questions, like how many times he'd moved in the last five years.

When the interrogation ended, he shifted in the booth, rubbing circles on my back. Pulling my head out of my hands, I gazed across the table at Emma, mouthing that I would kill her. She waved it away and excused herself.

"Did I pass?" Michael asked.

"I didn't know she was going to call you. She grabbed my phone. And I'm sorry. You can leave. I won't blame you. She had no right. I should have stopped her."

"She's looking out for you." His fingers grazed my cheek, and his blue eyes bore into mine. "She cares about you. I care about you too." He kissed me, and I hugged him tightly.

"Ahem," Emma cleared her throat, holding an order of buffalo wings, "enough with the kissy face. I brought a peace offering." She studied me. "Lex, your mascara's all over the place. Go freshen up."

"Em," I warned.

"It's okay," Michael insisted, sliding out of the booth so I could get out. "I'm not going anywhere."

Emma raised a challenging eyebrow, but I couldn't take it anymore. I didn't have the energy to argue with her. Typically, I avoided conflict, which made my career choice that much stranger. At least I tried to avoid conflict in my personal life, except it felt like Michael and I had already gone a few rounds. Eh, maybe conflict wasn't that bad.

I went into the bathroom and checked my reflection in the mirror. "Dammit, Emma," I snarled, "I'm not even wearing mascara." She had me so flustered about this awkward impromptu meet and greet that I didn't know if I was coming or going.

Storming out of the bathroom, I slowed as I approached the table.

"They were together for six years. While you were having six different relationships and however many one night stands, Lexie was dating the only man she ever loved. She fell for him in high school. And the entire time she was in the police academy, he was screwing someone else. I've tried to tell her to play the field, but she isn't wired that way. And dealing with perverts who've asked her to do all kinds of nasty things has only made this worse. So if you're not looking for something serious, walk away. Don't hurt her. She can't go through that again. I can't watch her go through that again. And you work together. Is that even allowed?" Emma stopped speaking when she spotted me, but I felt betrayed.

The butterflies were back, and my heart was racing. I had to know what Michael was going to say.

"I'd never do anything to hurt her or jeopardize her career. But she's stronger than you think. She needs to trust herself enough to take risks. She second guesses a lot of things and changes her mind often, but at least now I understand why."

Inhaling a breath, I tried to hide the hurt and betrayal away as I returned to the table. They fell silent, and Michael scooted in so I could sit.

"Are you okay?" he asked.

"Yeah." I stared at Emma, and she knew without a doubt that I had heard enough of their conversation to be reeling from the one, two punch that I never expected her to deliver.

"Lexie –" she began.

"Don't. Just don't." I held up my hand. "I want to call it a night, but you're leaving first before you stick your nose someplace else where it doesn't belong. I don't want or need you to fight my battles. I'm a fucking police officer for christ's sake. And I'm a big girl. I can take care of myself."

"I know that," she said, hanging her head. At least she had the decency not to defend her reasoning for spilling the beans to Michael about my previous relationship drama.

"Then go. And don't you ever do something like this again," I said, tired of her devious ways.

She smiled at Michael and picked up her purse. "I want you to know that I did this for your own good, Lexie. I'll call you tomorrow." She hugged me, even though I didn't make a move to reciprocate it, and then she was gone.

"Okay, for the record, I really don't understand women," Michael said. "Your friend's a handful, isn't she?"

"Yes. I'm sorry. I'm sorry she called. I'm sorry you showed up. And I'm sorry that she aired the unedited version of my dirty laundry all over the place. My baggage comes in a nice matching set, doesn't it?" I laughed, a bitter sound emanating from the painful void in my chest. "And my parents own a luggage store which makes this whole thing poetic in a sick and twisted way."

"Lexie?"

"What kind of cop doesn't know the man she's practically living with is banging the next door neighbor? Not once or twice. But three times, I found her slutty thongs in our laundry. Three times. The first time I dismissed it as something left in the washing machine by another resident. The second time, I started to get curious. But deep down, I knew, and I didn't do anything until I came home and found them in the shower."

"If it makes you feel any better, I found my ex-girlfriend sucking off one of my friends." He put his arms around me and kissed my temple. "Emma was only telling this story because she doesn't want you to end up with another douchebag. Regardless of what happens between us, trust your instincts. Don't let this define you. What that asshole did had nothing to do with you."

I licked my lips. "You're the only person, besides Emma, that knows all the gory details of my past. And you haven't left yet, even though you get how uptight, jealous, and neurotic this makes me."

"You, neurotic? No way," he teased.

I sighed and pushed away from him. "I really am ready to call it a night. I need to go home and hide under the covers, eat some ice cream, and cry. But pretend that I didn't just tell you that."

"Okay, so you have to go home and have a lingerie pillow fight with your best friend and talk about boys. I got it." He paid the tab for the evening, which I protested but he ignored, and walked me to my car. "Are you okay to drive?"

"I'm not drunk. Do you want me to walk a straight line or lean back and touch my nose?"

"No." He kissed me, a long, lingering kiss that made my heart ache. "But I'm going to call you in two hours. Is that enough time for you to get home and do all those things I'm not supposed to know about?"

"Probably." I smiled. "I only have a pint of chocolate swirl in the freezer. The container's small enough that it won't take that long to hit carton."

"Well, if you need someone to make an ice cream run for you, let me know." He looked like he wanted to say something else but didn't. Instead, he held my car door open while I slid inside.

THIRTEEN

Over the course of the next few days, Michael was attentive but not smothering. We spoke regularly on the phone. He even brought takeout and ice cream to my apartment two nights after the fiasco at the bar but was called back to work on account of a department store robbery.

Emma was apologetic, or as apologetic as my spunky best friend could be. Her apologies always came with qualified remarks, but I wasn't holding a grudge. That night forced me to talk about the past, and even though it'd been two years, I think I had subconsciously been holding a torch for Kevin, my ex. But now I realized he didn't deserve it. He didn't deserve me or even a second of my thoughts. I hadn't even turned twenty-four yet when we broke up. Back then, I was just a kid. And kids make mistakes. I just wasn't willing to repeat them. However, I finally forgave myself for letting him use me the way he did and for making me feel like I wasn't worthy. Screw him. I was strong and smart, and I deserved someone who respected that. I'd sought respect in my work life, and now I was seeking the same thing in my private life.

Detective Riley smiled when I walked into the squad room that morning. His eyes were so expressive, and now, they were screaming *I have a secret*. Before we had a chance to speak, Lieberman entered the room.

"Let's roll, people," he said, not giving anyone a chance to ask a question before he was out the door.

"You heard the man," Preston said as Kemper, Hawking, and I exchanged confused looks. "That means you guys too."

Outside the precinct, Lieberman was barking orders at a dozen uniformed officers. Sweeping arrest warrants had been signed for the V7Ts after weeks had been spent compiling evidence, determining identities, and surveilling the parties involved. Mr. Wolfe and three other pawn shop owners had been arrested but agreed to provide us with valuable information and testimony in exchange for reduced sentences. The district attorney's office had agreed, and we were moving in this morning.

"We want to bring everyone in at one time. No one will escape that way. And this thing will finally be over. You've each been assigned a location and suspect. Do not come back here until that man or woman is handcuffed in the back of your squad car. Do you understand me?" Lieberman asked, making eye contact with everyone.

A round of nods and 'yes, sir's echoed through the parking lot. However, I didn't know what I was supposed to do. And from the confused looks my two fellow officers had, they didn't know what to do either.

"Sir?" Hawking asked, drawing Lieberman's attention. "What do you want the three of us to do?"

"That's a good question." Lieberman focused on me. "Sarcone, you're with me. You seem to have some shitty luck, and I don't want anything to go wrong this time." My eyes shot to Riley who looked ready to protest, but Preston put her hand on his shoulder and whispered something in his ear. He pressed his lips together and forced a tight smile on his face. He didn't like it either. "The two of you," Lieberman continued, "are staying here and assisting the officers downstairs in booking. Keep these assholes separated as best you can. We don't need them to corroborate each other's statements."

"Yes, sir," Hawking said, leading the way back inside.

"And the two of you, get a hold of dispatch and listen for radio calls. If something goes sideways, you'll respond."

"Nothing better go sideways," Riley growled, but Lieberman didn't say a word.

Michael gave me one last look before Preston pushed him toward one of the unmarked cruisers. I followed Lieberman to his car and climbed into the passenger's seat. I didn't like this. Michael didn't like this. But from the self-satisfied look on Lieberman's face, at least I knew someone was having a good time.

"Now you're gonna see what real police work looks like," Lieberman said as he drove away from the precinct. "You've earned it. After all, how many officers can keep their cool when a gun's pointed at their head?"

"All of us," I responded, feeling a bit brazen.

"No. That's just what they want you to think. I've seen men, men twice your size, shit themselves in situations like that." He glanced at me. "You've got a pair of brass ones dangling between those shapely legs of yours."

I remained silent, not mentioning the inappropriate nature of his comment. It was sexist on a few levels. But we were about to make a bust, so now wasn't the time.

"Who's our target?" I asked, hoping to derail the one-sided conversation.

"The big gun himself, Alfonso Sigfried." Lieberman looked at me. "That should be no sweat for someone as brave as you. Hell, you don't worry about anything, do you? You spoke with the detectives from internal affairs after the shooting. Then you spoke to Riley and Preston about what you thought might have happened at the pawn shop. But for some reason, it must have slipped your mind to talk to me about it." My stomach clenched, but I did my best to appear outwardly calm. "Is there any particular reason why you're trying to jam me up?"

"I'm not, sir. I simply didn't understand how someone as experienced as you could let a perp escape."

"Are you afraid of me?"

"Should I be?" Even as the words left my mouth, the voice in my head screamed out, *Yes*.

"We're on the same side. That would be stupid." He parked the car and turned to face me directly. "Don't pretend you have any idea how easy it is to chase down a suspect. You've never had to do that before. Those jerk-offs you used to collar for vice probably had their pants around their ankles by the time you announced, so they were easy pickings. Fish in a barrel. Shit like that. But this is trench warfare. Stay on my six, do what I say, and do not question me. It's about time someone trained you properly."

"Yes, sir." I opened the car door, my insides quaking at the idea of what was about to happen.

I followed Lieberman down a long narrow walkway

to a townhouse. He stood to the side, gesturing that I stand on the other while he knocked. Before he could say or do anything else, a shotgun blast tore through the wood of the door, and he ducked to the side.

Automatically, my hand went to my firearm, and I drew my handgun. He kicked what remained of the door down and went in high. I knelt next to the door, scanning for the shooter. Once I was positive it was clear, I followed. He was fifteen feet ahead, and he pointed to the next room as we began clearing the house. Once we determined there was only one hiding place left, Lieberman announced our presence.

"This is the police, throw down your weapon, and open the door," Lieberman insisted.

"Whoa. Hold up. Don't shoot, dude." A teenager, probably fifteen or sixteen, opened the bathroom door.

"Drop it," Lieberman insisted, stepping forward and grabbing the barrel and yanking the shotgun out of the kid's hand. "What are you doing shooting at police officers? You're just a kid."

"My cousin told me to fire at the first person who rang the doorbell," the kid said. Lieberman pushed him onto the ground, frisked him, and gestured for my handcuffs. "How was I supposed to know it was gonna be a couple of cops?"

"What if it was the mailman or one of your neighbors wanting to borrow a cup of sugar? Who did you think it'd be?" I asked.

"I thought it'd be some gangbanger from another gang," the kid said.

"Alfonso Sigfried, is he your cousin?" Lieberman asked.

"Yeah. He told me to keep his place safe because he was leaving town for a while. Things got too hot around here."

"Where did he go?" Lieberman asked.

"He didn't say. And I have nothing else to say." The kid suddenly sounded tough, probably because guns were no longer pointed in his direction.

"Oh, I'll make you say something," Lieberman threatened.

"He's a kid," I pointed out, hoping Lieberman would realize we couldn't question him without a guardian or someone from child services present.

"Fine." Lieberman hauled him to the car, shoved him into the back seat, and returned to the precinct. "He fired a shotgun round at us. That's attempted murder of a police officer. They'll try him as an adult. He's looking at a few decades of hard time. Do you really believe he'll survive?"

I knew what Lieberman was doing, and even if it was borderline unethical, I had no choice but to play along. "That's doubtful. Well, unless his cousin hears about it and puts the word out that no one touches him."

"You really think Sigfried's got clout like that? The power on the inside resides with the big gangs and organized crime, not some street punks that think they're so bad because they smoke crack and break into little old ladies' homes," Lieberman replied.

"Yeah, I guess you're right." I glanced back at the handcuffed adolescent. "I'm sorry, kid. Maybe you'll get a lenient judge. I hear juvenile detention facilities are improving."

Lieberman smirked but remained facing forward the rest of the ride. By the time we unloaded the boy from the back of the car, he was begging for a phone call. And soon after, he was spilling his guts concerning Alfonso Sigfried's last known whereabouts.

"Nice save," Lieberman whispered as we watched

Preston question the kid and his counsel. “After today, we’re straight. But next time you have some kind of misgiving about something that went down, find me, so we can talk about it. Bad cops are a blemish on the entire department, but it’s worse when a good cop gets wrongly accused.” He moved closer, whispering in my ear, “This is your only free pass. Don’t cross me again. I’ve dealt with enough misunderstandings recently and will not tolerate another one.” And then he was gone.

I remained in the observation room, holding myself up by leaning against the glass. My heart was pounding. Did that really just happen? Did Detective Lieberman threaten me? I had no proof and no way of knowing exactly what he meant by it. The only thing I knew was that I shouldn’t speak a word of this to anyone.

“Lexie?” Michael appeared in the open doorway as if sensing that this was the worst moment for him to show up. “Is everything okay?”

“Yeah.”

“How’d things go with Lieberman?”

“Fine. Alfonso’s nephew gave us a lot of useful information. A BOLO’s been issued for him and his vehicle. And we’ve contacted the area precincts to keep an eye out. How did everything else go?”

“Like clockwork. Everyone we set out to arrest was brought in. A few punks have already squealed on their pals, and we’ve practically disbanded the entire gang. Narcotics division is stepping in to deal with the non-burglary related issues, but this should be enough to permanently stop the string of robberies.” He smiled. “Police department, one. V7Ts, zilch.”

“Is this why you looked like you were in such a good mood this morning?”

“No.” The smile from earlier returned to his face.

"What are you doing tonight?"

"I don't know yet. Did you have something in mind?"

"You're coming to my place for dinner. And if you just happen to bring an overnight bag, I won't tell Emma."

"Didn't you say that you weren't allowed to have guests in your apartment?"

"No, I said my house was too messy for guests, but that was before I cleaned." He grinned. "I did it just for you." He stepped closer, caressing my arm. "And I changed the sheets before coming to work this morning, put groceries in the fridge, and I have an entire meal planned. I even bought a bottle of wine."

"That sounds wonderful, but what are you going to drink?"

He laughed. "Just don't overthink it. After today, we have a ton to celebrate. Come over for dinner and stay for breakfast." He saw the hesitation on my face. "You're not ready. That's okay. I'll settle for cuddling. I can be patient, even if you've practically molested me on two prior occasions."

"Are you sure?"

"I'm pretty sure that was you tugging down my zipper and fumbling with my belt, unless you have an identical twin or a clone." He pecked my cheek and stepped toward the door. "Seriously, there's no pressure for dessert. Dinner and breakfast are okay with me."

"What time?" I asked.

"Seven."

"I'll see you then."

FOURTEEN

"Taste it," Michael insisted, putting his hand on the back of my head and pulling my mouth closer. "Lean forward a little bit more, I don't want it to drip down your shirt."

"Oh my god," I put my hand to my mouth, licking my lips, "your sauce is amazing. Where in the world did you learn to cook like that?"

"My mom." He placed the spoon carefully on the counter. "I should have warned you not to wear white when I was making her famous and infamous red sauce."

"Why is it infamous?"

"Somehow, it always manages to stain some article of clothing during the cooking process. Mom said it was because it spatters upward while it simmers, but I think it drips off the bottom of the spoon when being tasted." He lifted the spoon off the counter, demonstrating an oval patch of tomato sauce sticking to the countertop. "See, that's why I'm a detective."

"I thought it was because you look sexy in a dress

shirt."

"That too." He filled a pot with water and set it on the stove, next to the sauce. "If you want an apron or splatter guard or something, I'll get you one of my shirts to wear. But the safest thing to do is to go into the other room, take off your shirt, and hang it in the closet. The tomatoes aren't wily enough to get to it in there."

"What about my bra?"

"Is it white?"

"What do you think?" He scrutinized my chest, enjoying having permission to ogle me.

"Nude."

"You really are a detective. I guess that badge didn't come out of a crackerjack box. Does that mean the handcuffs are real too?"

"Everything's real." The sexual innuendo and tension coursed through the air, crackling between us. "Why don't you grab a glass of wine and relax? I'm just going to cook the pasta, and then we can eat."

"I can't believe you made your own pasta from scratch. And my parents claim we're Italian. What a joke."

"I don't want to start a family feud." Michael laughed. "I'm not claiming anything other than the fact that my mom is an awesome cook. She worked in a few restaurants when I was growing up. She always made sure there was extra at work, so she could bring it home and feed the five of us."

"Wow. Three sons, a police officer for a husband, and a full-time job. She sounds amazing."

"She is. And whenever you meet her, you'll have to tell her that her son is a terrific cook. Whenever I tell her that, she doesn't seem to believe me."

I uncorked the wine and filled two glasses. Was Michael seriously talking about letting me meet his mom? We'd barely even known each other for a month, and I wasn't even sure how long we had been dating. Surely, he wasn't speaking about anytime in the near future.

"Perhaps it's because you use her sauce as an excuse to get women to take off their clothes."

"Maybe." He stirred the pasta. "Is al dente okay? I don't want the noodles to turn into mush."

"Sure, that's great. But don't call them noodles. That's why she doubts your cooking acumen. And never call sauce gravy, unless you happen to be in a few certain households that feel completely different on the subject," I said, giggling at the absurdity that had been a few of my family gatherings in the past.

"Are those Italian family secrets you're sharing?"

"Yes, and if you tell anyone where you heard them, you'll be sleeping with the fishes."

"You need to work on your *Godfather* impression. You sound a little too *Jersey Shore*."

"Is there a difference?"

"I really hope so." He put the serving bowl on the table. Then he took a napkin, unfolded it, and tucked it into the top of my shirt. "It's for your own protection. Trust me."

"I do."

He met my eyes and kissed me briefly. "I'm glad." Then he sat across from me, offering the serving utensils. "Dig in."

The meal was amazing, and I gorged myself. At this rate, I might never leave Michael's apartment. He knew how to cook. He had excellent taste in wine, and the conversation was great. Damn, I was falling hard. And it scared me.

"Hey," he ran his fingers along the back of my hand, "you zoned out on me again. Is everything okay?"

"It's fine. I was just reliving the great sauce versus gravy debate. It's scary how adamant my uncle can be."

Michael looked like he didn't believe me, but he didn't push the issue. Instead, he finished cleaning the table and picked up the pot to pour the leftovers into a container. When he returned to the table after cleaning the kitchen, I burst out laughing.

"What?"

"You weren't kidding. Those tomatoes are pretty damn wily." I pointed at the red splotches covering the lower half of his shirt.

He sighed. "Another casualty in the battle of man against tomato. And again, the tomato is victorious."

"Take that off," I insisted, standing up and working on undoing the top buttons. "The trick is to rinse the stain out before it has time to set in."

"Oh, I thought the point was to convince you to rip my clothes off." Once his shirt was off, my hands ran along his chest. Somehow, a few specks of tomato sauce managed to bleed through his shirt and onto his skin, and I licked at a spot along his sternum. "The shirt can wait." He dropped it between us and kissed me. "You can say stop anytime you want, okay?"

I didn't say anything, and he grasped my chin, refusing to kiss me again until I nodded. He lifted me onto the table, standing between my legs as we continued to kiss. When his hand moved to my belt, I broke the kiss.

"Stop," I whispered, and he nodded, moving his hands to my shoulders. I rested my cheek against his shoulder for a moment. "I'm sorry. This is happening too fast. How long have we been dating?"

"Don't apologize, honey. I didn't mean to push." He stepped backward and grabbed the shirt, holding it strategically in front of himself. "I don't know what counts as our first date? We could start with hot dogs in the car."

"That was not a date." I slid off the table and went into his laundry room, which was basically a large utility closet, turning the dials on the machine to presoak and searching his cabinet for a stain remover. "And the two nights we made out inside my apartment weren't dates either."

"Then we'll start from the morning I first spoke to Emma," he said, handing me the shirt. "Because I don't want to start with the night we had our first fight. I'd like to pretend that didn't happen."

"Me too."

"Okay, so clean slate up until the six a.m. phone call. Deal?" Michael asked.

"That sounds good." After scrubbing the tomato sauce off his shirt and dropping it into the washing machine, I found Michael's bare chest to be a wonderful distraction. "My clothes are staying on tonight because if they come off, I won't want to stop. And I know myself well enough to know that I'll have doubts if things happen this quickly. It's been less than two weeks since our first date. But that doesn't mean your clothes can't come off."

"Lexie, that's not necessary." His breath hitched when I rubbed along his hard length. "Sexual favors aren't a quid pro quo." I didn't stop, and he moaned, leaning back against the washing machine as I unzipped his pants and slid them down his legs.

"Kiss me, Michael," I insisted, freeing him from his boxer briefs.

I pressed myself against his side, and his hands tangled in my hair. He claimed my mouth with his tongue while I squeezed and stroked him until he came in hot spurts in my hand. He broke our kiss, gasping.

"Lex," his lips brushed against mine again, and he laughed, "that was unexpected."

"Really? Because I had a feeling something like that might happen." I crinkled my nose playfully and washed my hands in the sink while he cleaned himself up and put his pants back on. "So do you still want me to spend the night?"

"Yes." He kissed the back of my neck and wrapped his arms around my waist. "But only if you want to."

"I want to."

"Good." He let out a content sigh. "I'll take you on a tour of the bedroom." He led me through the living room and into the bedroom. He opened the door and pointed. "That's the bed."

"Okay."

"That's the dresser. And television." He looked around. "Nightstand. Closet." He picked me up and tossed me onto the bed. "That's pretty much it."

"Remote?"

"I can't believe I almost forgot the most important part." He tossed it to me. "Anything else?"

I laid back and snuggled against the pillow. "No, that does it. Now just don't expect me to move from this spot."

"I wouldn't dream of it." He left the room and brought my overnight bag to me. "Do you mind if I take a quick shower? Y'know, on account of the sauce."

"Are you sure it's not gravy?" I smirked. "I'll get changed, and maybe I'll still be awake when you get out." A thought crossed my mind. "Did we finish the wine?"

"Not yet."

"Then take your time. A girl needs a chance to get her drink on."

Michael returned ten minutes later. His dark

brown hair now looked completely black since it was still wet, and he shook it like a dog, earning a round of giggles. We spent the rest of the evening in his bed, watching a movie, eating snacks, and finishing the bottle of wine.

That night, I slept well. My belly was full. My heart was light. And Michael made me feel safe and loved. Even though we didn't know each other for very long and had been dating for even less time, a part of me felt foolish for making him wait. It was like we'd known each other forever, but I was still too scared to rush into what I considered the ultimate sign of commitment – sex.

FIFTEEN

With the numerous V7Ts arrests, the spree of home invasions declined. Of course, there were still robberies and break-ins but not nearly as many as there had been. I didn't feel like I did much to contribute to the case, but all three detectives, even Lieberman, thanked Hawking, Kemper, and me for assisting. And based upon the lack of unfamiliar faces inside the precinct, the internal affairs investigation also concluded. We still didn't have eyes on Alfonso Sigfried, but without his groupies to do his dirty work, he didn't pose much of a threat. Before I could ask if I should return to my normal tour for the day, the burglary lieutenant called me into his office.

"Sarcone, have a seat," Lieutenant Peterson said. "We need to talk about Big Bill and Stryker King."

"Wasn't that investigated internally?" I asked, suddenly queasy and nervous.

"Yes, and it was ruled purely accidental. We still aren't sure how exactly King got inside the precinct and managed to get to the interrogation room without anyone noticing, but the camera feeds show him walking through the place. He's probably been here so often that he knew where to go and how not to get caught. Damn frequent flyers."

I remained silent, unsure what else the lieutenant had to say.

"Detective Lieberman says you're a good cop and you'll be a real asset to this division. But he also said you can be headstrong and jump to the wrong conclusions at times."

"I guess I'm still figuring things out," I admitted.

"Yeah." He rubbed his brow and went around the desk in order to stand in front of me. "I also know that you work well under pressure, and despite how you might be figuring things out, you've got the chops for this job." He picked up my personnel file and flipped through a few pages.

"Thank you, sir."

"Don't thank me. This was the second time you've been held at gunpoint. There was that incident when you were with vice. Thankfully, that issue resolved differently. And then a few days ago when you and Lieberman went to arrest Sigfried, that kid nearly blew the two of you away. I don't want to see one of my most promising officers get burnt out because of the stresses of the job."

"I'm fine, sir."

"No, you aren't. No one is okay after things like this. What we do isn't normal, and you aren't expected to deal with it like it's just another normal day. Department regulations require officers to seek counseling after a shooting. You didn't fire, so technically, you're clear. I can't make you talk to the department's headshrinker, but I want to strongly encourage you to talk to someone. My door is always open."

"Thank you."

He nodded. "If you have a problem, come see me. And I'm talking about more than the fallout from the shooting. I run a tight ship. This is a team, and everyone needs to be on board." He smiled, easing the implication of his words. "Take it easy today. You've earned yourself a break. Go downstairs and redirect the phone calls that come in. The desk sergeant's been a bit overwhelmed."

I nodded, leaving. Apparently even if internal affairs decided our precinct was clean, the lieutenant didn't seem quite so certain. I didn't know what that meant, but I didn't want to get bogged down in thinking about it. Work was returning to normal, and Lieberman and I would be parting ways. There was no reason why I had to be involved in his business or why he would be involved in mine. Obviously, someone was monitoring him to make sure he wasn't dirty, and if he was, he'd be caught eventually. I was just relieved that I was out of the picture.

"What'd you do?" Kemper asked. "The lieutenant doesn't normally speak to us. We're just lowly officers. You must have really screwed up."

"He told me to work the phones today," I replied, not getting dragged into the childish rhetoric.

"Even a trained monkey can do that," Kemper remarked, sticking his tongue out at me.

"Obviously not or you'd be on the phones," Riley said, his tone icy. "And I don't want to hear any more disrespect coming from you. It's one thing to kid around, but you just don't know when to quit. Should I recommend they send you back to the academy for some sensitivity training or personal communication skills classes?"

"No, sir," Kemper replied, and Riley went back to what he was doing.

It was sweet that Michael was defending me, but I didn't want that to turn into something either. Wow, figuring out this workplace romance thing wouldn't be easy. He glanced up as I went past his desk on my way to the lobby. He didn't say anything, but I felt his appreciative gaze on my back.

A few minutes later, calls were coming in left and right. The city's power grid was experiencing technical difficulties, and the technicians were shutting down power to parts of the city in an organized pattern in order to fix the glitch. The precinct was now officially in a blackout zone. All available officers had to be called to report in, and all nonessential personnel were being rerouted to the other precincts.

While the sergeant began calling all off duty personnel, Riley and Preston walked past the desk. Michael told Preston to wait a moment and came over to me, standing close so he wouldn't be overheard.

"It looks like we're not working together any longer. It's a shame really," he whispered.

"Is that why you put Kemper in his place?"

"Someone needed to." He glanced behind him, watching Preston tap her foot impatiently. "I have to go investigate a potential Sigfried sighting, but the caller doesn't seem particularly reliable. He also said he saw a little green man riding an elephant."

"Have fun." He snorted at my words and stepped away. "Hey, the city's having power issues, so try to get back before it gets dark. The crazies will be out."

"Thanks," Preston said. "We'll be careful."

"See you later, Officer," Riley added, winking.

After they left, I felt myself blush. Michael needed to stop being so flirtatious at work. Sure, we spent last night together. And he had brought me breakfast in bed this morning, but the more he flirted, the more difficult it was to separate my work life from my private life.

"Wipe that smile off your face, Officer Sarcone," the sergeant said. "That pretty boy detective isn't worth your time." She smiled. "But damn, I do like watching him walk away." She was an older woman, in her mid-forties with graying hair. From the gold band around her finger, it was also obvious she was married. "We need to have all the crooks in holding transported to central booking until this thing plays through. We don't need any lawyers saying this is cruel and unusual punishment. So phone over there for a transport van and pass word to the different departments that they should set up shop at the neighboring precinct for the rest of the day."

"Right away, ma'am."

I made a few calls and then went upstairs to pass word along. After returning to the front desk, I helped field calls for the rest of the day. Most were from civilians who were afraid that the power outage would cause a riot that would lead to vandalism and break-ins.

As the sun set and the sky grew darker, more reports started coming in. The rolling blackouts brought the lunatics out of the woodwork. Every available officer was responding to calls. Burglary division seemed to be the busiest. Shop owners reported thefts, vandalism, and suspicious activity. Calls had been coming in nonstop from the security firms, informing us that the power surges were wreaking havoc. One company, in particular, wasn't sure if the places they serviced were being robbed or if the system had reset, which meant the police had to check each location as soon as possible. Thankfully, I wasn't on the front lines, and instead, I was redirecting everyone to areas that still had regular power.

"The power company said three more hours," the sergeant muttered. "I can't wait for this to be over."

"Me too."

She glanced up at the lights which had flickered a few times but were still holding strong. "I know we have emergency generators, but just to be on the safe side, the captain said we'll shut down and reroute until the power's back up. It's probably a bigger pain in the ass than holding down the fort, but with all the rioting that's been happening throughout the country, we don't want to take any chances."

The phone rang again, but the caller only had a question on an unrelated matter. After dealing with that, I noticed a tense silence had settled around me. The sergeant was on the line with dispatch and whispers were being shared by the few police personnel that remained. Something serious was happening.

"Okay, if you need additional units, I'll find the manpower myself," the sergeant declared, hanging up.

"What's going on?"

"That was Detective Preston. They found Alfonso Sigfried. He's barricaded himself inside a bar and claims he has a bomb."

"Oh my god." My mind immediately went to Michael. He had to be okay. He just did.

"ESU is on the way, along with the bomb squad. We've sent officers to cordon off the area. Detective Preston's coordinating things from the outside."

"And Detective Riley?"

"He went inside to try to talk Sigfried down."

My stomach clenched, and I swallowed the bile. This morning, my biggest dilemma was whether or not the people at work would catch on to our relationship, but suddenly, everything else seemed so much more important. The fear that I could lose him at any moment shook my very foundation. Would I ever see him again?

"What can I do?" I asked.

"Nothing. We just have to wait it out." She grabbed my hand, and I realized I was shaking. "Pretty boy's a smart one. He'll be fine."

I nodded, but I couldn't focus on any other tasks. Thankfully, the calls had stopped coming in as power was restored to part of the blackout area while other parts not in our jurisdiction were cast into darkness. My only thoughts were on Michael.

"Why don't you go upstairs and see if anyone's heard anything," she said after we sat in silence for a full five minutes. "I can handle the rest here."

"Thank you, ma'am." I went up the steps, hoping someone would know something, but the squad room was practically empty. The only face I recognized was Kemper's.

"Yo, Lexie, did you hear about the bomb threat?" Kemper asked. I sunk into my chair and looked at him. "Riley snuck in a back way and got the jump on Sigfried. It turns out he didn't really have a bomb, and the civilians inside were evacuated."

"So Riley's safe?"

"I'm not sure. I haven't heard what happened to him or Sigfried yet. All I know is that the building was cleared of potential hostages and the bomb squad didn't find anything."

"They must have taken Sigfried into custody if they know there aren't any bombs," I surmised, hoping the words held true.

My mind was processing through Kemper's limited information, trying to make sense of it. His story was lacking. Logic needed to be applied in order to determine what already occurred.

"I don't know. It was on the news a few minutes

ago. But the last time the lights flickered, the TV turned off. And I got bogged down, talking to the lieutenant on the phone about that security firm that issued three dozen calls, so I didn't get a chance to turn the TV back on."

Getting out of the chair, I went across the room and hit the power button on the ancient contraption. A news anchor was in the forefront of the screen, talking about the gang leader that was fatally wounded during tonight's bomb scare. She brought a man onto the screen that I assumed was one of the civilians from inside the bar.

"When he reached for the guy's gun, somehow the dude got the slip on him and held him at gunpoint. The rest of us ran out, but it was obvious something bad was gonna happen," the witness said. "We're lucky to be alive. You hear a lot of bad things about the police, but that detective saved all of our lives."

The news anchor faced the camera sputtering some line about the bravery the men in uniform exhibit and how they're taken for granted before saying that the responding officer failed to comment.

"Holy shit," I cursed, my stomach clenching at the news that Riley could have easily been killed. "But that means he's okay, right?"

Maybe taking it slow wasn't the way to go. Our careers were dangerous, and waiting for some arbitrary length of time to pass before entertaining the thought of consummating our relationship seemed juvenile and stupid.

The phone rang, and Kemper answered, muttering a few uh-huhs before hanging up. "Yeah, dispatch just phoned. It's a mess, but at least our guy is okay."

"Thank god," I murmured. The lights flickered again, and the TV went out. I got up to turn it back on, and the power went completely out. The emergency lights flickered on, but the back-up generator didn't kick in like it was supposed to. "Does anything in this place work?"

"Piece of shit," the sergeant cursed from downstairs. She hit the intercom button, making an announcement to the entire stationhouse. "Okay, everyone we had in holding was transferred earlier since we're in a blackout zone, so now we're shutting down and moving to the nearest precinct to continue working until all systems are restored."

The few police personnel on the premises collected their belongings and began heading for the stairs.

"Are you coming?" Kemper asked as I rummaged through my desk for my cell phone.

"I'm not feeling well. If I duck out early, will you cover for me?"

"Sure, no problem. I hope you feel better." Kemper followed the others out of the building, and I slumped back in my chair.

Michael's okay. He's okay. I repeated this in my head as I dialed his number. Ringing sounded in the distance, and I got up, searching for the source. I went to the stairwell, spotting Michael coming inside as everyone else was going out. He glanced at his phone and then at me. When he made it onto our floor, I rushed into his arms and hugged him.

"Are you okay?" I asked.

"Yeah, I'm fine." He didn't sound fine, but he was in one piece. He scratched his head and edged toward his desk. "I got my ass handed to me for improper procedure. I was supposed to wait for back-up. How stupid is that? Where would back-up be when we're in the middle of a freaking blackout? The lieutenant threatened to suspend me for a few days. Can you believe that? Luckily, he's going to think about it and let me know what punishment seems fit after these damn blackouts are resolved." He pulled out a notepad and started writing in the dim light provided by the emergency lights. "At least we got Sigfried. It's taken us long enough." He muttered expletives under his breath.

I sat down in my chair and watched him write his report. He was stressed. I could see it in the way his shoulders tensed and the way he white-knuckled the pen. The precinct was eerily quiet since almost everyone had left. The only cops still inside the building were the officers downstairs that were assigned to redirect civilians to one of the other police stations. Silently, I waited for Michael to finish his report. He threw the pen down and let out a frustrated growl.

"Hey," I said softly, pushing away from my desk and crossing the room in order to be close to him, "you're okay. I was worried sick."

"It wasn't that big of a deal." He shook his head, swallowing and looking away. "Thing got blown out of proportion."

"Liar."

He chuckled.

"I get it if you don't want to talk about it. But you could have been killed tonight." I pushed his chair back and sat on his lap, straddling him. "I don't want to lose you." I began massaging his shoulders, and he leaned his head against my chest as I rubbed out the kinks and the knots. "It's over now," I whispered. "You can relax. It's just the two of us. Everyone else is gone. No one's here except me."

He looked up. "I thought I could reason with him. Instead, he starts shouting out crazy things like how he has the place wired with explosives and he's going to kill everyone." He looked away, and I grasped his chin in my hand and made him face me.

"I understand why you had to go inside. It's what we do. It's what we're trained to do. But I'd rather it be someone else. At the end of the day, it's more important to me that you're still standing," I insisted. "Maybe that's selfish, but I don't care. I don't want to lose you."

"Me neither."

He turned his head to look at the security camera which was dead, just like all the other electrical equipment in the precinct. Then he kissed me, soft and gentle, and I parted my lips and let his tongue explore. He needed to feel grounded the same way I did after dealing with Stryker King that horrible night a few weeks ago, and I wanted to give him the solace we both desperately needed.

"Michael," my voice was barely a whisper as he kissed down the column of my neck and his fingers undid the buttons on my shirt.

He pulled my tucked-in shirt free from my pants and smiled at the front-clasp on my bra and unhooked it. The material immediately fell away, and he kissed my breasts, paying equal attention to each rosy red peak. I moaned and threw my head back as he moved at a slow, tender pace. When his lips moved back to mine, my hands made fast work of his shirt, rubbing random patterns along his abdomen.

He pushed my back against the desk, and even though I was still seated in his lap, he ran his hand along my abdomen before slowly undoing my belt. He pulled me into an upright position, and I stood up so he could shove my pants down my legs. His hands massaged my calves, my thighs, and he pressed his mouth against my lace thong, teasing me through the material. I quivered, and my legs shook. He smiled at the effect he was having on me.

"Lexie," he met my eyes, and I saw just how badly

he needed this, "please."

"Good thing someone bought a box of condoms the other day." I smirked, bending down and opening his desk drawer to find his wallet. I removed the foil package and put it on the desk behind me.

I knelt on the floor, undoing his fly with my teeth. He inhaled sharply and lifted me off the ground. He stood and shoved his pants and boxer briefs down in one fluid motion. He was already fully erect and ready to go. I opened the packet and slid the condom down his shaft, hearing him sigh as he thrust into my hand.

He sat back down in the chair and pulled me onto his lap, groaning as his member came into contact with my thigh. He kissed me for a time, teasing me with his hands until I was begging for him to enter me. He pushed my panties to the side, and slowly, pressed into me. I slid inch by inch down onto his manhood, allowing my body time to get used to his size and girth as we both gasped and moaned at the intimate contact. He reached between us and rubbed his thumb in lazy circles against my clit, encouraging my inner walls to accept all of him. He only stopped once he was balls deep inside of me, neither of us moving.

"Are you okay?" he asked, touching my lips to his.

"More than okay," I responded, rocking slightly against him.

He leaned forward and kissed me again. "Wrap your legs around me," he instructed, standing up and carrying me, impaled on his cock, across the room. He pressed my back against the wall and slowly withdrew three-fourths of the way before easing back inside. I hadn't expected this man to be so gentle and careful, especially after a day like today, but he moved slowly, allowing me time to adjust to this intimate invasion. Easing slowly in and out, I began thrusting forward to meet him, and we found a steady pace.

Briefly, I considered how insane it was that we were having sex for the first time in the middle of the squad room. But no one was around, and Michael was nearly killed tonight. That thought made me tremble, and I clung to him, never wanting to let go. I felt the build-up in my stomach as my muscles started to clench and constrict, gripping him harder and trying to stop his rhythmic retreat.

He was close, and he picked up the pace. He shifted his angle, hitting the sensitive bundle of nerves on my front wall and sending me cascading over the edge. I cried out, and he covered my mouth with his, swallowing my screams in a kiss that had his tongue mimicking the actions of his cock. His lower back tensed beneath my calves, and he jerked inside of me, finding his own release.

Sated, we crumpled onto the floor, a mess of clothing, sweat, and limbs. He kissed me gently and cradled me against his chest. My heartbeat pounded in time to his.

He brushed my hair from my face. "I love you. I know it's too soon to say it, but I do." He planted kisses across my shoulder. "Forgive me. This wasn't the way I wanted our first time to go. You deserve so much better. I know you didn't want this to happen yet." He squeezed me tighter. "I shouldn't have asked."

"Oh, Michael," I looked up and kissed him, "if you didn't, I would have. I wanted this too. The only thing I could think about tonight was how stupid it was to wait. What we have is real. And that's all that matters." I blinked, pushing the overwhelming emotions back. "I think I fell for you the moment I saw you." I giggled. "Damn you, and those gorgeous good looks. How the hell could I resist?"

He smiled. “In that case, I’m all yours.” He glanced around the room. “We better get dressed before the power comes back, or else we’ll both be looking at reprimands.”

“Worse things could happen,” I retorted, untangling myself from his arms and going back to the desk to put my bra and uniform back on. “Lieberman could have walked in on us.”

“That would have been worse but almost worth it, just to see the look on his face.”

“Ugh.” I rolled my eyes and began buttoning my shirt. Michael fastened his belt, and we both checked to make sure our badges and guns were in place. “The best part of solving this case is that I don’t have to see him anymore.”

“But you won’t get to see me as much either.” Michael made a sad puppy face, and I laughed. We kissed again as if we couldn’t get enough of each other in our postcoital bliss. “How about we go somewhere on an actual date? Since we aren’t working together anymore, there’s no reason why we can’t be seen together.”

“Let’s just keep it on the down low at work, okay?” I asked.

“Okay. So where shall we go on our date? I’m thinking a romantic dinner, tablecloths, and candlelight. We can take things slow again if you want, now that we’ve taken the edge off.” He offered a sly grin.

“Oh no, you don’t.” I ran my fingers through my hair, untangling the knots. “You can’t put the genie back in the bottle after what just happened. I’m an all or nothing girl. And you just went all in.”

“That I did.” He snickered at the innuendo. “So let’s get the hell out of here and go someplace romantic.”

“The fancy dinner will have to wait. The city’s on

lockdown. But we can go back to my place, heat up some frozen pizza, and see if you're just as good horizontally as you are vertically," I suggested.

"Really?"

"Really."

SIXTEEN

"This has to be the best frozen pizza I've ever tasted," Michael cooed.

"You're crazy. It's soggy. I wonder if it thawed and refroze when my apartment lost power."

"Well, I was starving, so it's delicious." He glanced at the flashing display on the stove and then his watch. "The electric wasn't out that long." He cut another piece and took a big bite. "Although, it might have had something to do with the length of time we left it on the counter." He grinned. "Unfortunately, it seems we had more pressing matters to deal with while we were waiting for the oven to preheat." He nudged my thigh with his knee. "How come you were preheated but the oven wasn't?"

I slapped his arm, blushing. "Shut up. You were just as ready to go."

"I warned you what happens to the male anatomy when things get dicey at work." He finished off the last piece, and we snuggled on the couch. "So what happens now?"

"I guess I call Emma and tell her I have a boyfriend."

"Oh, wow. We should make it facebook official and everything." He snorted, enjoying the mockery.

"Sure, except for the fact that neither of us uses social media and we've agreed that no one at work needs to know."

"True, but Kemper better keep his distance. And he better be nicer to you."

"And you better be a little less alpha male. I'm entitled to have my own opinion and free will."

"I wouldn't have it any other way," he replied, finding the phrase amusing given the context. He yawned. "How do you feel about having tons of sleepovers? With the way work is, the only chance we'll have to see each other will be at night, and you know how often we get late night calls."

"Toothbrushes. Deodorant. Body wash." I was listing the toiletries I'd need to buy. "Do you have conditioner at your place?"

"Why? Does my hair seem dry or unmanageable?"

"No. You have great hair."

"It's because I condition." He hoisted me off the couch. "I'm exhausted, let's sleep now, and we'll work on the shopping list tomorrow." He watched as I found an oversized t-shirt and changed in front of him. "Oddly enough, I'm guessing you'll have fewer things to keep at my place. After all, you can sleep in my clothes, but I can't say the same."

I inhaled sharply, the familiar unease hitting again, but this time I forced it away. There was no set timeframe for things to happen. We could move just as fast or slow as we wanted, and I would do my best not to compare it to the way my previous relationship had progressed. This was different. I was different. And things were different when it came to the situations Michael and I faced.

"Is everything okay, Lex?" Michael asked, once

again reading my mind. “Are you second guessing things?”

“Not anymore. I love you, Michael.”

Enjoy this sneak peek from *Break-ins and Bouquets*

Chapter One

As I was coming home from another late night shift, the sky started to brighten, but it did nothing to improve my mood. Working nights in the middle of winter sucked. What sucked even more was the fact that my schedule was completely opposite from Michael's. *Let it go, Lexie,* I thought. I should consider myself lucky to be working for burglary division instead of vice. At least the police uniform was warm, unlike the outfits I'd worn as a decoy hooker. I sighed. That felt like a lifetime ago. A lot had changed in the last three months.

Unlocking my apartment door, I couldn't help but smile at the man who was sound asleep in my bed. Quietly, I grabbed something to sleep in and padded into the bathroom. Once I was freshly showered, having washed off the grime and annoyance of the night, I dried my long brown hair and crawled under the covers just as the sun was coming up.

I was exhausted. My partner and I had fielded calls from the time our shift started until it was time to go home. It was nonstop complaints and break-ins. But I was home now. Pressing my cheek against Michael's toned chest, I let the sound of his heartbeat lull me to sleep. Unfortunately, the tranquility was short-lived when something buzzed across the nightstand and Michael eased away from me, taking his cell phone and going into the living room.

"Stupid job," I hissed to the now empty room before closing my eyes and drifting back to sleep.

"Lexie," Detective Michael Riley whispered in my ear as he leaned over the bed and kissed my cheek, "I have to go to work."

I forced my eyes open. Just looking at Michael took my breath away. He stood next to the bed, still buttoning his shirt. His taut, sinewy muscles bunching as his hands moved effortlessly over the material. His blue eyes sparkled, and his gorgeous lips formed a playful grin. I had barely even fallen asleep, and he had to leave.

"Weren't you supposed to have the day off?" I asked.

"Yeah, tell that to Lieutenant Peterson." He rolled his eyes. "Apparently there was a smash and grab at a jewelry store that connects to one of my cases, so I have to get down there before someone screws it up."

With the holidays fast approaching, there had been a lot of recent break-ins, keeping all of us in burglary division busy. Last night, my partner and I responded to the same robbery that Michael had been called in early this morning to investigate. Sometimes, it really sucked to be a cop and to be dating a cop.

"Check my notepad before you go." I pointed at the police insignia covering the paper. "I might have something useful written down. Half the division was down there, so we were sent packing after a quick canvas. Last night was insane, so be careful today." I wished he didn't have to leave.

"I'm always careful."

He kissed me on the mouth, sending chills down my spine. Ever since we officially became a couple, consummating our relationship during a city-wide power outage that had left the precinct completely abandoned, we had barely gotten to spend any real time together. At work, there had been a few stolen glances and longing looks, but we did our best to maintain professional boundaries.

Michael's ex-girlfriend, Detective Samantha Preston, tended to appear at the most inopportune times, and since I had no desire to be on anyone's shit list, we were trying to keep a low profile. Plus, relationships within the same department were typically frowned upon. Official paperwork was supposed to be filed, and other obstacles were in the way. But since I was new to the division and our relationship was even newer, it seemed wise to keep it to ourselves for now. We could worry about the rest in the future.

I watched him turn, clip his handcuffs, shield, and gun to his belt, and put his jacket on. He skimmed through my notes and placed my notepad back on the nightstand. *It must be nice to be a detective and get to wear actual clothes instead of the annoying uniform*, I thought bitterly. He went to the door, and I stared at his perfectly formed, tight ass. He turned and smirked, probably having felt my eyes on him, before flipping the lock back in place and closing the door behind him.

Sighing, I scooted across the bed, nestling against the remaining warmth from where he had been asleep all night. I buried my face in his pillow and inhaled. It was the perfect intoxicating mixture of aftershave, soap, and something purely Michael. Letting out a frustrated growl, I closed my eyes and went back to sleep.

~*~

Waking up, I stared at the neon glow from the digital clock. I hated working third shift, particularly in the winter. It meant there was no chance to see actual sunlight. By the time I got up, the sun had already set. As I pulled my clothes out of the closet, I wondered if Michael was going to stay at my place again tonight or if he was going back to his place. It seemed the only way we managed to see one another was by having daily sleepovers, and even then, it was only an hour or two before he'd have to leave for work. When was the last time we even had sex?

Okay, maybe it wasn't just the job, the winter, and the uniform that were grating on my nerves. Maybe it was the fact that we had started out hot and heavy, and now we were like an old married couple. Sure, we lay beside each other in bed, but there was no touching. No intimacy. No time to do anything except sleep and work. Whatever happened to being young and vibrant? We were both in our twenties. Obviously, there was something wrong with this picture.

After eating breakfast or maybe it was actually dinner, it was hard to keep up given my crazy sleep schedule, I filled my travel cup with coffee and headed for the station. At the precinct, I found Officer Will Kemper waiting for me. He looked agitated.

"Hey, Sarcone," he called, "did you finish your report from last night's break-in?"

"Which one?"

"All of them." He snorted derisively. "But specifically, the jewelry store heist. I don't know what the hell's going on with that, but the brass is bitching." He rolled his eyes. "I was afraid it was something we had done."

"We didn't do anything." I was already being defensive. "We responded to the call, took the owner's statement and information, and waited for Detective Lieberman to take over the scene."

"Then I guess it's Lieberman's ass on the line." Kemper's lips curled into a cruel smile.

It was no secret that none of us liked Lieberman. He thought he was god's gift to crime fighting and everyone else was an incompetent hindrance. What made this even more irritating was the fact that he didn't hesitate to share his point of view with the rest of us whenever the opportunity presented itself.

"So," I threw a cautious glance around the squad room, hoping to spot Detective Riley, but we had probably missed each other, "do you have any idea why the white shirts are up in arms about the jewelry store? It seemed like a run-of-the-mill smash and grab to me. No one was hurt. No one was there. The robbers broke open the main display case, took whatever was inside, and ran off a minute after the alarm sounded, according to the security footage."

"The whispers around the bullpen make it sound like professionals."

"Makes sense." I bit my lip, remembering Michael saying it was connected to another one of his cases. Shaking off the thought since it was beyond my pay grade, I forced a neutral expression onto my face. "What have we been assigned to do this tour, partner?"

"Same old, same old," Kemper responded. "Do you want to drive tonight?"

"Not particularly." We were stuck patrolling the neighborhood and waiting for dispatch to send us out on calls. "Let me get ready and grab my gear. I'll meet you at the car."

Retreating to the locker room, I changed into my uniform and grabbed the thick study guide I picked up for the detective's exam. I still wasn't certain if I wanted to be a detective or even if I had what it took to investigate more serious crimes, but Michael had been a constant source of encouragement for the last couple of weeks. And a promotion might give us more opportunities to work together in the future. Even if it didn't, it would mean our schedules would be more likely to coincide, and that was enough incentive for me.

"Studying up?" Kemper asked when I met him beside the squad car we had been assigned.

"Yeah. It can't hurt, right? Worst case, I stay where I am, and best case, I get out of this itchy uniform and receive a nice salary hike. What do you think?"

"It sounds great. Why don't you quiz me while I drive? Then we'll trade off after our break, and I'll quiz you while you drive."

"You're taking the exam too?"

"I don't know. Maybe. Let's see how much I know before I give you a definitive answer."

~*~

Kemper and I stopped at a twenty-four hour Greek diner and ordered lunch. Well, it seemed like lunch to me. To the normal world, it would have seemed ridiculous. We both ordered submarine sandwiches and fries. As we waited for our food to be prepared, my gaze traveled to a shop across the street. It was four a.m., and while it wasn't unusual to encounter people still out and about, the two men standing around in dark clothing sent my radar buzzing.

"Maybe we should take a stroll while we wait for our lunch," I suggested, nudging Kemper in the ribs and directing his eyes to the suspicious looking men.

"Good idea. After all that riding around, I need to stretch my legs anyway. It would be a shame if I developed a clot or a DVT or whatever they're called. The lieutenant would be so annoyed if he had to fill out the workman's comp forms when I could have prevented it just by walking a few blocks." He raised an eyebrow, understanding precisely what needed investigating.

Casually, we headed across the street; although, it was hard for two uniformed police officers to appear casual at four in the morning. The two men spotted us and took to leaning against the brick wall, pretending they weren't casing the place.

I read the sign above the storefront. It was an adult novelty shop which meant there would probably be a lot of cash on hand since most people didn't want charges like that to appear on their bank statement or credit card bill. The shop closed six hours ago and didn't open again until ten a.m. There was no reason for these two men to be loitering outside, at least none that was legal.

"Evening," Kemper greeted as we approached. One of the two men nodded in response. "Can I help either of you gentlemen with anything?"

"Nah. We're good," the one who nodded replied.

"Sir, would you mind showing me some identification?" Kemper asked in a polite, authoritarian tone.

"What for?" the other guy asked. "We're not bothering anybody. It's not illegal for us to hang around or go for a walk."

His friend turned and gave him an angry glare, signaling he should shut up. "You don't need to see our IDs. We aren't doing anything wrong," the first guy insisted. He cast his eyes upon me, staring far too long at my breasts. I was used to behavior like that when I was working undercover for vice but not when I was in full police uniform. "Don't you think you and the little lady should get back to work and stop hassling us?"

"Little lady?" My eyebrows went skyward. "Do you see this badge? Or were your eyes unable to make it past my tits? That's officer to you."

The most annoying thing about this job was the lack of respect. Having started my career in vice, I thought my barely concealed breasts and ass were the reason for the disrespect. Apparently it had more to do with lacking a dick, or maybe it was just because men could be dicks. Kemper shot a warning glance in my direction, indicating that I cool it and be more professional.

"Whatever. We're going," one of the men said, and they both took off down the street.

"Crisis averted," Kemper whispered as we went back to the diner to pick up our meals. "But do me a favor and stick a post-it on my desk so I don't mistakenly call you 'little lady'."

"Ha ha." I gave him a withering glare, and he held up his hands, crossing his pointer fingers in an X. "I think that gesture only works on witches, not bitches," I teased, and he cracked a smile. "It's possible I overreacted. But that goon thought he could intimidate me by leering, and I refuse to bow to his will. Men always think that they can get whatever they want or do whatever they want. I don't get it."

"I've seen you spar in the precinct's gym. I would never think that," Kemper replied. "You're a cop. You know how to handle yourself."

"I hope so," I admitted quietly. "Frankly, running into some guys in a dark alley isn't on my list of things to do."

"Mine either."

Returning to the car, we sat inside and ate while I skimmed through the next chapter in the study guide.

After an encounter like this, I realized how much I wanted to get away from patrol and do something slightly less dangerous.

Chapter Two

"Sarcone. Kemper. Get your asses in here," Lieutenant Peterson bellowed as soon as we set foot inside the precinct. Obediently, we went into his office. "We received a civilian complaint against the both of you. Why were you harassing two men this morning?"

"Two men?" Kemper considered the calls we had responded to, but I realized what two men the lieutenant was talking about.

"We weren't harassing them. They looked suspicious. They were wearing dark clothing and loitering outside a closed shop at four a.m. We went over and asked if they needed any assistance," I began, but Kemper jumped in.

"I asked if I could see their IDs. They declined, and that was it."

Lt. Peterson studied each of us for a moment, sighing loudly. "Don't let it happen again." His sentiment made little sense. We hadn't done anything wrong, and it was impossible to prevent some hooligans from phoning in a complaint, even if nothing happened and it was wholly unsubstantiated. Peterson looked at the roster. "I'm rescheduling the two of you. Things around here have been a little too hot lately, so take the next shift off. I don't want the idiots from internal affairs thinking that I'm overlooking civilian complaints, even if they are bogus." He glowered at us. "This better be bogus," he warned.

"Aye, sir," I responded, equally irate and thrilled to have a day off.

Kemper was angry and muttered under his breath as he followed me to the locker rooms. "Can you believe this shit?" he asked. "We didn't do anything. Hell, we might have thwarted a burglary. And what thanks do we get? Oh yeah, we get our wrists slapped and end up suspended for a day. This is bullshit." He kicked the locker room door.

"We're not suspended. Suspension looks bad, and we would have been forced to sign something official. Instead, we're being rewarded for our diligence with a day off."

I wasn't an optimist by any stretch of the imagination, but for once, I was trying to put a positive spin on the situation, particularly since there was nothing we could do about it. Plus, there was a good chance with the unexpected time off that I could work my womanly wiles on Michael. My body ached for him. *Cool it, Lexie*, I chided, trying to get my mind out of the gutter and away from all the slutty things I wanted to do with my boyfriend.

"Yeah, an unpaid day off." Kemper continued to gripe as we parted ways, slipping into our respective locker rooms.

After I changed back into my street clothes, I made a beeline for the exit. The sun was coming up, and I wanted to call Michael to tell him the good news. As I was on my way out of the building, Michael was coming in.

"Hey, stranger," he greeted, smiling lecherously. "What are you still doing here?" He looked at his watch. “I know I’m thirty minutes early, but you should have been home an hour ago.”

“Our last call ran late, and then I got chewed out because of a civilian complaint.” I rolled my eyes.

“Ouch. Are you okay? Do you want me to go kick someone’s ass?” Michael was kidding, but I still appreciated the protective sentiment.

“Yes, please,” Kemper replied, interrupting us as he bounded down the steps. “Those two douchebags were casing that place. I don’t care what anyone says. We confronted them, and they reconsidered committing the crime. So where the hell does the lieutenant get off reprimanding us?”

“Will, let it go. It’s a day off,” I insisted, wanting him to disappear so I could talk to Michael.

“I’d suggest you keep your protest to a minimum,” Michael said, slipping into his formal police persona. “You’d hate to have that one day turn into two because you sound like an insubordinate rookie.”

“C’mon, Riley,” Kemper whined, “I have every right to be pissed. It isn’t fair.” Kemper glanced from Michael to me. “You sounded far more understanding when Sarcone was the one voicing a complaint.”

“She wasn’t blaming the brass,” Michael said.

“Whatever.” Kemper shook his head. “I’ll see you guys in a day or two.”

Once he was gone, I let out a sigh of relief. “Well, Detective,” my voice sounded sultry, and Michael’s eyes darkened, “it seems I’m off duty for an entire day. Whatever will I do with so much free time?”

“I have some suggestions,” he growled in my ear. “Meet me at my place at seven. I should be finished by then.”

“I’d like to be there when you finish,” I purred, blushing at my own brazen innuendo.

“God, Lexie, you’re killing me.” His voice sounded

hoarse, and he gave me a quick peck. "Seven o'clock. If I'm not home by then, let yourself in."

"Detective Riley," I said, suddenly sounding formal since a few officers just entered the double doors we were standing next to, "have a good day."

"Oh, I will." He cast a sideways glance at me and continued inside.

At least I found a way to salvage my unofficial suspension.

~*~

I went home, took a two hour nap, and forced myself out of bed at ten a.m. It was important that I find a way to avoid sleeping the rest of the day. Since I was spending the night with Michael, I wanted to be on the same sleep schedule. Our evening together would be utterly pointless if I was passed out when he came home, and he was unconscious by the time I woke up.

After brewing a pot of coffee, I decided the best way to combat the fatigue would be to keep busy, so I spent the entire day reading through the study guide for the detective's exam. After completing all the practice questions and rereading my notes, I was starting to believe this was something I could do. No more uniforms. No more patrols. And a lot more time on the job with Detective Riley. Smiling, I checked the time and hopped into the shower in preparation for our evening together.

When I got out, I dug through the bottom of my underwear drawer, looking for my lace thong and matching see-through bra. They were brand new. I had been saving them for a special occasion, and tonight seemed special enough. Despite the fact Michael might be tired after getting home from work, he would still enjoy the surprise.

Sliding into my little black dress, I studied my reflection in the mirror. My long brown hair was curled in loose waves, and the physical demands of my job ensured my waist and thighs stayed trim and strong while my C-cup sized rack added just the right amount of curve. *Damn, I was hot,* I giggled at the conceited thought. It was funny because most days I looked in the mirror and thought *blah*. It was rare that I actually thought I was something special. Pondering if that meant my self-image was healthy, I packed an overnight bag, found my keys, checking that I had my key to Michael's place, and headed for his apartment.

When the clock on the dashboard clicked to seven, I stepped out of my car and made my way to his building and knocked on his apartment door. There was no answer. I tried again. I strained to hear sounds of the television or shower, but no noise emanated from inside. Obviously, he had been delayed. I dug through my purse for his spare key, realizing that having a key to his place might be a step beyond where our still new relationship was but grateful not to have to stand outside his apartment all night in heels and a dress, looking pathetic and wanton.

Inside, his place looked like it had been hit by a tornado. Apparently he expected to get home early since he normally didn't let me visit unless he had the opportunity to straighten up first. I went to the fridge, helping myself to a glass of wine. Then I scanned the room for something to do. Dishes were piled up in the sink, and a basket of clean laundry waited to be folded.

"You better appreciate me," I said, starting on the dishes.

Once they were washed, dried, and put away. I moved to the laundry basket. My last boyfriend had been a lying, cheating sack of shit, and it had become painfully obvious after finding his conquest's unmentionables in our laundry. So being an investigator by trade and neurotic by design, I sifted through Michael's laundry, finding nothing out of the ordinary. He had some t-shirts, jeans, socks, and boxer briefs, all of the male variety and all in his size. If he was stepping out on me, he was much smarter about it than Kevin had been, but considering the fact that we were either at work or asleep, Michael didn't have time to cheat. Plus, I doubted he'd do that to me, particularly after my best friend, Emma, threatened to cut off his dick if he so much as looked at another woman. Yeah, Emma could be an overprotective handful. It was a good thing she was a nurse and not a cop, or people might end up dead.

Snooping wasn't exactly the best idea, but Michael should have known better than to leave me unsupervised in his apartment. I looked through his kitchen cabinets, checked out his movie collection, read through the products in his medicine cabinet and bathroom, and stumbled upon a case file sitting atop his desk. Even if it was my night off, I couldn't help but wonder what he was working on. The detectives always investigated the much more complex cases, and being a lowly officer, it was rare that we were privy to the bigger operations, unless we were tasked to assist.

Apparently the smash and grab at the jewelry store was the fourth one in the last two weeks. The surveillance footage I had watched showed two masked men breaking into the building, destroying the largest display case, scooping up as much jewelry as possible, and escaping within a minute of the alarm sounding. This was our suspects' M.O., and from the case file and Michael's notes, something was off about the robberies. Each location used the same security system, and since the alarm wasn't triggered until the jewelry cases were destroyed, it appeared that the perpetrators knew how to bypass the security measures that covered the front door.

I thought about the scene. There had been no obvious signs of tampering or a break-in at the front entrance. I assumed the burglars used a window or other entry point, like a side or rear door. Kemper and I hadn't gotten to review the security footage in any real detail, other than to make sure the robbers had been caught on tape and to pass a rudimentary description of them over the wire, but from Detective Riley's notes, there was a third man on the crew that provided technical support to bypass the exterior security systems. On gut instinct alone, it seemed obvious that he must work for the security firm since all locations used the same system. It was an inside job.

Flipping through the pages, I didn't see any transcripts or logs indicating that the security firm had been contacted, nor did I find a list of other potential targets – locations that used the same security system. Granted, that information could be in an official folder inside the precinct and not sitting on Michael's desk at home, but it was the most likely avenue to explore. I pulled a sticky note from the dispenser and wrote down my theory, leaving it next to the folder. Michael didn't like to talk about work outside of work since he felt it was a waste of our time together, but he would find my note eventually. And if he thought my hints were foolish or sophomoric, I wouldn't be around to see him crumple up the note and toss it away.

Now that I was through reading the case file, I was bored again. As the hours ticked by, the fatigue began to set in. If I wasn't so tired, I would have been livid, but it was hard to maintain the anger when I just as easily could be delayed by a work snafu. It was the job, and it was a dangerous job. I swallowed, hoping that Michael was okay. *It would be stupid to worry,* I told myself, feeling the unease settle in the pit of my stomach.

"Screwed up job," I bitched to the empty room, noting that it was already after eleven.

The dress was starting to get uncomfortable, and I dug through the pile of clean laundry for one of Michael's shirts. Slipping out of my dress and into his t-shirt, which fit like a dress, I sprawled out on the couch. I'd rather have him delayed than hurt. The fact that he wasn't home yet and hadn't called wasn't necessarily cause for alarm, but we didn't have the best track record either. Anything could have happened, and in the last two months, we'd both had a few close calls. No, I refused to believe anything was wrong. He just got held up with a last minute call. It happened all the time. I turned on the television, hoping to distract myself as my mind began racing through all the possible things that could have happened to him.

When I couldn't silence the negative thoughts, I poured another glass of wine. He was okay. Everything was okay. Normally, I didn't worry. But he said he'd be finished by seven, and it was now four and a half hours later. Maybe he went to my place instead, or Detective Lieberman was making him work late on the jewelry store heist. After all, Kemper had said the brass was bitching about the jewelry store thing, and that was before we'd had the civilian complaint launched against us. There was a lot going on at the precinct, but Michael was fine. I repeated this a few times while I finished my wine. Putting the glass down, I took a deep, calming breath. The wine had done the trick to relax me, and now my eyelids were getting heavy from lack of sleep. So much for getting on the same schedule.

Continue Michael and Lexie's story with *Break-ins and Bouquets* now available in print and e-book.

ABOUT THE AUTHOR

Elisa Archer has always loved reading, writing, and romance. On most days you can find her hiding behind a computer screen, frantically typing away at her latest story. She's always been an avid reader and enjoys everything from techno-thrillers to erotica. In fact, there isn't a genre of book she doesn't like. Writing just seemed to be the natural progression of her passion for books.

Elisa's romantic suspense series, featuring Officer Lexie Sarcone and Detective Michael Riley, is a compilation of action, mystery, and romance. Just like the lattes she drinks every day, Elisa likes her sex scenes steamy, hot, and sweet. But more importantly, she doesn't want to sacrifice a great story or plot for nothing but fluff. She hopes that readers will find her tales to be satisfying in more ways than one. Hopefully, you'll take the chance to find out for yourself.

For updates on future releases and promotions, visit http://www.elisaarcher.com

Manufactured by Amazon.ca
Bolton, ON

14615822R00104

...FOR DUMMIES®

References for the Rest of Us!®

COMPUTER BOOK SERIES FROM IDG

Are you intimidated and confused by computers? Do you find that traditional manuals are overloaded with technical details you'll never use? Do your friends and family always call you to fix simple problems on their PCs? Then the *...For Dummies®* computer book series from IDG Books Worldwide is for you.

...For Dummies books are written for those frustrated computer users who know they aren't really dumb but find that PC hardware, software, and indeed the unique vocabulary of computing make them feel helpless. *...For Dummies* books use a lighthearted approach, a down-to-earth style, and even cartoons and humorous icons to diffuse computer novices' fears and build their confidence. Lighthearted but not lightweight, these books are a perfect survival guide for anyone forced to use a computer.

"I like my copy so much I told friends; now they bought copies."

Irene C., Orwell, Ohio

"Quick, concise, nontechnical, and humorous."

Jay A., Elburn, Illinois

"Thanks, I needed this book. Now I can sleep at night."

Robin F., British Columbia, Canada

Already, hundreds of thousands of satisfied readers agree. They have made *...For Dummies* books the #1 introductory level computer book series and have written asking for more. So, if you're looking for the most fun and easy way to learn about computers, look to *...For Dummies* books to give you a helping hand.

IDG BOOKS WORLDWIDE™

7/96r

MORE WORD 97 FOR WINDOWS® FOR DUMMIES®

by Doug Lowe

IDG BOOKS WORLDWIDE

IDG Books Worldwide, Inc.
An International Data Group Company

Foster City, CA ♦ Chicago, IL ♦ Indianapolis, IN ♦ Southlake, TX

MORE Word 97 For Windows® For Dummies®

Published by
IDG Books Worldwide, Inc.
An International Data Group Company
919 E. Hillsdale Blvd.
Suite 400
Foster City, CA 94404
`http://www.idgbooks.com` (IDG Books Worldwide Web site)
`http://www.dummies.com` (Dummies Press Web site)

Library of Congress Catalog Card No.: 97-70744

ISBN: 0-7645-0137-2

Printed in the United States of America

10 9 8 7 6 5 4 3 2 1

1E/RX/QU/ZX/IN

Distributed in the United States by IDG Books Worldwide, Inc.

Distributed by Macmillan Canada for Canada; by Transworld Publishers Limited in the United Kingdom and Europe; by WoodsLane Pty. Ltd. for Australia; by WoodsLane Enterprises Ltd. for New Zealand; by Longman Singapore Publishers Ltd. for Singapore, Malaysia, Thailand, and Indonesia; by Simron Pty. Ltd. for South Africa; by Toppan Company Ltd. for Japan; by Distribuidora Cuspide for Argentina; by Livraria Cultura for Brazil; by Ediciencia S.A. for Ecuador; by Addison-Wesley Publishing Company for Korea; by Ediciones ZETA S.C.R. Ltda. for Peru; by WS Computer Publishing Company, Inc., for the Philippines; by Unalis Corporation for Taiwan; by Contemporanea de Ediciones for Venezuela. Authorized Sales Agent: Anthony Rudkin Associates for the Middle East and North Africa.

For general information on IDG Books Worldwide's books in the U.S., please call our Consumer Customer Service department at 800-762-2974. For reseller information, including discounts and premium sales, please call our Reseller Customer Service department at 800-434-3422.

For information on where to purchase IDG Books Worldwide's books outside the U.S., please contact our International Sales department at 415-655-3023 or fax 415-655-3299.

For information on foreign language translations, please contact our Foreign & Subsidiary Rights department at 415-655-3021 or fax 415-655-3281.

For sales inquiries and special prices for bulk quantities, please contact our Sales department at 415-655-3200 or write to the address above.

For information on using IDG Books Worldwide's books in the classroom or for ordering examination copies, please contact our Educational Sales department at 800-434-2086 or fax 817-251-8174.

For press review copies, author interviews, or other publicity information, please contact our Public Relations department at 415-655-3000 or fax 415-655-3299.

For authorization to photocopy items for corporate, personal, or educational use, please contact Copyright Clearance Center, 222 Rosewood Drive, Danvers, MA 01923, or fax 508-750-4470.

About the Author

Doug Lowe has written something like 35 computer books, including *PowerPoint 97 For Windows For Dummies, Word For Windows 95 SECRETS,* and *Internet Explorer 3 For Dummies*. Doug enjoys presenting boring technostuff in a style that is both entertaining and enlightening. He is a contributing editor for the magazine *DOS World*.

ABOUT IDG BOOKS WORLDWIDE

Welcome to the world of IDG Books Worldwide.

IDG Books Worldwide, Inc., is a subsidiary of International Data Group, the world's largest publisher of computer-related information and the leading global provider of information services on information technology. IDG was founded more than 25 years ago and now employs more than 8,500 people worldwide. IDG publishes more than 275 computer publications in over 75 countries (see listing below). More than 60 million people read one or more IDG publications each month.

Launched in 1990, IDG Books Worldwide is today the #1 publisher of best-selling computer books in the United States. We are proud to have received eight awards from the Computer Press Association in recognition of editorial excellence and three from *Computer Currents*' First Annual Readers' Choice Awards. Our best-selling *...For Dummies®* series has more than 30 million copies in print with translations in 30 languages. IDG Books Worldwide, through a joint venture with IDG's Hi-Tech Beijing, became the first U.S. publisher to publish a computer book in the People's Republic of China. In record time, IDG Books Worldwide has become the first choice for millions of readers around the world who want to learn how to better manage their businesses.

Our mission is simple: Every one of our books is designed to bring extra value and skill-building instructions to the reader. Our books are written by experts who understand and care about our readers. The knowledge base of our editorial staff comes from years of experience in publishing, education, and journalism — experience we use to produce books for the '90s. In short, we care about books, so we attract the best people. We devote special attention to details such as audience, interior design, use of icons, and illustrations. And because we use an efficient process of authoring, editing, and desktop publishing our books electronically, we can spend more time ensuring superior content and spend less time on the technicalities of making books.

You can count on our commitment to deliver high-quality books at competitive prices on topics you want to read about. At IDG Books Worldwide, we continue in the IDG tradition of delivering quality for more than 25 years. You'll find no better book on a subject than one from IDG Books Worldwide.

IDG BOOKS WORLDWIDE

John Kilcullen
CEO
IDG Books Worldwide, Inc.

Steven Berkowitz
President and Publisher
IDG Books Worldwide, Inc.

VIII WINNER — *Eighth Annual Computer Press Awards 1992*

IX WINNER — *Ninth Annual Computer Press Awards 1993*

COMPUTER CURRENTS 1995 READERS' CHOICE 1995

X WINNER — *Tenth Annual Computer Press Awards 1994*

XI WINNER — *Eleventh Annual Computer Press Awards 1995*

IDG Books Worldwide, Inc., is a subsidiary of International Data Group, the world's largest publisher of computer-related information and the leading global provider of information services on information technology. International Data Group publishes over 275 computer publications in over 75 countries. Sixty million people read one or more International Data Group publications each month. International Data Group's publications include: **ARGENTINA:** Buyer's Guide, Computerworld Argentina, PC World Argentina; **AUSTRALIA:** Australian Macworld, Australian PC World, Australian Reseller News, Computerworld, IT Casebook, Network World, Publish, Webmaster; **AUSTRIA:** Computerwelt Osterreich, Networks Austria, PC Tip Austria; **BANGLADESH:** PC World Bangladesh; **BELARUS:** PC World Belarus; **BELGIUM:** Data News; **BRAZIL:** Annuário de Informática, Computerworld, Connections, Macworld, PC Player, PC World, Publish, Reseller News, Supergamepower; **BULGARIA:** Computerworld Bulgaria, Network World Bulgaria, PC & MacWorld Bulgaria; **CANADA:** CIO Canada, Client/Server World, ComputerWorld Canada, InfoWorld Canada, NetworkWorld Canada, WebWorld; **CHILE:** Computerworld Chile, PC World Chile; **COLOMBIA:** Computerworld Colombia, PC World Colombia; **COSTA RICA:** PC World Centro America; **THE CZECH AND SLOVAK REPUBLICS:** Computerworld Czechoslovakia, Macworld Czech Republic, PC World Czechoslovakia; **DENMARK:** Communications World Danmark, Computerworld Danmark, Macworld Danmark, PC World Danmark, Techworld Denmark; **DOMINICAN REPUBLIC:** PC World Republica Dominicana; **ECUADOR:** PC World Ecuador; **EGYPT:** Computerworld Middle East, PC World Middle East; **EL SALVADOR:** PC World Centro America; **FINLAND:** MikroPC, Tietoverkko, Tietoviikko; **FRANCE:** Distributique, Hebdo, Info PC, Le Monde Informatique, Macworld, Reseaux & Telecoms, WebMaster France; **GERMANY:** Computer Partner, Computerwoche, Computerwoche Extra, Computerwoche FOCUS, Global Online, Macwelt, PC Welt; **GREECE:** Amiga Computing, GamePro Greece, Multimedia World; **GUATEMALA:** PC World Centro America; **HONDURAS:** PC World Centro America; **HONG KONG:** Computerworld Hong Kong, PC World Hong Kong, Publish in Asia; **HUNGARY:** ABCD CD-ROM, Computerworld Szamitastechnika, Internetto online Magazine, PC World Hungary, PC-X Magazin Hungary; **ICELAND:** Tolvuheimur PC World Island; **INDIA:** Information Communications World, Information Systems Computerworld, PC World India, Publish in Asia; **INDONESIA:** InfoKomputer PC World, Komputek Computerworld, Publish in Asia; **IRELAND:** ComputerScope, PC Live!; **ISRAEL:** Macworld Israel, People & Computers/Computerworld; **ITALY:** Computerworld Italia, Macworld Italia, Networking Italia, PC World Italia; **JAPAN:** DTP World, Macworld Japan, Nikkei Personal Computing, OS/2 World Japan, SunWorld Japan, Windows NT World, Windows World Japan; **KENYA:** PC World East African; **KOREA:** Hi-Tech Information, Macworld Korea, PC World Korea; **MACEDONIA:** PC World Macedonia; **MALAYSIA:** Computerworld Malaysia, PC World Malaysia, Publish in Asia; **MALTA:** PC World Malta; **MEXICO:** Computerworld Mexico, PC World Mexico; **MYANMAR:** PC World Myanmar; **NETHERLANDS:** Computer! Totaal, LAN Internetworking Magazine, LAN World Buyers Guide, Macworld Netherlands, Net, WebWereld; **NEW ZEALAND:** Absolute Beginners Guide and Plain & Simple Series, Computer Buyer, Computer Industry Directory, Computerworld New Zealand, MTB, Network World, PC World New Zealand; **NICARAGUA:** PC World Centro America; **NORWAY:** Computerworld Norge, CW Rapport, Datamagasinet, Financial Rapport, Kursguide Norge, Macworld Norge, Multimediaworld Norge, PC World Ekspress Norge, PC World Nettverk, PC World Norge, PC World ProduktGuide Norge; **PAKISTAN:** Computerworld Pakistan; **PANAMA:** PC World Panama; **PEOPLE'S REPUBLIC OF CHINA:** China Computer Users, China Computerworld, China InfoWorld, China Telecom World Weekly, Computer & Communication, Electronic Design China, Electronics Today, Electronics Weekly, Game Software, PC World China, Popular Computer Week, Software Weekly, Software World, Telecom World; **PERU:** Computerworld Peru, PC World Profesional Peru, PC World SoHo Peru; **PHILIPPINES:** Click!, Computerworld Philippines, PC World Philippines, Publish in Asia; **POLAND:** Computerworld Poland, Computerworld Special Report Poland, Cyber, Macworld Poland, Networld Poland, PC World Komputer; **PORTUGAL:** Cerebro/PC World, Computerworld/Correio Informático, Dealer World Portugal, Mac*In/PC*In Portugal, Multimedia World; **PUERTO RICO:** PC World Puerto Rico; **ROMANIA:** Computerworld Romania, PC World Romania, Telecom Romania; **RUSSIA:** Computerworld Russia, Mir PK, Publish, Seti; **SINGAPORE:** Computerworld Singapore, PC World Singapore, Publish in Asia; **SLOVENIA:** Monitor; **SOUTH AFRICA:** Computing SA, Network World SA, Software World SA; **SPAIN:** Communicaciones World España, Computerworld España, Dealer World España, Macworld España, PC World España; **SRI LANKA:** Infolink PC World; **SWEDEN:** CAP&Design, Computer Sweden, Corporate Computing Sweden, Internetworld Sweden, it.branschen, Macworld Sweden, MaxiData Sweden, MikroDatorn, Nätverk & Kommunikation, PC World Sweden, PCaktiv, Windows World Sweden; **SWITZERLAND:** Computerworld Schweiz, Macworld Schweiz, PCtip; **TAIWAN:** Computerworld Taiwan, Macworld Taiwan, NEW ViSiON/Publish, PC World Taiwan, Windows World Taiwan; **THAILAND:** Publish in Asia, Thai Computerworld; **TURKEY:** Computerworld Turkiye, Macworld Turkiye, Network World Turkiye, PC World Turkiye; **UKRAINE:** Computerworld Kiev, Multimedia World Ukraine, PC World Ukraine; **UNITED KINGDOM:** Acorn User UK, Amiga Action UK, Amiga Computing UK, Apple Talk UK, Computing, Macworld, Parents and Computers UK, PC Advisor, PC Home, PSX Pro, The WEB; **UNITED STATES:** Cable in the Classroom, CIO Magazine, Computerworld, DOS World, Federal Computer Week, GamePro Magazine, InfoWorld, I-Way, Macworld, Network World, PC Games, PC World, Publish, Video Event, THE WEB Magazine, and WebMaster; online webzines: JavaWorld, NetscapeWorld, and SunWorld Online; **URUGUAY:** InfoWorld Uruguay; **VENEZUELA:** Computerworld Venezuela, PC World Venezuela; and **VIETNAM:** PC World Vietnam.

3/24/97

Dedication

To Bethany.

Author's Acknowledgments

I'd like to thank project editor Tere Drenth for keeping this book on track and for offering many excellent suggestions, and also Jennifer Davies, Stephanie Koutek, and Ray Werner for their technical and editorial prowess. I'd also like to thank Tim Gallan, Leah Cameron, Mary Goodwin, Jim McCarter, Kezia Endsley, Kristin Cocks, Becky Whitney, Michael Partington, and Michael Simsic for their help with previous editions.

Oh, and thanks to Margie Nunez and Linda Wilson for various and sundry contributions. And thanks to Dan Gookin for authoring the most excellent *Word For Windows 97 For Dummies*, without which this sequel would not be possible.

Publisher's Acknowledgments

We're proud of this book; please send us your comments about it by using the IDG Books Worldwide Registration Card at the back of the book or by e-mailing us at feedback/dummies@idgbooks.com. Some of the people who helped bring this book to market include the following:

Acquisitions, Development, and Editorial

Project Editor: Tere Drenth

Acquisitions Editor: Mike Kelly

Copy Editors: Jennifer Davies, Stephanie Koutek

Technical Reviewer: Raymond Werner

Editorial Manager: Seta K. Frantz

Editorial Assistants: Chris H. Collins, Michael D. Sullivan

Production

Project Coordinator: Sherry Gomoll

Layout and Graphics: Brett Black, J. Tyler Connor, Angela F. Hunckler, Jane E. Martin, Drew R. Moore, Elizabeth Cárdenas-Nelson, Mark C. Owens, Anna Rohrer, Brent Savage

Proofreaders: Henry Lazarek, Karen York

Indexer: David Heiret

General and Administrative

IDG Books Worldwide, Inc.: John Kilcullen, CEO; Steven Berkowitz, President and Publisher

IDG Books Technology Publishing: Brenda McLaughlin, Senior Vice President and Group Publisher

Dummies Technology Press and Dummies Editorial: Diane Graves Steele, Vice President and Associate Publisher; Judith A. Taylor, Brand Manager; Kristin A. Cocks, Editorial Director

Dummies Trade Press: Kathleen A. Welton, Vice President and Publisher; Stacy S. Collins, Brand Manager

IDG Books Production for Dummies Press: Beth Jenkins, Production Director; Cindy L. Phipps, Supervisor of Project Coordination, Production Proofreading, and Indexing; Kathie S. Schutte, Supervisor of Page Layout; Shelley Lea, Supervisor of Graphics and Design; Debbie J. Gates, Production Systems Specialist; Tony Augsburger, Supervisor of Reprints and Bluelines; Leslie Popplewell, Media Archive Coordinator

Dummies Packaging and Book Design: Patti Sandez, Packaging Specialist; Lance Kayser, Packaging Assistant; Kavish + Kavish, Cover Design

♦

The publisher would like to give special thanks to Patrick J. McGovern, without whom this book would not have been possible.

♦

Contents at a Glance

Cartoons at a Glance

By Rich Tennant • Fax: 508-546-7747 • E-mail: the5wave@tiac.net

"THAT'S RIGHT, DADDY WILL DOUBLE YOUR SALARY IF YOU SHOW HIM HOW TO MAIL MERGE."

page 7

"I TOLD HIM WE WERE LOOKING FOR SOFTWARE THAT WOULD GIVE US GREATER PRODUCTIVITY, SO HE SOLD ME A WORD PROCESSING PACKAGE THAT CAME WITH THESE SIGNS."

page 329

Software Obsolescence Syndrome-The need to own only the latest version of any program.

page 239

"IT'S A MEMO FROM SOFTWARE DOCUMENTATION. IT'S EITHER AN EXPLANATION OF HOW THE NEW SATELLITE COMMUNICATIONS NETWORK FUNCTIONS, OR DIRECTIONS FOR REPLACING BATTERIES IN THE SMOKE DETECTORS."

page 261

The new desktop publishing software not only lets Rags produce a professional looking greeting card quickly and inexpensively, but it also allows him to say it his way.

page 165

Table of Contents

Introduction

Welcome to *MORE Word 97 For Windows For Dummies,* the book for people who lie awake at night pondering questions of cosmic significance, such as “What if my head explodes?” and “How do you do footnotes in Word?”

This book won’t help you with the first question, but it surely will help with the second, and dozens of other questions like it. What the heck are styles? How do you make an outline? Is there happiness to be found in the Mail Merge feature?

If such questions boil your blood, this book is just what you need. It lets you catch your breath and count to ten before putting your fist through the monitor. After it calms you down, it shows you how to use the so-called “advanced features.” When you’re done, you’ll say, “Geez Louise, that wasn’t so bad. Why was I so upset?”

This book talks about “advanced” Word features in everyday — and often irreverent — terms. No lofty prose here. I have no Pulitzer Prize expectations for this book, although I was kind of hoping it would be made into a major motion picture starring Harrison Ford so that maybe I could retire. Other than that, my goal is to make an otherwise dull and lifeless subject at least tolerable, if not kind of fun.

About This Book

This isn’t the kind of book you pick up and read from start to finish, as if it were a cheap novel. If I ever see you reading it at the beach, I’ll kick sand in your face. This book is more like a reference; it’s the kind of book that you can pick up, turn to just about any page, and start reading. I’ve included 28 chapters, each one covering a specific aspect of using Word — like using styles, drawing pictures, creating macros, or making an index. Just turn to the chapter you’re interested in and start reading.

Each chapter is divided into self-contained chunks, all related to the major theme of the chapter.

For example, the chapter on creating an index contains nuggets like these:

- Marking index entries
- Creating an index
- Marking a range of pages
- Building an index from a list of words
- Creating subentries
- Creating cross-references
- Updating an index

You don't have to memorize anything in this book. It's a "need-to-know" book: You pick it up when you need to know something. Need to know how to create a three-column layout? Pick up the book. Need to know how to generate a table of contents? Pick up the book. Otherwise, put it down and get on with your life.

What about Word 97 For Windows For Dummies?

Ah . . . now we're getting somewhere. This book is actually the sequel to *Word 97 For Windows For Dummies* by Dan Gookin. It picks up where Dan's book leaves off. If you're totally new to Word, you should probably check out Dan's book first. (Well, actually, you should get *both* books!)

As a special bonus and at no extra charge, you'll find references to topics covered not only in this book, but in *Word 97 For Windows For Dummies* as well.

How to Use This Book

This book works like a reference. Start with the topic you want to learn about; look for it in the table of contents or in the index to get going. The table of contents is detailed enough so that you should be able to find most of the topics you're looking for. If not, turn to the index where you'll find even more detail.

After you find your topic in the table of contents or the index, turn to the area of interest and read as much or as little as you need or want. Then close the book and get on with it.

On occasion, this book directs you to use specific keyboard shortcuts to get things done. When you see something like this,

Ctrl+Z

it means hold down the Ctrl key while pressing the *Z* key, and then release both together. Don't type the plus sign.

Sometimes I'll tell you to use a menu command, like this:

File⇨Open

This line means use the keyboard or mouse to open the File menu; then select the Open command. (The underlined letters are the keyboard *hot keys* for the command. To use them, first press the Alt key. In the preceding example, you would press and release the Alt key, press and release the *F* key, and then press and release the *O* key.)

Whenever I describe a message or any other information that you see on the screen, it will look like this:

```
Are we having fun yet?
```

Anything you are instructed to type appears in bold, like this: Type **b:setup** in the Run dialog box. Type exactly what you see, with or without spaces.

Another little nicety about this book is that when you are directed to click one of the many little buttons that litter the Word screen, a picture of the button appears in the margin. This way, you can see what the button looks like to help you find it on the screen.

This book rarely directs you elsewhere for information — just about everything you need to know about using Word is right here. On occasion, I'll suggest that you turn to *Windows 95 For Dummies* (by Andy Rathbone) for more specific information about global warming and Klingon relaxation techniques — oops — I mean Windows 95. I may also refer you to *Word 97 For Windows For Dummies* on occasion. These books are published by IDG Books Worldwide.

Oh, I almost forgot. In the interest of saving trees, I will frequently abbreviate *Word 97 for Windows* to simply *Word* or sometimes *Word 97*.

Foolish Assumptions

I'm going to make only three assumptions about you:

1. **You use a computer.**
2. **You use Windows 95.**
3. **You use Word 97.**

Nothing else. I don't assume that you're a computer guru who knows how to change a controller card or configure memory for optimal usage. Such computer chores are best handled by people who *like* computers. Hopefully you are on speaking terms with such a person. Do your best to keep it that way.

How This Book Is Organized

Inside this book, you find five parts arranged into chapters. Each chapter is broken down into sections that cover various aspects of the chapter's main subject. The chapters are arranged in a logical sequence, so it makes sense to read them in order if you want. But you don't have to read it that way. You can flip the book open to any page and start reading.

Here's the lowdown on what's in each of the five parts:

Part I: Wait! There's More!

The chapters in this part dive head-first into the subtle nuances of features that you thought you already knew all about: character and paragraph formatting, styles, templates, and so on. You'll be so excited about the new things you discover in these chapters that you'll want to write home, or maybe even call.

Part II: Word's Gee-Whiz Desktop Publishing Features

Word is a surprisingly good desktop publishing program — good enough so that you can create pretty fancy newsletters, brochures, and other documents without the need for a separate desktop publishing program. The chapters in this part show you how.

Part III: Webbing with Word

Word 97 sports several new features that allow you to create documents that can be published on the Internet's World Wide Web. The two chapters in this part show you how to use Word as a Web document editor and how to access documents published on the Internet.

Part IV: I've Always Wondered How to Do That

This part shows you how to use those features you've heard about but never had the nerve to try.

Part V: Shortcuts and Tips Galore

When it comes to Word, you can always learn more shortcuts. Some of them are even kind of fun.

Icons Used in This Book

Pay special attention to this icon — it lets you know that some particularly useful tidbit is at hand, perhaps a shortcut or a way of using a command you might not have considered.

Watch out! Some technical drivel is just around the corner. Read only if your pocket protector is firmly attached.

Danger! Danger! Danger! Stand back, Will Robinson!

Did I tell you about the memory course I took?

Where to Go from Here

Yes, you can get there from here. With this book in hand, you're ready to charge full speed into the strange and wonderful world of Word. Browse through the table of contents and decide where you want to start. Be bold! Be courageous! Be adventurous! Above all else, have fun!

Part I

Wait! There's More!

The 5th Wave By Rich Tennant

"THAT'S RIGHT, DADDY WILL DOUBLE YOUR SALARY IF YOU SHOW HIM HOW TO MAIL MERGE."

In this part . . .

Some people get by for years knowing only the basics. They learn to open and save files, make text bold and italic, hit the Enter key at the end of paragraphs, and that's about it. If your Word skills are just enough to get you by, this part is for you. The chapters in this part show you how to do things you've always known you should be able to do, but were afraid to ask about.

Chapter 1

More Editing Madness

In This Chapter

- Efficient methods of editing your documents
- Using Navigational tools
- Reviewing the Reviewing Toolbar
- Selecting text via mouse or keyboard
- Getting from one place to another fast
- Using the Go To command and bookmarks
- Discovering a simple macro that cures a serious defect in the Go To command
- Using the Find and Replace commands
- Using AutoText
- Counting your words
- Creating desktop scraps

Editing is what you hate most about Word 97. Word processing is made up of basically two chores: editing and formatting. Formatting is fun because you get to ditz around with fonts and sizes and alignments until your one page memo about office lockup procedures is suitable for framing. Editing, on the other hand, is work, because instead of fooling around with appearances, editing requires that you focus on actual words. Bother.

This chapter is a quick review of the basics of editing your fine prose. You probably already know most of the basics of editing documents — such as deleting unwanted text, inserting a word here or there, and rearranging sentences. Otherwise, you'd be reading *Word 97 For Windows For Dummies* instead of *MORE Word 97 For Windows For Dummies*. Still, a little review never hurts now and then, especially on a topic as important as editing. After all, editing is probably how you spend most of your time with Word.

Getting Around

Other than actual typing, the most basic editing skill is moving the insertion point around within a document. You undoubtedly know how to do that by using the arrow keys and the PgUp (PageUp) and PgDn (PageDown) keys. However, Word provides plenty of keyboard shortcuts that enable you to move around your document even more quickly. The most useful of these keyboard shortcuts are summarized in Table 1-1.

Table 1-1 Keyboard Shortcuts for Navigating through Documents

Keyboard Shortcut	*What It Does*
Up/Down Arrows	
Up	Previous line
Down	Next line
Ctrl+Up	Previous paragraph
Ctrl+Down	Next paragraph
Alt+Up	Previous object
Alt+Down	Next object
Left/Right Arrows	
Left-arrow	Left one character
Right-arrow	Right one character
Ctrl+Left-arrow	Left one word
Ctrl+Right-arrow	Right one word
Alt+Left-arrow	Left one word (same as Ctrl+Left-arrow)
Alt+Right-arrow	Right one word (same as Ctrl+Right-arrow)
Page Up/Page Down	
PgUp	Previous screen
PgDn	Next screen
Ctrl+PgUp	Top of window
Ctrl+PgDn	Bottom of window
Ctrl+Alt+PgUp	Previous page
Ctrl+Alt+PgDn	Next page
Alt+PgUp	Top of column
Alt+PgDn	Bottom of column

Keyboard Shortcut	What It Does
Home/End	
Home	Beginning of line
End	End of line
Ctrl+Home	Beginning of document
Ctrl+End	End of document
Other	
Alt+F1	Next field
Shift+F1	Previous field
F11	Next field (Same as Alt+F1)
Shift+F11	Previous field (Same as Shift+F1)
Ctrl+F6	Next document window
Shift+Ctrl+F6	Previous document window
F5	Go to; calls up the Go To dialog box
Shift+F5	Go back to the previous insertion point

Selecting Text with Mouse and Keyboard

After typing and moving the insertion point around your document, the next most basic editing skill is selecting text. In Word, you must always select text before you can apply any formatting or editing to the text. For example, to make text boldface, you must first select the text and then use a formatting command to apply the boldface formatting.

The easiest way to select text is by dragging the mouse over the text you want to select. You can also use the following mouse actions to select text:

- Another way to select a block of text with the mouse is to click at the start of the block, hold down Shift, and click at the end of the block. This action selects all text in-between the clicks.
- To select a single word, double-click the mouse anywhere on the word. Click, click.
- To select an entire paragraph, triple-click the mouse anywhere on the paragraph. Click, click, click.
- To select an entire sentence, hold down Ctrl and click the mouse anywhere in the sentence.

- To select a column of text, hold down Alt, press and hold the left mouse button, and drag. Drag the mouse left or right to increase or decrease the width of the column selected, and drag the mouse up or down to extend the column up or down. (This technique is most useful after you've arranged text into columns by using tabs and you want to rearrange the columns.)

Some mouse selection techniques require you to click the *selection bar*, that invisible but ever-present narrow band to the left of the text. (By the way, your mouse pointer turns into a right-pointing arrow when it's in the selection bar.)

- Click the selection bar once to select an entire line of text. Click.
- Double-click the selection bar to select an entire paragraph. Click, click.
- Triple-click the selection bar to select the entire document. Click, click, click.
- To select several paragraphs, double-click the selection bar to select the first paragraph, hold the mouse button down after the second click, and drag the mouse up or down the selection bar to select additional paragraphs.

If you are allergic to the mouse, you can use the keyboard shortcuts summarized in Table 1-2 to select text.

Table 1-2 Keyboard Shortcuts for Selecting Text

Keyboard Shortcut	*What It Does*
Ctrl+A	Selects entire document.
Ctrl+NumPad5	Selects entire document.
Alt+NumPad5	Selects entire table.
F8	Extends the selection, similar to holding down the Shift key or dragging the mouse. After pressing F8, the selection is extended as you move the insertion pointer.
Ctrl+Shift+F8	Extends a column selection.

Rolling Around with the Microsoft IntelliMouse

Along with Office 97, Microsoft introduced a new mouse, called the *IntelliMouse*. The new IntelliMouse looks pretty much like the old mouse, with the addition of a rolling wheel control that sits atop the mouse,

between the left and right mouse buttons. You can roll the wheel forward or backward, or you can click it as if it were a third mouse button.

Word 97 supports the IntelliMouse's wheel control in the following ways:

- You can scroll your document by rolling the wheel. This is equivalent to clicking on the up or down arrow buttons in the scroll bar.
- You can *pan* the document by pressing and holding the wheel, then dragging the mouse up or down. When you do so, the document scrolls in the direction you slide the mouse. The farther you drag the mouse, the faster the document scrolls.
- You can *autoscroll* the document by clicking the mouse wheel once. The document starts to slowly scroll down and continues to scroll down until you click any mouse button (including the wheel) or press any key. (As with panning, you can increase the speed of autoscrolling by dragging the mouse. The farther you drag the mouse, the faster the document scrolls. You can also reverse the autoscroll direction by dragging the other way.)
- You can zoom in or out by holding down the control key while rotating the mouse wheel.
- You can expand or collapse portions of an outline while working in Outline View or with the Document Map by pointing at the portion of the outline you want to expand or collapse, holding down the shift key, and rotating the mouse wheel.

Going Places with Edit⇨Go To

The Go To command is the Word equivalent of the "Go Directly To Jail" card in Monopoly. This command enables you to jet over to any of several specific locations in your document, without passing Go or collecting $200.

You can call up the Go To command from the Edit menu (Edit⇨Go To) by pressing F5 or by double-clicking on the page number portion of the status bar at the bottom of the Word window. Whichever way you choose, the Go To dialog box appears, as shown in Figure 1-1.

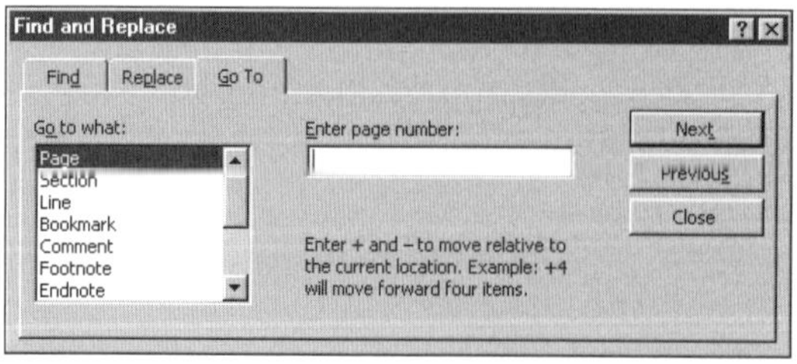

Figure 1-1: The Go To dialog box.

The Go To dialog box is used most often to go to a specific page number. To do that, simply type the page number into the Enter Page Number field, click Go To (the Next button changes to a Go To button the moment you type a page number) and click Close or press the Esc key to dismiss the Go To dialog box.

TIP

Besides going to a specific page, you can also go forward or backwards a certain number of pages. To go forward, type a plus sign followed by the number of pages you want to skip. For example, to go 3 pages forward, type **+3.** To go backwards, type a minus sign instead of a plus sign. For example, type **-20** to go backwards 20 pages.

In addition, besides going to a specific page, the Go To command enables you to go to a particular section or line, or any of several types of goodies that may reside in your document, such as bookmarks, annotations, footnotes, and so on. To go to something other than a page, just change the setting of the Go To What drop-down list box.

One of the most annoying bugs to be found in Word is right here in the Go To dialog box. The problem is that the Go To dialog box stays on the screen after Word has found the page and taken you to it. If you Go To Page 11, you have to press the Esc key to dismiss the Go To dialog box before you can begin working on page 11. Microsoft would probably tell you that it designed the feature that way; that is, most users, after going to page 11, don't want to do anything to page 11 but want instead to go to page 23 (and making them press F5 again would be a nuisance). Nonsense! The Go To dialog box should disappear after taking you to wherever you want to go. It shouldn't stick around like an unwanted houseguest.

Using the New Browse Control

Word 97 sports a new control located at the bottom of the scroll bar. It's called the *browse control,* and it is pictured in the margin. As you can see, the browse control consists of three buttons. The top and bottom buttons allow you to navigate forward and backwards through your document. Normally, these buttons move your document to the previous or next page. However, you can use the middle button to change the way these buttons work.

When you click the Select Browse Object button (sandwiched between the two double-arrow controls), a menu appears that lets you access several navigation features from one convenient location, as shown in Figure 1-2.

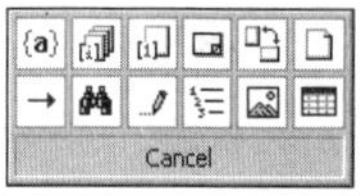

Figure 1-2: The Select Browse Object menu.

The first two buttons on the second row of this menu invoke the familiar Edit⇨Goto and Edit Find commands. The ten remaining buttons change the unit by which the document is browsed when you click the double up or double down arrow controls immediately above and below the Select Browse Object button. Table 1-3 describes the function of each of the twelve buttons that appear on the Browse menu:

Table 1-3: Options on the Select Browse Object Menu

Button	*What it does*
	Invokes the Edit⇨Goto command
	Invokes the Edit⇨Find command
	Browse by edits (works in conjunction with revision tracking)
	Browse by headings as indicated by standard heading styles
	Browse by graphic objects
	Browse by Word table objects
	Browse by Word fields
	Browse by endnote
	Browse by footnote
	Browse by comments
	Browse by section
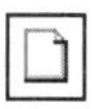	Browse by page

Yes, You Can Go Back

A funny thing about Word is that it has more than a few useful commands that aren't accessible from the menus or toolbars. One such command is the Go Back command. Most Word users don't know about the Go Back command because they can only access it via its keyboard shortcut, Shift+F5, and if they didn't read the manual, they'd probably never stumble across it on their own. Yet the Go Back command can be very useful. Word remembers the last five locations at which you've edited your document, and each press of Shift+F5 returns you to one of those previous editing locations.

The Magic of Undo and Repeat

The Undo command is one of the best ways to become a Word guru. Without the Undo command, you would be afraid of experimenting with Word for fear of losing your document. But with this command at hand, you can try anything you want, knowing that the worst that can happen is that you may have to use the Undo command to undo your mistake.

You can access the Undo command from the Edit menu (Edit⇨Undo), but Undo is used frequently enough that you should simply memorize its keyboard shortcut: Ctrl+Z. While you're at it, go ahead and memorize the keyboard shortcut (Ctrl+Y) for an almost equally useful command: Repeat. The Repeat command, as its name implies, repeats the last action. If you just used the Format⇨Font command to make a bevy of formatting changes all at once, select some nàer text that you want similarly formatted and then press Ctrl+Y. By using this Repeat command, you can apply the same formats to the other text.

The Repeat command repeats just about any action you can do in Word, including Undo. When the most recent command is Undo, the Repeat command becomes the Redo command: It redoes the action undone by the Undo command. Undo and Redo are a perfect combination for people who can't decide whether they like something or not.

Unlike most word processors, Word keeps track of more than one recent action. In fact, you can undo up to 100 recent actions. To undo more than one action at a time, click on the down-arrow in the standard toolbar's Undo button to reveal a list of the 100 recent undoable actions. Drag the mouse to select the actions you want to undo and release the mouse to undo them all in one fell swoop.

The Redo button in the standard toolbar has a similar capability to redo up to 100 recently undone actions.

Working with Bookmarks

A *bookmark* is a name you assign to a location in a document or to a selection of text so that you can easily return to that location at a later time. Using a bookmark is a safer and more effective method than attempting to fold down the corner of your monitor to mark a page.

To create a bookmark, position the insertion point where you want to place the bookmark and press Ctrl+Shift+F5. This key combination brings up the Bookmark dialog box, as shown in Figure 1-3. Type the name of the bookmark and click the Add button.

The bookmark name can be a maximum of 20 characters in length and can include letters and numbers, but no spaces, punctuation, or special symbols except the underscore character (_). The bookmark name must begin with a letter. Notice that the Add button doesn't become active until you start typing a valid bookmark name, and if you type an incorrect bookmark name (for example, if you include a space or any special character except the underscore), the Add button is deactivated.

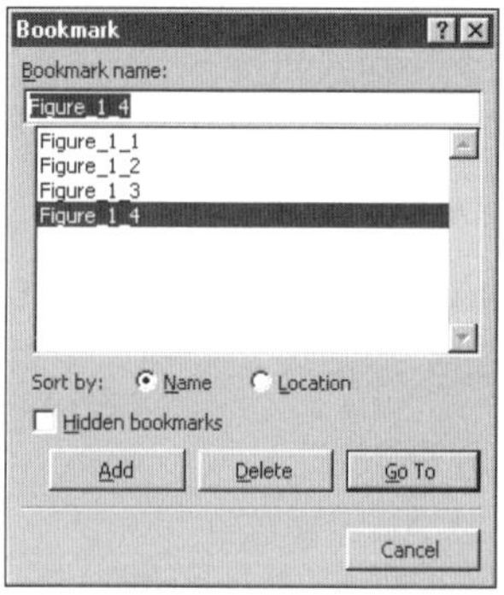

Figure 1-3: Adding a bookmark.

You can create a bookmark for a selection of text rather than for a specific insertion point location, but you usually have little reason to bother selecting the text. If the only reason you are creating the bookmark is to go to it later, don't bother selecting a range of text; just place the insertion point at the location you want to return to and create a bookmark.

After you create a bookmark, you can go to it at any time by pressing Ctrl+Shift+F5 to call up the Bookmark dialog box, clicking on the bookmark you want to go to, and clicking the Go To button.

You can also go to a bookmark by calling up the Edit⇨Go To command, selecting Bookmark in the Go To What list, selecting the bookmark in the Enter Bookmark Name drop-down list, and clicking Go To. Going to the bookmark using Ctrl+Shift+F5 is a lot easier, though.

Actually, you don't have to select Bookmark in the Go To What list if you remember the bookmark name. Simply type the bookmark name in the Enter Page Number field and press the Enter key. Word is smart enough to figure out that what you entered was a bookmark, not a page number.

To delete a bookmark, press Ctrl+Shift+F5 to call up the Bookmark dialog box, select the bookmark you want to delete, and click Delete.

Using the Find Command

The Edit⇨Find command enables you to search for text anywhere in your document. The command also lets you search for specific formats, such as a particular font or style, and for special symbols such as paragraph marks or annotations.

You summon the Find command by choosing Edit⇨Find from the menu or by pressing Ctrl+F. Unfortunately, the Find command has no toolbar button, but you can add one if you're willing to customize your toolbars. Word even supplies a predefined toolbar button image that looks like a set of binoculars.

However you invoke it, the Find command displays the Find tab in the Find and Replace dialog box, as shown in Figure 1-4. The following sections explain how to use this dialog box for various searches.

Figure 1-4: The Find dialog box.

Finding missing text

You can use the Edit⇨Find command to find text anywhere in a document. Just follow these steps:

1. **Choose Edit⇨Find or press Ctrl+F to summon the Find dialog box.**

   Refer to Figure 1-4 for a glimpse of this dialog box.

2. **Type the text you want to find in the Find what field.**

   For example, "Bandersnatch."

3. **Click the Find Next button.**

4. **Wait a second while Word searches your document.**

   When Word finds the text, it highlights that text on-screen. The Find dialog box remains on-screen so that you can click Find Next to find yet another occurrence of the text.

5. **Stop when you see the message indicating that no more occurrences of the text could be found.**

You can bail out of the Find dialog box at any time by clicking Cancel or pressing the Esc key.

Advanced searches

To gain additional control over the Find operation, click the More button. This expands the dialog box to the larger form shown in Figure 1-5. The following sections explain the advanced search options that are available when you click the More button.

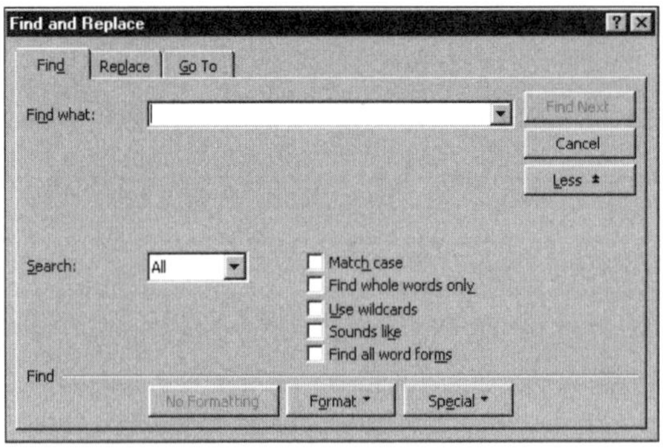

Figure 1-5: Clicking the More button shows additional search options.

You can shrink the expanded Find dialog box down to size by clicking the Less button.

Changing the search direction

You can change the direction of Word's search by changing the setting in the Search drop-down box. Three choices are available:

- **Down:** Starts the search at the position of the insertion point and searches forward toward the end of the document.

- **Up:** Searches backward from the insertion point, toward the beginning of the document.

  Both the Down and Up options search until they reach the bottom or top of the document; then they ask whether you want to continue searching the rest of the document.

- **All:** Searches the entire document without regard to the position of the insertion point.

Check the Matc<u>h</u> case check box before beginning the search if it matters whether the text appears in uppercase or lowercase letters. This option is handy when you have, for example, a document about Mr. Smith the black-smith.

Speaking of Mr. Smith the blacksmith, use the Find whole words onl<u>y</u> option to find your text only when it appears as a whole word. If you want to find the text where you talk about Mr. Smith the blacksmith's mit, for example, type **mit** in the Fi<u>n</u>d what text box and check the Find whole words onl<u>y</u> check box. That way, the <u>F</u>ind command looks for *mit* as a separate word and doesn't show you all the *mit*s in *Smith* and *blacksmith*.

Check the <u>U</u>se wildcards check box if you want to include wildcard characters or other search operators in the Fi<u>n</u>d what field. Table 1-4 summarizes the search operators that you can use if you select this option.

Table 1-4 Advanced Search Operators for the Find Command

Operator	*What It Does*
?	Finds a single occurrence of any character. For example, f?t finds *fat* or *fit.*
*	Finds any combination of characters. For example, b*t finds any combination of characters that begins with *b* and ends with *t,* such as *bat, bait, ballast,* or *bacteriologist.*
#	Any numerical digit.
[*abc*]	Finds any one of the characters enclosed in the brackets. For example, b[ai]t finds *bat* or *bit,* but not *bet* or *but.*
[*a-c*]	Finds any character in the range of characters enclosed in the brackets. For example, b[a-e]t finds *bat* or *bet,* but not *bit* or *but.*
[!*abc*]	Finds any character except the ones enclosed in the brackets. For example, b[!ai]t finds *bet* or *but,* but not *bat* or *bit.*
@	Finds one or more occurrences of the preceding character. For example, 10@ finds *10, 100,* or *1000.*

Operator	*What It Does*
{*n*}	Specifies that the preceding character must be repeated exactly *n* times. For example, 10{2} finds *100,* but not *10* or *1000.*
{*n*,}	Specifies that the preceding character must be repeated at least *n* times. For example, 10{2,} finds *100* or *1000,* but not *10.*
{*n*,*m*}	Specifies that the preceding character must be repeated from *n* to *m* times. For example, 10{2,3} finds *100* or *1000,* but not *10* or *10000.*
<	Finds the following text only if it appears at the beginning of a word. For example, <pre finds *predestined* and *prefabricated,* but not *appreciate* or *apprehend.*
>	Finds the preceding text only if it appears at the end of a word. For example, ing> finds *interesting* and *domineering,* but not *ingenious* or *ingest.*

Check the Sounds like check box if you're not sure exactly how to spell the text for which you're searching. Word can search for words that are pronounced the same as the word you're searching for. For example, if you search for **your** with the Sounds like option on, Word stops when it finds *you're*. Don't expect too much from this option, however. For example, if you typed **low** in the Find what field, you'd expect the option to find *Lowe* (well, *I* would anyway). But it doesn't.

If you select the Find all word forms, Word looks for alternate forms of most verbs. For example, if you search for **run**, Word finds *runs, running,* and *ran.* And the program is smart enough to know about certain oddball words such as go: If you search for **go**, Word finds not only *goes, going,* and *gone,* but also *went.* Searching for **be** finds *is, was, am, were, being,* and *been.*

Don't expect miracles, however. Find all word forms doesn't pick up every imaginable word form, especially where nouns are concerned. For example, a search for **introduction** doesn't pick up *introductory,* and **religion** doesn't catch *religious*. Find all word forms is more adept at finding alternate word forms for verbs than for nouns.

Finding formats

To find specific types of formatting, choose the Edit⇨Find command or press Ctrl+F, then click the More button to display the advanced search options as shown back in Figure 1-6. Click the Format button and choose the type of format you want to search for from the pop-up menu. The following options are available:

- **Font:** Enables you to search for specific font formatting. You can search for specific fonts or for font formatting such as bold, italics, font size, and so on.
- **Paragraph:** Enables you to search for specific paragraph formatting, such as indentation and alignment.
- **Tabs:** Enables you to search for paragraphs with specific tab settings.
- **Language:** Enables you to search for paragraphs formatted for a particular language.
- **Frame:** Enables you to search for specific frame formatting.
- **Style:** Enables you to search for paragraphs formatted with a particular style.
- **Highlight:** Enables you to search for highlighted text.

Make sure that the Find What field itself is blank; otherwise, the Find command searches for specific text that's formatted with the style you specify.

Finding special characters

You can also use the Find command to search for special characters such as em dashes or annotation marks. Call up the Find command (Edit⇨Find or Ctrl+F), click the More button to reveal the advanced Find options, then click the Special button to reveal a list of special characters that you can search for, as shown in Figure 1-6. Select the character you want to search for and click Find Next to begin the search.

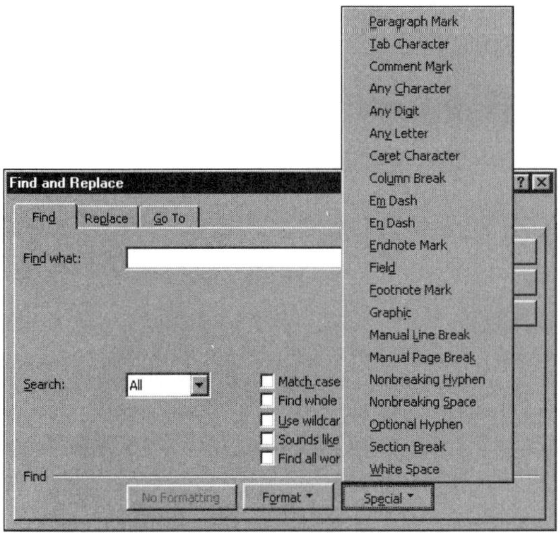

Figure 1-6: Searching for special characters.

When you select a special character, Word inserts a code into the Find what text box. If you know the code, you can bypass the Special button and its huge menu by typing the code directly into the Find what field. Table 1-5 summarizes the codes.

Table 1-5 Search Codes for Special Characters

Character	*Code*
Paragraph mark	^p
Tab character	^t
Comment mark	^a
Any character	^?
Any digit	^#
Any letter	^$
Caret character	^^
Column break	^n
Em dash	^+
En dash	^=
Endnote mark	^e
Field	^d
Footnote mark	^f
Graphic	^g
Manual line break	^l
Manual page break	^m
Nonbreaking hyphen	^~
Nonbreaking space	^s
Optional hyphen	^-
Section break	^b
White space	^w

Replacing Text

You can use the Edit⇨Replace command to replace all occurrences of one bit of text with other text. The following steps show you the procedure:

1. **Choose Edit⇨Replace or press Ctrl+H.**

   The Replace tab in the Find and the Replace dialog box appears, as shown in Figure 1-7.

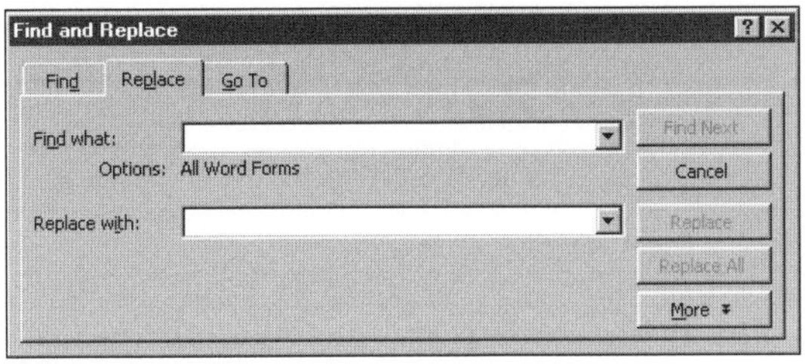

Figure 1-7: The Replace dialog box.

2. **Type the text you want to find in the Find what text box.**
3. **Type the text you want to substitute for the Find what text in the Replace with text box.**
4. **Click the Find Next button.**

   When Word finds the text, it highlights that text on-screen.

5. **Click the Replace button to replace the text.**
6. **Repeat the Find Next and Replace sequence until you're finished.**

If you're absolutely positive that you want to replace all occurrences of your Find what text with the Replace with text, click the Replace All button. Taking this step automatically replaces all remaining occurrences of the text. The only problem is that you're bound to encounter at least one spot where you didn't want the replacement to occur. Replacing the word **mit** with **glove**, for example, changes *Smith* to *Sgloveh* (and no, *Sgloveh* is not the Czechoslovakian form of the name *Smith*).

As for the Find command, you can click the More button to expand the dialog box so that additional options are visible, as shown in Figure 1-8. You can then use the Match case, find whole words only, Use Wildcards, Sounds like, and Find all word forms options. The last option is even smart enough to properly replace alternate word forms with the correct version of the replacement text. For example, if you replace **run** with **walk**, Word replaces *running* with *walking* and *ran* with *walked*.

WARNING!

Because Word is not 100 percent confident in its capability to properly replace all alternate word forms, you get a warning message if you select the Find all word forms option and click Replace All. Find all word forms is tricky enough that you should verify each replacement.

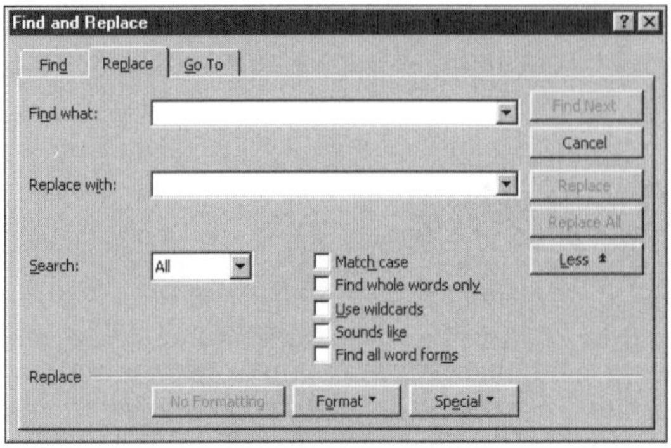

Figure 1-8: Advanced options for the Replace command.

Copy, Cut, and Paste

Copying, cutting, and pasting are the basic editing operations not only in Word, but in all Windows applications. These operations rely on a special storage area called the *clipboard,* which Windows uses to temporarily stash information you have copied or cut so that you can paste that information to another location.

You can access the Copy, Cut, and Paste commands from the Edit menu, or from the standard toolbar. However, these commands are important enough that you should endeavor to commit their keyboard shortcuts to memory. Table 1-6 lists the keyboard shortcuts for the Copy, Cut, and Paste commands.

Table 1-6 The Three Most Important Word Keyboard Shortcuts

Keyboard Shortcut	*What It Does*
Ctrl+C	Copies the selected text to the Clipboard.
Ctrl+X	Cuts the selected text to the Clipboard. The original text is removed from the document.
Ctrl+V	Pastes the contents of the Clipboard at the insertion point.

Memorizing these keyboard shortcuts will prove worth the effort. Not only will they save you time when working in Word, you'll soon discover that just about all Windows programs — including Windows itself — honor these keyboard shortcuts.

If you have trouble remembering these shortcuts, consider first that they are positioned adjacent to one another on the bottom row of the keyboard.

Dragging and Dropping

Drag-and-drop editing (or *dragon dropping*) helps you to move text from one location in a document to another by using only the mouse, without using the Clipboard. You simply highlight the text you want to move and use the mouse to drag the text to a new location. When you release the mouse button, the text is cut from its original location and pasted to the new location.

If you hold down the Ctrl key while dragging text, you can copy the text, instead of moving it, to the new location. In other words, the text is not deleted from its original location.

You can drag and drop text between two open documents, but both documents must be visible on the screen. To ensure that both documents are visible, use the Window⇨Arrange All command.

Before you step in the dragon dropping, consider the following:

- If you don't like this feature — and you may well find that you don't — you can disable it via the Tools⇨Options command. Select the Edit tab and then uncheck the Drag-and-Drop Text Editing check box.
- On the other hand, if you can't get the dragon drop technique to work, check the Tools⇨Options command Edit settings to make sure that the Drag-and-Drop Text Editing check box is checked.

Using the Spike (A Fancy AutoText Feature)

You can't get very far in Word without learning how to use the basic cut-and-paste keys: Ctrl+X to cut text to the Clipboard, Ctrl+C to copy text to the Clipboard, and Ctrl+V to paste text into your document from the Clipboard. These keys are great as far as they go, but at times you really need a more powerful cut-and-paste feature.

Suppose, for example, that you want to create a new document by moving information from a half-dozen existing documents. Using regular cut-and-paste, you would employ a procedure something like the following:

1. **Create a new document.**
2. **Open a document containing something you need to move.**
3. **Cut the text you need to the Clipboard.**
4. **Switch back to the new document.**
5. **Paste the text from the Clipboard into the new document.**
6. **Repeat Steps 2 through 5 until the new document is assembled.**

This procedure works, but it involves a great deal of unnecessary switching back and forth between documents. What if you could just cut text to the Clipboard without obliterating the Clipboard's existing contents? Then you could simply cut the text you need from one document, open another document and cut some more text, and so on, until you've cut all the text you need. Then you switch to the new document and paste in all that text with one swift keystroke.

Word enables you to do precisely that by using an obscure little feature known as the Spike. The Spike has nothing to do with volleyball, punk rock hairstyles, or Snoopy's little cousin. Rather, the Spike is a kind of super-clipboard, which accumulates bits and pieces of text, graphics, or whatever else you place on it. Then, with a single keystroke, it inserts its entire contents into a document. Follow this procedure to use the Spike:

1. **Select the text, graphics, or whatever else you want to move from the initial document and place on the Spike.**
2. **Press Ctrl+F3.**

   Ctrl+F3 is the magic "Cut-to-Spike" key. The selected text or graphics is deleted from the document and added to the Spike.
3. **Perform Steps 1 and 2 again for other bits of text and graphics you want accumulated on the Spike.**

   You can open other files to collect information from several documents to put on the Spike.
4. **After you've gathered up all the text and graphics you need, position the cursor at the point in the target document where you want everything inserted.**
5. **Press Ctrl+Shift+F3.**

   Ctrl+Shift+F3 is the magic "Put-the-Spike-Here" key. All the text and graphics on the Spike are inserted into the target document.

The Spike is kind of a peculiar gadget. Keep the following thoughts in mind while using it:

- You cannot place anything on the Spike without simultaneously deleting it from the document's text. (Too bad. Word really should have a "Copy-to-Spike" key to complement its "Cut-to-Spike" key. But it doesn't.)
- TIP: One way around the problem of not being able to copy text to the Spike is to use the following sequence of keys: Ctrl+C, Ctrl+F3, Ctrl+V. This procedure copies the selection to the Clipboard, cuts the selection to the Spike, and then inserts the copy of the selection from the Clipboard back into the document at its original location. This leaves a copy of the text in the Spike, which you can later paste into a document by pressing Ctrl+Shift+F3. (If you're really adventurous, record this key sequence as a macro and assign it to the keyboard combination Ctrl+Alt+F3 — your very own "Copy-to-Spike" command.)
- The Spike is actually a special AutoText entry. To view the contents of the Spike, choose the Tools⇨AutoCorrect command, click the AutoText tab, then select Spike from the list of AutoText entries (you'll have to scroll through the list to find it).

Creating Desktop Scraps

In Word, you can drag text completely away from Word into another application. The target application for this type of drag-and-drop edit is usually Windows 95 itself, or more precisely, the Windows 95 desktop. When you drag text out of Word onto the Windows 95 desktop, the text is placed in a *document scrap* and given its own icon, as shown in Figure 1-9. You can then drag the text back into a Word document at a later time: a few minutes later or a few days later. The scrap can sit on the desktop indefinitely. You can also double-click the scrap icon to open the scrap as a document.

Document scraps are a great way to move bits and pieces out of one or several documents for use later in another document. In essence, scraps enable your desktop to double as a super-clipboard, capable of holding not just one, but many text snippets that you can paste together later. (Just be careful that your Windows 95 desktop doesn't become cluttered with scraps just like your real desk!)

TIP: If you need to create more than a few scraps and you don't want your desktop to become cluttered, create a folder called *Scrapbook* (or whatever name suits your fancy) and drag the scraps into the folder instead of to the desktop. Then, you can close or minimize the Scrapbook folder to hide the scraps.

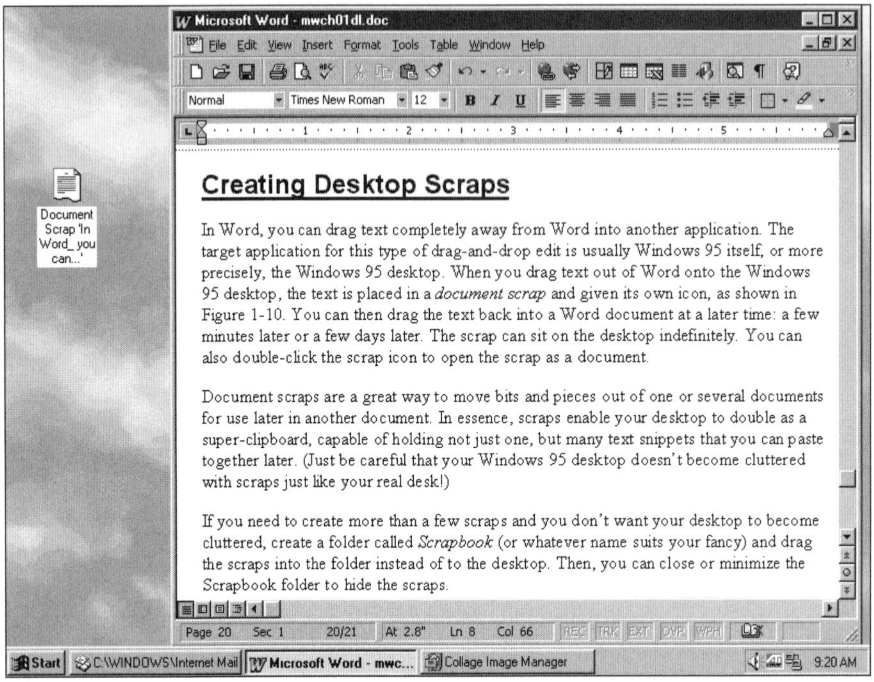

Figure 1-9: A document scrap sitting on the desktop.

Shrinking Text to Fit the Page

Have you ever been frustrated by a document with a last page that contains only a line or two of text? Of course you have. There's no shame in admitting it. Fortunately, Word provides relief in the form of a feature called Shrink-to-fit. This nifty little feature nips and tucks your document in a bold effort to eliminate that last short page. Sometimes it works; sometimes it doesn't. But if you want to get rid of that silly-looking one-line page, it's at least worth a try.

Here's the entire "make-it-fit-better" procedure in a nutshell:

1. **Choose the File➪Print Preview command.**

   Shrink-to-fit is available only in Print Preview mode.

2. **Click the Shrink-to-fit button in the Print Preview toolbar.**

   Word tries like mad to shorten the document by a page. If the procedure works, you see the document reformatted so that it's one page shorter. (You may have to scroll through the document to verify that the short page is really gone.) If it doesn't, you instead see an apologetic tail-between-the-legs dialog box telling you that it didn't work.

- You may not be happy with the results of Word's reformatting efforts. It may do something really crazy, such as change the text font size from nicely legible 10-point to eye-squinting 8-point. If so, press Ctrl+Z to undo the damage.
- If Shrink-to-fit doesn't work, you can always try manually shortening the document. Adjust the margins, point sizes, line spacing, space between paragraphs, and so on. You may also try rewriting your prose to be a wee bit more concise, rather than long and verbose in a rambling sort of way, an obvious victim of the three cardinal sins of succinct writing, these being, of course, repetition, redundancy, and reiteration, which can leave your readers understandably wondering if you were voted "most talkative" in high school and — gee, where did the time go? — will this sentence ever *end?*
- If Shrink-to-fit doesn't give satisfactory results and manually shortening the document doesn't seem to work either, consider doing just the opposite: Instead of shortening the document to get rid of that last one- or two-line page, try rewriting or reformatting to make the document longer so that the last page isn't quite so embarrassingly short. Add a few points of extra space between paragraphs, increase the margins, or do whatever else has to be done to lengthen that annoying final page.

Word and Character Counts

An important part of editing is knowing how long your document is. Trust me, I know. When a magazine editor says she needs a 1,750 word article on the mating habits of Australian slugs, she means 1,750 words. Don't try to cheat by delivering an article of only 1,749 words. You won't get paid.

To find out if you've written enough, or if you've written too much, all you have to do is pop up the Tools⇨Word Count command. This will display the dialog box shown in Figure 1-10, which is loaded with all the information you need.

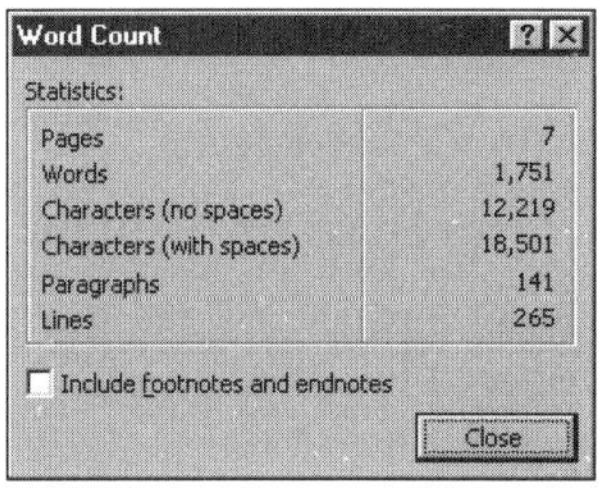

Figure 1-10: Oops, this document is way too long.

Chapter 2

More Spelling and Grammar Checking Goodies

In This Chapter

- Checking your spelling on-the-fly
- Setting the spell checking options
- Using the grammar checker
- Marking text for no-proofing or foreign language proofing
- Using AutoCorrect
- Cheating at crossword puzzles

I was voted Worst Speller in the Sixth Grade. Not that this qualifies me to run for Vice President or anything, but it shows how much I appreciate computer spell checkers. Spelling makes no sense to me. I felt a little better after watching *The Story of English* on Public Television. Now at least I know who to blame for all the peculiarities of English spelling: the Angles, the Saxophones, and the Norms (especially the guy from *Cheers*).

Thank goodness for Word's spell checker. It works its way through your document, looking up every word in its massive list of correctly spelled words and bringing any misspelled words to your attention. It performs this task without giggling or snickering. It gives you the opportunity, in fact, to tell it that *you* are right and *it* is wrong and that it should learn how to spell words the way you do.

You can use Word's spell checker in one of two fundamentally different ways. You can have it watch over your shoulder as you type and gasp in horror every time you commit a spelling error, or you can wait until the document is finished, then have it check the spelling for the entire document. Either way, the spell checker is pretty thorough. Hope you have thick skin.

On-the-Fly Spell Checker

The easiest way to check your document's spelling is to enable Word's new on-the-fly spell checking option. If Word doesn't already check your spelling as you type, call up the Tools⇨Options command, click the Spelling and Grammar tab, and check the Check spelling as you type check box. Also, make sure the Hide spelling errors in this document option is *not* checked.

When you enable the Automatic Spell Checking option, Word underlines any misspelled words with a wavy red line as shown in Figure 2-1. (I tried to convince IDG Books to pop for an expensive four-color printing process so that you could actually see the red lines in Figure 2-1. The folks at IDG informed me that they would be glad to oblige, but the cost would be deducted from my next royalty check. I then realized that you could probably figure out that the wavy line under the misspelled words in Figure 3-1 is supposed to be red.)

TIP

Word doesn't beep, chime, or yell at you when you misspell a word. As a result, unless you watch the screen as you type, you may not immediately notice a spelling error. So it's a good idea to periodically check the screen, even if you are a 90-word-per-minute touch typist who never looks up.

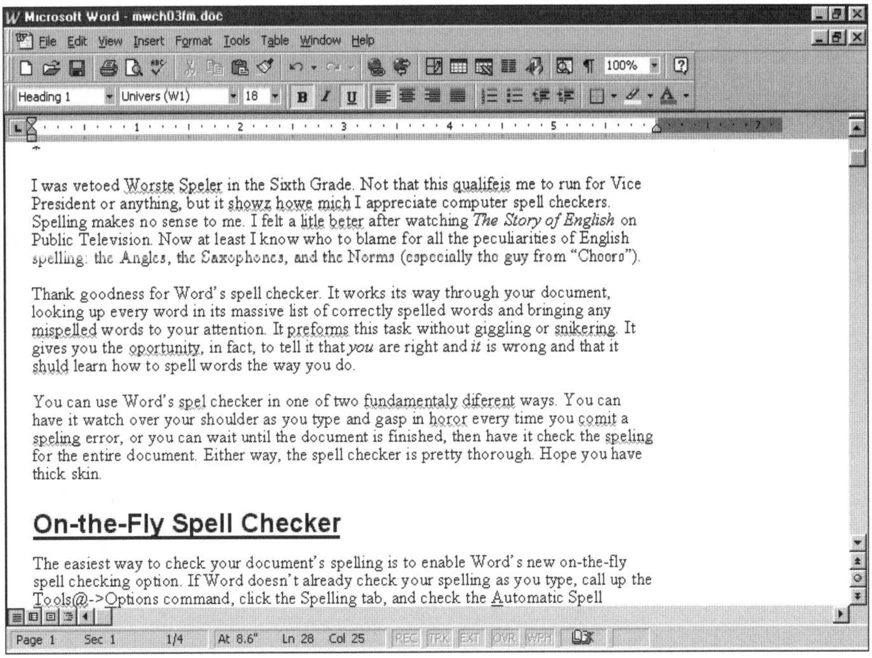

Figure 2-1: Automatic Spell Checking in action.

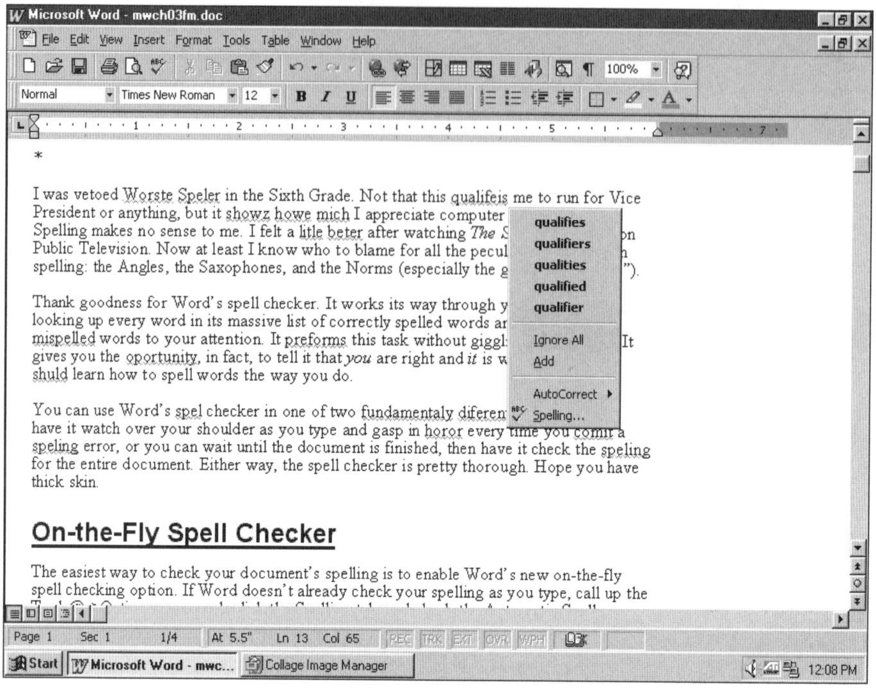

Figure 2-2: Correcting a spelling mistake.

If you make a spelling mistake, you can go back and correct the word. After you do that, Word removes the wavy red underline. Alternatively, you can right-click the word to bring up a quick menu of suggested spellings, as shown in Figure 2-2. Click the correct spelling for the word to replace the misspelled word with the correct spelling automatically.

The quick menu that appears when you right-click a misspelled word also shows the following commands:

- **Ignore all:** This command tells Word to ignore this misspelling, not only here but throughout the document. When you ignore the misspelling, Word removes the wavy red underlines.
- **Add:** This command tells Word to add the misspelled Word to a custom dictionary so that Word will not flag it as a misspelling in the future. Use this command for those rare occasions when you come across a word that is spelled correctly but that Word doesn't recognize. (This occurs frequently with proper names or in technical writing.)

- **AutoCorrect:** If you realize that you make the same mistake over and over again, choose AutoCorrect, then select the proper spelling for the misspelled word. Word will not only correct the underlined word but will automatically correct this spelling mistake whenever you make it in the future.
- **Spelling:** This command brings up the Spelling dialog box for a full-fledged spell check.

Manually Spell Checking a Document

If you don't use the Automatic Spell Checking feature, you can still check the spelling for a document after the fact. There are three ways to begin a spell check:

- Call up the Tools➪Spelling and Grammar command.
- Press F7.
-  Click the Spelling button in the standard toolbar.

Whichever you choose, Word begins checking your spelling. When Word finds a misspelled word, it displays the Spelling and Grammar dialog box shown in Figure 2-3.

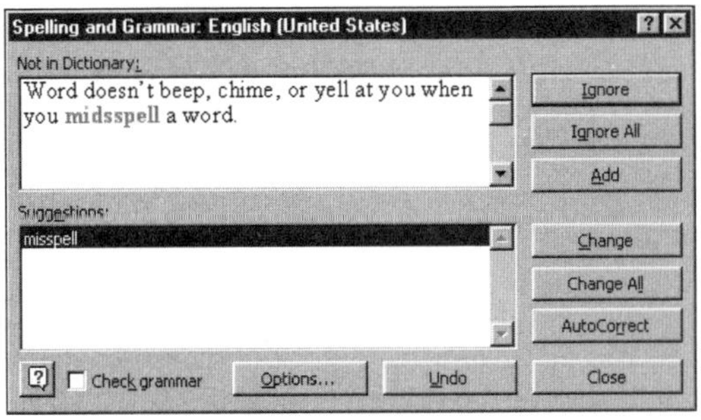

Figure 2-3: The Spelling and Grammar dialog box.

You then have the following options:

- **Ignore:** If the word is correctly spelled as it is or if you want to spell it incorrectly on purpose (for example, if you're creating a menu for a restaurant called *The Koffee Kup*), click the Ignore button.
- **Ignore All:** Click this button to tell Word to ignore not only this occurrence of the word but subsequent occurrences of the word in this document, too.

- **Add:** If the word is correctly spelled and you want to add it to a custom dictionary, click Add. Word adds it to the current custom dictionary, as indicated in the Add Words To list box. (Custom dictionaries are explained later in this chapter.)
- **Change:** If the word really is misspelled, choose the correct spelling from the list of suggested spellings that appear in the dialog box and click the Change button. If the correct spelling doesn't appear among the suggestions, type the correct spelling in the Change To field and click the Change button.
- **Change All:** If you think the spelling error may crop up again, click Change All. This tells Word to automatically correct any subsequent occurrences of the same error.
- **AutoCorrect**: If you realize that you make this same spelling mistake over and over again, click AutoCorrect. Word adds the misspelled word and its correct spelling as an AutoCorrect entry. That way, Word automatically corrects the soÃ$ling error without even bothering to ask.
- **Options**: Brings up the Spelling options dialog box, the same as if you had chosen the Tools➪Options and clicked the Spelling and Grammar tab.
- **Undo:** Reverses the action you took for the last misspelled word displayed by the Spelling dialog box.
- **Close:** Closes the spell checker.

Using the Spelling Icon

When you enable automatic spell checking, you find a spelling icon in the form of an open book at the bottom of the Word window, near the right edge of the status bar. This icon indicates the status of your document's spelling:

Word is spell checking the document. The pencil is animated to give the feeling of motion. When you enable the Automatic Spell Check option, the pencil moves whenever you type.

The document contains one or more spelling errors. You can go directly to the next spelling error by double-clicking on the Spelling icon.

The document does not contain any spelling errors.

Using the Grammar Checker

Word also includes a grammar checker that can make sure that your prose is properly composed. Previous versions of Word also included a grammar checker, but the grammar checking in Word 97 is a major improvement over the older versions. In fact, Word 97 is (in my humble opinion) the first word processor available that comes with a grammar checker worth using.

The grammar checker is integrated with the spell checker so that whenever you spell check a document, the grammar checker kicks in and checks your document's grammar as well, provided you have activated the grammar checking feature.

To activate on-the-fly grammar checking, call up the Tools⇨Options command, click the Spelling and Grammar tab, then check the Check grammar as you type option and uncheck the Hide grammatical errors in this document option. When you enable the on-the-fly grammar checking, any grammatical errors in your document are underlined with a wavy green line. You can right-click the grammar error to bring up a quick menu that offers one or more alternatives to the underlined words.

If you want to manually check your document's grammar, call up the Tools⇨Options command, click the Spelling and Grammar tab, and check the Check grammar with spelling option. Grammatical errors are flagged along with spelling errors when you check your document's spelling.

Skipping Text While Spell Checking

Sometimes, you don't want to spell and grammar check all of the text in a document. For example, you may have a paragraph of Chaucer's poetry, in which every word would likely be flagged as a spelling error. Or, you may have a list of phone numbers that would all be marked as spelling errors. Fortunately, there are several ways to exclude certain portions of your document from the spell checker's scrutiny.

You can exclude numbers, words spelled with all capitals (such as acronyms like ACCT or NCAA), and Internet addresses (like www.idgbooks.com) from spell checking via the Tools⇨Options command. Call up Tools⇨Options, click the Spelling and Grammar tab, then check the Ignore words in UPPERCASE, Ignore words with numbers, and Ignore Internet and file addresses options. Then click OK.

To ignore a range of text, such as a paragraph of Chaucerean poetry, follow these steps:

1. **Highlight the section of text you want to spare the burden of spell checking.**
2. **Call up the Tools⇨Language⇨Set Language command.**

   The Language dialog box appears, as shown in Figure 2-4.

Figure 2-4: The Language dialog box.

3. **Choose (no proofing) in the Mark selected text as list box.**

   The (no proofing) entry is found at the beginning of the list box, so you may have to scroll the box up to find it.

4. **Click OK.**

You can also use the Tools⇨Language⇨Set Language command to indicate that a range of text is written in a different language. For example, if you normally write in English, but you want to include a Russian quotation in your document, use the Tools⇨Language⇨Set Language command to set the quotation to Russian.

Word's Foreign Language Features

The fact that Word 97 includes a Tools⇨Language⇨Set Language command might lead you to believe that Word can spell check documents written in foreign languages. Unfortunately, that's not the case. Although you can mark text as being written in a foreign language, Word comes with only one dictionary for spell checking. Setting the language does not by itself enable Word to spell check in that language.

To spell check a document in a foreign language, you must purchase and install a separate language kit for the language you want to check. These kits are available for $79.95 from a company called Alki Software. You can locate them on the World Wide Web at `http:\\www.alki.com`. The language kit includes a spelling dictionary, thesaurus, and hyphenation file.

So what good is the Set Language command if you haven't purchased a language kit? Although Word can't spell check a language without the appropriate dictionary, setting the text's language prevents Word from trying to spell check the text as English and thereby marking every word as misspelled.

Changing the language for text also enables the following international features:

- Word formats dates according to the conventions of the set language. For example, if you set the language to German, a date such as February 10, 1997 appears as 10/02/97.
- Word formats punctuation correctly for the set language. For example, if you type an exclamation mark at the beginning of a sentence and set the language to Spanish, Word turns the exclamation mark upside down. ¡Olé!
- Setting the language affects how the Table➪Sort command works. Word sorts text into alphabetical order based on the language you set.
- How did I create the accent mark over the "e" in "Olé?" By using one of the keyboard shortcuts listed in Table 2-1.

Table 2-1: Keyboard Shortcuts for Accent Marks

Accented Character	*Keyboard shortcut*	*Note*
à, è, ì, ò, ù	Ctrl+`, *letter*	The ` is the leftmost key in the top row of the keyboard.
á, é, í, ó, ú, ý	Ctrl+`, *letter*	The ` is the apostrophe key.
â, ê, î, ô, û	Ctrl+Shift+^, *letter*	The ^ is the caret, located on the 6 key.
ã, ñ, õ	Ctrl+Shift+~, *letter*	The tilde is the leftmost key in the top row of the keyboard.
ä, ë, ï, ö, ü, ÿ	Ctrl+Shift+:, *letter*	The : is the colon key.

Using AutoCorrect

AutoCorrect is a cool Word feature that monitors your typing, watches carefully for common typing mistakes, and fixes them quicker than you can say "Bob's your uncle." It's even better than on-the-fly spell checking, because it doesn't wait for you to tell it to correct your spelling mistakes. Instead, it just corrects them automatically, without asking permission. For example, type **adn,** and AutoCorrect changes it to *and*. Typing **teh** becomes *the;* **recieve** becomes *receive*.

AutoCorrect has other features as well: It corrects capitalization including accidental use of the Caps Lock key — also known as the cAPS lOCK KEY — and it lets you insert special symbols.

AutoCorrect is controlled from the Tools➪AutoCorrect command, which brings up the dialog box shown in Figure 2-5. This dialog box lets you activate specific AutoCorrect features — in the figure, all AutoCorrect features are enabled, but you might find that one feature or another doesn't suit your fancy. If that's the case, use the Tools➪AutoCorrect command to disable the feature you don't like.

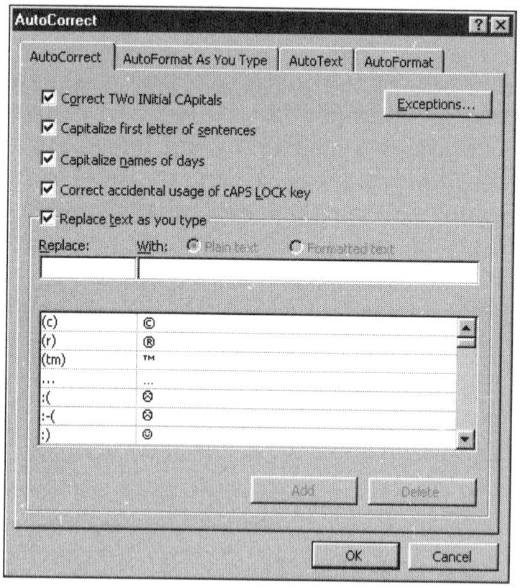

Figure 2-5: The AutoCorrect dialog box.

The following paragraphs describe each of the AutoCorrect options in detail:

- **Correct TWo INitial CApitals:** If you're an average typist, you probably have the bad habit of occasionally leaving the Caps key down a bit too long when typing the initial capital letter of a sentence or a proper noun. The result is that two letters of the word wind up being capitalized rather than just one. If this option is enabled, AutoCorrect watches for this mistake and changes the second capital letter to lowercase.
- **Capitalize first letter of sentences:** If you choose the Capitalize first letter of sentences option, Word automatically ensures that the first letter of each sentence is capitalized. The poet e.e. cummings should have used this feature.
- **Capitalize names of days:** If this option is enabled, Word always capitalizes the first letter of the names of days: Monday, Tuesday, Wednesday, and the like. Thus, if you type **thursday**, Word automatically changes it to *Thursday.*

- **Correct accidental usage of cAPS LOCK key:** I love this feature. I frequently press the Caps Lock key by mistake when reaching for the Shift key. With this option enabled, Word watches for the tell-tale pattern of inverted capitalization: a word that begins with a lowercase letters, then continues with uppercase letters. When it detects the pattern, it corrects the incorrectly capitalized letters and disables the Caps Lock key.
- **Replace text as you type:** This option activates a list of replacements that should be made whenever certain words are typed. For example, whenever you type **adn**, Word should automatically substitute *and.* Word only makes these substitutions if the Replace text as you type check box is selected.

To add your own AutoCorrect entries to the AutoCorrect replacement list, call up the Tools⇨AutoCorrect command and type the text you want to replace in the Replace field, followed by the text you want to replace it with in the With field. For example, if you want to set up an AutoCorrect entry so that every time you type *february,* Word replaces it with *February,* type **february** in the Replace field, type **February** in the With field, and click Add.

If you want Word to preserve the formatting for an AutoCorrect entry, first type the replacement text in your document and format it however you wish. Then, select the text and call up the Tools⇨AutoCorrect command. The replacement text is placed in the With field. All you have to do is type the Replace field and click Add.

Using the Spell Checker to Solve Crossword Puzzles

Hmm. A nine-letter word meaning "loss" whose first letter is D, fourth letter is R, and last two letters are NT.

Been stuck on that one for hours? No problem. Word's spell checker can find the word for you. All you have to do is substitute a question mark for each letter that you don't know, and Word finds every word in its dictionary whose spelling matches the pattern.

For example, to find all the nine-letter words whose first letter is D, fourth letter is R, and last two letters are NT, use the spell checker to look up **d??r???nt**. It finds two words: *decrement* and *detriment.*

TIP

The question mark represents one character. You can also use an asterisk to represent any number of characters. For example, to find all the words that start with *pro* and end with *ent,* no matter how many characters are in between, look up **pro*ent**. You find a bunch of words, including *procurement, proficient, prominent, pronouncement, proponent,* and *provident.*

Chapter 3

More Formatting Factoids

In This Chapter

- Understanding formatting in Word
- Formatting characters
- Formatting paragraphs
- Understanding text flow
- Learning all about tabs
- Living with fonts
- Exploring the ten commandments of formatting

How I loved my first computer. It had one of those daisy-wheel printers that created pages that looked like they had been typed on an actual typewriter. And my word processing software was so advanced that I could actually underline individual words and even set tab stops. And it could print out an entire page of letter-quality text faster than Congress can give itself a pay raise!

Those were the good old days. Back then, you didn't worry too much about what your text looked like, because you didn't really have that much control over appearances. So instead, you had to focus on — brace yourself — your actual words. Your document's words were actually more important than your document's appearance.

Nowadays, it seems as if appearance is everything. Who cares what your document says, as long as it looks great. The most brilliantly conceived proposal can go unread unless it looks like it was produced by a Madison Avenue ad agency. Sigh.

If you need a refresher in the basics of formatting text with Word, you've landed in the right chapter. The formatting stuff in this chapter is pretty basic, so much of it may be review if you've been using Word for awhile. But heck, a little review never hurt, and you may find a few juicy formatting tidbits in here that you didn't know you didn't know.

I hate this stuff as much as you do. Because I'm a writer, I like to concentrate on what my words *say* rather than how they look. If you agree, I highly recommend that you plow straight on to Chapter 4, where you will be thrust into the world of *styles.* It turns out that styles are the secret to freedom from the bondage of all the formatting nonsense presented in this chapter.

Understanding Formatting in Word

Before getting into the details of applying specific formats to your document, you should review the gestalt of how Word formats your text. In Word, there are three basic types of formats: characters, paragraphs, and sections.

Characters: Characters are the smallest element that you can format in Word. You can make characters bold, italic, or underlined, change their font size, and more! If you're deranged enough, you can format every character of your document differently. Doing so gives your documents a ransom-note appearance, which is something you probably want to avoid.

Paragraphs: The next biggest element you can format in Word is a paragraph. You can format each paragraph so that it has its own tab stops, line spacing, extra space before or after the paragraph, indentation, alignment (left, right, centered, or justified), and more. Paragraphs also have default character formats. So the only time you need to apply a character format is when you want your characters to vary from the paragraph's default character format, such as when you want to italicize a word or make it boldface.

Sections: Word also enables you to control the layout of pages. You can format each page by setting the top, bottom, left, and right margins, setting the number of columns and the size of each column, setting the paper size, controlling the placement of headers and footers, and more. You can format your document so that all pages have the same layout, or you can divide your document into *sections,* each with a different page layout. That's why Word refers to these formats as *section formats.*

- Unlike some other word processors who shall remain nameless but whose initials are *W-O-R-D-P-E-R-F-E-C-T*, Word does not depend on codes that have been handed down from medieval chambers of formatting torture. If you're an experienced WordPerfect user, you'll be constantly looking for the Reveal Codes command until you figure this out. In Word, formats are applied to portions of your document — characters, paragraphs, and sections — and are not controlled by codes that are embedded within the text that you can see and edit.

TIP

- Paragraph formatting information is contained within the paragraph mark at the end of the paragraph, which looks like this:

  ¶ If you can't see these marks on the screen, call up the Tools➪Options command and click the View tab. Then check the Paragraph Marks command. You can also refer to Chapter 18 for nauseating detail on setting various Word options.

- If you delete that paragraph mark, the paragraph is merged with the following paragraph. Any formatting that was applied to the paragraph mark you deleted is lost — the text assumes the formatting of the following paragraph.

- If you use more than one page layout in a document, the document is divided into two or more sections. Each section except the last one ends with a *section break,* which looks like this:

  ::::::::::::::::::::::::::::::::End of Section::::::::::::::::::::::::::::::::

  Section marks work much like paragraph marks: If you delete one, the text before the section mark assumes the page layout of the section following the mark.

- Every document has at least one section, but you see section marks only if you divide the document into two or more sections. Where's the section mark for the last section of a document? There is none. The formatting information for the last section of a document is stored in the last paragraph mark in the document.

Formatting Characters

The sections that follow show you how to apply various formats to characters. Like most things in Word, you discover that there's more than one way to apply these formats. The easiest way is to use keyboard shortcuts (if you can remember them) or the various buttons and gizmos on the Formatting toolbar. Otherwise, you can use the Format➪Font command if you like to play with dialog boxes.

Applying character formats the easy way

You can apply character formats before or after you type the text you want to format. To apply a character format to text as you type it, follow these steps:

1. **Type text up to the point where you want to apply a format.**
2. **Turn on the special character formatting by using one of the keyboard shortcuts or toolbar buttons listed in Table 3-1.**

   Nothing happens at first, but wait . . .

3. **Type away.**

   Anything you type assumes the format you applied in Step 2.

4. **Turn off the special character formatting by using the keyboard shortcut again.**

   Or, if you clicked one of the buttons on the Formatting toolbar, click it again. Either way, Word discontinues the special formatting. Any text you subsequently type is formatted as usual.

Table 3-1 Character Formatting the Easy Way

Toolbar Button	*Keyboard Shortcut*	*What It Does*
B	Ctrl+B	Bold
I	Ctrl+I	*Italic*
U	Ctrl+U	Underline (continuous)
	Ctrl+Shift+W	Word underline
	Ctrl+Shift+D	Double underline
	Ctrl+Shift+A	ALL CAPS
	Ctrl+Shift+K	SMALL CAPS
	Shift+F3	Change case
	Ctrl+=	Subscript
	Ctrl+Shift+=	Superscript
Times New Roman	Ctrl+Shift+F	Change font
12	Ctrl+Shift+P	Change point size
	Ctrl+]	Increase size one point
	Ctrl+[	Decrease size one point
	Ctrl+Shift+>	Increase size to next available size
	Ctrl+Shift+<	Decrease size to previous available size
	Ctrl+Shift+Q	Switch to Symbol font (Γρεεκ Τραγεδψ)
	Ctrl+Shift+Z	Remove character formatting
	Ctrl+spacebar	Remove character formatting

To apply a character format to text you've already typed, follow these steps:

1. **Highlight the text you want to format.**

   To highlight a single word, double-click anywhere in the word. To highlight an entire paragraph, triple-click anywhere in the paragraph. Otherwise, highlight the text that you want formatted by dragging the mouse over it while holding down the left mouse button or by using the arrow keys to move the cursor while holding down the Shift key.

   TIP

   If Word's Automatic Word Selection option is enabled, you don't have to double-click to select an entire word; Word automatically selects the entire word if the insertion point is anywhere in the word. To activate this option (or to deactivate it if it is already activated), use the Tools⇨Options command, click the Edit tab, and then click the Automatic Word Selection button. Click the OK button or press Enter to close the Options dialog box.

2. **Apply the format using one of the keyboard shortcuts or toolbar buttons listed in Table 3-1.**

   The effects of your formatting should be immediately apparent.

3. **Move on.**

   Disperse. There's nothing more to see here. Return to your homes.

Some other tidbits on character formatting:

- You can gang tackle text with formats, if you want. For example, you can format text as ***bold italic double-underlined*** if you're really desperate for attention.
- To remove *all* character formatting, highlight the text that you want to return to normal; then press Ctrl+spacebar or Ctrl+Shift+Z.
- To remove a specific character format, such as bold or italic, but leave other character formats intact, highlight the text and type the keyboard shortcut or click the toolbar button for the format you want to remove.
- To paraphrase Chuck Yeager, there are old Word users, and there are bold Word users, but there are no old bold Word users.

Using the Format⇨Font command

The character formatting options you're likely to use most — bold, italics, underlining, font, and point size — are all readily accessible from the Formatting toolbar or easy-to-remember keyboard shortcuts. Most of the other character formatting options don't dare show their faces on the Formatting toolbar, and you probably won't use them enough to learn their keyboard shortcuts. Bother.

If you find yourself in the unenviable position of needing to apply a character format that's not on the toolbar and you can't remember the shortcut, you have three alternatives. First, you can try to talk yourself out of it. Who needs double-underlining, anyway? If that doesn't work, you can flip open this book, turn to Table 3-1, and look up the keyboard shortcut.

As a last resort, you can use the Format⇨Font command. Yes, I know it pops up a dialog box that looks like it was designed by Bill Z. Bub himself, but it does give you one-stop shopping for all of Word's character formatting options.

The Format⇨Font command is the only way to apply the following formats to characters:

- Dashed underline
- Color
- Strikethrough
- Shadow
- Emboss
- Engrave
- Character spacing

These formats do not appear on any of the standard toolbars, and they have no keyboard shortcuts. So if you want to apply them, you have to use the Format⇨Font command. (If you use any of these weird formats regularly, consult Chapter 19 to learn how to assign a keyboard shortcut to them.)

Here's the procedure for applying mystifying, strange formatting:

1. **Highlight the text you want to mangle with oddball formatting.**
2. **Conjure up the Format⇨Font command.**

   Press Alt+O and then *F* to activate the command. Or use its convenient and easy-to-remember mnemonic keyboard shortcut, Ctrl+D. (Just remember that the *D* stands for *those demonic character formats*. Works for me.)
3. **Tremble before the Font dialog box.**

   After all, it was designed by Bill Z. Bub himself. Figure 3-1 shows its ghastly appearance.
4. **Play with the controls.**

   Fiddle with the various controls to set the Font, the Font Style (bold, italic, and so on), and the Size. Click the Effects you want (Strikethrough, Superscript, and so on). Use the drop-down list boxes to set the Underline and Color. Have a ball.

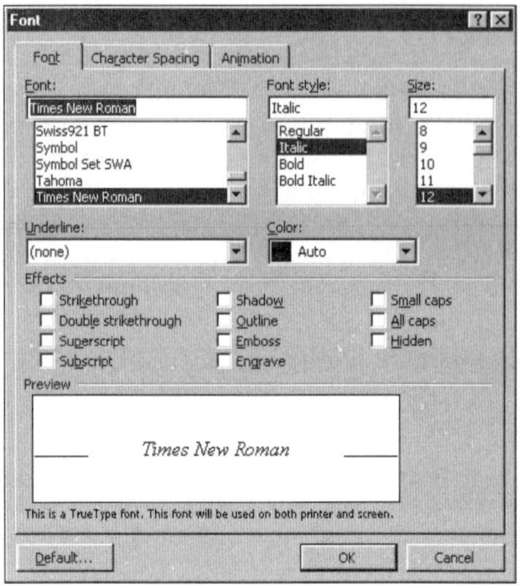

Figure 3-1: The Font dialog box.

5. **Click OK when you've had enough.**

   The dialog box vanishes, and your text is magically transformed with the formats you selected.

Some notes about using the Font dialog box:

- If you haven't yet typed the text you want to mangle, use the Format⇨Font command, choose the formats you want, click OK, and then start typing. When you're done, press Ctrl+spacebar or Ctrl+Shift+Z to resume normal type.
- To remove oddball formats that you've applied with the Format⇨Font command, select the text and press Ctrl+spacebar or Ctrl+Shift+Z. Or conjure up the Format⇨Font command once again and uncheck the formats you want to get rid of.
- Notice the tabs across the top of the Font dialog box? They enable you to switch between basic font formatting controls, character spacing controls, and animation controls. If you click the Character Spacing tab, you see options to control the spacing between characters, raise or lower characters from the baseline, and apply a spiffy desktop publishing feature called *kerning*. These options are in the realm of desktop publishing, so ignore them for now. If you can't wait, skip ahead to Chapter 11 for information about using these options. Animation settings are covered in the next section.

Animating your text

Word 97 has the ability to add simple animation effects to your text. These animation effects won't make your document look like it was produced by Disney animators, but it can draw attention to text you want highlighted. Of course, animations are visible only when you view the document on your computer using Word 97, so there's no point in using them for documents that will be printed rather than viewed online (check out Chapters 16 and 17 for more online stuff).

Word 97 offers the following text animation effects:

- Blinking Background: The background flashes.
- Las Vegas Lights: The text is surrounded by dots that flash on and off in changing colors.
- Marching Black Ants: The text is surrounded by a series of black dashes that appear to march around the text.
- Marching Red Ants: Same as Marching Black Ants, only the "ants" are red. (Watch out — Red Ants bite.)
- Shimmer: The text flashes with a fuzzy effect that makes you wonder if you had too much beer last night.
- Sparkle Text: Little dots of color flash on and off in and about the text giving it a festive party look.

To animate your text, follow these steps:

1. **Highlight the text you want to animate.**
2. **Choose the Format⇨Font command.**

   The Font dialog box appears.
3. **Click the Animation tab.**

   The Animation controls appear, as shown in Figure 3-2.
4. **Select the type of animation you want from the Animations list box.**

   Word displays a preview of the animation effect in the Preview area.
5. **Click OK.**
6. **Say "Ooh" and "Aah" when you see the animation in action.**

To remove an animation effect (which you'll probably end up doing after you realize that the whole idea is kind of silly), repeat the above procedure and select (none) in Step 4.

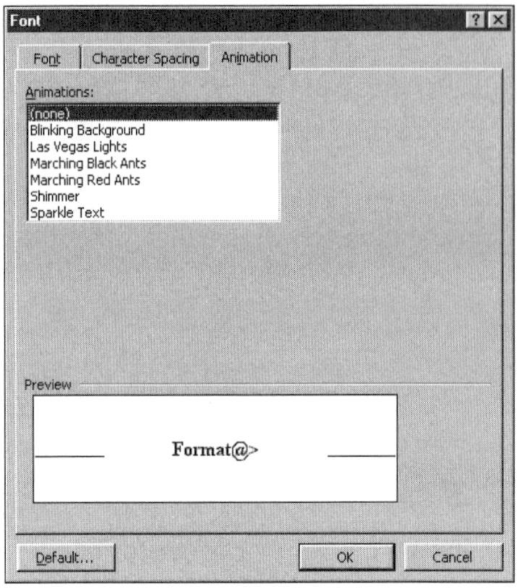

Figure 3-2: The Animation controls in the Font dialog box.

Inserting Special Characters

You probably already know about the Insert⇨Symbol command. Did you know that several of the special symbols accessible from this command are assigned keyboard shortcuts? Table 3-2 lists the more useful of these symbols and their shortcuts.

Table 3-2 Keyboard Shortcuts for Special Symbols

Symbol	*Name*	*Keyboard Shortcut*
©	Copyright	Alt+Ctrl+C
®	Registered mark	Alt+Ctrl+R
™	Trademark	Alt+Ctrl+T
—	Em dash	Alt+Ctrl+– (minus sign on the numeric keypad)
–	En dash	Ctrl+– (minus sign on the numeric keypad)
. . .	Ellipsis	Alt+Ctrl+. (period)

- You can add a keyboard shortcut to any special character by choosing the Insert⇨Symbol command, clicking the Symbols tab or the Special Characters tab in the Symbol dialog box that appears, and choosing the Shortcut Key button.

- An em dash is a dash that is the width of the letter M. An en dash is as wide as a letter N. If using a dash as a punctuation mark — like this — you should use an em dash instead of two hyphens. The old double-hyphen treatment is a carryover from the days of manual typewriters.
- The minus sign required for the em dash and en dash shortcuts is the minus sign on the numeric keypad, way off to the far-right side of the keyboard. (This would probably be Rush Limbaugh's favorite key if he used a PC, but he's a Mac fanatic.) The shortcut won't work if you use the hyphen that's between the 0 and the equal sign (=) at the top of the keyboard.

Formatting Paragraphs

The following sections show you how to apply various formats to a paragraph. Once again, there's more than one way to apply these formats. The easy way is to use keyboard shortcuts or toolbar buttons, but if you must, you can resort to the Format⇨Paragraph, Format⇨Tabs, or Format⇨Borders and Shading commands.

Applying paragraph formats the easy way

To apply a paragraph format, follow this painless procedure:

1. **Click anywhere in the paragraph that you want to format.**

   It matters not where in the paragraph, as long as the cursor is somewhere in the paragraph.

2. **Use one of the keyboard shortcuts or toolbar buttons summarized in Table 3-3.**

   The effect of your formatting should be obvious.

3. **There is no third step. You're done.**

   Made you look!

Table 3-3 Paragraph Formatting the Easy Way

Toolbar Button	*Keyboard Shortcut*	*What It Does*
	Ctrl+L	Left-aligns a paragraph
	Ctrl+R	Right-aligns a paragraph
	Ctrl+J	Justifies a paragraph
	Ctrl+E	Centers a paragraph
	Ctrl+M	Increases left indent

Table 3-3 (continued)

Toolbar Button	*Keyboard Shortcut*	*What It Does*
	Ctrl+Shift+M	Reduces left indent
	Ctrl+T	Creates hanging indent
	Ctrl+Shift+T	Reduces hanging indent
	Ctrl+1	Single-spaces paragraph
	Ctrl+2	Double-spaces paragraph
	Ctrl+5	Sets line space to 1.5
	Ctrl+0 (zero)	Removes space before or sets space before to 1 line
	Ctrl+Q	Removes paragraph formatting

Keep these notes in mind when formatting your paragraphs:

- As with character formats, you can heap paragraph formats atop one another. Just keep typing keyboard shortcuts or clicking toolbar buttons until the paragraph is formatted just right.

- To remove paragraph formatting, use the easy-to-remember Ctrl+Q keyboard shortcut (the *Q* stands for *quit using those diabolical paragraph formats*).
- Paragraph formats are stored in the paragraph marker at the end of the paragraph. Don't make the mistake of spending hours polishing a paragraph's appearance and then deleting the paragraph marker to merge the text into the following paragraph. If you do, all the formatting you so carefully applied is lost. (If that happens, quickly press Ctrl+Z to undo the deletion.)

Using the Format⇨Paragraph command

If you find yourself in the unenviable pickle of needing to use a formatting option that's not on the Formatting toolbar and you can't remember its keyboard shortcut, you can always conjure up the Format⇨Paragraph command and pick and choose your paragraph formats from a palette of delightful formatting treasures.

Here's the procedure for using the Format⇨Paragraph command:

1. **Click anywhere in the paragraph that you want to format.**

   It doesn't matter where in the paragraph, just so the cursor is somewhere in the paragraph.

2. **Summon the Format➪Paragraph command.**

   Press Alt+O and then *P*. The Paragraph dialog box appears, shown in Figure 3-3.

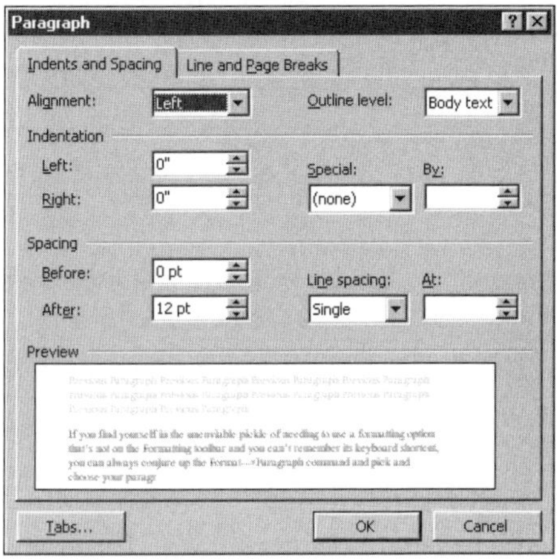

Figure 3-3: The Paragraph dialog box.

3. **Play with the controls.**

   You can set the paragraph alignment (Left, Right, Centered, or Justified) from the Alignment drop-down list. You can increase the Left or Right indentation, or you can choose a First Line or Hanging indent from the Special drop-down list box. You can also increase or decrease the amount of spacing Before and After the paragraph and set the Line Spacing.

   As you play with the controls, keep an eye on the Preview box to see the effect of your changes.

4. **Click OK when you're done.**

   Presto change-o! You're done.

REMEMBER

You can set left and right indentation as well as first line and hanging indents by playing with the ruler. See the section "Setting tabs with the ruler" later in this chapter for details.

Here's some additional info on using paragraph formatting options:

- You can change the unit of measure that's used for setting indentation by using the Tools➪Options command, clicking the General tab, and setting the Measurement Units field to the unit of measure you want to use. See the sidebar "Measuring up" for more information about units of measure.

- In the Line Spacing drop-down list, you can select several options for the paragraph's line spacing. The ones you'll use most are Single, 1.5 Lines, and Double. You can use Multiple to set some other line spacing, such as 3 lines. At Least lets you specify a minimum measurement for the line spacing, such as "At Least 14 Points." You can also use Exactly to set an exact measurement, but I recommend you avoid it. You can get into trouble if you use 12 point type in a paragraph, but set the line spacing to "Exactly 10 Points."
- Notice the Line and Page Breaks tab at the top of the Paragraph dialog box. Click it and you see options for controlling how paragraphs are positioned on the page. More information on these options is in the section "Line and Page Breaks," coming up in a jiffy.
- Oh, and the Paragraph dialog box has a Tabs button that zaps you over to the Tabs dialog box so that you can set tab stops. This too is covered later, in the section "All about Tabs."

Line and Page Breaks

When you conjure up the Format⇨Paragraph command, you can click the Line and Page Breaks tab to awaken a different set of paragraph formatting options. Figure 3-4 shows the Line and Page Breaks tab of the Paragraph dialog box.

Measuring up

The way Word measures things, such as line spacing and indentations, is confusing if you don't understand the terminology. Here are the units of measure Word accepts:

in Inches. You know what they are.

Cm Centimeters. You should know by now, but in case you're not sure, there are 2.54 centimeters in an inch.

Pt Points, a term used by typographers to measure type. There are 72 points in an inch and 12 points in a pica.

pi Pica, another wacky term used by typographers. There are roughly 6 picas in an inch and 12 points in a pica.

Li Line — the same as a pica.

cb Cubit, 17.5 inches. There are 105 picas in a cubit, and 1,260 points in a cubit. (Just kidding. Word doesn't really accept cubits as a valid measurement unless the filename extension for the document you're working on is ARC.)

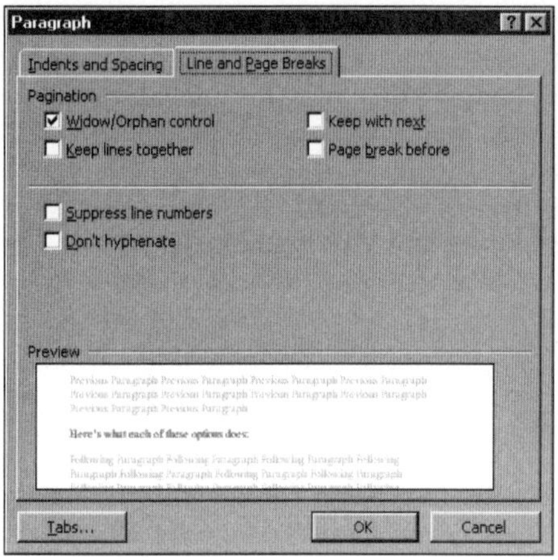

Figure 3-4: Setting the Line and Page Break options.

Here's what each of these options does:

Widow/Orphan control: If a paragraph falls at the bottom of the page, Widow/Orphan control prevents Word from splitting the paragraph if it means that one line would be left stranded at the bottom of one page or the top of the next page. Instead, the entire paragraph is bumped to the next page. Widow/Orphan control is on by default; you should leave it on.

Keep lines together: Sometimes you have a paragraph that you don't want split up across pages. For example, suppose you want to quote a work of fine literature, such as a classic poem from Winnie-the-Pooh:

Cottleston, Cottleston, Cottleston Pie,
A fly can't bird, but a bird can fly.
Ask me a riddle and I reply:
"*Cottleston, Cottleston, Cottleston Pie.*"

Obviously, you would lose the stunning emotional impact of this powerful poem if you allowed Word to split it across two pages. Give it the Keep lines together option so Word moves the whole thing to the next page if it doesn't fit in its entirety on the current page.

Keep with next: This option prevents Word from inserting a page break between a paragraph and the one that follows it. You use it mostly for headings, to prevent a heading from being stranded at the bottom of a page.

Page break before: This option forces Word to place the paragraph at the top of the next page. Use it for chapter or section headings when you want each chapter or section to start on a new page.

Suppress line numbers: If you use Word's line numbering feature, this option tells Word to skip the paragraph when numbering lines.

Don't hyphenate: If you use Word's hyphenation feature, this option tells Word to not hyphenate any words in the paragraph. Hyphenation is explained ad nauseam in Chapter 12.

All about Tabs

You can set tab stops in one of two ways: by dropping them directly on the ruler or by ditzing around with the Format⇨Tabs command. Dropping tabs directly on the ruler is far and away the easier method of the two. You should get involved with the Format⇨Tabs command only when you want to use *leaders* (little rows of dots that run across the page).

Setting tabs with the ruler

Here's the procedure for setting tabs with the ruler:

1. **If the ruler isn't visible, use the View⇨Ruler command to make it visible.**
2. **Type some text that you want to line up with tab stops.**

   Type several paragraphs if you want. Hit the Tab key once and only once between each column of information that you want lined up. Don't worry if everything doesn't line up at first. You'll fix it later.
3. **Select the paragraph or paragraphs whose tabs you want to set.**

   If you're setting tabs for just one paragraph, click the mouse anywhere in the paragraph. If you're setting tabs for more than one paragraph, drag the mouse to select at least some text in each paragraph.
4. **Click the mouse on the ruler at each spot where you want a new tab stop.**

   Watch as the text you selected in Step 2 lines up under the tabs you create. Add one tab stop to the ruler for each column of information you want aligned.
5. **Adjust.**

   Nothing works quite right the first time. If you dropped a tab at $1^1/_2$ inches and want to move it to $1^3/_4$ inches, just click and drag the tab marker with the mouse and slide it to the new location. When you release the mouse button, text in the currently selected paragraphs is adjusted in the new tab position.

Here's more fascinating information about tabs:

- Default tab stops are placed every half an inch. However, each time you create a new tab stop, any default tab stops to the left of the new tab stops are deleted. In other words, default tab stops exist only to the right of tab stops you create.
- Word enables you to create four types of tab alignments: left, center, right, and decimal. To change the type of tab that's created when you click the ruler, click the Tab Alignment button at the far left edge of the ruler. Each time you click the button, the picture on the button changes to indicate the alignment type:

Left tab; text is left aligned at the tab stop.

Center tab; text is centered over the tab stop.

Right tab; text is right aligned at the tab stop.

Decimal tab; numbers are aligned at the decimal point over the tab stop.

Here are some miscellaneous thoughts to ponder concerning tab stops:

- Rush Limbaugh fans often refuse to use left tab stops.
- You can quickly summon the Tabs dialog box by double-clicking the lower-half of the ruler. Watch where you double-click, though, because the first click adds a tab stop.
- If you want to add a tab leader (a row of dots, dashes, or a solid line that precedes the tab, as is often found in a restaurant menu), first create the tab stop by dropping it on the ruler. Then conjure up the Format⇨Tabs command, select the tab stop you want the leader added to, and select a leader type (dots, dashes, or solid line). Then click OK and check the results.
- To remove a tab stop from the ruler, click the tab stop you want to remove and drag it straight down, off the ruler. When you release the mouse, the tab stop is deleted.
- To quickly remove all tab stops, issue the Format⇨Tabs command or double-click in the bottom half of the ruler to summon the Tabs dialog box. Click the Clear All button to remove the tabs and then click OK to return to the document.

Running a bar tab

You must be 21 to use this feature in most states.

One of the more unusual things you can do with tabs is create vertical bars between columns of information, like this:

Star Trek	Happy Days	All In The Family
Star Trek: The Next Generation	Laverne and Shirley	The Jeffersons
Star Trek: Deep Space Nine	Mork and Mindy	Archie's Place

Here, the vertical bars between the columns are actually special deviant versions of tab stops. To create them, here's what you do:

1. **Create some tab stops on the ruler.**

   Create *two* tab stops for each column of information you need, about 1/8 inch apart.

2. **Conjure up the Format⇨Tabs command.**

   The Tabs dialog box, shown in Figure 3-5, appears.

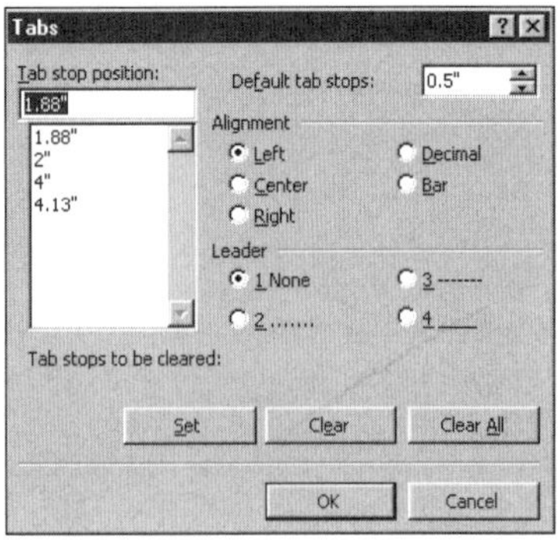

Figure 3-5: The Tab dialog box.

3. **Yell, "Norm!"**

4. **Convert every other tab stop to a bar tab.**

   Click the first tab stop; then select Bar as the alignment type. Click the Set button to make the change permanent; then click the third tab stop and make it a bar tab, too. Repeat for every other tab stop.

   You must click the Set button after changing each tab stop to a bar tab. Otherwise, Word doesn't run your bar tab.

5. **Click OK.**

   When the Tabs dialog box vanishes, check out the vertical bars between text columns. Notice that the tab marker in the ruler appears as a small vertical line.

6. **Adjust.**

   If you don't like the way the tab stops are positioned, move 'em in the ruler by clicking them and dragging them.

All you ever wanted to know about bar tabs is found in these three small bullets:

- Bar tabs aren't like regular tab stops in that the Tab key doesn't stop at them. Try it. Create a bar tab; then press the Tab key. The cursor zooms right past the bar tab to the next available tab stop.
- If the bar tab extends above or below the line, it's because the paragraph format calls for extra space above or below the paragraph. Use the Format⇨Paragraph command to remove the Above or Below space. (If you need the extra space, add it to the adjoining paragraphs instead.)
- Bar tabs are a crude way of making tables. Word has a special feature just for making tables, called — believe it or not — the Table Feature. It's a lot easier to work with than bar tabs. It's covered in Chapter 10.

Formatting Pages

To control the layout of text on the page, use the File⇨Page Setup command. This command displays the Page Setup dialog box.

The Page Setup dialog box has four tabs, which control the following options:

Margins: The options on this tab enable you to set the margins. Normally, this tab contains options to set the Top, Bottom, Left, and Right margins. However, if you click the Mirror Margins button, the Left and Right options change to Inside and Outside. Then the margins for each page alternate: On odd numbered pages, the inside margin is on the left; on even-numbered pages, the inside margin is on the right. The Margins tab also enables you to set the position of headers and footers.

Paper Size: The options on the Paper Size tab enable you to specify the size of the paper (for example, 8$^1/_2$ x 11 inches, 8$^1/_2$ x 14 inches, and so on) and the orientation — whether the page is printed normally (*portrait*) or sideways (*landscape*).

Paper Source: The Paper Source options enable you specify that the first page of the document is to be printed on paper drawn from a different source than the paper used for the rest of the document. For

example, you may specify that the first page be printed on paper manually fed to the printer, and the rest of the document printed on paper drawn from the paper tray. This is used mostly for two-page letters, where the first page is printed on manually fed letterhead, and subsequent pages are printed on plain paper in the printer's paper tray.

Layout: This oddball tab enables you to set up different headers for the even- and odd-numbered pages, control how text is aligned between the top and bottom page margins, suppress endnotes (more on this in Chapter 9), and number the lines on the page. Hmph.

The Apply To option in the Page Setup dialog box can be set to Whole Document or This Point Forward. If you choose This Point Forward, a new section is created at the current cursor location. If you selected a range of text before calling up the File⇨Page Setup command, the Apply To choices will be Whole Document and Selected Text.

If you want to change the layout of just one page — for example, to print on page of a document sideways — follow these steps:

1. **Move to the top of the page you want to apply special page formatting to, then use the mouse to select the entire page.**
2. **Call up the File⇨Page Setup command.**

   The Page Setup dialog box will appear.
3. **Change whatever settings you want to change.**

   For example, change the orientation to "Landscape" to print this one page sideways.
4. **Change the Apply To list box to Selected Text.**
5. **Click OK.**

Word inserts two section breaks: one before the text you selected, the other after the selected text. The section created for the text you selected will specify the page layout changes you made. Then, the second section will revert to the original page layout settings.

AutoFormat (Or, Make It Stop!)

Word's AutoFormat watches everything you type and steps in when it thinks you are trying to format something but you aren't doing it right. Here are just some of the changes AutoFormat might make to your document as you type along:

- If you type a quotation mark, AutoFormat will change it to a left (“) or right (”) quotation mark depending on whether you use it before or after a word.
- If you type (c) — that is, the letter “c” in parentheses — AutoFormat will convert it to a Copyright symbol: ©.
- If you type an asterisk followed by a tab and some text, AutoFormat will remove the asterisk and convert the paragraph to a bullet list.
- If you type a number followed by a period and a space, AutoFormat will remove the number and convert the paragraph to a bullet list.

The list goes on and on. Some of the changes are helpful, but some can be annoying. Fortunately, you can selectively disable most of the AutoFormat feature by following these steps:

1. **Choose the Tools⇨AutoCorrect command.**

   The AutoCorrect dialog box will appear.

2. **Click the AutoFormat As You Type tab.**

   The AutoFormat As You Type options will appear, as shown in Figure 3-6.

3. **Turn off thc AutoFormat options that annoy you.**
4. **Click OK.**

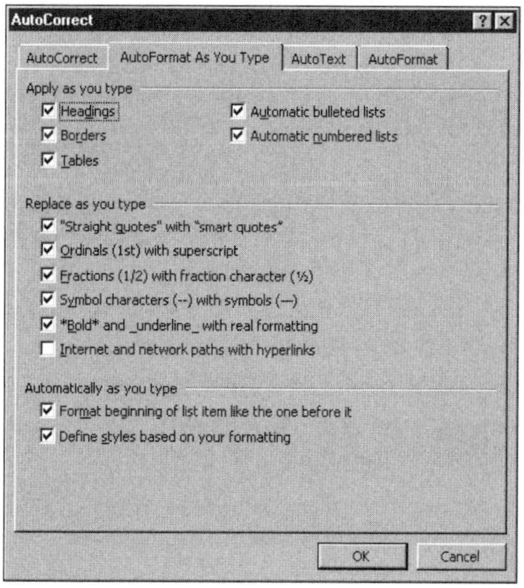

Figure 3-6: Changing the AutoFormat As You Type options.

The Ten Commandments of Formatting

When Bill Gates came down from the mountain, he originally had 15 formatting commandments. But he dropped one of the three tablets, shattering it to pieces, so now we have but ten.

I. Thou shalt remember thy keyboard shortcuts to speed thy way

Don't bother memorizing the keyboard shortcuts for formats you rarely or never use. But do memorize the shortcuts for the formats you use frequently. It's much faster to press Ctrl+B than it is to click the mouse button or contend with menus and dialog boxes. Make a short list of the shortcuts you want to learn and tape them to your computer or somewhere within eyesight.

II. Thou shalt not press Enter at the end of each line

You defeat the whole purpose of word processing if you press the Enter key at the end of each line you type. Let Word figure out where to break each line.

III. Thou shalt not create empty paragraphs

Don't press the Enter key twice to leave extra space between paragraphs. Instead, format the paragraph with $1^1/_2$ or 2 blank lines before the first line.

IV. Thou shalt not use extraneous spaces

On a typewriter, you're supposed to hit the spacebar twice between sentences. With proportional fonts, you should use only one space following the period at the end of a sentence. Also, don't use spaces to align text in columns. Use tabs instead.

V. Thou shalt not use extraneous tabs

Don't hit the Tab key two or three times to move text across the page. Instead, hit the tab key once and then set a tab stop where you want the text aligned.

VI. Thou shalt not underline when italics will do

Underlining is for typewriters. Italics is for computers. You paid lots of hard-earned money for your computer, so you may as well get your money's worth.

VII. Thou shalt not use more than three fonts on a page

Avoid the ransom note look at all costs. Use one font for your text, a second font for headings, and maybe a third font for emphasis. But no more than three fonts altogether, please.

VIII. Thou shalt not use Exact Line Spacing

The Exact Line Spacing option (found under the Format⇨Paragraph command) is a source of much trouble. Use Single, 1.5 lines, or Double instead.

IX. Thou shalt use the AutoCorrect feature

The AutoCorrect feature can correct typos on the fly, as well as help with simple formatting chores such as making sure sentences start with capital letters and using "curly quotes" properly.

To activate this feature, use the Tools⇨AutoCorrect command. When the AutoCorrect dialog box appears, check the things you want Word to automatically correct; then click OK.

X. Thou shalt use styles

The best way to deal with all this formatting nonsense is to put all the formatting you'll ever need into styles. Then you don't have to worry about line spacing, hanging indents, fonts and font sizes, or anything else. Just apply the correct style and everything is taken care of. (Styles are discussed in detail in Chapter 4. Aren't you lucky?)

Chapter 4

More Style Sensations

In This Chapter

- Understanding styles
- Creating a new style
- Applying a style
- Changing a style
- Assigning a shortcut key to a style
- Basing one style on another
- Setting the style for the next paragraph automatically
- Using character styles
- Storing styles in a template
- Learning the ten commandments of styles

Styles are what Tiggers like best. They are the secret to freeing yourself from the tyranny of Word's Format menu. With styles, you toil at a paragraph's formatting until you get the paragraph just right; then you type a name by which Word remembers all of the formatting you've applied to the paragraph. From then on, you can apply the same formatting to other paragraphs simply by calling up the style. No more hunting and pecking your way through the Format menu commands, trying to recall how you got the paragraph to look so good.

I like Microsoft's styles so much, I *almost* bought the company. If you're not yet using styles, I suggest you learn how to use them right away. Although the concept of styles may be confusing at first, they aren't really that hard to learn. An hour or so invested in learning how styles work pays off in many saved hours of unnecessary formatting time later.

Understanding Styles

The basic idea behind styles is to store all of the formatting information for a paragraph under a single name. That way, you can quickly apply the saved formats to other paragraphs simply by referring to the style's name. For example, suppose that you want to format headings using 16-point Arial Bold, with 18 points of space above the heading and 6 points below, and with a line drawn beneath the paragraph. You'd have to bounce the mouse all over the place to format a heading like this manually. But if you've stored the formats in a style, you can apply all of them with a single mouse click or a keyboard shortcut.

Styles contain all of the formatting information specified with the following Word commands:

- **Format⇨Font:** Includes the font name, style (regular, bold, italic, or bold italic), and special character attributes such as small caps or superscripts, as well as character spacing and kerning.
- **Format⇨Paragraph:** Includes left and right indentation, first line indentation and hanging indents, line spacing, before and after spacing, and text flow (widow/orphan control, keep with next, and so on).
- **Format⇨Tabs:** Includes tab stop positions, tab types, leader tabs, and bar tabs.
- **Format⇨Borders and Shading:** Includes borders and line styles as well as fill shades.
- **Tools⇨Language:** Enables you to use an alternate dictionary for spelling and hyphenation or to tell Word that a paragraph specified with this style should be skipped when the document is spell checked.
- **Format⇨Bullets and Numbering:** Enables you to set up numbered or bulleted lists. (See Chapter 6 for more information about bullets and numbers.)

With all these formats stored together under one name, you can imagine how much time styles can save you. Styles are an integral part of the way Word works. Even if you think you don't use styles, you do: Word documents start off with several predefined styles, including the ubiquitous Normal style. The Normal style governs the default appearance of paragraphs in your document.

Here are some other benefits of using styles:

- Suppose you don't know how to drop a line three points beneath the paragraph, and you don't want to learn how. No problemo. Just bribe your friendly Word guru into creating the style for you. After the style is created, you don't have to know how to use the formatting instructions contained in the style. All you have to know is how to apply the style, and that's as easy as clicking the mouse.
- The real beauty of styles comes when you decide that the headings are too small — can't you make them 18 point instead of 16 point? Without styles, you'd have to adjust the size of each heading separately. With styles, you simply change the style and — voilà! — all the paragraphs assigned to that style are automatically adjusted.
- Styles are stored along with your text in the document file. Thus, each document can have its own collection of styles, and styles with the same name can have different formatting characteristics in different documents. For example, a style named Bullet List may have ordinary round bullets in one document but check marks or pointy index fingers in another.
- You can also store styles in special types of documents called templates. This method makes it easier to set up styles and use them over and over again. You find everything you ever wanted to know about templates in the next chapter.
- Word comes with 28 templates already set up to format various types of documents, such as letters, reports, proposals, memos, and so on. If one of these templates suits your fancy, you may not need to create your own styles. Just apply the template you like to your document and then use the styles it contains. See Chapter 5 for more information about templates.
- Oops, 18 point is too big for the headings. How about 14 point? Once again, no need to change each heading paragraph individually. Just change the style, and each heading paragraph is changed automatically.
- Another benefit of using styles is that some Word features, most notably Table of Contents and Outline view, work best when you use styles for your headings and body text. Don't even attempt to use these features if you don't use styles. (Outlines are covered in Chapter 7; tables of contents are covered in Chapter 19.)

Basic Style Stuff

The basics of working with styles are not difficult to master. The following sections detail the various procedures you need to get comfortable working with styles.

Creating a new style

To create a new style, follow these steps:

1. **Tweak a paragraph until it is formatted just the way you want it.**

   Select the entire paragraph and set the font. Then use the Format⇨Paragraph command to set the line spacing, before and after spacing, and indentation for the paragraph. If you use tabs for the paragraph, set them using the ruler or the Format⇨Tabs command. Add any other formatting you need, such as bullets, numbering, shading, borders, and so on.

2. **Press Ctrl+Shift+S.**

   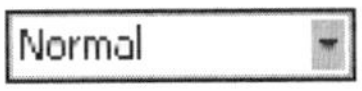

   Or click the style list box on the Formatting toolbar (the style list box is the left-most box on the Formatting toolbar and is shown in the margin). ***Note:*** Don't click the arrow that's at the right side of the style list box; that will drop down the list to show all of the available styles. Instead, click in the text portion of the list box.

3. **Type a name for the style.**

   Be descriptive. You can use more than one word, but avoid typing a name that's so long it doesn't fit in the style list box.

4. **Press Enter.**

   The style is added to Word's list of styles for the document so that you can reuse it.

Keep these points in mind when creating styles:

- When thinking up a name, try to come up with a name that describes the function of the paragraph in the document (for example, *Salutation* or *Vogon Poetry*) or that describes the type of formatting the style contains (like *Dbl Indent* or *Bullet List*).
- You can access the style you create only in the current document. To make the style accessible in other documents, you need to put it in a template. Templates are covered in Chapter 5.

- So far, I've avoided the Format⇨Style command. I'm trying to avoid it as long as possible.

Applying a style

To apply a style to a paragraph, follow these steps:

1. **Put the cursor in the paragraph that you want to format.**

   You don't have to select the entire paragraph; just move the cursor anywhere in it.

2. **Choose the style you want from the style list box.**

   Click the down arrow next to the style list box or press Ctrl+Shift+S; then scroll through the list of styles until you find the one you want. Then click it. The formatting contained in the style is applied to the paragraph.

You can use the preceding procedure to change the style assigned to a paragraph. When you do that, all the formatting drawn from the original style is replaced with formatting from the new style.

To apply a style to two or more adjacent paragraphs, simply select a range of text that includes all the paragraphs you want formatted. Then choose the style. When you press the Enter key to create a new paragraph, the new paragraph normally assumes the same style as the preceding paragraph. See the section "Setting the style of the next paragraph" later in this chapter for an important — and useful — exception.

Every paragraph in a document is assigned to a style. The default style for the first paragraph in a new document is called *Normal.*

You can tell which style is assigned to a paragraph by clicking anywhere in the paragraph and looking at the style list box. It shows the name of the style assigned to the paragraph. Or, if the style area is revealed, you can see the name of each paragraph's style to the left of the paragraph. Use the Tools⇨Options, View command to reveal the style area.

Here are some helpful hints to using styles effectively:

- The little graphic that appears next to each style name in the style list gives you some useful information about the style. For example, if you saw the graphic that appears in the margin next to this paragraph, you'd know that the style is a paragraph style because of the paragraph symbol (¶), and you'd know that paragraphs formatted with this style will be left aligned and that the paragraph's text is 10-point.
- If the style that you are looking for doesn't appear in the style list, hold down the Shift key and click the down arrow next to the style list box. Sometimes Word doesn't list all the available styles unless you do this.

- To quickly return a paragraph to Normal style, press Ctrl+Shift+N.
- To assign the built-in Heading 1, Heading 2, or Heading 3 styles, press Ctrl+Alt+1, Ctrl+Alt+2, or Ctrl+Alt+3.
- You can create keyboard shortcuts for any style that you create. See the section "Assigning shortcut keys to styles" later in this chapter.

Overriding style formatting

Ordinarily, all the formatting you need for a paragraph should come from the paragraph's style. However, there are occasions when you want to add additional formatting to a paragraph or change some aspect of a paragraph's formatting. The most common example of this is applying character formats such as bold or italics to characters within the paragraph. However, you can also apply paragraph formats to a paragraph that is formatted with a style. Any formats you apply simply augment or replace formats specified in the style.

Here are some guidelines:

- Formats that you apply to a paragraph directly rather than via a style are called, naturally enough, *direct formats*.
- Any direct paragraph formatting you apply is lost if you later decide to apply a different style to the paragraph. For example, if you apply the Normal style to a paragraph and then add 12 points of space above the paragraph, the extra 12 points of space above is lost if you apply a different style to the paragraph.
- Character formats are a little different. In most cases, Word preserves character formatting that you've applied directly even when you change the paragraph's style. For example, if you create a paragraph formatted with the Normal style, italicize a few words in the paragraph, and then apply another style to the paragraph, the italic words remain italicized.
- Sometimes, however, Word negates direct character formatting that you've applied. This happens when you select a block of text in the paragraph and change the style. Word examines the text you selected, and if more than half the text has had direct formatting applied, all the direct formatting in the paragraph is removed. This is a strange rule that makes no sense to me, so I just ignore it. (This strategy works for many of life's little problems, doesn't it?)
- Notice how I still haven't touched the Format➪Style command?

Changing a style

There are two ways to change the formatting of an existing style: with or without the Format➪Style command. Because the Format➪Style command is a cumbersome beast, I recommend staying away from the Format➪Style command.

TIP: The following procedure for changing an existing style without using the Format➪Style command works for any style other than Normal. To change the Normal style, you must unfortunately use the Format➪Style command.

Here's the procedure for changing a style without using the Format➪Style command:

1. **Find a paragraph that is formatted with the style you want to change.**
2. **Change its formatting.**

   Use keyboard shortcuts, toolbar buttons, or commands on the Format menu if you must. To change the character format for a style, first select the entire paragraph by triple-clicking it; then apply the character format.

   TIP: Besides triple-clicking, there are other ways to select an entire paragraph. You can double-click in the selection area just to the left of the paragraph. If the style area is revealed, you can click the paragraph's style name in the style area.
3. **Select at least one character in the paragraph.**

   The next step won't work if you simply place the insertion point within the paragraph without actually selecting some text.
4. **Reapply the style to the paragraph.**

   Click the down arrow next to the style list box, or press Ctrl+Shift+S; then click the name of the style.
5. **When the Modify Style dialog box appears, click OK.**

   Figure 4-1 shows the Modify Style dialog box. It presents you with two options: You can either update the style with the changes you've made to the paragraph, or you can discard the changes and reapply the style as it was. Assuming you want to update the style to reflect the changes you've made (that's the default choice), just click OK or press Enter.
6. **Notice how other paragraphs formatted with the same style are changed automatically.**

   Aren't styles great?

TIP: If you fiddle with a paragraph a bit and then decide you liked it the way it was, reapply the style, but pick the second choice in the Reapply Style dialog box (return the formatting of the selection to the style).

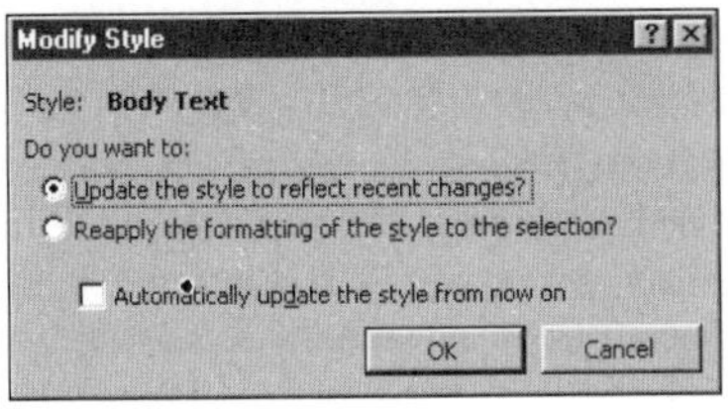

Figure 4-1: The Modify Style dialog box.

In some cases, you might discover that when you make format changes to the text in a paragraph, the style is automatically changed to reflect your formatting changes. This happens when you (or your evil twin) goes into the Format➪Style command and sets the Automatically Update option for the style. When this option is activated, any formatting changes made to a paragraph formatted with the style will be applied to the style automatically. (This is one of several new style features for Word 97.)

Giving in to the Format➪Style Command

So far, I've conveniently avoided the Format➪Style command. I could only put off the inevitable for a short time, however. Now it's time to pay the piper. The following procedure describes how you can use the Format➪Style command to change a style.

1. **Summon the Format➪Style command.**

   Remember how to do this? Simply click the menu commands or press Alt+O and then *S*. The Style dialog box appears, as shown in Figure 4-2.

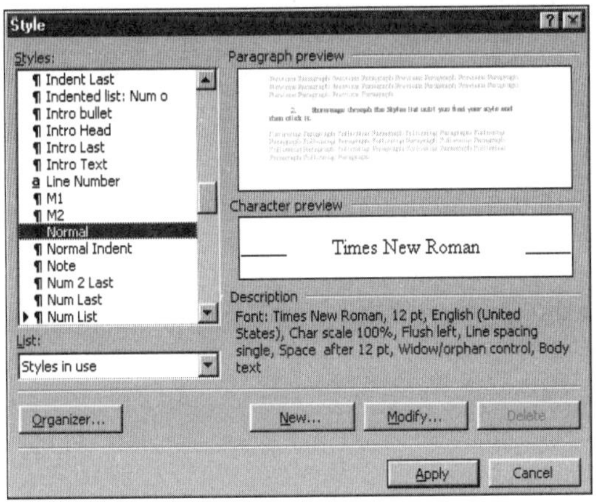

Figure 4-2: The Style dialog box.

2. **Rummage through the Styles list until you find your style and then click it.**

   If you selected a paragraph formatted with the style you want to change before calling up Format⇨Style, that style appears in the Style dialog box. (To find styles quickly, type the first letter of the style you want to find. The style list jumps to the first style that starts with that letter.)

3. **Click Modify.**

   The Modify Style dialog box appears, as shown in Figure 4-3.

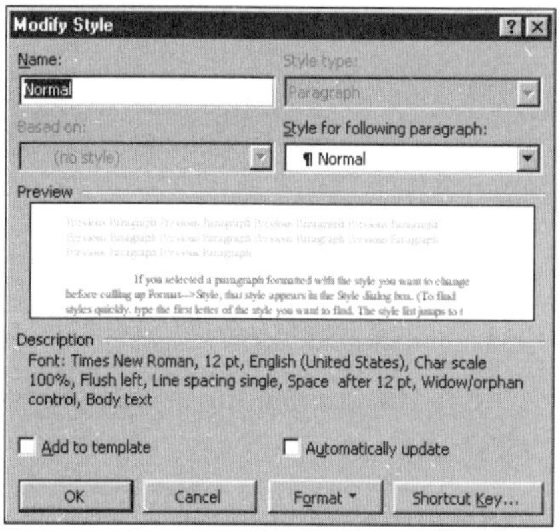

Figure 4-3: The Modify Style dialog box.

4. **Change the format of the style.**

   Click the Format button to reveal the mini-Format menu, shown in Figure 4-4. Choose any of these menu commands to summon an appropriate formatting dialog box. (The dialog boxes that appear when you choose one of these commands are identical to the ones that appear when you choose the corresponding command from the main Format menu.)

5. **After you have made your formatting changes, click OK.**

   Doing so returns you to the Style dialog box. The Cancel button changes to a Close button.

6. **Click Close.**

   The style is updated and any paragraphs formatted with that style are updated to reflect the new style.

If you don't like the results of your style changes, press Ctrl+Z to undo them.

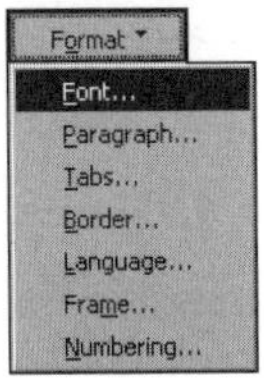

Figure 4-4: The Modify Style dialog box's Format menu.

Deleting a style

Styles can be very useful, so useful in fact that you may soon start creating them at the drop of a hat. Pretty soon, your documents are filled with styles you no longer use. When that happens, it's time to prune your style garden back, deleting styles you no longer use.

Fortunately, deleting styles is easy. Just follow these simple steps:

1. **Conjure up the Format⇨Style command.**
2. **When the Style dialog box appears, choose the style that you want to delete from the Styles list box.**
3. **Click the Delete button.**
4. **That's all!**

When you delete a style, any paragraphs formatted with the style return to Normal style. Styles go in and out of fashion all the time, so don't feel bad about deleting them.

Neat Things to Do with Styles

There's much more to using styles than creating and applying them. The sections that follow chronicle some of the more interesting things you can do with styles.

Assigning shortcut keys to styles

Word enables you to assign keyboard shortcuts to your favorite styles. Then you can apply those styles by simply pressing the keyboard shortcut. There

are two ways to assign keyboard shortcuts: with and without the Format⇨Style command.

To create a keyboard shortcut using the Format⇨Style command, follow these steps:

1. **Conjure up the Format⇨Style command.**
2. **Choose the style that you want to create a shortcut for.**
3. **Click the Modify button.**
4. **When the Modify Style dialog appears, click the Shortcut Key button.**

   The Customize Keyboard dialog box appears, ready for you to assign a keyboard shortcut for the style. (See Figure 4-5.)

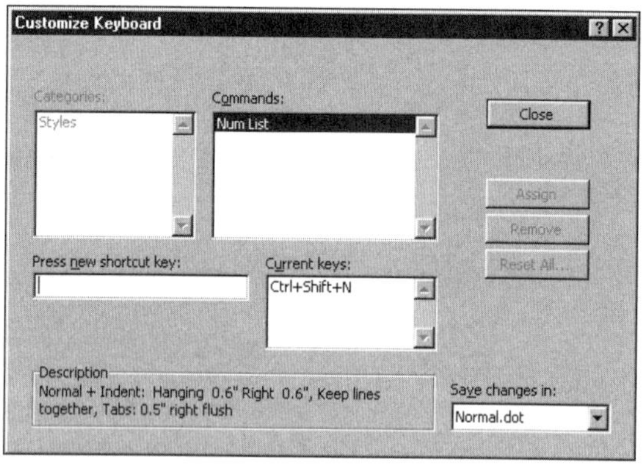

Figure 4-5: Assigning a keyboard shortcut to a style.

5. **Type the keyboard shortcut you want to assign to the style.**

   For example, Ctrl+Shift+N.
6. **Click Assign to assign the keyboard shortcut.**
7. **Click Close; then click OK and then Close again to get all the way out of there.**

To assign a keyboard shortcut without using the Format⇨Style command, follow these steps:

1. **Press Ctrl+Alt+gray plus.**

   That's the gray plus sign key on the numeric keypad, way over at the far right side of the keyboard.

2. **Check out the mouse pointer that looks like a pretzel.**

   Avoid the temptation to douse it with mustard.

3. **Choose the style from the style list box on the Formatting toolbar.**

   Click the down arrow next to the style list box; then click the style you want to assign a shortcut to. Word displays the Customize dialog box, ready for you to type a shortcut.

4. **Type the keyboard shortcut that you want to use.**

   Like Ctrl+Alt+R.

5. **Click Assign to assign the shortcut to the style.**

6. **Click Close; click OK; then click Close.**

   You're done.

Keep these tidbits in mind when using keyboard shortcuts:

- You can assign more than one keyboard shortcut to a style if you want.
- To remove a keyboard assignment you previously assigned, click it in the Current Keys list in the Customize dialog box; then click the Remove button.
- The four predefined paragraph styles already have keyboard shortcuts associated with them:

Shortcut	Style
Ctrl+N	Normal
Ctrl+Alt+1	Heading 1
Ctrl+Alt+2	Heading 2
Ctrl+Alt+3	Heading 3

- You can create keyboard shortcuts using virtually any combination of keys on the keyboard. The shortcuts can utilize the Shift, Ctrl, and Alt keys, either alone or in combination. For example, you could assign Ctrl+K, Alt+K, Ctrl+Shift+K, Ctrl+Alt+K, or even Ctrl+Alt+Shift+K.
- You also can create complex keyboard shortcuts such as Ctrl+Shift+I, 1. To activate this shortcut, the user must press Ctrl+Shift+I; then release those keys and press the 1 key.
- When you type a keyboard shortcut in the Customize dialog box, Word displays the current command assigned to the keyboard shortcut you press. Take note of this assignment to make sure that you aren't

stepping on some other useful function's toes. However, if the keyboard shortcut is preassigned to a Word function you hardly ever use, don't hesitate to use the shortcut for your style.

TIP

- You can also assign styles to toolbar buttons or custom menus. See Chapter 25 for details.

Basing one style on another

Suppose you create 20 different styles for various types of paragraphs in a complicated document, only to discover that your boss wants the entire document to use Palatino rather than Times New Roman as the base font. Do you have to change all 20 styles to reflect the new font? Not if you set your styles up using *base styles*.

A base style is a style that provides formatting information for other styles. For example, suppose you have a style named Bullet List, and you want to create a similar style named Bullet List Last that you use for the last paragraph of a series of bulleted paragraphs. The only difference between Bullet List and Bullet List Last is that Bullet List Last has additional space after the paragraph. Otherwise, the styles are identical. Base styles enable you to do this. In this case, Bullet List Last consists of all the formatting from its base style, Bullet List, plus 6 points of space after.

A style *inherits* all the formats that are specified in its base style. If the base style changes, the changes are inherited, too. However, a style can override the formats that it inherits from the base style. For example, if a style does not specify a point size, any paragraphs formatted with the style inherit the point size from the base style. However, if a style specifies a point size, then the point size of the base style is ignored.

Here's the procedure for creating a style that's based on another style:

1. **Choose the paragraph you want to format.**
2. **Apply the style that you want to use as the base style to the paragraph you selected.**
3. **Change the formatting of the paragraph.**

   Add whatever extra formats you want to be applied to the new style. These formats are added to the base style's formats.
4. **Create the new style.**

See the earlier section "Creating a new style" for help with this step. The new style is based on the style that was originally applied to the paragraph.

TIP: You can also set the base style by using the Format➪Style command. Click Modify on the Style dialog box; then choose the base style in the Based On text box of the Modify Style dialog box.

Any changes you make to a style are automatically reflected in any styles that are based on the style you change. Thus, if all 20 of your paragraph styles are based on the Normal style, you can change the font for all 20 styles simply by changing the font for the Normal style. (Except for any styles that are based on Normal, but they specify their own font to override the font picked up from the Normal style. In that case, those styles retain their own fonts.)

TIP: You can quickly tell what a style's base style is and what additional formats are added to the base style by looking at the style's description displayed at the bottom of the various style dialog boxes. For example, you may see a style description that resembles this one:

```
Normal + Indent: Hanging 0.6  Right 0.6 , Keep Lines
Together, Tab stops 0.5  Right Flush
```

Here, you can tell that this style is based on the Normal style, but adds a hanging indent, Keep Lines Together, and a right tab stop.

TIP: A style does not have to be based on another style. If you don't want a style to be based on another style, use the Format➪Style command, choose the style you want to modify, and click the Modify button. Then change the Based On drop-down list box to "(no style)."

A style that serves as a base style may itself have a base style. For example, Bullet List Last may be based on Bullet List, which in turn may be based on Normal. In that case, the formats from Normal, Bullet List, and Bullet List Last are merged together whenever you apply the style.

Setting the style of the next paragraph

When you press the Enter key to create a new paragraph, the new paragraph normally assumes the same style as the previous paragraph. In some cases, that's exactly what you want it to do. However, for some styles, the style of the following paragraph is almost always a different style. For example, a

paragraph formatted with the Heading 1 style is rarely followed by another Heading 1 paragraph. Instead, a Heading 1 paragraph is usually followed by a Normal paragraph.

Instead of always changing the style assigned to a new paragraph in situations like this, you can specify the style to be assigned to the next paragraph with the Format⇨Style command. Then, when you press Enter, the new paragraph is assigned the style you specified. This little trick can almost completely automate the chore of formatting your documents.

To set the style for a following paragraph, follow these steps:

1. **Conjure up the Format⇨Style command.**

   The Style dialog box appears.

2. **Choose the style you want to modify.**

   Scroll through the list of styles until you find the one you want. For example, Heading 1.

3. **Click the Modify button.**

   The Modify Style dialog box appears.

4. **Choose the style for the next paragraph in the Style for Following Paragraph text box.**

   Click the arrow to reveal a drop-down list of all available styles in the document. Click the one that should ordinarily follow paragraphs formatted with the style you're modifying. For example, Normal.

5. **Click OK.**

   You return to the Style dialog box.

6. **Click Close.**

   You're done.

- Examine the Style for Following Paragraph setting for each of your styles to see whether you can save yourself some work. Heading styles should specify Normal for the following paragraph, as should any other type of paragraph that usually occurs in singles. You may find other styles that should have this field set, too. For example, I have a Chapter Number style that specifies Chapter Title as Style for Following Paragraph.
- This is such a great time-saver that I wish I had about eight more things to add to this short bullet list to make it look more important. But the only thing of note to say here is — just do it!

Viewing style assignments by enabling the style area

If you want to have a bird's-eye view of the styles applied to each paragraph, open up the style area — a narrow band on the left-hand edge of the document window. Figure 4-6 shows what Word looks like with the style area activated.

Follow these simple steps to enable the style area:

1. **Choose the Tools⇨Options command.**

   The Options dialog box appears.

2. **Find the View tab and click it.**

   The Options dialog box has 12 tabs, so you may have to hunt for a moment to find the View tab.

3. **Set the Style Area Width text box to at least 0.6 inch.**

   The Style Area Width text box is located at the bottom left of the dialog box. You can set it to any width you want, but 0.6 inch is just about wide enough to accommodate most style names.

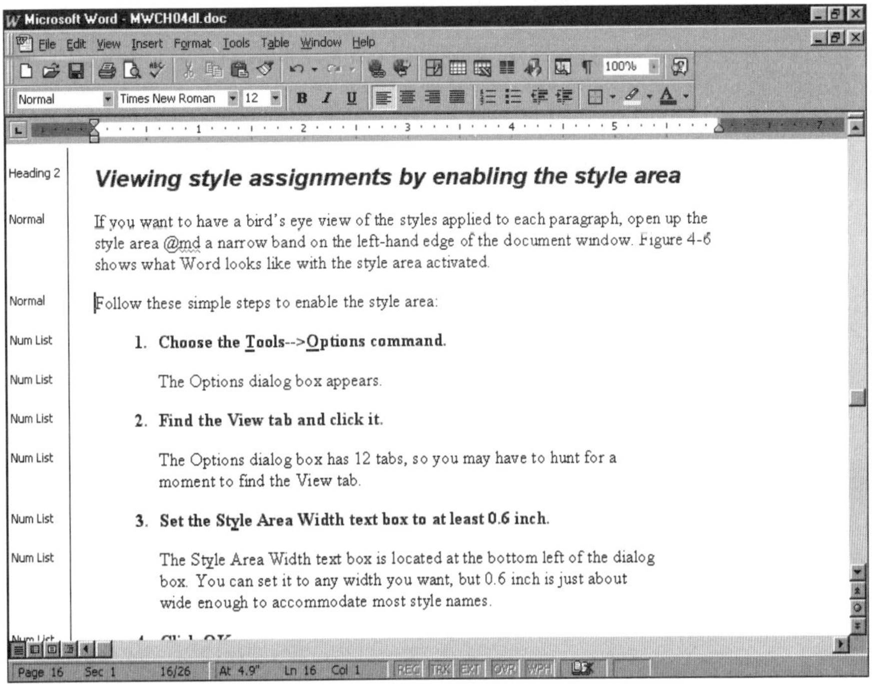

Figure 4-6: Using the style area.

4. **Click OK.**

   The style area should appear.

Here are some helpful hints:

- You can adjust the width of the style area by dragging the line that separates it from the rest of the document window. Just position the mouse over the line and press the mouse button when the pointer changes shape. Drag the line to increase or decrease the width of the style area.
- To remove the style area altogether, drag the line all the way to the left of the window or invoke the Tools➪Options command and set the Style Area Width text box to 0.
- You can select an entire paragraph by clicking the paragraph's style name in the style area.
- The problem with the style area is that it restricts the width of the document window. If you can't see the entire width of your text with the style area enabled, you may want to leave it off. Or, beg your boss for a brand new 17" monitor so that you'll have plenty of room on the screen for the Word document with the style area enabled.
- The style area is visible only in Normal and Outline View. If Word is in Page Layout View when you call up the Tools➪Options command, you won't see the Style Area Width field. Use the View➪Normal or View➪Outline commands to switch to Normal or Outline View.

Automatic Style Definition

One of the new features of Word 97 is the ability to automatically create styles for you based on formatting you apply to text paragraphs. For example, if you start with a Normal paragraph, but then apply a bunch of formatting — say, you center it, change the font, make it bold and italic, Word 97 creates a new style for you, utilizing the formats you applied to the paragraph. You can then use the newly created style to quickly apply the same formatting to other paragraphs.

Word uses the name *Body Text* for the new style. If you already have a Body Text style, the new style is called Body Text 1; if you already have a Body Text 1, Body Text 2 is used, and so on.

Note that this feature works only with paragraphs that are longer than one line. If the paragraph is shorter than one line, Word instead applies one of the built-in heading styles to the paragraph.

If you find this automatic style definition feature annoying (as I do), you can turn it off by following these steps:

1. **Choose the Tools⇨AutoCorrect command.**

   The AutoCorrect dialog box appears.

2. **Click the AutoFormat As You Type tab.**

   The AutoFormat As You Type options appears.

3. **Uncheck the Define styles based on your formatting option.**

4. **Click OK.**

Viewing Formatting by Using the What's This? Command

Unsure about the formatting you applied to a paragraph or character? Fear not. You can use the Help⇨What's This? command to find out which formats have been applied and whether those formats came from a style or were directly applied.

Here's the procedure for examining formats using the What's This? command:

1. **Choose the Help⇨What's This? command.**

   The mouse pointer picks up a question mark riding piggyback.

2. **Click the character whose format you want to examine.**

   If you're interested in the paragraph formatting, click any character in the paragraph. For the formatting applied to a specific character, you must click directly on that character.

3. **Check it out.**

   A big cartoon bubble appears, showing the formats applied to the paragraph and character (see Figure 4-7).

4. **Click Esc when you're done.**

   The bubble vanishes.

The formatting bubble shows paragraph and character formatting separately. The top part of the bubble shows the formatting applied to the paragraph from the paragraph style and applied directly. The bottom part displays the character formatting taken from the paragraph style, the character style (if any), and direct character formatting.

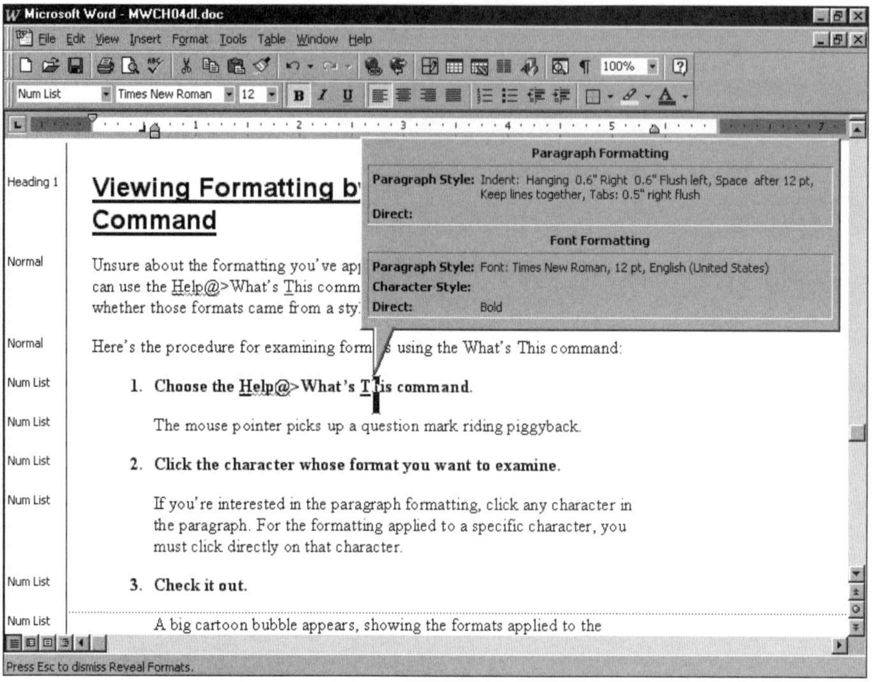

Figure 4-7: Using the What's This? command to examine formats.

- To see formatting information for another character, click again. The What's This? function remains active until you dismiss it by pressing the Esc key.
- Character style? He never said anything about character styles. What's he talking about? (See the next section.)

Creating and using character styles

The vast majority of Word styles are *paragraph styles,* which affect formatting for an entire paragraph. Word has a little-known and seldom-used feature called *character styles,* which enables you to create styles applied to specified characters rather than entire paragraphs.

Here's the blow-by-blow account of how you create a character style:

1. **Summon the Format⇨Style command.**

   The Style dialog box appears.

2. **Click the New button.**

   The New Style dialog box appears, as shown in Figure 4-8.

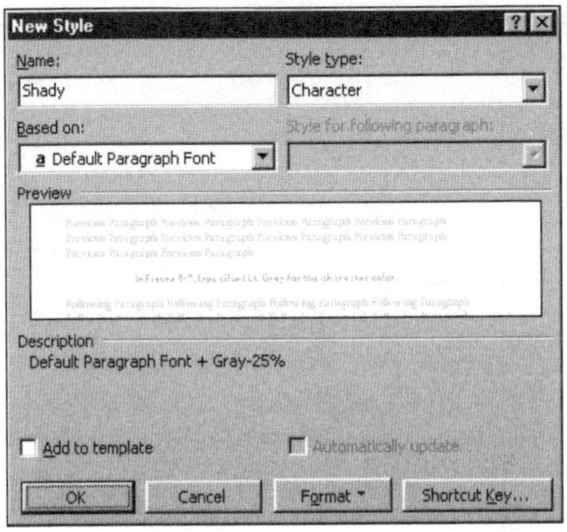

Figure 4-8: Creating a new character style.

3. **Change the Style Type text box to Character.**
4. **Type a name for the new character style in the Name text box.**

   In Figure 4-8, I typed Shady in the Name text box.
5. **Use the Format button to specify the character formats you want for the style.**

   In Figure 4-8, I specified 25% Gray for the character color.
6. **If you want to assign a keyboard shortcut to the style, use the Shortcut Key button.**

   When the Customize dialog box appears, type your shortcut key, click the Assign button, and then click the Close button.
7. **Click OK; then click Close.**

To apply a character style, select the range of characters you want to apply the style to and then apply the style using the style list box on the Formatting toolbar or by typing the keyboard shortcut for the style.

TIP

- Like paragraph styles, you can base character styles on other styles. You can use a special style name, such as *Default Paragraph Font,* to make the character style inherit the font formats of the underlying paragraph style.
- The shady character style is best used in documents written by shady characters.

Don't let me tell you the difference between direct character formats and character styles

The difference between a character style and direct character formatting is subtle. When you assign a new style to a paragraph, any formatting applied by character styles is preserved. Formatting applied by direct character formats (bold, italic, and so on) is usually preserved, but not if you selected a block of characters before applying the new paragraph style, and more than half the characters in the block were directly formatted. In that case, all direct formatting for the paragraph is removed.

If you frequently assign paragraph styles by marking a block of text in the paragraph, and you're annoyed when you lose direct character formatting, consider using character styles instead of direct formatting. Create the following character styles:

Bold text: Default Paragraph Font + Bold, keyboard shortcut Ctrl+B.

Italic text: Default Paragraph Font + Italic, keyboard shortcut Ctrl+I.

Bold Italic text: Default Paragraph Font + Bold Italic, keyboard short cut Ctrl+ Shift+ B.

By specifying Ctrl+B and Ctrl+I as keyboard shortcuts for bold text and italic text, you apply them in exactly the same way that you apply direct bold and italic formatting.

However, the need for a separate bold italic text style points out another difference between character styles and direct character formats. You cannot gang-tackle text with character styles. If you type Ctrl+B to apply the bold text style and then type Ctrl+I to apply the italic text style, the bold format is replaced with the italic format. With direct character formats, the sequence Ctrl+B, Ctrl+I results in bold italic text.

If you use any other character formats routinely, create character styles for them, too. For example, if you frequently use the Strikethrough format, create a Strikethrough character style and assign a keyboard shortcut to it. If you like to interject a little Greek here and there, create a Greek Text character style that sets the font to Symbol and assign it a keyboard shortcut.

Searching for and replacing style formatting

Want to quickly find every paragraph formatted with the Heading 1 style? You can activate the style area and scroll through the document, watching the style area to see whether the Heading 1 style comes up. But there's an easier way: Just use the Edit⇨Find command.

Here's the procedure for finding paragraphs tagged with a particular style:

1. **Invoke the Edit⇨Find command.**

   The keyboard shortcut is Ctrl+F. Either way, the Find dialog box appears.

2. **Click the More button.**

   Additional controls will appear on the Find dialog box.

3. **Click the Format button and then choose the Style command from the pop-up menu.**

   The Find Style dialog box appears, as shown in Figure 4-9.

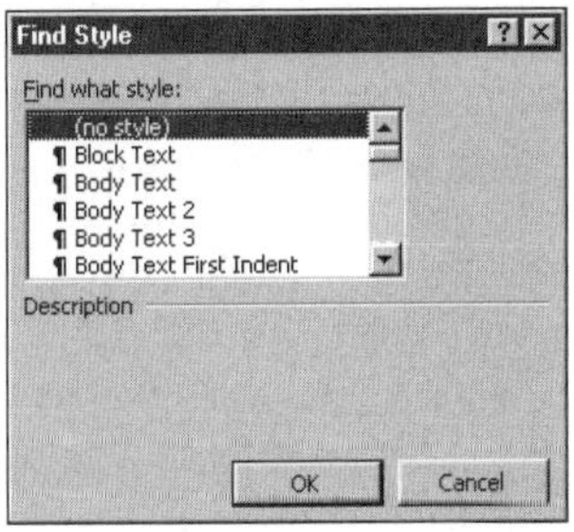

Figure 4-9: The Find Style dialog box.

4. **In the Find Style dialog box, scroll through the list of styles until you locate the one you're looking for. Click it; then click OK.**

   Make sure that the Find What text box in the Find dialog box is blank; otherwise, the Find command searches for specific text that's formatted with the style you specify.

5. **Click the Find Next button to find the next occurrence of the style.**

   Click it again to find the next occurrence. It's like déjà vu all over again.

6. **Press Esc when you're done.**

To replace paragraph styles, follow a similar procedure with the Edit⇨Replace command:

1. **Invoke the Edit⇨Replace command.**

   The keyboard shortcut is Ctrl+H. The Replace dialog box appears.

2. **Click the More button to reveal the additional Replace controls.**

3. **Click in the Find What text box; then use the Format button to choose the style you want to find and replace.**

4. **Click in the Replace With text box; then use the Format button to choose the style you want to replace the Find What style with.**

5. **Click the Find Next button.**

   Word finds the first paragraph formatted with the style you specified and asks whether you want to replace its style.

6. **Click Replace if you want to replace the style.**

   Word replaces the style; then it finds the next paragraph formatted with the style and asks again. If you don't want to replace it, click Find Next. Either way, Word finds the next paragraph and asks again. Keep it up until all paragraphs have been found.

TIP: When replacing one style with another, you can click the Replace All button to have Word replace all occurrences of the style without asking your permission. I suggest you start by clicking Find Next just to make sure that Word is finding and replacing styles the way you intended. After you're sure, click Replace All to finish the laborious Find and Replace operation without your intervention.

WARNING! Make sure that you leave both the Find What and Replace With fields blank. You're looking for all paragraphs formatted with a particular style; it doesn't matter what text is in the paragraphs. If you accidentally leave text in the Replace With text box, Word replaces the entire paragraph with the Replace With text. If that happens, press Ctrl+Z and go fishing.

Storing styles in a template

You can store styles directly in a document file or in a *template* file. When you apply a template to a document, you can copy all the styles in the template into the document, replacing any existing styles with the same name. You can change the entire look of a document simply by applying a different template.

Keep these hints in mind when using templates:

- To store a style in the current template rather than the current document, check the Add to Template button in the New Style dialog box when you use the Format⇨Style command to create the style.
- To copy styles from the document to the template, use the Format⇨Style command and then click the Organizer button.
- To apply a different template to the document, use the File⇨Templates command.
- For much more information about using templates, read ahead to Chapter 5.

Ten Points to Remember about Using Styles

Here are ten (or so) points to remember when you use styles, in no particular order.

Always use styles

This is kind of redundant, because with Word, you *have* to use styles. Whether you realize it or not, all paragraphs in Word are based on a style. If you don't use styles, the paragraphs are based on the utilitarian Normal style.

My point here is that for all but the simplest of documents, create and apply styles instead of applying direct formatting to your paragraphs. In the long run, using styles rather than direct formatting saves you a great deal of time and grief. You may curse the computer while you climb the steep-at-times learning curve that comes along with using styles, but when you get to the top, you'll say to yourself, "That wasn't so hard."

Avoid the Format⇨Style command at all costs

I hate the Format⇨Style command. It's much easier to create styles by example: Format a paragraph, click in the style list box on the Formatting toolbar, and type a new style name. To apply a style, use a keyboard shortcut or choose the style name from the style list box.

The Format⇨Style command is useful in the following circumstances:

- You want to assign a keyboard shortcut to a style, or you can't remember that Ctrl+Alt+gray plus is the shortcut.
- You want to specify a style for the following paragraph.
- You want to use a different base style.
- You want to delete a style.

You can perform most other routine style chores more easily without the Format⇨Style command.

Check out the templates that come with Word

Microsoft has already done a great deal of the hard work creating styles for you. Check out the various templates that come with Word to see whether any of them are suitable. If not, pick one that's close and modify it to suit your needs. For a bunch of information on using templates, check out Chapter 5.

Use the Style for Following Paragraph field to automate your formatting

The fastest way to assign styles is to have Word do it automatically. Set the Style for Following Paragraph field in the Modify Style or New Style dialog box. Then, when you press the Enter key to create a new paragraph, Word automatically assigns the style.

Use keyboard shortcuts to assign styles quickly

The second fastest way to assign styles is to use keyboard shortcuts. Assign a keyboard shortcut to each style that you use frequently. Don't bother with the ones you use infrequently, though. It's hard enough to remember the keyboard shortcuts that you use frequently.

Use the built-in Heading 1, Heading 2, and Heading 3 styles for your headings

Word has three predefined heading styles. If you don't like the way they look, redefine them. By using Heading 1, Heading 2, and Heading 3, you can work with your headings in Outline view or use them to create a table of contents. (See Chapters 7 and 19 for more information.)

Base all text variants on the Normal style

Most documents have several different types of paragraphs that are minor variations on normal text. For example, the bullet-list paragraphs in this book are variations of the book's normal-text paragraphs: They have the same typeface, point size, and line spacing, but the margins are different and they have bullets. Paragraphs like this should be formatted with styles that are based on the Normal style. That way, if you decide to make a sweeping change, such as moving from 10 to 11 point type or switching from Times New Roman to Palatino, you can change the Normal style rather than changing each style individually.

Use Space Before or Space After, but not both

When you create your paragraph styles, decide in advance whether you prefer to add extra space before or after the paragraphs. As much as possible, stick to your decision. If you have two adjacent paragraphs, the first with extra space after and the second with space before, you may end up with more space than you intended between the paragraphs.

Chapter 5

More Template Temptations

In This Chapter

- Understanding templates
- Applying a template to a document
- Creating a new template
- Using global templates
- Using the Organizer to move stuff between templates

A *template* is not a place of worship, though an occasional sacrifice to the Word gods may make your word-processing life a bit easier. Rather, a template is a special type of Word document that holds styles, boilerplate text, macros, keyboard shortcuts, and other customized Word settings.

You can probably get by for years without knowing or caring about templates, but a solid understanding of what templates are and how they work helps remove the shroud of mystery from many of Word's most useful features, especially styles. As a result, this chapter presents the basics of working with templates: what they are, how to create them, and how to use them.

Understanding Templates

A template is a special type of document file used as the basis for formatting your documents. Whenever you create a new document, a template file is used as the starting point for the new document. The following items are copied from the template into the new document:

- The template's styles
- Margins and other page layout information specified in the File⇨Page Setup command, including paper size and orientation, headers and footers, and so on
- Columns set by the Format⇨Columns command

- AutoText entries
- Text and graphics
- Macros
- Keyboard shortcuts, as well as menu and toolbar customizations

A template is really no different than a normal document, except that it is saved with a filename extension of DOT rather than DOC, as normal documents are. You can open a template and edit it just as you can any other document, and you can convert a document to a template simply by saving it as a template rather than as a document. The real difference between templates and documents is in how they are used.

TIP

Each document has one and only one template attached to it. If you don't specify a template to attach to a new document, Word attaches the generic template normal.dot, which contains the standard styles such as Normal, Heading 1, Heading 2, and Heading 3, plus default margins, keyboard shortcuts, toolbars, and so on. You can attach a different template to a document later, and you can copy the styles from the new template into the existing document, if you wish. Then you have access to the styles from the new template as well as the existing document.

The normal.dot template is always available in Word, even if you're working with a document that's based on some other template. Computer nerds call normal.dot a *global template.* (Computer nerds love the term *global* because they have visions of dominating the planet someday.)

Attaching Templates to Your Documents

Before you get into templates too deep, here's a quick review of the basics of attaching templates to your documents.

Creating a new document based on a template

To create a document based on a template other than normal.dot, follow these steps:

1. **Conjure up the File⇨New command.**

   You are greeted by the ever-familiar New dialog box, shown in Figure 5-1.

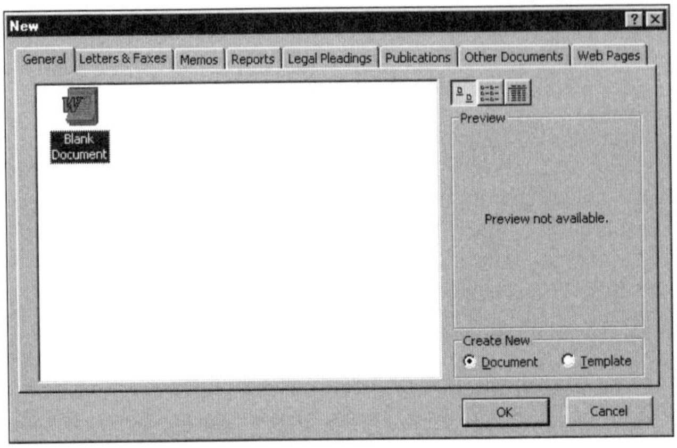

Figure 5-1: The New dialog box.

2. **Select the template you want to base the new document on.** If the template doesn't appear in the New dialog box, click one of the tabs that appears at the top of the dialog box.
3. **Click OK.**

   You're done.

If you create a new document using the New button on the Standard toolbar or the Ctrl+N shortcut, Word automatically assigns the normal.dot template. The only way to create a new document based on a different template is to wade through the murky menu waters.

If you choose the Blank Document template, which appears under the General tab of the New dialog box, your document is created using the normal.dot template. I guess someone at Microsoft decided that showing the Normal.dot template in the New dialog box would be confusing, so they call normal.dot Blank Document here.

When you create a new document, any text or graphics that appears within the template is copied into the new document. This is a great way to include a letterhead in all your letters, a standard header in all your memos, a title on all your reports, and so on. When you attach a different template to an existing document (see the next section), text and graphics contained in the template are *not* copied into the document.

TIP

If you pick a wizard rather than a template from the New dialog box, the wizard leads you through a series of prompts to gather information about the document that you want to create. It then creates the document for you. When the wizard is finished, the document is fully formatted and loaded with styles, but it is based on the Normal template. In this case, the formatting and styles are created by the wizard, not drawn from a template.

The Letter Wizard

Word comes with a colorful collection of Wizards. The most useful is the Letter Wizard, which is found in the New dialog box under the Letters & Faxes tab. To summon this wizard, choose File⇨New, click the Letters & Faxes tab, then double-click Letter Wizard.wiz.

The Letter Wizard starts by asking if you want to create just one letter or if you want to do a mail merge. If you choose to do a single letter, a Letter Wizard creates a skeleton letter for you, then displays a dialog box that allows you to select one of several letter formats and prompts you through the process of filling in the standard parts of the letter, such as the Recipient name and address, greeting, and salutation. But if you elect to do a mail merge, the Letter Wizard calls up the Mail Merge Helper (which is described in detail in Chapter 8).

Because the Letter Wizard is so popular, Microsoft decided that they should include a link to it directly on the Tools menu. In Word 97, you can invoke the Letter Wizard by choosing the Tools⇨Letter Wizard command. This Letter Wizard is actually a scaled back version of the one accessed from the File⇨New command. The Tools⇨Letter Wizard command takes you directly to a dialog box that steps you through the process of creating a single letter. You are not given the choice of doing a mail merge.

Sometimes the Letter Wizard appears all by itself, too. Word 97 watches as you type, and if it thinks you are typing a letter, the Office Assistant (the animated help feature that is new in Word 97) appears, offering to help you type the letter. If you agree that you need help with the letter, the Letter Wizard appears.

Attaching a different template

If you decide that you want to change the template assigned to a document, follow these steps:

1. **Fire up the Tools⇨Templates and Add Ins command.**

   You are greeted by the Templates and Add-ins dialog box, shown in Figure 5-2.

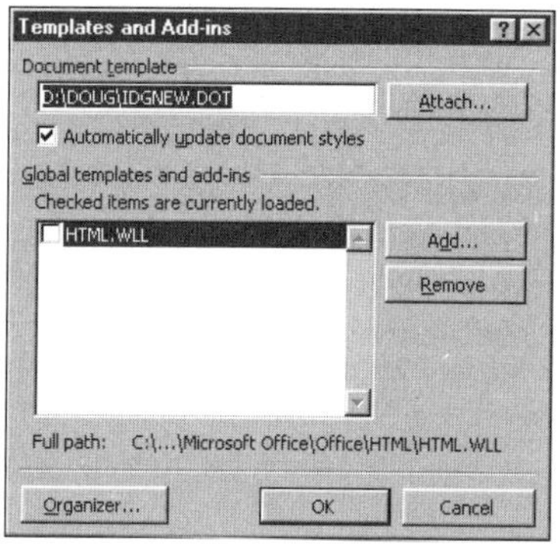

Figure 5-2: The Templates and Add-ins dialog box.

2. **Click the Attach button.**

   A dialog box listing available templates appears.

3. **Choose the template that you want to attach.**

   You may have to rummage around your disk a bit to find the template you want.

4. **Click Open to return to the Templates and Add-ins dialog box.**

5. **If you want to copy styles from the new template, check the Automatically update document styles check box in the Templates and Add Ins dialog box.**

   If you leave this box unchecked, the styles from the new template are ignored. Usually, the reason you're attaching a new template is to get its styles, so you probably want to check this box.

6. **Click OK.**

   You're done. If you updated styles, the results of attaching the new template should be immediately apparent as the paragraphs are reformatted according to the new styles.

Here are some idiosyncrasies about using templates that you should know:

TIP

- When you attach a different template to an existing document, text and graphics from the template are not copied into the document. To include text and graphics from a template, create a new document based on the template.
- If you want to see the effects of applying styles from a template without actually attaching the template, use the Format⇨Style Gallery command. It displays a preview of your document formatted with styles from a template you choose. From the gallery, you can copy styles into your document from a template, but you can't actually attach the template to your document. To do that, you must note the name of the template you want to attach, exit the gallery (click Cancel), and then use the Tools⇨Templates and Add Ins command to attach the template.
- The Organizer button whisks you off to the Organizer, the ultimate tool for managing templates. The Organizer is described in detail later in this chapter, in the section "Using the Organizer."

Creating Your Own Templates

If you're not content with the templates provided with Word, you can create your own. The sections that follow explain the ins and outs of creating templates.

Creating a new template to store your styles

Let's say you've toiled for hours on a document, and now you want to make its styles available to other documents that you may someday create. The simplest solution is to create a template that contains the styles in your document. Here's how:

1. **Open the document that has all the styles you want to save in a template.**
2. **Invoke the File➪Save As command.**

   The Save As dialog box appears.
3. **Way down at the bottom of the Save As dialog box, find the Save File as Type drop-down list box. Choose Document Template as the file type.**
4. **Choose the folder in which you wish to store the template.**

   If you want to create a new folder for the template, click the Create New Folder button and type a name for the new folder.
5. **Type a filename for the template.**

   Don't forget that, with Windows 95, you aren't limited to eight characters anymore. So instead of SLSRPT.DOT, you can use a more meaningful name such as Sales Report.dot.
6. **Click OK.**

   The document is saved as a template file.
7. **Delete unnecessary text from the file.**

   Press Ctrl+A to select the entire document and then press Del to delete it. Or, if you prefer, leave a small amount of boilerplate text behind.

   All the text that you leave in the document appears in your new document when you use the template to create a new document.
8. **Save the file again.**

   Click the Save button on the Standard toolbar or press Ctrl+S.

Don't forget that besides text and styles, templates also store page setups, column settings, keyboard shortcuts, macros, and toolbars.

Creating a new template from scratch

To create a new template from scratch, follow these steps:

1. **Use the File⇨New command.**

   The New File dialog box appears.

2. **Choose the Template radio button.**

   That way, Word creates a new template rather than a new document file.

3. **If you want the new template to be based on an existing template, select the existing template now.**

   Otherwise, base the new template on normal.dot (Blank Document).

4. **Click OK.**

5. **Create whatever styles you want to include in the template.**

   See Chapter 4 for detailed instructions on creating styles.

6. **Type some text if you want to include boilerplate text in your template.**

7. **Save the file.**

   Use the File⇨Save command. Type a name for the template and click Save.

8. **Close the file.**

   Use the File⇨Close command.

Modifying an existing template

If you want to create a template that's similar to an existing template, the easiest way is to open the template and save your modifications under a new name. Here's the procedure:

1. **Invoke the File⇨Open command.**

   Or click the Open button or press Ctrl+O. The Open dialog box appears.

2. **Change the List Files of Type field to Document Templates (*.DOT).**

3. **Find the template that you want to model the new template on.**

   You may have to switch to the \MSOffice\Templates folder or the folder that contains your templates.

4. **Open it.**

   Click the template file; then click Open.

Boring details about where to store templates

By default, Word 97 stores its templates in the \Program Files\Microsoft Office \Templates folder. But how does Word know how to divvy up the templates among the zillions of tabs that appear across the top of the New dialog box? The answer is actually pretty easy: Each of those tabs represents a folder within the Templates folder. Thus, the memo templates are located in \Program Files\Microsoft Office\Templates\Memos, and the Letter templates are located in \Program Files\Microsoft Office\Templates \Letters.

You can change the location where templates are stored by calling up the Tools⇨Options command, clicking the File Locations tab, and double-clicking the User Templates option.

You can also specify a location for Workgroup Templates, which are templates that can be accessed via a network. This comes in handy if you and other network users need to share a set of common templates. In that case, place the common templates on a network file server, then use the Workgroup Templates option under the File Locations tab to indicate the location of the shared templates.

When you create your own templates, you can store them in one of four locations:

1. In \Program Files\Microsoft Office\ Templates, so that they appear along with "Blank Document" (that is, Normal.dot) under the General tab. This is probably the best place to store your templates, especially if you only need a few. (If you need more than a few custom templates, you may be beyond help anyway.)
2. In one of the existing folders under \Program Files\Microsoft Office\Templates. For example, if you create a template named Angry Letter to The Editor.dot, store it in \Program Files\Microsoft Office\Templates \Letters & Faxes folder. That way, the new template appears with your other letter templates under the Letters & Faxes tab.
3. In a new folder. Click the Create New Folder button when you save the template. The folder you create appears as a tab in the New dialog box.
4. In the folder indicated by the Workgroup Templates option under Tools⇨Options. Templates in this folder is merged with the Templates folder when the New dialog box is displayed.

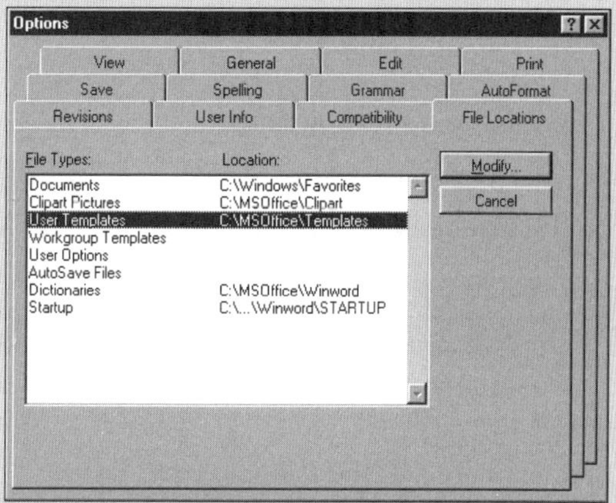

5. **Use the File➪Save As command to save the template under a new name.**

   It's best to do this step before you make any modifications. That way, you don't run the risk of accidentally changing the existing template on disk.

6. **Make your changes.**

   Use the Format➪Style command to modify the styles, and make any other changes you want to the template.

7. **Save your changes.**

   Press Ctrl+S or click the Save button.

8. **Close the file.**

   Use the File➪Close command.

Using Global Templates

The normal.dot template is a *global template,* which means that it is always available when you're working in Word, even if you're working with a document that is attached to a different template. You can specify that other templates become global ones, too, so that they are available even if you're not working with a document that's attached to them.

The styles and text contained in a global template are not available unless the current document is attached to that template. However, any macros, AutoText entries, toolbars, and customized menus are available whenever the global template is active.

Follow these steps to activate a global template:

1. **Summon the Tools➪Templates and Add Ins command.**

   The Templates and Add-ins dialog box appears.

2. **Locate the Global Templates and Add-ins list box.**

   It contains a list of all the currently available global templates, along with buttons to Add or Remove global templates.

3. **Click the Add button.**

   The Add Templates dialog box appears.

4. **Choose the template that you want to make global; then click OK.**

   When you return to the Templates and Add-ins dialog box, the template you chose appears in the Global Templates and Add-ins list box.

5. Click OK.

You're done.

Some tidbits about global templates follow:

- To disable a global template temporarily, conjure up the File➪Templates command and uncheck the template's check box in the Global Templates and Add-ins list box. To remove the template from the list, choose it and click the Remove button.
- After you've made a template global, it remains global until you quit Word. The next time you start Word, the template is included in the Global Templates and Add-ins list box, but its check box is unchecked so that it is not active. To activate the template to make it global, use the File➪Templates command and check the template's check box. See the sidebar, "Stop me before I tell you about the startup directory," to find out how to set up a global template that's active each time you start Word.
- It's best not to mix global templates and templates attached to documents. If you want to create a bunch of custom macros, toolbars, and menus for global use, place them in a separate template that you don't use for documents.

Stop me before I tell you about the startup directory

When you add a template to the Global Templates and Add-ins list, the template remains in the list each time you start Word. However, you must use the Tools➪Templates and Add Ins command and check the check box next to the template in the list to make the template global. If you don't want to do that each time you start Word, follow these steps:

1. Exit Word using the File➪Exit command.
2. Double-click on the My Computer icon on your desktop. Navigate to the folder that contains the template you want to make global.
3. Double-click on My Computer again to open a second My Computer window. Double-click on the C drive, then navigate to the \Program Files\Microsoft Office\Office\Startup folder.
4. Drag any templates you want to be global ones from the template folder to the Startup folder. Use the right mouse button to drag the template. When you release the right mouse button, a pop-up menu will appear; choose the Create Shortcut Here command when this pop-up menu appears.
5. Close both My Computer windows and then start Word.

Any template files in the \Program Files\Microsoft Office\Office\Winword\Startup folder are automatically loaded and made global. If you previously added the template to the Global Templates and Add-ins list, you should remove it before following the preceding procedure.

Using the Organizer

If you want to move styles en masse from one document or template to another, the easiest way to do it is to use the Organizer — Word's tenacious tool for taming templates. The organizer is especially useful when you create several new styles in a document and you want to copy those files to the document's template.

To copy styles from your document to a template, follow these steps:

1. **Summon the Format⇨Style command.**

   The Style dialog box appears.

2. **Click the Organizer button.**

   The Organizer dialog box, shown in Figure 5-3, appears.

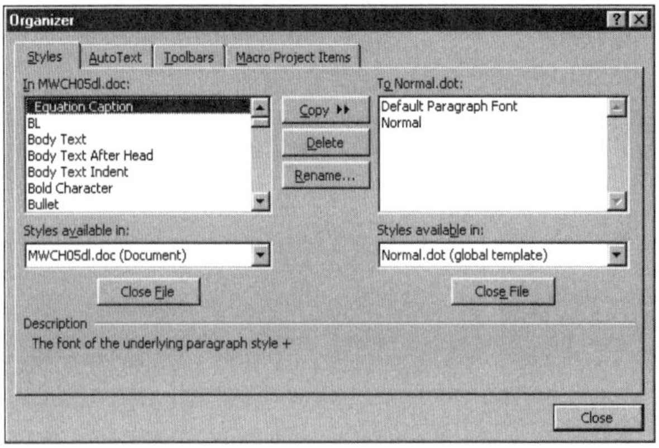

Figure 5-3: The Organizer dialog box.

3. **If you want to copy styles to a template other than normal.dot, click the right Close File button, click the Open File button, select the template file, and click Open.**

4. **Choose the styles you want to copy in the left style list (the In list box).**

   To choose several styles, hold down the Ctrl key while clicking style names. To choose a block of styles, click the first style in the block; then hold down the Shift key and click the last style.

5. **Click the Copy button.**

   The styles are copied from the document to the template.

6. **Click the Close button.**

The Organizer is a helpful beast:

- You can copy styles from either list in the Organizer dialog box. If you choose styles in the right box, the In and To designations switch and the arrows on the Copy button change to indicate that styles are copied from the right list to the left list.
- To move styles from the current document to normal.dot, skip Step 3 in the preceding procedure.
- Click the down arrow next to the Styles available in list box on the left side of the Organizer dialog box to reveal a list of style sources that includes the current document, the currently attached style, and normal.dot. To move styles from the attached template to normal.dot, choose the template in the Styles available in list.
- TIP: You can also use the Organizer to delete or rename styles. To delete styles, choose them in either the left or right list; then click the Delete button. If you've been good, Word asks for confirmation before it deletes the styles. To rename a style, choose it and click the Rename button. When Word asks for a new name, start typing. (Notice that you can rename only one style at a time.)
- The Organizer is also handy for copying AutoText, toolbars, and macros from one template to another. Just click the appropriate Organizer tab and have at it.

Chapter 6

More Bullet and Number Morsels

In This Chapter

- Creating bulleted lists or numbered lists the easy way
- Allowing Word to automatically format bulleted and numbered lists
- Using deviant bullets
- Using crazy numbering schemes
- Creating an outline list

Bullets and numbered lists are great ways to add emphasis to a series of important points or to add a sense of order to items that fall into a natural sequence. Glance through this book and you see what I mean. It's loaded with bulleted and numbered lists.

In Word, you can add a bullet or a line number to each paragraph. The bullet or number is a part of the paragraph format, and Word adds the bullet character or the number so that you don't have to. Word even keeps the numbers in a numbered list in sequence, so if you add or delete a paragraph or rearrange paragraphs in the list, the numbers are automatically reordered.

For Word 97, Microsoft put a lot of time and effort into rewriting the underlying *engine* that powers the bullets and numbering feature. Microsoft didn't add any new features to the bullets and numbering feature, but they managed to clean up a number of bugs that plagued earlier versions of Word. As a result, the bullets and numbering feature is more useful than ever before.

The Easy Way to Create a Bulleted or Numbered List

Nothing is easier than clicking a toolbar button, and that's about all there is to creating a simple bulleted or numbered list. With the click of a button, you can create a bulleted list like this one:

- Cheery disposition
- Rosy cheeks
- No warts
- Plays games, all sorts

Click another button, and you transform the whole thing into a numbered list:

1. Cheery disposition
2. Rosy cheeks
3. No warts
4. Plays games, all sorts

Do *not* type bullet characters (either asterisks or special Wingdings characters) or numbers yourself. Instead, use the following procedures to create bulleted or numbered lists.

Creating a bulleted list the easy way

To create a bulleted list, follow this procedure:

1. **Type one or more paragraphs that you want to add bullets to.**
2. **Select the paragraphs that you want to add bullets to by clicking and dragging the mouse over them.**

3. **Click the Bullet button on the Formatting toolbar (shown in the margin).**
4. **You're done.**

When you create a bulleted list this way, Word uses a default bullet character (normally a small dot) and creates a $^{1}/_{4}$-inch hanging indent. (If the paragraphs already have hanging indents, the original indentation settings are preserved.) To learn how to use oddball bullets, find the section "Using Deviant Bullets" later in this chapter.

Here are a few additional tricks for bulleting your lists:

- To add additional items to the bulleted list, position the cursor at the end of one of the bulleted paragraphs and press Enter. Because the bullet is part of the paragraph format, it is carried over to the new paragraph.
- You can remove bullets as easily as you add them. The Bullet button works like a toggle: Press it once to add bullets, press it again to remove them. To remove bullets from an entire list, select all the paragraphs in the list and click the Bullet button.
- TIP: Ever notice how the good guys never run out of bullets in the movies? Bad idea. The old notion of the six shooter is a pretty good one. Placing more than six bullets in a row pushes the limits of just about any reader's patience. (Of course, I've routinely disregarded that advice throughout this book, but what are you going to do, shoot me?)
- Oh, and by the way, you probably shouldn't leave one bullet standing by itself. Bullets are used to mark items in a list, and it takes more than one item to make a list.
- If you want to create a bulleted list as you go, start by formatting the first paragraph with a bullet. Then, when you press Enter to start the next paragraph, the new paragraph will automatically be formatted as a part of the bullet list. When you're done, press Enter and then click the Bullet button again to deactivate bullets.
- TIP: Without doubt, the best way to work with bullets is to create a bullet style. This way, you can customize the bullet style all you want. With a bit of work, you can even mimic the check mark and gray-line look of the bullets in this book or create your own custom bullet design. Assign a keyboard shortcut such as Ctrl+Shift+B to your custom bullet style, and you're on your way.

Creating a numbered list the easy way

To create a numbered list, follow this procedure:

1. **Type one or more paragraphs that you want numbered.**
2. **Select them all.**

   Drag the mouse over all the paragraphs you want numbered.
3. **Click the Numbering button on the Formatting toolbar.**
4. **That's all!**

When you use the Numbering button to create a numbered list, Word uses a default numbering format and establishes a 1/4-inch hanging indent for each paragraph. (If the paragraphs are already formatted with hanging indents, the original indentation settings are kept.) You can use all sorts of crazy numbering schemes if you want; to find out how, skip ahead to the section "Using Crazy Numbering Schemes."

Word is really cool about keeping the list in order. If you add or delete a paragraph in the middle of the list, Word renumbers the paragraphs to preserve the order. If you add a paragraph to the end of the list, Word assigns the next number in sequence to the new paragraph.

The Numbering button works like a toggle: Click it once to add numbers to paragraphs, click it again to remove them. To remove numbering from a numbered paragraph, select the paragraph and click the Numbering button. To remove numbering from an entire list, select all the paragraphs in the list and click the Numbering button.

Automatic Bullets and Numbers

Word's AutoFormat feature can create bulleted and numbered lists automatically whenever Word determines that you are trying to create a bullet or numbered list. Specifically:

- Word automatically formats text as a bulleted list whenever you begin a paragraph with an asterisk, period, or hyphen followed by a space or tab.
- Word automatically formats text as a numbered list whenever you type a number followed by a period, hyphen, right parenthesis, or greater-than sign (>) and a space or tab.

If you do not want this automatic formatting to occur, call up the Tools⇨AutoCorrect command, click the AutoFormat As You Type tab, and uncheck the Automatic bulleted lists and Automatic numbered lists options.

Using Deviant Bullets

If you don't like the default bullet format that you get when you click the Bullet button, change it! Here's how:

1. **Invoke the Format⇨Bullets and Numbering command.**

   The Bullets and Numbering dialog box appears, as shown in Figure 6-1. This dialog box has three tabs. If the bullet options don't appear, click the Bulleted tab to bring them forth. The Bulleted tab presents six possible bullet formats.

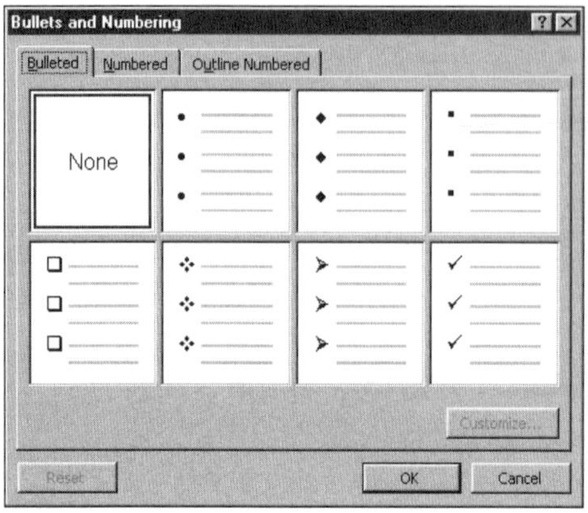

Figure 6-1: The Bullets and Numbering dialog box (Bulleted tab).

2. **If one of the seven bullet formats shown in the dialog box suits your fancy, click it and then click OK. You're done.**
3. **Otherwise, click one of the bullet formats, then click the Customize button.**

   The Customize Bulleted List dialog box appears, as shown in Figure 6-2.

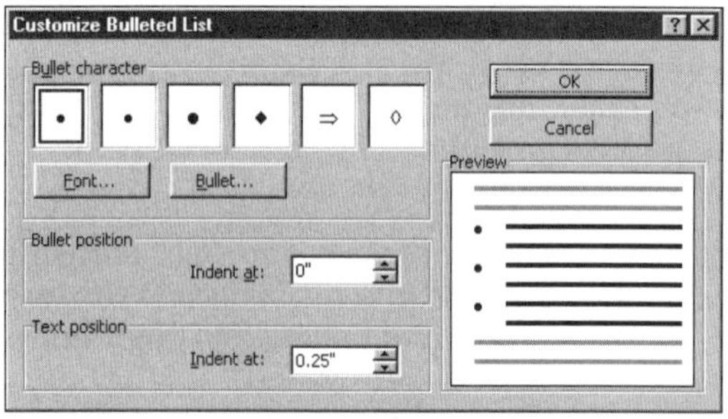

Figure 6-2: The Customize Bulleted List dialog box.

4. **Modify the bullet format as you see fit.**

   Play with the bullet character, font settings, bullet position, and text position. As you play, the preview box shows you how your bulleted list appears.
5. **If you don't like any of the bullet characters shown in the Modify Bulleted List dialog box, click the Bullet button.**

   The symbol dialog box appears.
6. **Pick the bullet character you want; then click OK.**

   TIP: You can change the fonts displayed by choosing a different font from the the Symbols From list box: You find the best bullet characters in the Wingdings font. Click the character you want to use and then click OK.

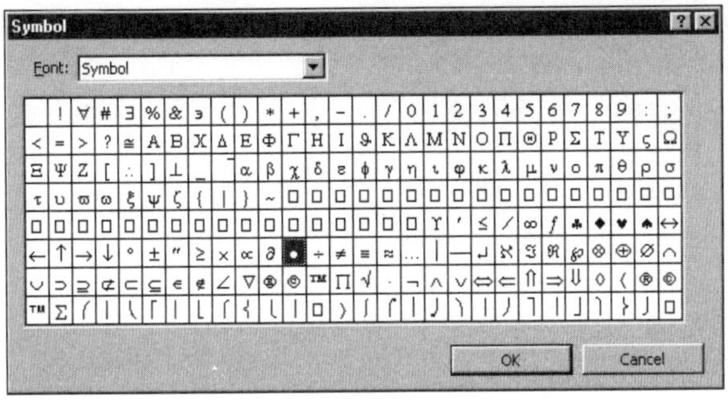

Figure 6-3: The Symbol dialog box.

7. **OK your way back to the document.**

   Click OK to return to the document and to see the results of your bullet formatting efforts.

TIP

This is a lot of work, isn't it? Better do it once and then save it in a style.

Keep these points in mind when changing your bullets:

- If the characters in the Symbol dialog box seem too small to read, fear not. When you click one of them, Word blows it up about four times normal size so that you can see it.
- The Wingdings font, which comes with Windows 95, is filled with great bullet characters: pointing fingers, smiley faces, grumpy faces, thumbs up, thumbs down, peace signs for folks who were at Woodstock, time bombs, and a skull and crossbones. (Yo ho, yo ho, a pirate's life for me!)
- You can apply any font formatting options you want to the bullet character by clicking the Font button. This brings up the normal Font dialog box, which was described in detail back in Chapter 3.

Using Crazy Numbering Schemes

Most of us like to count 1, 2, 3, and so on. But some people count A, B, C, or maybe I, II, III, like a Roman. Not to fear. With Word, you can count just about any way you like.

Follow these prudent steps to create your own crazy numbering schemes:

1. **Invoke the Format⇨Bullets and Numbering command.**

   The Bullets and Numbering dialog box appears. Figure 6-4 shows the Bullets and Numbering dialog box with the Numbered tab up front. (If the Numbered tab isn't showing, click it.)

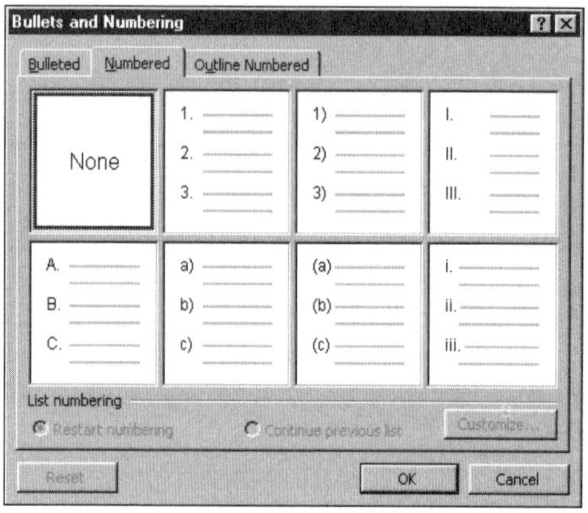

Figure 6-4: The Bullets and Numbering dialog box with the Numbering options shown.

2. **If one of the seven numbering formats shown in the dialog box is acceptable, click it; then click OK.**

   You're home free.

3. **Otherwise, select one of the numbering schemes and click Customize.**

   The Customize Numbered List dialog box appears, as shown in Figure 6-5.

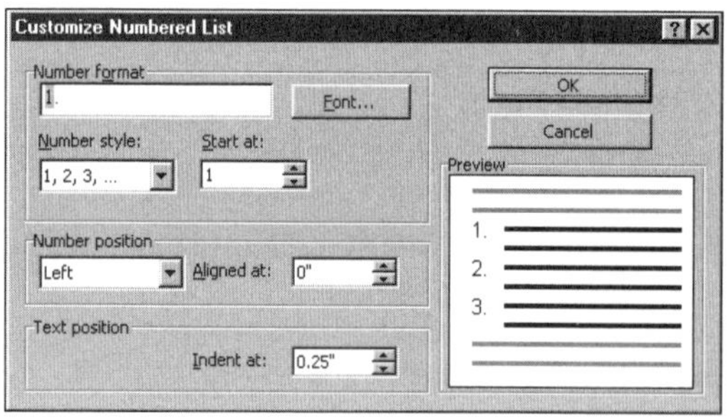

Figure 6-5: The Customize Numbered List dialog box.

4. **Modify the numbering scheme to suit your fancy.**

   You can type text to be included before and after the number, change the number format, and play with the indentation.

5. **Click OK.**

   Happy numbering!

I wouldn't want to do this more than once. Put it in a style so that you can call up your hard-earned number format with the touch of a key (see chapter 4 for the low-down on styles).

Keep these points in mind when using numbered lists:

- Besides normal number formats like 1, 2, 3 . . . or A, B, C . . . or I, II, III . . ., you can specify One, Two, Three . . .; 1st, 2nd, 3rd; or even First, Second, Third as the number format. Believe it or not, these oddball formats work even with unreasonably long lists. Try it and see for yourself: Word knows how to spell one thousand one hundred eighty-seventh. It also knows that the Roman numeral equivalent is MCLXXXVII. Isn't that amazing?
- You can add text that will appear before or after the number by typing the text into the Number format text box. Note that the number itself is shown in the Number format text box with a gray background.
- If you want to specify a different font for the numbers, click the Font button when the Modify Numbered List dialog box appears. The font is applied not only to the number but also to any text that appears before or after the number.

Creating an Outline List

You can create compulsive outline lists that would satisfy even the most rigid anthropology professor using Word's numbering feature. I wouldn't wish this task on anyone, but if you must create these types of lists, this feature is a godsend.

Here's an outline of the procedure for creating a multilevel list (I created my own outline list in the text for a visual example):

1. **Type the text that you want to make into an outline list.**

   a) Type the top-level paragraphs as you normally do.

   b) Don't worry about numbers yet.

2. Adjust indentation using the Increase and Decrease buttons to reflect numbering levels.

a) Use the Increase Indent button to create second- or third-level paragraphs.

b) Use the Decrease Indent button to promote a paragraph to a higher numbering level.

3. Use the Format⇨Bullets and Numbering command, then click the Outline Numbered tab to apply the outline list format.

a) The Outline Numbered tab of the Bullets and Numbering dialog box appears, as shown in Figure 6-6.

b) Click the outline numbering format that you like.

c) Click OK.

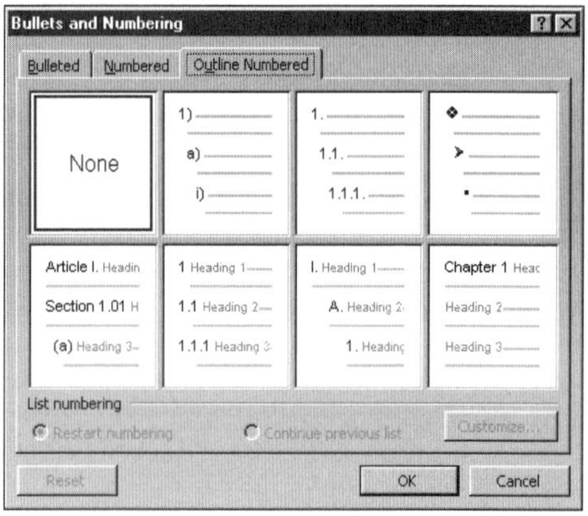

Figure 6-6: The Outline Numbered tab of the Bullets and Numbering dialog box.

4. To create a custom outline numbering scheme, select one of the outline numbered formats, then click the Customize button.

a) The Customize Outline Numbered List dialog box appears, as shown in
Figure 6-7.

b) This dialog box enables you to customize each level of an outline list.

c) The Level box indicates which level is shown. To change levels, move the scroll bar.

d) You can format each level as a bullet or a number. Choose the bullet or number format from the Bullet or Number drop-down list box.

e) When you've had enough, click OK.

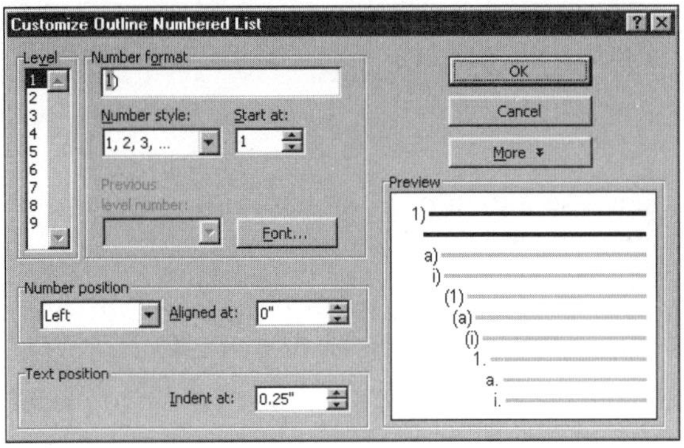

Figure 6-7: The Customize Outline List dialog box.

Here are some notes on outline lists:

TIP

- You can create styles for bulleted or numbered lists, but not for outline lists. Too bad.
- The outline list feature is good for small lists with two or three levels. But if what you really want to do is create an outline, use the Outline feature instead. See Chapter 7 for details on how to create an outline.
- Did you notice in the Outline Numbered tab of the Bullets and Numbering dialog box (Figure 6-6) that the four outline numbered formats listed in the second row of formats all include the text "Heading 1," "Heading 2," and "Heading 3" in the outline. These outline number formats work in conjunction with Word's built-in heading styles to format an outline list. Any paragraphs that are formatted with the built-in heading styles will be numbered accordingly in the outline list. (In previous versions of Word, numbered lists based on heading styles was a separate feature.)

Breaking and Continuing a List

In Word 97, the Bullets and Numbering dialog box includes the following new options:

- **Restart numbering:** Use this option when you want to start the numbering scheme at 1 again.
- **Continue with previous list:** Use this option when you want to insert a non-numbered paragraph in the middle of a numbered list, but you want to continue the numbering from a previous list.

Chapter 7

More Outlining Oddities

In This Chapter

- Switching to Outline view
- Understanding Outline view
- Collapsing and expanding an outline
- Promoting and demoting paragraphs
- Editing in Outline view
- Printing an outline
- Working with the Document Map

Some writers have the outlining gene — others don't. Some writers manage to concoct at least a rudimentary outline only through an extraordinary act of self-will. Other writers spend days polishing the world's most perfect outline before they write a word. Their outlines are so good that they can write with their eyes closed after finishing the outline. Hmph. I fall somewhere in between. I spin a fairly decent outline up front, but I'm not compulsive about it. I rarely write with my eyes closed and usually revise the outline substantially as I go, sometimes beyond the point of recognition.

Word has a built-in outlining tool that's handy whether you like to create detailed outlines in advance, or you just want to check occasionally on the overall structure of your document to see how it is evolving. I use it all the time, even though I'm not an outline fanatic. If you use Word to create reports, proposals, or other types of documents that have some sense of structure to them, you owe it to yourself to learn the basics of working with outlines.

Switching to Outline View

Word usually runs in *Normal view,* which displays your document in a manner that's most convenient for on-screen editing. *Outline view* shows the contents of your document in the form of an outline. You can switch to Outline view in three ways:

- Using the View⇨Outline command
- Clicking the Outline View button (shown in the margin) next to the horizontal scroll bar, near the bottom-left corner of the document
- Typing the keyboard shortcut Ctrl+Alt+O

Figure 7-1 shows an example of a document in Outline view.

To return to Normal view, use the View⇨Normal command, click the Normal button (shown in the margin), or press the keyboard shortcut Ctrl+Alt+N.

In Word 97, there is also another way to work with a document's outline: by turning on the Document Map. Flip to the last section in this chapter to learn more about the Document Map.

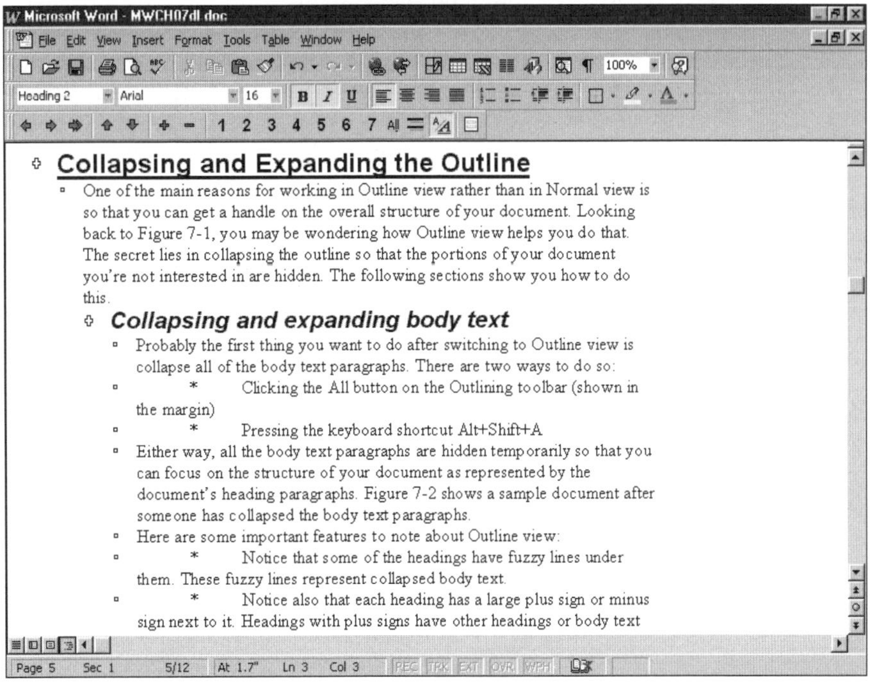

Figure 7-1: A document in outline view.

Understanding Outline View

The key to understanding Word's Outline view is realizing that an outline is just another way of looking at a document. The outline is not a separate entity from the document. Instead, when you switch to Outline view, Word takes the headings from your document and presents them in the form of an outline. Any changes you make to your document while in Outline view are reflected automatically in the document when you return to Normal view, and any changes you make in Normal view automatically appear when you switch to Outline view. The reason is because Normal view and Outline view are merely two ways of displaying the contents of your document.

There are some important concepts to note about Outline view:

- The outline is made up of the headings and body text of the document. Any paragraph formatted with one of the built-in heading styles (Heading 1, Heading 2, Heading 3, and so on) is considered to be a heading; any other paragraph is considered body text.
- When you switch to Outline view, an extra toolbar appears on-screen, replacing the ruler (which isn't needed in Outline view). This toolbar, appropriately called the Outlining toolbar, contains buttons for performing routine outlining tasks. You can see the Outlining toolbar in Figure 7-1.
- Initially, a document in Outline view may not appear dramatically different than it does in Normal view. That's the case in Figure 7-1. Just wait, though: In the following sections, you see how Outline view enables you to view your document quite differently from the way you view it in Normal view.
- While in Outline view, you can type new text or edit existing text just as you do in Normal view. You can also apply character formatting such as bold or italic, and you can apply styles to paragraphs. However, you can't apply direct paragraph formats like indentation, tab stops, alignment, and so on. To apply these types of formats, you must return to Normal view.
- Outline view has its own set of keyboard shortcuts to help you move things along. They are summarized in Table 7-1.

Table 7-1 Keyboard Shortcuts for Outline View

Keyboard Shortcut	*What It Does*
Ctrl+Alt+O	Switches to Outline view
Ctrl+Alt+N	Switches back to Normal view

(continued)

Table 7-1 *(continued)*

Keyboard Shortcut	*What It Does*
Alt+Shift+A	Collapses or expands all text
Alt+Shift+hyphen	Collapses the selection
Alt+Shift+plus	Expands the selection
Alt+Shift+1	Collapses/expands to Heading 1
Alt+Shift+*(number)*	Collapses/expands to specified heading level
/ (on numeric keypad)	Hides/shows formatting
Shift+Tab	Promotes the selection
Alt+Shift+left arrow	Promotes the selection
Tab	Demotes the selection
Alt+Shift+right arrow	Demotes the selection
Ctrl+Shift+N	Demotes selection to body text by applying Normal style
Alt+Shift+up arrow	Moves the selection up, similar to cutting and pasting it
Alt+Shift+down arrow	Moves the selection down, similar to cutting and pasting it

Collapsing and Expanding the Outline

One of the main reasons for working in Outline view rather than in Normal view is so that you can get a handle on the overall structure of your document. Looking back to Figure 7-1, you may be wondering how Outline view helps you do that. The secret lies in collapsing the outline so that the portions of your document you're not interested in are hidden. The following sections show you how to do this.

Collapsing and expanding body text

Probably the first thing you want to do after switching to Outline view is collapse all of the body text paragraphs. There are two ways to do so:

- Clicking the All button on the Outlining toolbar (shown in the margin)
- Pressing the keyboard shortcut Alt+Shift+A

Either way, all the body text paragraphs are hidden temporarily so that you can focus on the structure of your document as represented by the document's heading paragraphs. Figure 7-2 shows a sample document after someone has collapsed the body text paragraphs.

Here are some important features to note about Outline view:

- Notice that some of the headings have fuzzy lines under them. These fuzzy lines represent collapsed body text.
- Notice also that each heading has a large plus sign or minus sign next to it. Headings with plus signs have other headings or body text subordinate to them. Headings with minus signs do not. Body text paragraphs always have a hollow square bullet next to them.
- To restore body text paragraphs, click the All button or press the Alt+Shift+A keyboard shortcut again.

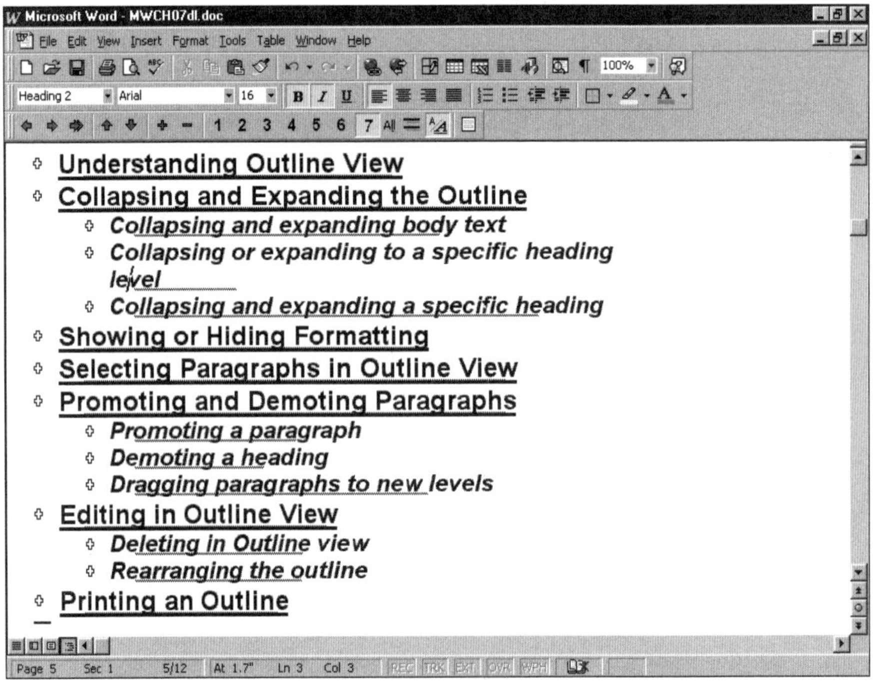

Figure 7-2: A document in Outline view with body text collapsed.

Collapsing or expanding to a specific heading level

The eight numbered buttons on the Outlining toolbar enable you to collapse or expand an outline to a specific heading level. For example, if you want to see just the top level headings (paragraphs formatted with the Heading 1 style), click the Show Heading 1 button (shown in the margin).

Collapsing and expanding a specific heading

You also can selectively collapse or expand specific headings in Outline view so that you can focus on specific portions of your document. For example, you can collapse the entire document to Heading 1 and then expand only the heading that you want to work on.

To collapse and subsequently expand a heading, follow these simple steps:

1. **Select the heading that you want to collapse.**

   Click anywhere in the heading to select it.

2. **Click the Collapse button (shown in the margin).**

   All the subordinate heading and body text paragraphs text for the heading are hidden temporarily.

3. **To expand the heading again, click the Expand button (shown in the margin).**

   The hidden paragraphs reappear.

TIP

Another way to collapse a heading is to double-click the big plus sign next to it. Double-click it again to expand the heading. You can also use the keyboard shortcuts:

Alt+Shift+hyphen	Collapse
Alt+Shift+plus	Expand

Showing or Hiding Formatting

Collapsing body text from an outline gives you a bird's-eye view of a document's structure, but you can focus more closely on the structure if you remove the formatting associated with each heading style.

To remove formatting from an outline, click the Show Formatting button or press the gray slash key on the numeric keypad. Figure 7-3 shows what an outline looks like with formatting removed.

Keep these tips in mind when using the Show Formatting button:

- To restore formatting, click the Show Formatting button or press the gray slash key again.
- You don't need the formatting to distinguish among heading levels because the headings are indented for you. So I usually work in Outline view with formatting off.
- When you hide formatting, you're doing just that: hiding it. You're not actually removing it. When you click the Show Formatting button again or return to Normal view, all the formatting that you so carefully applied to your document is restored.

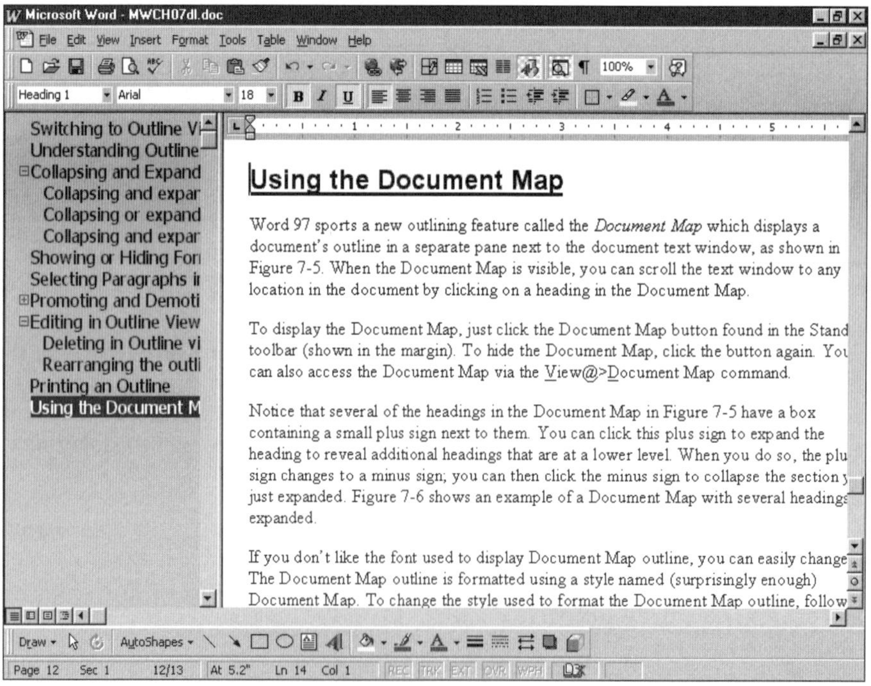

Figure 7-3: A document in Outline view with all formatting removed.

Selecting Paragraphs in Outline View

When you work in Outline view, it's easy to become confused about how to select various portions of the document. This section is a quick summary of the techniques.

Most of the techniques for selecting text that work in Normal view also work in Outline view. For example, you can select a block of text by dragging the mouse or holding down the Shift key while using the keyboard arrows.

To select an entire heading or body text paragraph, point the mouse to the left of the paragraph in the invisible zone (actually, the left margin) called the *selection bar* and click. (The mouse arrow points Northeast when it's in the selection bar.)

To select a heading paragraph and all its subordinate paragraphs, click the big plus sign next to the paragraph or double-click to the left of the paragraph in the selection bar. This action selects subordinate heading paragraphs as well as body text paragraphs.

TIP

It isn't necessary to select an entire paragraph to perform most outline operations. For example, you can select a paragraph for promotion or demotion just by clicking anywhere in the paragraph.

Promoting and Demoting Paragraphs

To *promote* a paragraph means to move it up one level in the outline. If you promote a Heading 2, it becomes a Heading 1. If you promote a body text paragraph, it becomes a heading paragraph at the same level as the heading it is subordinate to. Thus, if you promote a body text paragraph that follows a Heading 2, the body text paragraph becomes a Heading 2.

To *demote* a paragraph is to move the paragraph down one level in the outline. If you demote a Heading 1, it becomes a Heading 2. Demote it again and it becomes a Heading 3. You cannot demote a body text paragraph, but you can demote any heading to a body text paragraph.

TIP

When you promote or demote headings, the body text paragraphs that fall under the heading always go along for the ride. There's no need to worry about losing a heading's body text. Whether or not subordinate headings get swept up in the move depends on how you handle the promotion or demotion.

Promoting a paragraph

To promote a paragraph, place the cursor anywhere in the paragraph and then perform any of the following techniques:

- Click the Promote button (shown in the margin) on the Outlining toolbar.
- Press Shift+Tab.
- Use the keyboard shortcut Alt+Shift+left arrow.

The paragraph moves up one level in the outline pecking order.

REMEMBER

You cannot promote a Heading 1; it is already at the highest level in the outline hierarchy.

If you want to promote a heading *and* all its subordinate headings, click the big plus sign next to the paragraph or double-click in the invisible selection bar to the left of the paragraph. Then promote it. If you promote a body text paragraph, it assumes the heading level of the heading paragraph it used to belong to.

You also can promote paragraphs by dragging them with the mouse. See the section "Dragging paragraphs to new levels" later in this chapter.

Demoting a heading

To demote a heading, place the cursor anywhere in the heading and then do one of the following:

- Click the Demote button (shown in the margin) on the Outlining toolbar.
- Press Tab.
- Use the keyboard shortcut Alt+Shift+right arrow.

The heading moves down a level in the outline pecking order.

To demote a heading *and* any headings unfortunate enough to be subordinate to it, click the paragraph's big plus sign or double-click in the hidden selection bar just left of the paragraph. Then demote it.

REMEMBER

Don't be insensitive when you demote a paragraph. It can be a traumatic experience.

You can also demote paragraphs by dragging them with the mouse. See the section "Dragging paragraphs to new levels" next in this chapter.

You can't demote a body text paragraph. It's already at the bottom of the rung.

You can quickly demote a heading paragraph to body text by clicking the Demote to Body Text button (shown in the margin) on the Outlining toolbar or by pressing the keyboard shortcut Ctrl+Shift+N. (Recognize this shortcut? Demoting a paragraph to body text is accomplished by assigning the Normal style to it.)

Dragging paragraphs to new levels

When you move the mouse pointer over the big plus or minus sign next to a heading or body text paragraph, the pointer changes from a single arrow to a four-cornered arrow. This arrow is your signal that you can click the mouse to select the entire paragraph (and any subordinate paragraphs) and then use the mouse to promote or demote a paragraph along with all its subordinates.

To promote or demote with the mouse, follow these steps:

1. **Point to the big plus or minus sign for the paragraph you that want to demote or promote.**

   The mouse pointer changes to a four-cornered arrow as shown in the margin.

2. **Click and hold the mouse button down.**

3. **Drag the mouse to the right or left.**

   The mouse pointer changes to a double-pointed arrow, as shown in the margin, and a vertical line appears that shows the indentation level of the selection. Release the button when the selection is indented the way you want. The text is automatically assigned the correct heading style.

If you mess up, press Ctrl+Z to undo the promotion or demotion. Then try again.

You can't demote a heading to body text using the preceding technique. You must use the Demote to Body Text button or Ctrl+Shift+N.

Editing in Outline View

Outline view is a great place to perform large-scale editing on your document, such as rearranging or deleting whole sections of text. If you edit a document while the body text is hidden, any edits you perform on headings are automatically extended to the body text that belongs to them. Thus, if you delete a heading, all its body text is deleted, too. If you move a heading to a new location in the document, the body text moves as well.

Deleting in Outline view

To delete large portions of your document quickly, switch to Outline view. Select the text that you want to delete; then press the Del key and — Pow! — the text is gone.

Some helpful hints when using Outline view to delete text:

- Click the mouse in the magic invisible selection bar just left of a heading paragraph to select the entire paragraph. Then press Del and kiss the paragraph good-bye.
- Click the big plus sign next to a heading paragraph to select it *and* all its subordinate headings and body text. Press the Del key to send everything — headings and body text alike — into oblivion.
- Click and drag the mouse over a block of heading paragraphs to select them and then press Del to delete everything that you selected.
- Obviously, using the Del key in Outline view is risky business. Don't do it unless you're certain that the body text and subordinate paragraphs are preserved. When in doubt, switch to Normal view and delete text the old-fashioned way.

Rearranging the outline

To rearrange your document on a large scale, switch to Outline view and move entire headings up or down in the outline. Remember, body text always travels with its headings. Whether subordinate headings travel as well depends on whether you select them before moving headings around.

To move just one paragraph, click anywhere in the paragraph. To move a paragraph along with its subordinates, click the big plus sign next to it. Then use one of the following techniques.

To move the selected paragraphs up, use one of these methods:

- Click the Up button (shown in the margin) on the Outlining toolbar.
- Press Alt+Shift+up arrow.
- U Drag the text with the mouse.

To move the selected text down, use one of the following techniques:

- Click the Down button (shown in the margin) on the Outlining toolbar.
- Press Alt+Shift+down arrow.
- Drag the text with the mouse.

REMEMBER

If you don't like the result of your move, you can always undo it by pressing Ctrl+Z.

Printing an Outline

You can quickly print an outline of your document by following this procedure:

1. **Switch to Outline view.**
2. **Click the All button (shown in the margin) to hide body text.**
3. **Collapse or Expand any other headings that you want to include or exclude in the printout.**
4. **Click the Show Formatting button if you don't want the outline to include heading formats.**
5. **Click the Print button on the Standard toolbar.**

   The outline prints.

TIP

A printed outline is no substitute for a table of contents. See Chapter 21 for details on printing a table of contents — complete with page numbers.

Using the Document Map

Word 97 sports a new outlining feature called the Document Map that displays a document's outline in a separate pane next to the document text window, shown in Figure 7-4. When the Document Map is visible, you can scroll the text window to any location in the document by clicking on a heading in the Document Map.

To display the Document Map, just click the Document Map button found in the Standard toolbar (shown in the margin). To hide the Document Map, click the button again. You can also access the Document Map via the View⇨Document Map command.

Notice that several of the headings in the Document Map in Figure 7-4 have a box containing a small plus sign next to them. You can click this plus sign to expand the heading to reveal additional headings that are at a lower level. When you do this, the plus sign changes to a minus sign; you can then click the minus sign to collapse the section that you just expanded.

If you don't like the font used to display Document Map outline, you can easily change it. The Document Map outline is formatted using a style named (surprisingly enough) Document Map. To change the style used to format the Document Map outline, follow these steps:

1. **Choose the Format⇨Style command.**

   The Style dialog box appears.

2. **Select Document Map from the list of styles.**

   You probably have to use the scroll bar to scroll through the list.

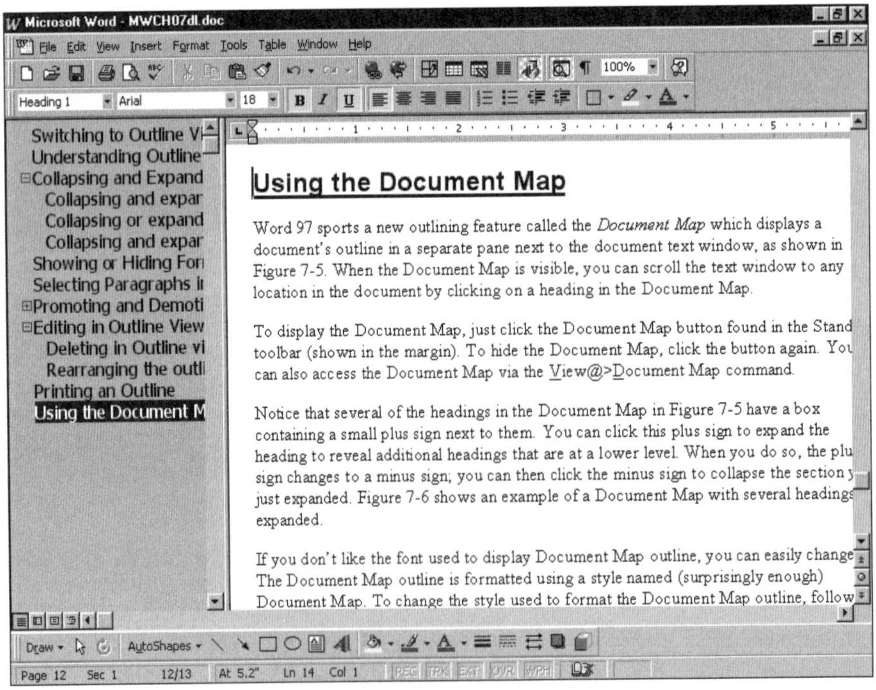

Figure 7-4: A Document Map with two headings expanded.

3. **Click the Modify button.**

   The Modify Style dialog box appears.

4. **Click the Format button, then choose Font from the pop-up menu that appears.**

   A standard Font dialog box appears.

5. **Choose whatever font settings you want for the outline.**

   The default setting for the Document Map font is 12-point Tahoma. I like to change to a smaller font, such as 9-point Arial.

6. **Click OK to dismiss the Font dialog box, then click OK again to dismiss the Modify Style dialog box.**

   You are returned to the Style dialog box.

7. **Click Close to dismiss the Style dialog box.**

You're done. Figure 7-5 shows how the Document Map appears when displayed with 9-point Arial type rather than the default Document Map style. As you can see, this smaller type style shows more of each heading in the Document Map.

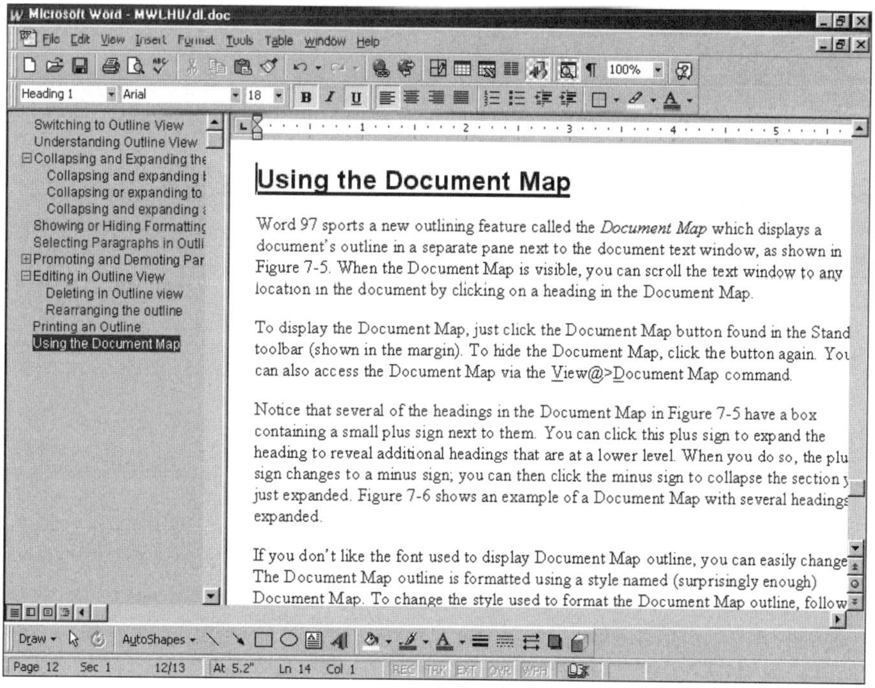

Figure 7-5: How the outline looks when the Document Map style is changed to 9-point Arial type.

Chapter 8

More Mail Merge Madness

In This Chapter

- Understanding mail merge
- Using merge fields in the body of a letter
- Using a condition test
- Printing mailing labels and envelopes
- Sorting the data source
- Using a query
- Editing the data source directly
- Importing data from another source

Mail merge. Just the sound of those two words is enough to drive even veteran Word users into a state of utter and complete panic. Just when you think that you've figured out enough about mail merge to put out a simple form letter, along comes Word with a bunch of additional mail-merge features. Arghhhh! What next?

This chapter covers some of the more interesting things you can do with Word's mail-merge feature, such as print mailing labels, choose only certain names to print letters for, use data from sources other than Word, and create an address directory.

This chapter is *not* a gentle introduction to mail merge. It does have a section called "Understanding Mail Merge" that quickly reviews the basics, but if you're completely new to mail merge, stop where you are. Back up very slowly, make no sudden moves, and get yourself a copy of *Word 97 For Windows For Dummies.* It has an entire chapter devoted to the basics of using mail merge.

Word 97 has a Tools➪Merge Documents command that is not related at all to the Mail Merge feature. Instead, the Tools➪Merge Documents command is a part of the revision marking feature, which is covered in Chapter 26. Don't get these two distinctly different features confused.

Understanding Mail Merge

When most people say *mail merge,* they mean merging a file that contains a list of names and addresses with another file that contains a model letter to produce a bunch of personalized form letters. Suppose that you decided to do some volunteer work for the local public library, and the library decided to put you in charge of getting deadbeats to return long overdue books. A personalized letter would be the ideal way to communicate your message to these good-for-nothings. And Word's mail-merge feature is ideal for preparing such a personalized letter.

Mail merge is a three-step affair, greatly assisted by the Mail Merge Helper dialog box, which appears when you summon the Tools➪Mail Merge command. Figure 8-1 shows the Mail Merge Helper.

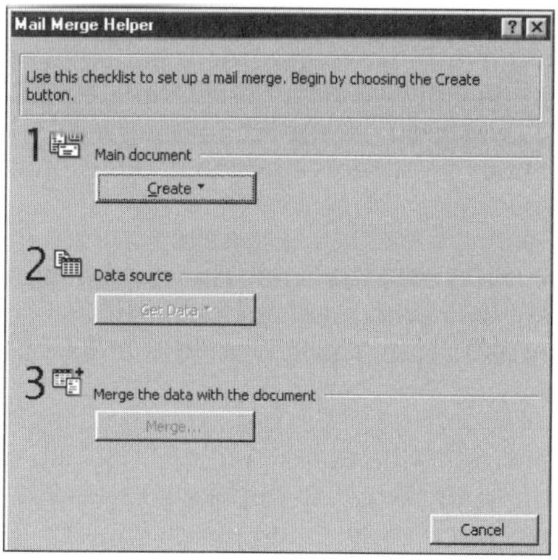

Figure 8-1: The Mail Merge Helper.

These steps summarize the three mail-merge steps the Mail Merge Helper guides you through:

1. **Write the form letter.**

   First you have to figure out what to say to all those recalcitrant patrons. You can create a new letter or call up the letter you sent last time when you volunteered for something. Either way, you have to create a *main document.* You toil over the letter for hours, trying to be firm yet

inoffensive. As you write the letter, you leave blank spaces in the spots that will be filled in with personalized information, such as the inside address and salutation ("Dear John"). Figure 8-2 shows an example of a typical form letter.

2. **Get the names and addresses.**

   Hope to God that someone has already typed the names and addresses of all the deadbeats into a computer. In the best of all worlds, that person typed the names into a Word document so that you're all set. In the OK-but-still-a-long-shot world, someone has indeed already entered the names, but he did it by using PC CheaperBase or some other database program you never heard of. You have to figure out a way to convert the data into a format you can use with Word.

   After the main document is composed, you return to the Mail Merge Helper and click the Get Data button, which enables you to set up a *data source:* a Word document that contains all the names and addresses neatly formatted in a table. The good news is that Word sets up this table for you; all you have to do is tell it which *fields* to include (such as first and last names, address lines, city, state, postal code, and so on). Then Word pops up the Data Form dialog box, shown in Figure 8-3. You spend the next two weeks working in this dialog box, typing names and addresses.

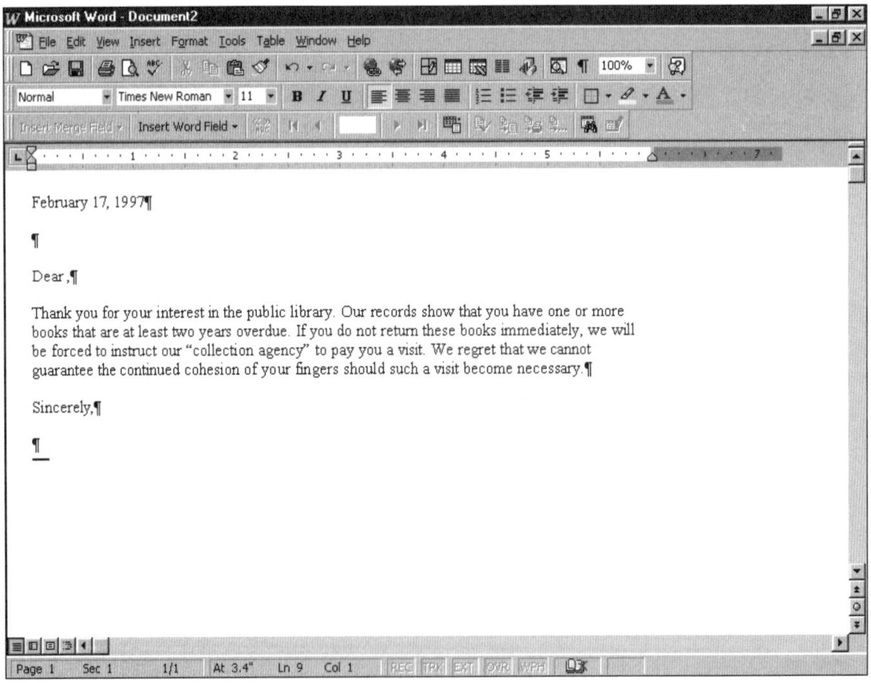

Figure 8-2: A typical form letter.

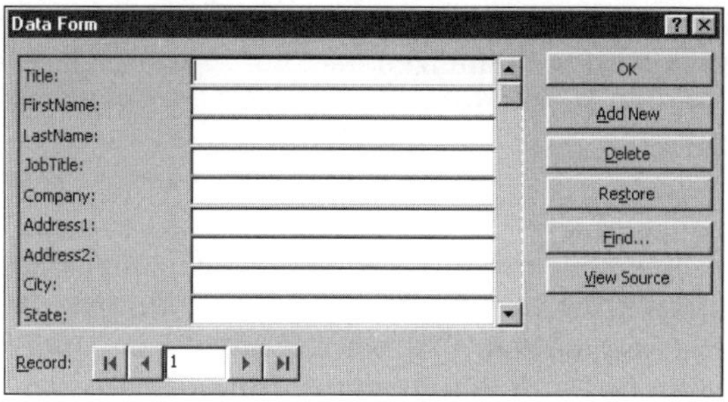

Figure 8-3: Using the Data Form dialog box to enter names and addresses.

2a. **Insert field names in the main document.**

Did I say that there were just three steps? I guess I didn't mention that some of the steps have substeps. Sorry.

After you enter all the names and addresses (saving the file frequently, of course), Word complains that you didn't enter any field names in your main document and whisks you back to your form letter. There you add the field names to the blank spaces you left in the form letter by positioning the cursor in one of the blank spots, clicking the Insert Merge Field button from the Mail Merge toolbar, and choosing the appropriate field name from the list of field names that appears. When you're finished, the document looks something like Figure 8-4.

3. **Merge the addresses with the form letter.**

This is the easy part. After you've set up the main document and the data source, click the Merge button in the Mail Merge Helper. Word creates a personalized letter for each name in the address list. You can send the personalized letters directly to the printer or you can put them all in a new document, which you can then examine before you print.

Creating Form Letters with Pizzazz

Usually, you think of mail merge only in terms of adding an inside address and personalized salutation to a form letter. You can also personalize the body of the letter, however, if you have information you want to include in the letter and you plan ahead carefully. You can include fields from the data source, for example, in the body of the letter. You can tell Word to pause as it prepares each merge letter so that you can type custom text. And you can include an IF field to customize each letter based on the results of a condition test.

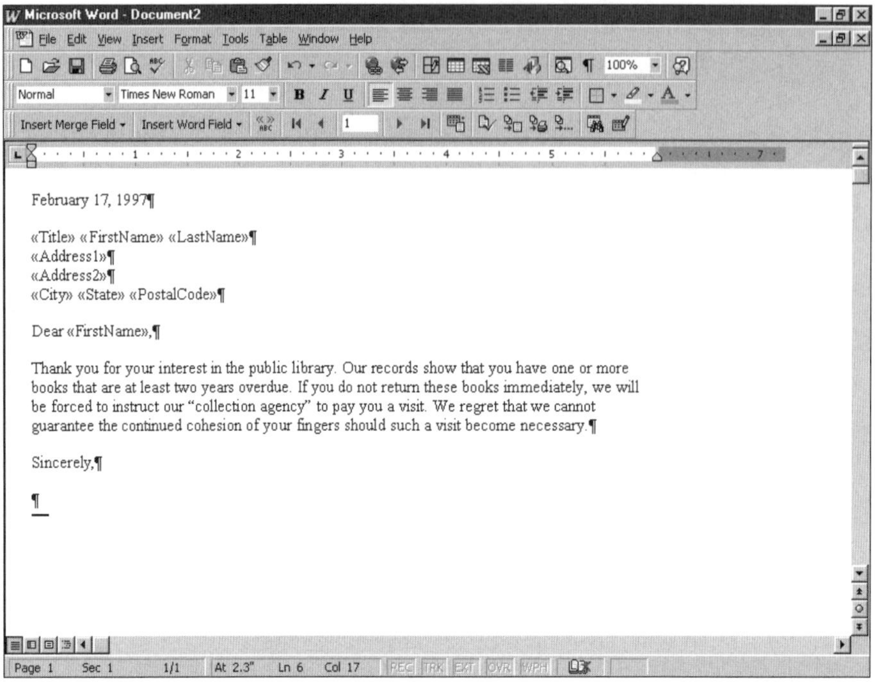

Figure 8-4: The form letter with field names inserted.

Using merge fields in the body of a letter

Suppose that in addition to the names and addresses of all the deadbeat library patrons, you also have the titles of their overdue books. To make the letter seem more personalized, why not mention the books in the body of the letter?

For this to work, of course, the name of the overdue book or books would have to be included as a field in the data source. The easiest way to do this would be to include a field named Books, which contains the titles of all overdue books with the book titles formatted in italic type. If a patron had just one overdue book, the Books field would contain the name of a single book, such as "*A Tale of Two Cities*." But if the patron had two or more overdue books, the Books field would contain all the names, such as "*The Killer Angels* and *Roots*."

Figure 8-5 shows how this type of letter looks. As you can see, I included the merge field Books in the body of the paragraph. When you merge the letters, the contents of each record's Books field is inserted into the middle of the sentence.

For example:

Our records show that you checked out *A Tale of Two Cities* more than two years ago, and we have not heard from you since.

Our records show that you checked out *The Killer Angels* and *Roots* more than two years ago, and we have not heard from you since.

Our records show that you checked out *Networking For Dummies, PowerPoint 97 For Windows For Dummies*, and *MORE Word 97 For Windows For Dummies* more than two years ago, and we have not heard from you since.

The secret to inserting fields in the middle of sentences is carefully planning all the grammatical possibilities to avoid an embarrassing faux pas. Suppose that you write a sentence like this one:

Our records show that you checked out the book "Books" more than two years ago and haven t returned it yet.

Then you'd end up with sentences like these:

Our records show that you checked out the book *A Tale of Two Cities* more than two years ago and haven t returned it yet.

Our records show that you checked out the book *The Killer Angels* and *Roots* more than two years ago and haven t returned it yet.

Our records show that you checked out the book *Networking For Dummies, PowerPoint 97 For Windows For Dummies*, and *MORE Word 97 For Windows For Dummies* more than two years ago and haven t re-

This works for the first sentence, but the second two aren't quite right.

People have been desensitized to personalized mail by Publishers Clearing House. Don't overdo the personalization; most people see right through it.

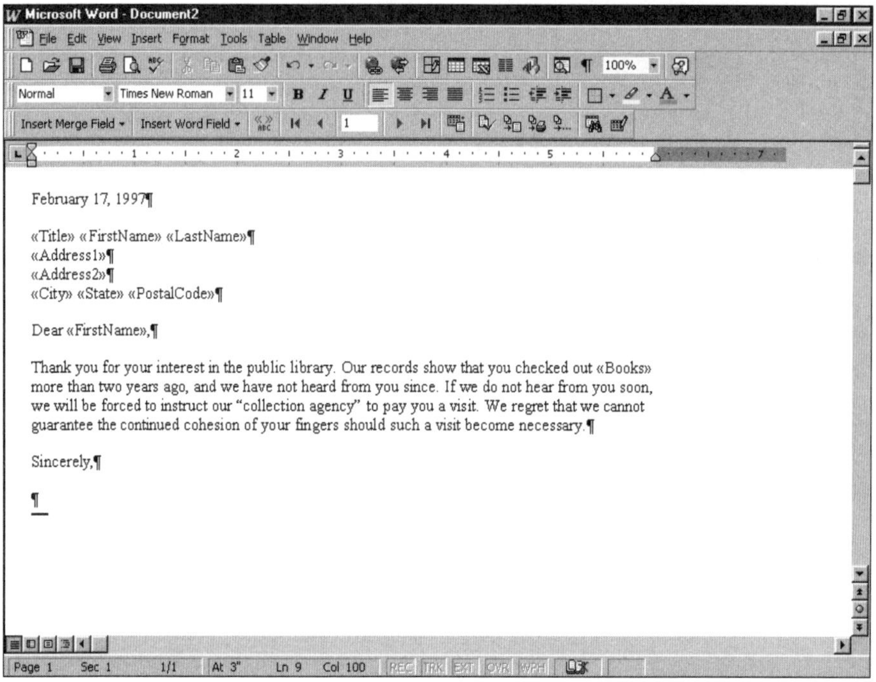

Figure 8-5: The form letter with a merge field inserted in the body of the letter.

Personalizing each letter

Suppose that you want to add a little personal note to each letter. You can merge the letters to a document and then edit the resulting document and add a personal note to each merged letter. That's the easy way, and probably the best way if you want to do it only once. But if you want to add a personal note to each letter of a mail merge you run every Friday, consider doing it the cool computer geek way: by adding a FILLIN field to your main document.

A FILLIN field causes Word to prompt you for text to be inserted into each document as the mail merge proceeds. A dialog box like the one in Figure 8-6 appears for each letter as it is merged. When you type a personalized message here, it is inserted into the letter.

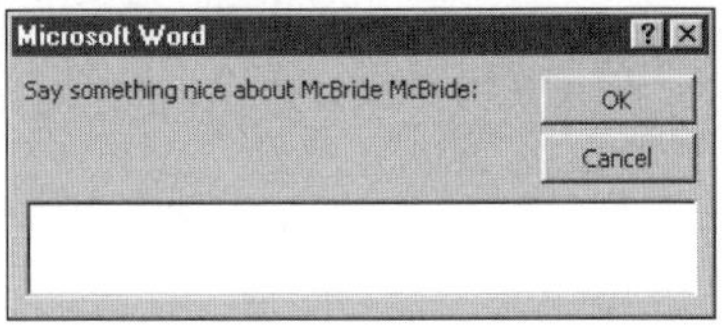

Figure 8-6: How Word prompts you to enter personalized text for each letter.

Follow these steps to prompt for personalized text for each letter:

1. **Set up a main document and data source as you normally do.**

   See the first section in this chapter, "Understanding Mail Merge," for a review of how to do that. If you're still completely perplexed, see *Word 97 For Windows For Dummies.*

2. **Edit the main document.**

   Use the Window command to switch to the window that holds the main document or use the Mail Merge Helper's Edit button to edit the main document.

3. **Call up the Tools➪Options command, click the View tab (if the View options are not already displayed), and check the Field Codes box if it is not already checked. Then click OK.**

   You must be able to see field codes as they are inserted into your document. All the beautiful merge field placeholders, such as `«FirstName»`, are replaced by less elegant merge fields, such as `{MERGEFIELD FirstName}`. Have no fear — the merge fields are intact. Checking the Field Codes box in the View Options dialog box simply tells Word to display these fields in greater detail.

4. **Position the cursor at the spot where you want personalized text to be inserted for each letter.**

   It's usually best to insert the personalized text in its own paragraph so that you don't have to worry about leaving too many or too few spaces before or after it.

5. **Click the Insert Word Field button in the Mail Merge toolbar and then choose Fill-in as the type of field to insert.**

   The Insert Word Field: Fill-in dialog box appears, as shown in Figure 8-7.

Figure 8-7: This dialog box appears when you insert a FILLIN field.

6. **Type a friendly prompt and then click OK.**

   Type whatever text you want Word to display when it prompts you for text during the merge. In Figure 8-7, I entered "Say something nice about:" as the Prompt text.

7. **Insert the FirstName and LastName merge fields in the FILLIN field so that you know to whom each letter is addressed.**

   This part of the procedure is the most difficult. You may have noticed that the prompt text in Figure 8-6 included the name of the person to whom the letter is addressed. These names are usually available as the merge fields FirstName and LastName. To insert the name, find the FILLIN field you inserted in Step 6. It should look something like this:

   ```
   { FILLIN  Say something nice about:  }
   ```

   Move the cursor to the point in the field's prompt text where you want the name inserted (in this case, just before the colon). Then click the Insert Merge Field button to insert the FirstName and LastName fields. Also, insert a space before each field. When you're finished, the FILLIN field should look like this:

   ```
   { FILLIN  Say something nice about { MERGEFIELD
         FirstName }  { MERGEFIELD LastName }:  }
   ```

8. **Use the File⇨Save command to save the main document. Then call up the Mail Merge Helper dialog box (Tools⇨Mail Merge) and click the Merge button to merge the letters.**

9. **When you're prompted, type a personal message for each letter.**

   Pay attention to the name that appears in the dialog box so that you know which message to type.

If you check the Ask once check box in the Insert Word Field: Fill-in dialog box, Word prompts you for the fill-in field just once. It then inserts the same text in each letter created during the mail merge. This procedure is useful if you want to insert a different message every time you run a mail merge, but the message is the same for each letter in the merge run.

Using a condition test

A *condition test* enables you to insert different text into a merge letter based on the contents of some field in the data source. If you have a field named *Party,* for example, you may include one message for records in which the Party field is Republican and a completely different message for records in which the field is Democrat. (I would offer appropriate messages for both cases, but I would probably offend half my loyal readers, so I'll pass.)

To incorporate a condition test into a mail-merge document, you use a Word IF-THEN-ELSE field. This procedure sounds like computer programming to me, so you had better grab your pocket protector and close your door. You don't want your friends to see you doing this or you'll lose their respect forever.

Follow these steps to add a conditional test to your mail merge:

1. **Set up a main document and data source as you normally would.**

   Look back to the section "Understanding Mail Merge" at the beginning of this chapter for a quick review. Or consult *Word 97 For Windows For Dummies.*

   Make sure that the data source contains a field that you can use as the basis for a condition test. If you want to include one message for people who owe you money and another for people who are all paid up, for example, make sure that the data source has a field that provides the balance due.

2. **Edit the main document.**

   Use the Window command to pop up the main document or use the Mail Merge Helper's Edit button.

3. **Summon the Tools⇨Options command. If the View options are not already displayed, click the View tab.** Then check the Field Codes box if it is not already checked and click OK.

   You need to see the merge codes that you insert into your document, so you may as well activate the Field Codes option now.

4. **Move the cursor to where you want to insert the conditional text.**
5. **Use the Insert Word Field button from the Mail Merge toolbar to insert an IF-THEN-ELSE field.**

   Click the Insert Word Field button and then choose If...Then...Else. A dialog box similar to the one in Figure 8-8 appears.

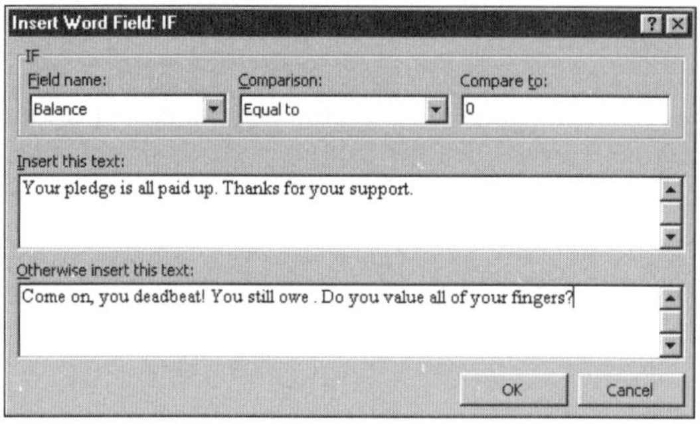

Figure 8-8: This dialog box appears when you insert an IF-THEN-ELSE field.

   If the conditional text is based on the balance due, for example, choose the Balance field (or whatever field contains the balance due).

6. **Set up the condition test in the Field Name, Comparison, and Compare To fields.**

   Start by choosing in the Field Name field the field you want to test. Then set the conditional equation in the Comparison field and the value to be compared in the Compare To field.

7. **In the Compare To text box, type the value to which you want to compare the field.**
8. **In the Insert this Text field, type the text you want inserted if the condition is true.**

   In Figure 8-8, I typed, "Your pledge is all paid up. Thanks for your support."

9. **In the Otherwise Insert this Text box, type the alternative text you want included if the condition is *not* true.**

   In Figure 8-8, I typed "Come on you deadbeat! You still owe . Do you value all your fingers?" (In this example, the second sentence is incomplete because I plan to insert the Balance field in the next step. Bear with me.)

10. **Edit the main document and insert field names into the IF-THEN-ELSE field.**

    The IF merge field inserted in Figure 8-8 should look like this in the main document:

    ```
    IF { MERGEFIELD Balance ] = 0  Your pledge is all paid
          up. Thanks for your support.   Come on you dead-
          beat! You still owe . Do you value all your
          fingers?
    ```

    Position the cursor after the word *owe* and then click the Insert Merge Button from the Mail Merge toolbar to insert the Balance field. When you're finished, the IF merge field should look like this:

    ```
    IF { MERGEFIELD Balance ] = 0  Your pledge is all paid
          up. Thanks for your support.   Come on you dead-
          beat! You still owe { MERGEFIELD Balance }. Do
          you value all your fingers?
    ```

11. **Save the main document by using the File⇨Save command; then call up the Mail Merge Helper dialog box and click the Merge button to merge the letters.**

12. **Put away your pocket protector and don't tell anyone that you did this.**

Printing Mailing Labels and Envelopes

Ever spent 30 minutes printing 50 personalized letters by using mail merge and then spent another 30 minutes hand-addressing envelopes? Never again! Word can easily transform a mail-merge address list into mailing labels or envelopes.

These steps show the procedure for creating mailing labels:

1. **Call up the Tools⇨Mail Merge command.**

   The familiar Mail Merge Helper dialog box appears.

2. **Click the Create button under Main Document and choose Mailing Labels.**

3. **When Word asks whether you want to use the active window or create a new main document, choose New Main Document.**

4. **Back at the Mail Merge Helper, click Get Data under Data Source and choose Open Data Source. Choose the file that contains your mailing addresses and click OK.**

   If you haven't yet created your mailing list, choose the Create Data Source option instead. Then choose the fields to be included in the mailing list and enter your names and addresses.

5. **When Word complains that it has to set up the main document, obey its wishes. Click the Set Up Main Document button.**

6. **When Word displays the Label Options dialog box, choose the label type you use and click OK.**

   Figure 8-9 shows the Label Options dialog box. Click "Dot matrix" if you use a dot-matrix printer or "Laser and ink jet" if you use a laser or ink jet printer. Then scroll through the Product number list to choose the specific Avery label type you plan to use.

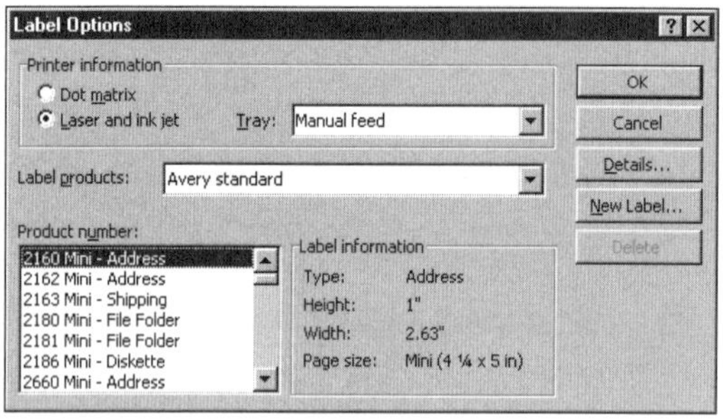

Figure 8-9: The Label Options dialog box.

   If the labels you use aren't in the list, choose Custom Dot Matrix or Custom Laser as the label type and then click the Details button. This step pops up a dialog box in which you type detailed measurements for the labels. Measure your labels carefully, type the measurements, and click OK.

7. **When Word displays the Create Labels dialog box, use the Insert Merge Field button to insert merge fields where you want them to appear on the labels. Then click OK.**

   As you insert each merge field, it is copied into the Sample Label box (see Figure 8-10). If you include more than one field on a line, be sure to press the spacebar to leave a space between the fields. To begin a new line, press Enter. Click OK when you're finished.

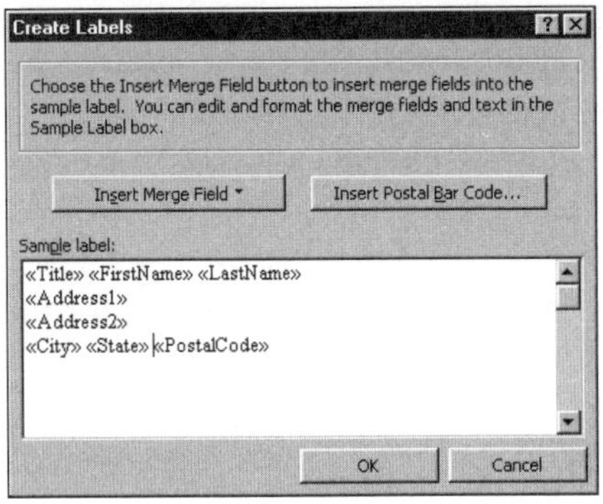

Figure 8-10: The Create Labels dialog box.

8. **Back at the Mail Merge Helper, click the Merge button to create the labels.**

   Word displays the Merge dialog box, from which you can tell Word to merge to a new document or directly to the printer. Choose the option you want, click the Merge button and watch while Word creates your labels.

The procedure for creating envelopes is the same, except that you choose Envelopes from the Create button under Main Document. Also, rather than specify Label Options, you specify Envelope Options. The procedures are otherwise identical.

TIP: If you want to include a postal bar code on your labels or envelopes, click the Insert Postal Bar Code on the Create Labels or Create Envelopes dialog box. This code is not a secret password that gets you into pubs where mail carriers hang out — it's a bar code that speeds mail delivery. If you do bulk mailing and have the proper permits, using this bar code can earn postage discounts.

TIP: You can use the same data source to print both personalized letters and labels or envelopes. If you do, however, be very careful to stuff each letter into its corresponding envelope. Nothing spoils a personalized mailing more than to send personalized letters to the wrong addresses.

When you print labels, you can save yourself a great deal of grief if you use Avery label products. Nope, I don't get an under-the-table kickback for this blatant endorsement. It just so happens that Word comes with most Avery label sizes and formats predefined.

Fun Things to Do with the Data Source

Mail merge would be useful enough if all you could do with the data source was use it to store your names and addresses. But Word's data sources have more tricks up their sleeves than meet the eye. With a little chutzpah and a bit of wrestling with the dialog boxes, you can do several cute and moderately useful tricks with the data source. The following sections explain these amazing feats.

Sorting data

Suppose that you enter all the names in whatever sequence they were sitting in the pile, but you want to print the letters in alphabetical order. No problem! Just sort the data source. Here's how you do it:

1. **Set up the mail merge as you normally would.**

   Call up the Tools⇨Mail Merge command, use the Create button in the Main Document section to set up the main document, and click the Get Data button to create the data source or open an existing data source.

2. **Don't click the Merge button yet!**

3. **Click the Query Options button instead to summon the Query Options dialog box. If the sort options aren't visible, click the Sort Records tab.**

   Figure 8-11 shows the sort options in the Query Options dialog box.

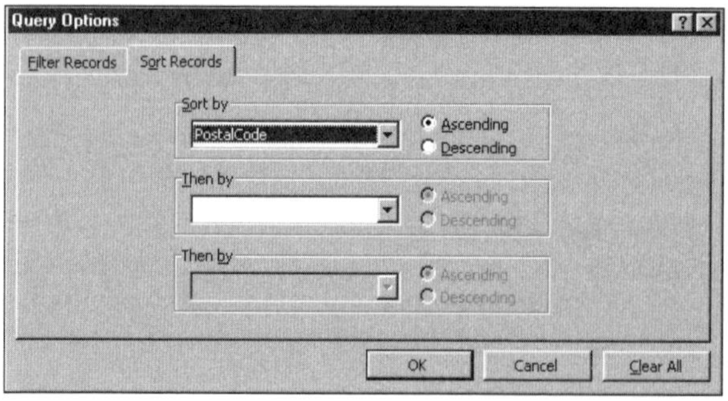

Figure 8-11: Sorting the data source.

4. **In the Sort By list box, choose the merge field that you want the data source to be sorted by.**

   Click the down arrow next to the sort field box to reveal a list of all the merge fields in the data source and then choose the one you want to sort the data by (LastName, for example).

5. **If you want a second or third sort field, set them in the Then By and Then By fields.**

   The Then By field is used as a tiebreaker when two or more records have the same main Sort By field. If the data source has more than one record with the same LastName, they are sorted into sequence by their first names, like this:

   ```
   King   Larry
   King   Martin Luther
   King   Stephen
   ```

   If you have a third field you can use as a tiebreaker, set it in the next Then By field.

6. **Click OK.**

   You return to the Mail Merge Helper dialog box.

7. **Click the Merge button to continue with the mail merge.**

   If you want to sort records in reverse order, click the appropriate Descending button. Records are then sorted on that field in reverse order, beginning with the *Z*s and working back up to the *A*s.

TIP: If you want to sort your data source on a particular field, such as LastName, make sure that you set that field up as a separate merge field. It may be tempting to replace the separate Title, FirstName, and LastName fields with a single Name field. But if you do, you can't sort your records by the last name.

Using a merge query

Merge query sounds like some ominous computer database feature that you have to have a Ph.D. to figure out, but all it really means is that you send letters to only a certain select group of names from your data source. You may want to send letters only to left-handed San Francisco 49er fans born in February, for example. Sending letters to this group is possible if you have fields in your data source for handedness, favorite football team, and birthday.

Word uses the term *filter* to mean the process of choosing the records you want to include in a mail merge. Unlike the filters in your car, mail-merge filters don't fill up with gunk, so you don't have to change them every 5,000 miles. You do have to be careful about how you set them up, though, to be sure that they choose just the records you want included in your mail merge.

To mail letters to only those lucky few, follow these steps:

1. **Set up the mail merge just like you usually do.**

   Summon the Tools⇨Mail Merge command and then click the Create button in the Main Document section and specify the main document. Then use the Get Data button to set up the data source.

2. **Don't click the Merge button yet!**

3. **Click the Query Options button instead to summon the Query Options dialog box. If the Filter Records options aren't visible, click the Filter Records tab.**

4. **Set the criteria for including records in the mail merge by specifying a Field, Comparison, and Compare To value for each criteria.**

   To create a letter only for people who live in the 93711 zip code, for example, set the first Field to PostalCode, the first Comparison to Equal To, and the Compare To field to 93711. This filter means that only records whose PostalCode field is equal to 93711 are included in the mail merge.

5. **Click OK.**

   You return to the Mail Merge Helper dialog box.

6. **Click the Merge button to continue with the mail merge.**

TECHNICAL STUFF

I've never been very good at relationships

You can set up different kinds of tests in the Comparison fields. Computerniks call these tests *relational tests* because they test the relationships between two things (in this case, a merge field and a specific value). You can use these relational tests to create different kinds of selection filters.

You can set up complicated queries that check the contents of several fields. You may want to mail letters only to people who live in a particular city and state, for example. You set up the query like this:

```
City Equal to Bakersfield
And State Equal to CA
```

In this query, only records whose City field is equal to *Bakersfield* and whose State field is equal to *CA* are included in the merge.

(continued)

(continued)

You can also set up queries that test the same field twice. To mail to addresses with zip codes 93711 or 93722, for example, set up the query like this:

```
PostalCode Equal to 93711 Or
   PostalCode Equal to 93722
```

Notice that I change the And/Or field from And to Or. That way, a record is selected if its PostalCode field is 93711 or 93722. If you test the same field for two or more specific values, do not leave the And/Or field set to And. If I had left the And/Or field set to And in the preceding example, a record would be selected only if its Postal Code was equal to 93711 and if it was also equal to 93722. Obviously, this can't be: Each record in the data source can have only one value for the PostalCode field. It's natural to want to leave the And/Or field set to And because you want to "mail letters to everyone in the 93711 *and* 93722 zip codes." But when you fill in the Query dialog box, you have to use Or, not And.

On the other hand, suppose that you want to mail to anyone whose zip code is 93711, 93722, or any value in between. In that case, you use two condition tests linked by And, as shown in this example:

```
PostalCode Greater Than or
Equal to 93711

And PostalCode Less Than or
Equal to 93722
```

Table 8-1 Relational Tests

Comparison Setting	*What It Means*
Equal To	Selects only those records in which the value of the specified Field exactly matches the Compare To value
Not Equal To	Selects only those records in which the value of the specified Field does not exactly match the Compare To value
Less Than	Selects only those records in which the value of the specified Field is less than the Compare To value
Greater Than	Selects only those records in which the value of the specified Field is greater than the Compare To value
Greater Than or Equal To	Selects only those records in which the value of the specified Field is greater than or equal to the Compare To value
Is Blank	Selects only those records in which the value of the specified Field is blank
Is Not Blank	Selects only those records in which the value of the specified Field is not blank

Editing the data source directly

When you edit the data source by clicking the Edit button in the Data Source portion of the Mail Merge Helper dialog box, you are presented with the Data Form dialog box, which provides a convenient way to add names and addresses to your mailing list. If you want, you can fiddle directly with the data in the data source by clicking the View Source button in the Data Form dialog box. When you do, the data source document is displayed in a document window so that you can edit it just like any other document (see Figure 8-12).

Data is stored in the data source as a Word table. Each field is represented by a table column, and each record is represented by a row. The first row of the table contains the field names. You can edit data directly in the table if you want, but I find it easier to edit the table data by using the Data Form dialog box.

TIP

Word formats the table so that most of the columns are not wide enough to display their contents on one line. However, the line breaks in the fields don't affect the way the merged letters are printed. If you want, you can adjust the width of each field by dragging the boxes between columns in the ruler.

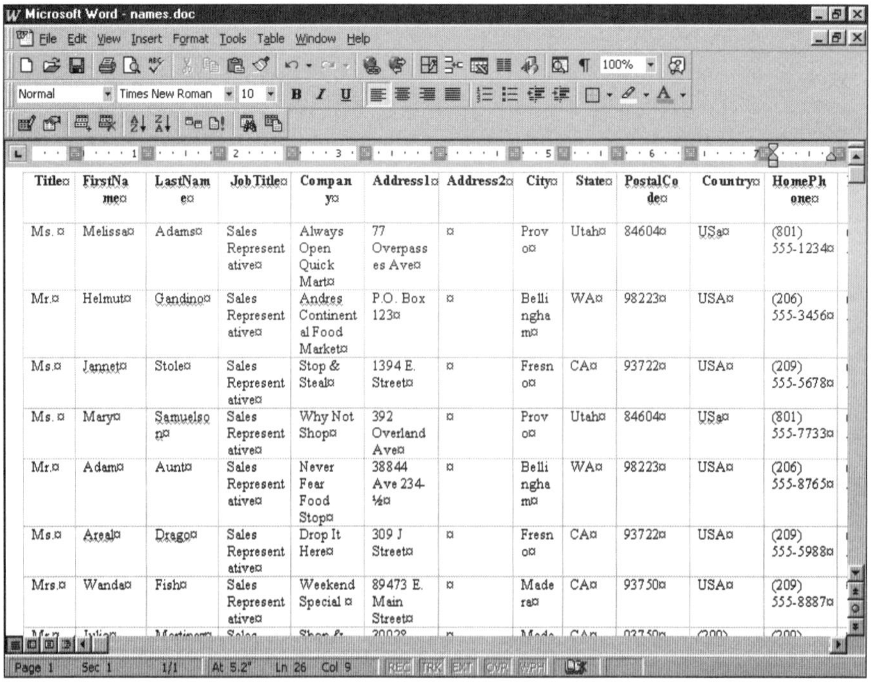

Title	FirstName	LastName	JobTitle	Company	Address1	Address2	City	State	PostalCode	Country	HomePhone
Ms.	Melissa	Adams	Sales Representative	Always Open Quick Mart	77 Overpasses Ave		Provo	Utah	84604	USa	(801) 555-1234
Mr.	Helmut	Gandino	Sales Representative	Andres Continental Food Market	P.O. Box 123		Bellingham	WA	98223	USA	(206) 555-3456
Ms.	Jannet	Stole	Sales Representative	Stop & Steal	1394 E. Street		Fresno	CA	93722	USA	(209) 555-5678
Ms.	Mary	Samuelson	Sales Representative	Why Not Shop	392 Overland Ave		Provo	Utah	84604	USa	(801) 555-7733
Mr.	Adam	Aunt	Sales Representative	Never Fear Food Stop	38844 Ave 234-½		Bellingham	WA	98223	USA	(206) 555-8765
Ms.	Areal	Drago	Sales Representative	Drop It Here	309 J Street		Fresno	CA	93722	USA	(209) 555-5988
Mrs.	Wanda	Fish	Sales Representative	Weekend Special	89473 E. Main Street		Madera	CA	93750	USA	(209) 555-8887

Figure 8-12: Editing the data source directly.

When you view the data source, Word activates the Database toolbar, just beneath the Formatting toolbar. The function of each button on the Database toolbar is summarized in Table 8-2.

Table 8-2 Buttons on the Database Toolbar

Button	*What It Does*
	Calls up the Data Form dialog box so that you can quickly enter new records
	Calls up the Manage Fields dialog box so that you can add new fields to the table or delete fields from the table
	Adds a new record to the table
	Deletes the chosen record
	Sorts the table into ascending sequence
	Sorts the table into descending sequence
	Imports data from a database program
	Updates the contents of any Word fields included in the data source
	Finds data in a specific field
	Switches to the mail-merge main document

TIP

You can add or delete fields from the table by clicking the Manage Fields button. When you do, the Manage Fields dialog box appears, as shown in Figure 8-13. To add a field to the table, type the field name in the Field Name box and click the Add button. To remove a field, choose the field in the Field Names in Header Row list and click the Remove button.

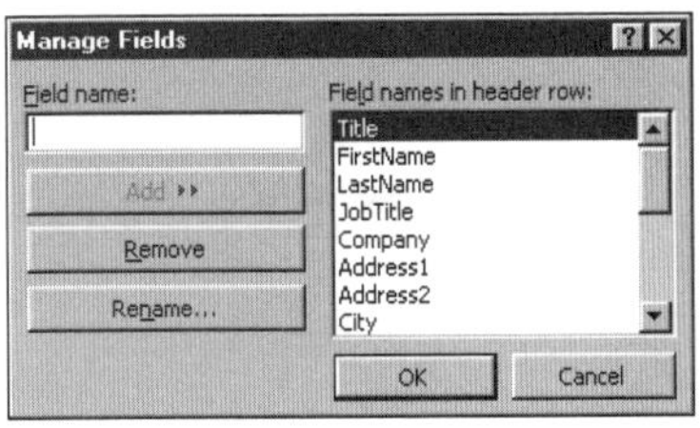

Figure 8-13: The Manage Fields dialog box.

Importing data from another source

Word enables you to use name and address records that you created with another program for your mail merges. If you use Paradox for Windows to keep a customer list, for example, you can open the Paradox database file as the data source. You can do the same with files created with dBASE, Microsoft Excel, Microsoft Access, Microsoft FoxPro, Lotus 1-2-3, WordPerfect, and earlier versions of Microsoft Word.

All you have to do to use a file created by one of the preceding programs as a mail-merge data source is follow these steps:

1. **Create a name and address database by using your program of choice.**

   Use whatever commands are necessary to create the data and keep it up-to-date.

2. **Call up Word and begin a mail merge.**

   Use the Tools⇨Mail Merge command to begin the mail merge. Click the Create button to create a new main document or open an existing one.

3. **Use the Get Data button to open an existing data source.**

4. **When the Open Data Source dialog box appears, use the List Files of Type field to choose the type of file you want to use.**

   If you create the database file with Paradox, for example, choose Paradox Files as the file type.

5. **Choose the file you want and click OK.**

   Word opens the database file and converts it to a mail-merge data source.

6. **Continue as usual.**

   Finish the mail merge by completing the main document (if necessary) and clicking the Merge button to begin the merge.

When you open a Microsoft Access file as a data source, Word asks whether you want to include the entire file or access specific records based on an Access query. If the data table is large and you don't need all the records, consider setting up an Access query to select just the records you want to include in the mail merge. This procedure is more efficient than importing the entire file into Word and then using a mail-merge query.

If the file you open is a Microsoft Excel worksheet, Word asks whether you want to include the entire worksheet file or whether you want to include only those cells that fall within a certain range.

You can also open text files in which the data for each field is separated by commas, tabs, or other characters. This is your bridge to foreign database programs that aren't included in the List Files of Type field. Almost all database programs let you *export* data to a text file. You can use the export feature to create a file that Word can open as a text file data source.

Unprecedented nonsense about precedence

If you set up a query that uses three or more field tests and mixes And and Or, you had better grab your pocket protector first so that you're prepared to deal with the advanced computer science graduate degree subject of precedence.

Precedence means, in layman's terms, "what to do first." You may suppose that Word would test the conditions you list in the Query Options dialog box in the order in which you list them. Not necessarily. Word groups any condition tests linked by And and checks them out before combining the results with tests linked by Or.

Confused? So am I. Let's walk through an example to see how it works. Suppose that you open the menu at a restaurant and see that the fried chicken dinner comes with a "leg or wing and thigh." Which of the following statements represents the two possible chicken-dinner configurations the restaurant could sell you:

- You can order a meal with a leg and a thigh, or you can order a meal with a wing and a thigh.
- You can order a meal with a leg, or you can order a meal with a wing and thigh.

Hmm. Tough one. According to the way Word processes queries, the answer is the second one. Word lumps together as a group the two options linked by And. If you were a computer science grad student, you would put parentheses around "wing and thigh," like this: "leg or (wing and thigh)."

If you want the first example to be the right answer, you have to state the menu choice as "leg and thigh or wing and thigh." Or, if you like to use parentheses, you could go with "(leg or wing) and thigh."

For a more realistic Word example, suppose that you want to mail to everyone who lives in Dallas or Fort Worth. To do that, you have to set up the query like this:

```
City Equal to Dallas
And State Equal to TX
Or City Equal to Fort Worth
And State Equal to TX
```

Chapter 9

More Footnote Foibles

In This Chapter

- Adding footnotes
- Changing the appearance of footnotes
- Changing the reference marks
- Changing the footnote separators
- Finding a footnote reference

Footnotes. Back when I was in college, typing them was a major pain in the derriere.[1] You had to count out the lines just right to make sure that you left enough room at the bottom of the page. I never did figure out how to deal with footnote references that fell right at the bottom of the page, too close to the margin to place the note on the same page.

Footnotes are one of the neatest features of word processors, at least while you're in college. After that, they're a pretty useless appendage, unless you happen to work at the college, in which case the footnote feature becomes a source of resentment — just one among many examples of how easy kids have it today. Hmph.

Adding a Footnote

There's really not much to using footnotes, unless you want to get fancy with them. Here's the down-and-dirty procedure for adding plain-vanilla footnotes:

1. **Put the cursor where you want the little footnote reference number to appear in your text.**
2. **Call up the Insert⇨Footnote command.**

---

[1]Hindpart; rear appendage; stern.

The Footnote and Endnote dialog box appear, as shown in Figure 9-1. You can choose between footnotes and endnotes (footnotes appear at the bottom of the page on which the footnote reference appears; endnotes are printed together at the end of the document) and fiddle with numbering options, but usually you just give this dialog box a bothered glance before clicking OK.

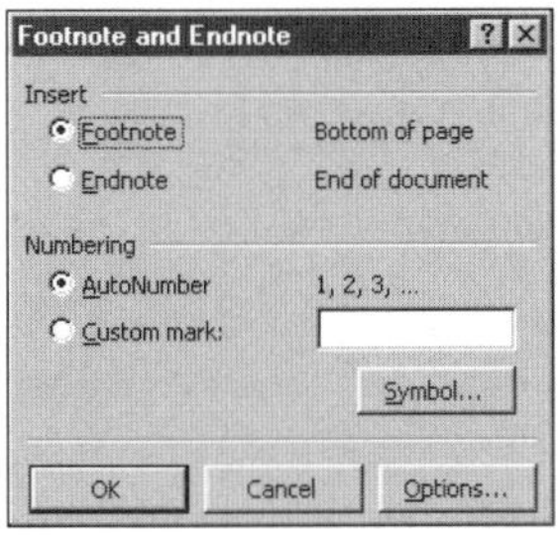

Figure 9-1: The Footnote and Endnote dialog box.

3. **Click OK.**

   This step opens a separate footnote window at the bottom of the screen, as shown in Figure 9-2. Type your footnote in the space provided.

4. **Click Close when you're finished.**

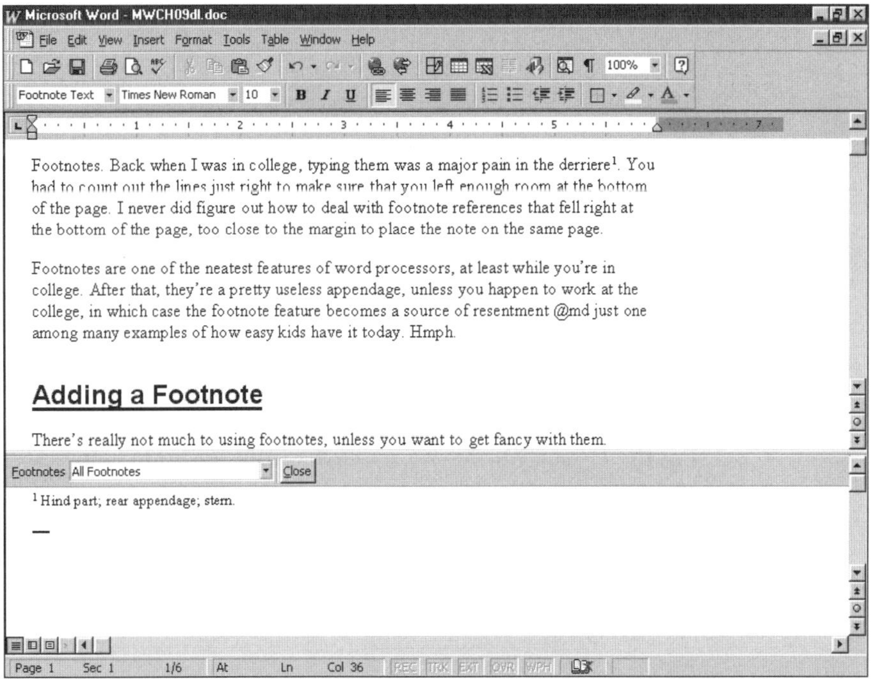

Figure 9-2: Typing a footnote in the footnote window.

Word automatically numbers footnotes for you. Heck, that's the point. When you use the Insert⇨Footnote command, Word inserts the little footnote reference number in the text and pairs it with a number in the footnote itself. If you go back later and insert a new footnote in front of an existing one, Word automatically juggles the footnote numbers to keep everything in sync.

Here are some more tips to remember when using footnotes:

- For an extra-quick way to create a footnote, use the keyboard shortcut Ctrl+Alt+F. This keyboard shortcut means "go directly to the footnote window. Do not display the Footnote and Endnote dialog box; do not collect $200."
- To look at your footnotes, use the View⇨Footnotes command.
- If you start off with Endnotes but then decide that you want to convert your endnotes to footnotes (or vice versa), fear not! Just call up the Insert⇨Footnote command, click the Options button, and then click the Convert button. When you click OK three times, your notes are converted.
- If you made a goof in the footnote, double-click the footnote reference in the text. That action pops open the footnote window so that you can fix the note.
- To delete a footnote, select its footnote reference number in the text and press the Del key.

Changing the Footnote Format

The formatting of footnotes is governed by the Footnote Text style. You can change the appearance of all the footnotes in your document by simply modifying the Footnote Text style.

Similarly, footnote reference numbers are formatted by using the Footnote Reference style. This style is a character style, so it doesn't affect formatting for the entire paragraph.

For details on how to change a style, see Chapter 4.

The initial setting for Footnote Text is Normal + 10 point. Therefore, footnotes are formatted by using the same font as in your Normal paragraphs, except that they are 10 point regardless of the Normal text size. If you want your footnotes to appear in a different font from the rest of the document, change the font for the Footnote Text style.

The initial setting for Footnote Reference is Default Character Format + Superscript. As a result, footnote reference numbers are printed using the same font as the rest of the text in the paragraph, except that the superscript attribute applies. If you would rather see footnote references in a different font, all you have to do is change the Footnote Reference style.

Both Footnote Text and Footnote References are applied automatically when you create footnotes, so you shouldn't have any cause to apply these formats directly.

Changing the Reference Marks

Most footnotes are numbered 1, 2, 3, and so on, but Word enables you to change this standard numbering format to use letters, roman numerals, or the special reference symbols *, †, ‡, and §.

Follow these steps to change reference marks:

1. **Summon the Insert⇨Footnote command.**

   The Footnote and Endnote dialog box appears.

2. **Click the Options button.**

   The Note Options dialog box appears, as shown in Figure 9-3.

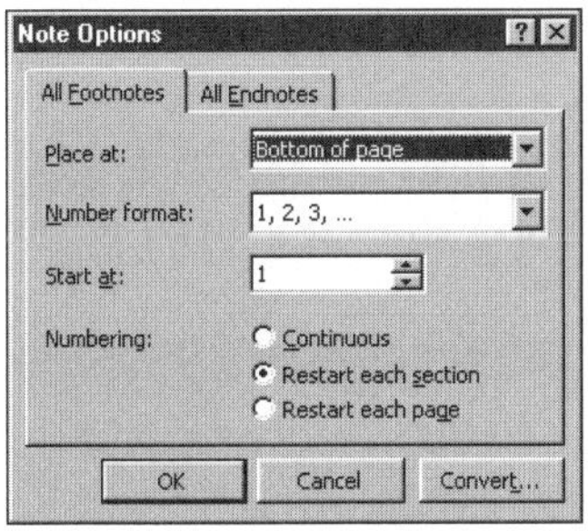

Figure 9-3: The Note Options dialog box.

3. **Choose the Number format you want.**

   This list shows your choices:

   1, 2, 3 . . .

   a, b, c . . .

   A, B, C . . .

   i, ii, iii . . .

I, II, III . . .

*, †, ‡, § . . .

4. Click OK all the way home.

You have to click twice — once to return to the Footnote and Endnote dialog box and then a second time to return to your document.

All the footnotes in a section must use the same numbering scheme. You can't mix and match.

If you choose the special symbols *, †, ‡, and § for your reference marks, Word doubles them if necessary to create unique reference marks. The first four footnotes use the symbols singly. The mark for the fifth through eighth notes are **, ††, ‡‡, and §§. After that, the symbols are tripled.

To keep this doubling and tripling of symbols in check, choose the Restart Each Page button in the Note Options dialog box. That way, the mark for the first note on each page is always an asterisk (*). Otherwise, you'll end up with reference marks like §§§§§§§§§§, which look really silly.

You can bypass Word's automatic footnote-numbering scheme at any time by checking the Custom Mark button in the Footnote and Endnote dialog box and then entering any text that you want to use for the mark in the Custom Mark text box. If you want to enter a symbol that's not readily available from the keyboard, click the Symbol button and choose the symbol you want from the resulting Symbol dialog box.

Changing the Footnote Separators

Word automatically adds a short horizontal line called the *footnote separator* to separate footnotes from the text on a page. If the footnote is too long to fit at the bottom of the page, Word automatically continues the footnote to the next page and adds a *footnote continuation separator,* a longer horizontal line. You can customize the appearance of these separators by following this procedure:

1. Create at least one footnote.

There's no point in bothering with customized separators for a document that doesn't yet have any footnotes. Word doesn't let you anyway.

2. Summon the View⇨Footnotes command.

The footnote window appears.

3. In the list box at the top of the footnote window, choose the separator that you want to edit.

You can choose the footnote separator, the footnote continuation separator, or the footnote continuation notice. (The continuation notice is printed beneath a footnote that is being continued to the next page; the continuation separator is printed atop the continued note on the next page.)

4. **Edit it.**

   Delete the horizontal line if you want. Add text, such as "Footnotes," above or below it. Or change the amount of space before or after the separator. Whatever.

5. **Click Close.**

   You're finished.

TIP: If you mess with a separator and then wish that you hadn't, use the View⇨Footnotes command, choose the separator you messed up, and click the Reset button.

Finding a Footnote Reference

To quickly find the reference mark for a particular footnote or endnote, follow these steps:

1. **Call up the Edit⇨Go To command.**

   The keyboard shortcut is Ctrl+G. The Go To command displays a dialog box that isn't worthy of a separate figure here.

2. **In the Go To What list box, choose Footnote or Endnote.**

3. **In the Enter Footnote Number text box, type the number of the footnote that you want to go to.**

   If the notes are numbered with reference symbols (*, †, ‡, and §), type the corresponding number (1, 2, 3, and so on).

4. **Click OK.**

   There it is.

Or, for an even easier method, click the Select Browse Object button located near the bottom of the scrollbar on the right edge of the document window. Then choose one of the following buttons from the pop-up menu that appears:

- Browse by endnote
- Browse by footnote

This changes the double-headed up and down arrow buttons that appear above and below the Select Browse Object button so that they go to the previous and next footnote or endnote, respectively.

Chapter 10
More Table Tidbits

In This Chapter

- Autoformatting a table
- Adding borders and shading to a table
- Merging cells to create headings
- Sorting rows in a table
- Pretending that a table is a spreadsheet
- Pretending that a table is a database

I couldn't figure out what to call this chapter: Setting the table? Turning the tables? Sliding under the table? Dancing on the table? Tabling the motion? The periodic table? Table for two? So I gave up and decided to call it just "More Table Tidbits."

All the basic kid stuff about using tables is in *Word 97 For Windows For Dummies.* Read this chapter when you're ready to move up from the kids' table to the grown-ups' table so that you can learn how to do grown-up table stuff, such as add borders, create headings, and pretend that the table is a spreadsheet or database. (After all, pretending that you're something you really aren't is what being at the grown-up table is all about, isn't it?)

REMEMBER

If you're going to sit at my table, you have to remember the same two rules of table manners I've been trying to teach my kids for years: No talking with your mouth open and no eating with your mouth full.

The Table Drawing Tool

New for Word 97 is a feature that lets you draw complicated tables on the screen using a simple set of drawing tools. The Draw Table command is ideal for creating tables that are not a simple grid of rows and columns but are instead a complex conglomeration where some cells span more than one row and others span more than one column. These complex tables were

difficult to create in Word 95, but Word 97 lets you create them with just a few mouse clicks.

Here's the procedure for creating a table using the Draw Table tool:

1. **Choose the Table⇨Draw Table command or click the Tables and Borders button on the standard toolbar.**

   This throws you into Page View (if you aren't already there) and brings up the Tables and Borders toolbar, shown in Figure 10-1.

2. **Draw the overall shape of the table by dragging the mouse to create a rectangular boundary for the table.**

   When you release the mouse button, a table with a single cell is created, as shown in Figure 10-2.

3. **Carve the table up into smaller cells.**

   For example, to split the table into two rows, point the mouse somewhere along the left edge of the table, then press the mouse button and drag a line across the table to the right edge. When you release the mouse, the table is split into two rows.

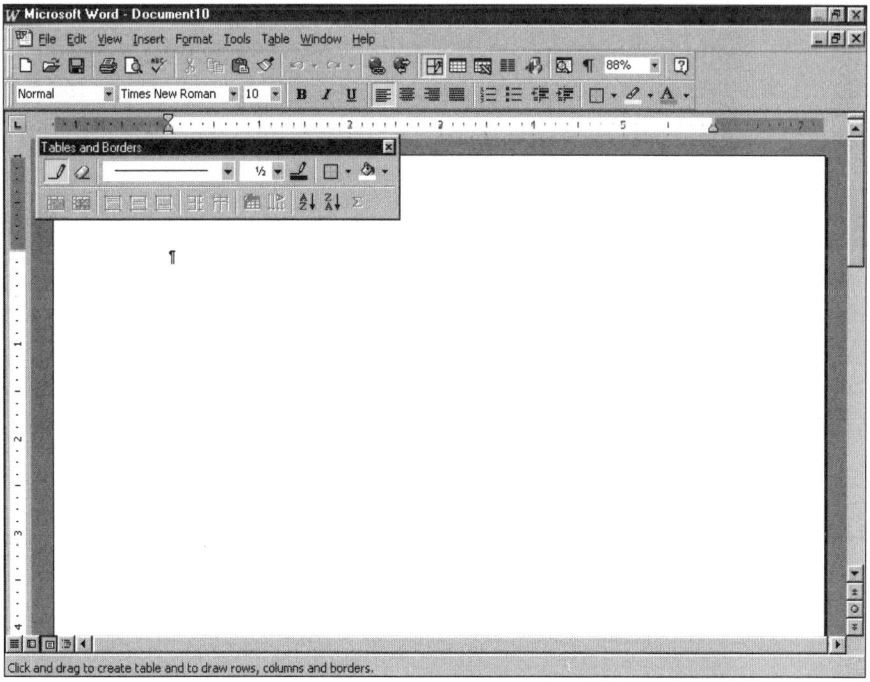

Figure 10-1: Drawing a table with the Tables Drawing tool.

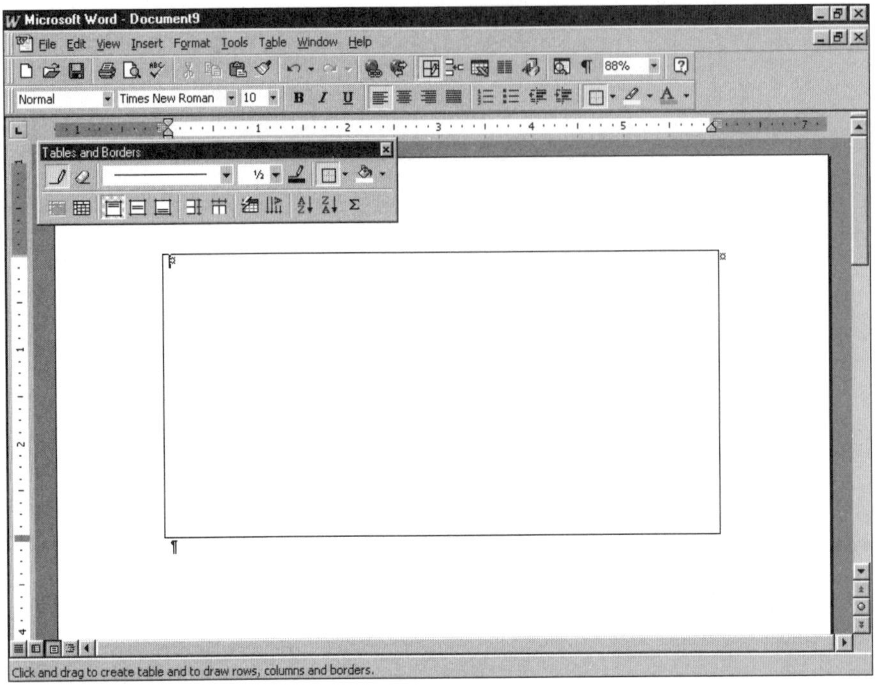

Figure 10-2: First draw a rectangle as the outline for the table.

You can continue to carve up the table into smaller and smaller cells. For each slice, point the mouse at one edge of where you want the new cell to begin and drag the mouse to the other edge.

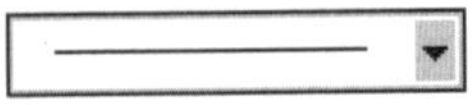

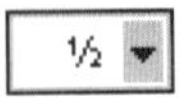

4. **If you want to change the line size or style drawn for a particular segment, use the line style and line weight drop-down controls in the Tables and Borders toolbar.**

   You can change the style of a line you've already drawn by tracing over the line with a new style.

5. **If you make a mistake while drawing the table cells, click the Erase button (shown in the margin) and erase the mistaken line segment.**

   Click the Draw Table button if you want to draw additional segments after using the Erase tool.

6. **When you're done, click the Tables and Borders button again to dismiss the Tables and Borders toolbar.**

Figure 10-3 shows a table carved up into several cells, with various types of line style and line weights.

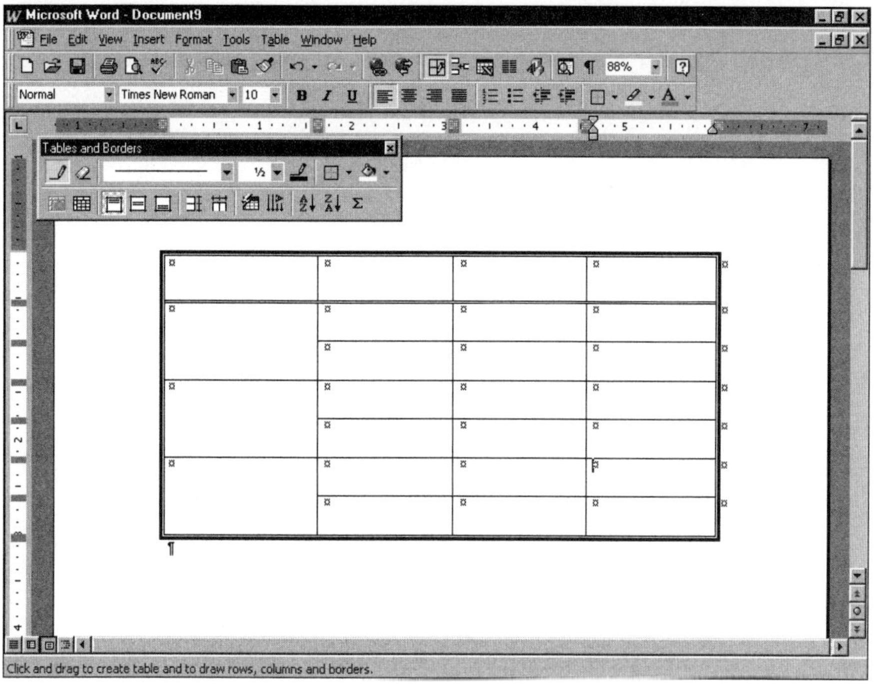

Figure 10-3: A finished table.

The Tables and Borders toolbar contains an assortment of tools that you can use not only to new draw tables but also to work with existing tables. Many of these tools are described in detail in later sections of this chapter. Table 10-1 summarizes the function of each tool on this toolbar.

Autoformatting a Table

You can create great-looking tables in two ways:

- Use the Table⇨Table AutoFormat command and skip the rest of this chapter.
- Pretend that you didn't read this section and toil away at the table for hours until you get it just the way you want.

Get the picture?

Table 10-1 The Tables and Borders Toolbar

Button	*Name*	*What it does*
	Draw Table	Draws the outline of the table, then draws line segments to create new cells within a table
	Erase	Erases line segments to remove cells from a table
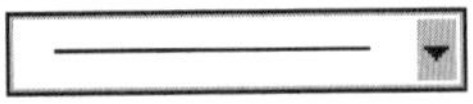	Line Style	Sets the line style for line segments drawn with the Draw Table tool
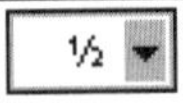	Line Weight	Sets the width of line segments drawn with the Draw Table tool
	Border Color	Sets the color of line segments drawn with the Draw Table tool
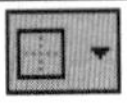	Outside Border	Shows or hides borders for selected cells
	Shading Color	Sets the background color for the selected cells
	Merge Cells	Merges adjacent cells to create one large cell
	Split Cells	Splits a merged cell into separate cells
	Align Top	Sets the vertical alignment of the selected cells to Top
	Center Vertically	Sets the vertical alignment of the selected cells to Center
	Align Bottom	Sets the vertical alignment of the selected cells to Bottom
	Distribute Rows	Adjusts the height of the selected rows so that the rows are distributed evenly
	Distribute Columns	Adjusts the width of the selected columns so that the columns are distributed evenly
	Table AutoFormat	Summons the Table AutoFormat dialog box
	Text Direction	Changes the direction of text in a cell
	Sort Ascending	Sorts the selected cells in ascending order
	Sort Descending	Sorts the selected cells in descending order
	AutoSum	Creates an AutoSum field

Here are the steps to instant awe-inspiring tables:

1. **Create a table.**

   Use the Insert Table button on the Standard toolbar or the Table➪Insert Table command. Create the correct number of rows and columns and type your data. If appropriate, devote the first row and column to headings.

   Or, use the Tables and Borders button and draw the table using the Draw Table tool.

2. **Click the mouse anywhere in the table.**

3. **Summon the Table➪Table AutoFormat command.**

   Or, if the Tables and Borders toolbar is visible, click the Table AutoFormat button (shown in the margin). Either way, the Table AutoFormat dialog box appears, as shown in Figure 10-4.

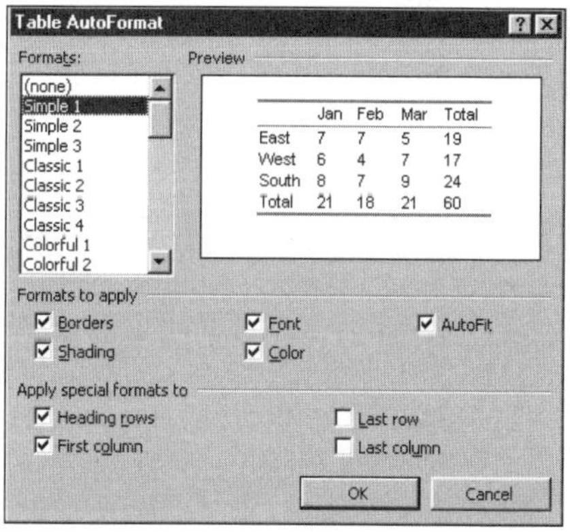

Figure 10-4: The Table AutoFormat dialog box.

4. **Choose the table format that you like from the Formats list box.**

   As you scroll through the list of available formats, a preview of how a sample table will appear with the format applied is shown in the preview box.

5. **If you want to change the formatting elements applied to the table, check or uncheck the appropriate check boxes.**

   If you don't have headings in the first column, for example, uncheck the First column check box. Or if you don't have a printer that can do justice to shading, uncheck the Shading check box.

6. **Click OK.**

   You return to the document, where you can admire your work.

7. **Don't tell your friends how you did it.**

   Make them think that you toiled for hours drawing the table.

You can change the AutoFormat applied to a table at any time. Just click anywhere in the table and summon the Table➪Table AutoFormat command again.

The Table➪Table AutoFormat command works by setting the formatting individually for each cell in the table. If you're still not satisfied, you can easily adjust the formatting by using the commands on the Format menu.

Amazingly, the formatting applied by the Table➪Table AutoFormat command can withstand severe table editing in the form of inserting and deleting entire columns and rows. Remarkable! Microsoft should patent some of this stuff.

Adding Borders and Shading to a Table

The Table AutoFormat command does an excellent job of formatting common types of tables. But to create a more complex table, you may need to revert to manual methods of adding borders and shading. Never fear; just follow these steps:

1. **If the Tables and Border toolbar isn't visible, click the Tables and Border button to summon it.**

2. **Select the cell or cells to which you want to add a border or shading.**

3. **To change the border style for a cell, first choose the border line style and weight using the drop-down controls in the toolbar, then drag over the line segment you want to change.**

   As you drag over the line segment, the line style and weight setting will be applied.

4. **To shade a cell, click the cell you want to shade, then click the Shading Color button.**

   This will apply the default shading color to the cell. To apply a different color, click the down arrow that's next to the Shading Color button to reveal a menu of color choices and select the color you want to use.

5. **You're finished.**

   Click the Border button again to make the Border toolbar go away.

You can also apply borders and shading by using the Format➪Borders and Shading command, although I'm not sure why you would when the tools on the Tables and Borders toolbar are so much easier to use.

You can remove borders as well as create them by using the Tables and Borders toolbar. Select No Border for the line style, then drag the mouse over the border you want to remove.

Merging Cells to Create Headings

Some tables have headings that span more than one column. For example, consider the table shown in Figure 10-5. In this example, the cell that contains the heading "Shipments By Region (millions)" spans three columns so that the heading is centered over those columns.

	Shipments By Region (millions)		
	Western	Eastern	Central
Paper bags	103	87	98
Plastic bags	120	93	92
Dirt bags	43	38	129
Scum bags	204	44	31

Figure 10-5: A table with a heading that spans three columns.

If you use the Draw Table tool to draw your tables, you can create cells that span several columns for these headings. But if you use the Insert⇨Table command to create a table, you must use the Table⇨Merge Cells command to create a cell that spans several columns.

To create a merged cell that spans several columns, follow these simple steps:

1. **Create the table using the Insert⇨Table command.**

   Type the data into the cells as usual. For the heading that spans several columns, type the text into the cell over the first column that you want the heading to span.

2. **Highlight the cells in the row in which you want to create a multicolumn heading.**

3. **Use the Table⇨Merge Cells command.**

   Or click the Merge Cells button (shown in the margin) if the Tables and Borders toolbar is visible. Either way, the cells are merged into one super cell that spans several columns.

4. **If you want the heading centered over the cells, click the Center button on the Formatting toolbar.**

   Or press Ctrl+C.

Change your mind? Select the big cell and use the Table➪Split Cells command or click the Split Cells button (shown in the margin). When Word asks you in how many columns to split the cell, specify the number of columns that the heading cell spans.

TIP

If you have a really long table, so long that it doesn't all fit on one page, select the heading row and use the Table➪Headings command. Then Word duplicates the heading row at the top of the table on each page.

TIP

Merged cells don't get along well with the Table➪Table AutoFormat command. Format the table with Table➪Table AutoFormat first; then merge the cells to create a multicolumn heading.

Sorting Data in a Table

If you enter rows into a table in the wrong order, you can sort them by using the Sort buttons found on the Tables and Borders toolbar. First, highlight the entire table (or just the rows you want to sort). Then, click one of the following buttons found on the Tables and Borders toolbar:

Sorts the table into ascending sequence.

Sorts the table into descending sequence.

If you need more precise control over how a table is sorted, follow these steps:

1. **Select the rows you want to sort.**

   It's best if you select entire rows and leave out any heading rows you don't want sorted.

2. **Summon the Table➪Sort command.**

   The Sort dialog box, shown in Figure 10-6, appears.

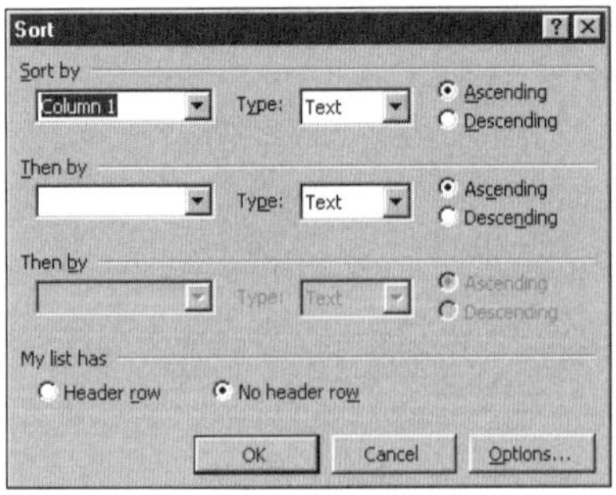

Figure 10-6: The Sort dialog box.

3. **Set both the column you want to sort the table by and the type of sort you want.**

   The Sort By list box allows you to choose any of the columns you selected. Under Type, you can choose Text, Number, or Date. And you can choose Ascending or Descending sequence.

4. **Click OK.**

   The data is sorted according to your specs.

TIP: Make a mistake? Table sorting is a little error-prone. It's all too easy to include heading rows accidentally in the sort range or to pick the wrong column. If you should be so unlucky, fret not. Just press Ctrl+Z to undo the whole thing.

You can sort as many as three columns. You can sort a table, for example, that shows sales data by Sales Rep within Region. You can specify a different sort type and sequence for each column, too.

TIP: Pay no attention to the My list has selections at the bottom of the dialog box. If your table has one or more header rows, just don't select them when you sort the table.

Turning Text Sideways

A new feature in Word 97 allows you to turn the text in a table cell on its side. Take a look at the table shown in Figure 10-7. The cell in the top row (which is merged, by the way) contains normal text. But the text in the cells in the second row is rotated so that it displays sideways.

Normal text is very boring			
But sideways text is really cool	But sideways text is really cool	But sideways text is really cool	But sideways text is really cool

Figure 10-7: Sideways text is cool.

To change the text direction, first select the cell containing the text you want to reorient, then click the Change Text Direction button (shown in the margin). Click the button once to rotate the text 90 degrees. Click it again to rotate the text an additional 180 degrees for a different orientation. Click the button a third time to restore the text to its normal orientation.

Pretending That a Table Is a Spreadsheet

If you can't afford a real spreadsheet program, you can pretend that Word's table feature is sort of like a spreadsheet. After all, it does let you enter data into rows and columns, just like a spreadsheet does. If only you could create simple formulas that total data in several cells — oh, I almost forgot — you can!

Follow these steps to total the contents of a row or column of cells:

1. **Create a table in which a row or column of adjacent cells contains numbers you want to add up.**
2. **Place the insertion point in the cell in which you want to place the sum.**
3. **Click the AutoSum button.**

   That's it! The sum will be placed in the cell.

Word's calculation abilities go beyond the ability to merely sum a row or column of figures. In fact, a Word table can include functions that are similar to the functions found in a more powerful spreadsheet program such as Microsoft Excel. To create a cell that contains a formula to calculate an average, a product, or some other value, follow these steps:

1. **Place the insertion point in the cell in which you want to place the calculated value.**
2. **Choose the Table⇨Formula command.**

   The Formula dialog box appears, as shown in Figure 10-8.

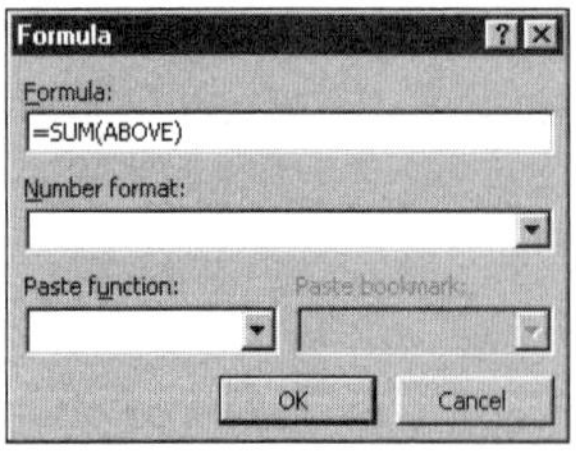

Figure 10-8: The Formula dialog box.

3. **Briefly review the formula and number format proposed by Word.**

   Word will initially propose to calculate the sum of values to the left of or above the selected cell. But you can substitute a different calculation by selecting one of the options listed in the Paste Function drop-down list.

4. **Click OK.**

   The formula is inserted into the cell, and the value is calculated.

5. **Double-check the results.**

   Make sure that the numbers look good. You can never trust a computer to add things up right.

You can also create simple math expressions in the Formula field, such as C3+C5*100. When you create expressions like this, you can refer to specific cells just as you would in a spreadsheet program: A1, C4, and so on.

Don't throw away your copy of Excel or Lotus just yet. Formulas are useful for summing or averaging cells in small tables, but that's about as far as their usefulness goes. A Word table is no substitute for an Excel spreadsheet.

Pretending That a Table Is a Database

Word also likes to pretend that it's a database program. After all, databases are nothing more than tables of information, so why not call a Word table a *data table?* This enables Microsoft to increase the price of Word by about $50.

To use a table as a database, use the first row in the table to specify a field name for each column. Then use the View➪Toolbars command to activate the Database toolbar. This toolbar has a bunch of useful buttons that let you treat a table like a database. The most useful is the Data Form button, which enables you to insert and delete table rows as though they were database records.

Isn't this what you do when you use the Mail Merge feature? You bet. So I'm not going to repeat myself here. If you want to know more about using a table as a database, shuffle on over to Chapter 8.

Part II

Word's Gee-Whiz Desktop Publishing Features

The 5th Wave By Rich Tennant

In this part . . .

Back in the old days, it was enough work just to get a document's tabs and margins set properly. Fancy desktop publishing features — using different text fonts or working with column formats — were best left to desktop-publishing gurus who used specialized page-layout programs that ran only on the Macintosh.

Alas, those days are gone. Now, anybody can be a desktop publisher. Word 97 contains all the desktop publishing features that you need to create spiffy-looking newsletters, brochures, manuals, and even full-length books. The chapters in this part show you how to use Word's desktop publishing features. It might be like trying to find gold in a silver mine or trying to drink whiskey from a bottle of wine, but it works. So get back.

Chapter 11

Bluffing Your Way through Typography School

In This Chapter

- Serif type
- Sans serif type
- Other kinds of type
- Point size, line length, and line spacing
- Picking type
- Avoiding typeface clash

Back where I came from, there were people who did nothing all day but study type. They were called *typographers*. They worked in musty type foundries that smelled of molten lead and spent most of their free time cleaning their hands and coming up with cute names for new type designs like *Pandemonium* or *Bologna Book* or *Vogon Old Style*.

Now, through the magic of Windows, you too can be a typographer. Why print all your documents using Arial and Times New Roman like everybody else, when typefaces that are more attractive and more useful are readily available? A surprising number of Windows application programs come with extra typefaces, so odds are that you already have a few alternatives to pick from. Some programs, such as CorelDRAW!, come with *hundreds* of typefaces. Just today I was in an office supply store and saw a collection of 400 typefaces on a CD-ROM for $29.95.

Of course, the dark side of this story is that after you have all those typefaces, you don't know what to do with them. The proper use of typefaces can make your documents look like they were done by a professional with impeccable taste. Improper use can have the same effect as hanging a yellow "Amateur Desktop Publisher On Board" sign on your computer.

Typography (the study of type) can be a fascinating subject. Whole books have been written about it, books that are worthy of a quiet evening read while resting in a lush, leather recliner with a glass of sherry and a pipe nearby. If you don't have a leather recliner and you're fresh out of sherry and quiet evenings, this chapter has to suffice. It gives you a few quick pointers that don't make you an expert in typography but should help you avoid the most obvious typographical blunders.

TIP

Two basic kinds of type fonts are used in desktop publishing: *PostScript* and *TrueType.* PostScript is the more popular among desktop publishing gurus, but TrueType is far and away the more popular among normal people, because support for TrueType is built into Windows 95. Using PostScript requires not only a more expensive PostScript printer, but also special software that you don't want to contend with. This chapter focuses on TrueType fonts, conveniently ignoring PostScript so that I don't have to buy an expensive printer.

Two Uses for Type

Before jumping into the various types of type, I want to distinguish between the two uses of type.

Body text: Body text is the main text of your document. The most important criteria for selecting a typeface for body text is legibility. In most documents, body text consists of paragraph upon paragraph of rather ordinary-looking words. You should choose a body text typeface that doesn't distract the readers as they read.

Display type: Display type is used for headings, captions, titles, and anything else that isn't body text. Text set in display type is usually brief — often just a few words — so legibility isn't the only factor to consider. The display type usually contrasts in some way with the body text type, adding variety to a page that would otherwise be filled with boring and lifeless body text.

When selecting type for body and display text, keep these points in mind:

- The typefaces you use for body text and display type need to be carefully coordinated. One of the easiest ways to mess up an otherwise good-looking page is *typeface clash.* (And the Typeface Clash Police are everywhere, you know.) See the section, "Avoiding Typeface Clash," later in this chapter for advice on picking typefaces for body text and display type that work well together.

- Some documents have more than one kind of display type. For example, a newsletter has display type in the nameplate, masthead, headings, pull quotes, jumplines, and so on. Try to limit the number of different typefaces you use for these elements. If you don't, your document ends up looking like a ransom note.
- When you set up the styles for a document, set the Normal style to the body text font and base other styles that are variations of body text on Normal. Then create a style named Display that uses the typeface you want for display type and base styles that define display text (such as Heading 1, Heading 2, and so on) on the Display style. This enables you to change your typefaces later simply by changing the Normal and Display styles. (For more information about styles, see Chapter 4.)

About face

To a normal person, the terms *font* and *typeface* mean the same thing. But don't use them interchangeably around typography nuts. They're liable to throw a case of hot lead type in your face. Here a rundown on the proper way to use these terms:

Typeface: A typeface is a design for a set of letters, along with numerals and punctuation marks to go along with it. The typeface includes both upper- and lowercase letters. For example, Times Roman is the name of one of the most popular typefaces.

Typeface family: A group of closely related typefaces. For example, Times Roman, Times Bold, Times Italic, and Times Bold Italic. The bold, italic, and bold italic forms of a family are considered separate typefaces, but members of the same family.

Font: A complete set of type for a particular typeface and size. For example, 10-point Avant Garde and 12-point Avant Garde are two distinct fonts.

In the days of lead type, the distinction between font and face was important because a typesetter had only certain fonts representing a particular family. For example, the typesetter had only 9-, 10-, 12-, and 14-point Times font for each face in the Times family. If you wanted 13-point Times Roman, you were out of luck.

The distinction between font and face is not so important anymore because Windows can create fonts of any point size you want. Thus, if you have the Times Roman typeface, you can display it in any size you want.

Windows actually muddles the terminology by using the term *font* to mean *typeface family.* When you format characters in Word, you specify the font (such as Times New Roman), the size (such as 11 point), and the style (bold, italic, or bold italic). Actually, all three of these characteristics combined is what a typographer calls a *font.*

Type Types

Typography is kind of like wine tasting: It has its own fancy terminology. Typographers say things like, "*Vogon Old Style* has a delicately balanced variation in stroke weight, with just a hint of angularity in the serifs to drive the message forward without being pretentious. This, combined with its full but gentle bouquet and a tangy but fruity finish, makes it the ideal choice for your yard-sale signs."

Then they'll look at you, expecting you to nod your head knowingly and say, "Ah."

You certainly don't need to have such refined taste when it comes to picking type, but you should at least understand the differences between the basic kinds of type — serif, sans serif, script, and decorative/novelty.

Serif type

Serif type is type that has little feet at the bottom of the letters. These little feet enable the type to walk smoothly across the page in Michael Jackson moon-walking style. Figure 11-1 shows the difference between a serif and sans serif *y* up close so that you can see what I am talking about.

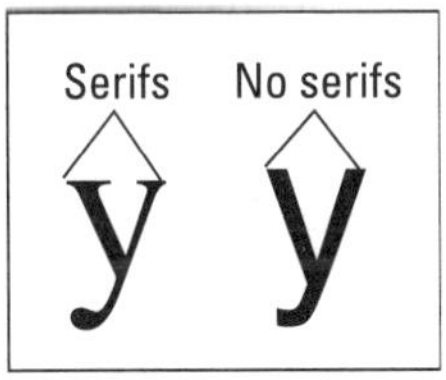

Figure 11-1: What a serif really is.

In each of the typefaces in Figure 11-2, the serifs at the bottoms of the letters create the faint illusion of a baseline that aids the eye as it moves across the page.

Serif type is usually the best kind of type to use in paragraphs of text. The serifs make it easier for the eye to follow a line of text across the page and then jump down to the next line.

Times New Roman is ubiquitous and universal, too.

Bookman Old Style is a classic.

Century Schoolbook is an excellent study.

Garamond is gentile.

Lucida Bright is a smart choice.

Figure 11-2: Some typefaces that include serifs.

Serifs also occur at the tops of some letters, like at the top of a capital *T* or *F* and a lowercase *p* or *y*. Serifs at the tops of letters are called *head serifs*. That means they get to boss the lowly *foot serifs* around.

TECHNICAL STUFF

Who cares about all those type parts?

Ever wonder what all the doohickeys and deelybobs found in a typical type design are called? Probably not. But just in case, the accompanying figure and the following definitions give you the lowdown.

Serifs: The little feet at the tops and bottoms of the letters.

Descender: The part of the letter than hangs down below the line (such as the lines in j, p, and y).

Ascender: The part of the letter that rises above the body of the letter (such as the lines in b, d, and h).

X-height: The height of a lowercase letter x, which usually governs the height of other lowercase letters and the appearance of the ascenders.

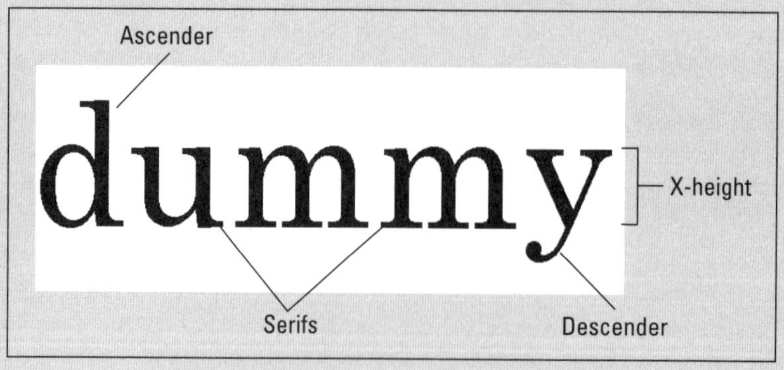

Sans serif type

Sans serif typefaces don't have serifs. Figure 11-3 shows some examples.

Arial is a bit overused.

Arial Narrow fits in tight places.

Century Gothic goes around in circles.

Haettenschweiler

Figure 11-3: Sans serif typefaces.

Here are some things to keep in mind concerning sans serif type:

TIP

- Without serifs to scoot the eye across the line, sans serif types are difficult to read in large stretches. Sans serif types are best used for headlines, captions, notes, and other short bursts of text. Use them in full paragraphs only if you want to appear trendy.
- The best-known sans serif typeface is Arial, which is built into many laser printers. Arial is a versatile typeface, but it's overused. Some designers would rather cut off their ear than use Arial. Suitable alternatives include Folio and Univers.
- Notice in Figure 11-3 how Century Gothic has a very geometrical look to it. It's almost as if the whole typeface is constructed of perfect circles and straight lines. Appearances can be deceiving, though. Study this typeface carefully and you'll notice subtle variations in the seemingly perfect circles and lines. (Try turning the book around and looking at the type upside-down.)

Scripts

Scripts are typefaces that are designed to mimic handwriting. Some scripts look like ornate, hand-drawn calligraphy; they are usually used in formal invitations. Other scripts look like they were spontaneously drawn. Figure 11-4 shows examples of both.

Brush Script

Lucida Caligraphy

Forte

Mistral

Viner Hand ITC

Figure 11-4: Various script typefaces.

Don't use script typefaces until you've considered these points:

- Scripts are usually difficult to read, especially in smaller sizes. Don't use them for large expanses of text.
- Don't use script types to imitate a hand-written signature. It's too much of a desktop cliché. If you want to add a computer printed signature to your documents, use a scanner to scan your signature and then include it as a graphic. If you don't have a scanner, take your signature to a copy center that has computers. They'll scan it for you, probably for about $10.

Novelty types

Novelty types are types that are so weird they defy categorization. Figure 11-5 shows some examples.

Ransom Has a Crazy Look

KEYSTROKES MT: BOXY BUT GOOD

Curlz MT Has a Fun Look

STENCIL REMINDS ME OF M*A*S*H

(Holidays MT)

Figure 11-5: Some really cool typefaces.

See? There are hundreds of typefaces like this to choose from.

Be careful about how you use these typefaces. Most of them are intended only for decorative use. Some of them can evoke a certain atmosphere, such as the Gold Rush days. Others just look goofy.

You can often find typefaces that represent your favorite TV show: *Star Trek, The Brady Bunch, The Flintstones, The Jetsons,* and so on. These are fun for a comical effect.

There's More to Typography Than Picking a Typeface

Picking a typeface is only the first step in creating type that looks good. Other aspects to consider are the point size, line length, line spacing, and alignment.

Point size

When you create a new document by clicking the New button, Word bases the new document on the Normal template (NORMAL.DOT). The default text format for documents based on the NORMAL.DOT is 10-point Times New Roman. Considering that the left and right margins in the Normal template are $^{1}/_{4}$-inch, creating text lines a full 6 inches long, this font is way too small. Type a few paragraphs of text in 10-point Times New Roman on a 6-inch line and you'll see what I mean.

One obvious way to improve the legibility of documents based on NORMAL.DOT is to increase the point size to 11- or 12-point type. As you increase the point size, the amount of text that fits on each line naturally goes down and the text becomes more readable. This increase eases the burden on the eye, probably saving you money in the long run by reducing your need for eyeglasses. (See Chapter 5 for details on how to modify the NORMAL.DOT template.)

Note, however, that not all typefaces appear to be the same size at a given point size. For example, consider the examples in Figure 11-6, both set in 12-point type.

Notice how much larger the second example looks, even though both samples are the same point size? This is partly because the design of Century Schoolbook has a slightly larger x-height than Times New Roman, but also because Century Schoolbook has longer serifs than Times New Roman, which leaves more space between the letters.

Times New Roman (12 point)

The Old Grey Donkey, Eeyore, stood by himself in a thistly corner of the forest with his front feet well apart and his head on one side, and thought about things.

Century Schoolbook (12 point)

The Old Grey Donkey, Eeyore, stood by himself in a thistly corner of the forest with his front feet well apart and his head on one side, and thought about things.

Figure 11-6: Some typefaces look bigger than others.

TIP

- Increasing the point size isn't the only way to make NORMAL.DOT more legible. Another alternative is to shorten the line length by increasing the margins. See the next section, "Line length," for more about the relationship between point size and line length.
- There is no magic point size to use in all circumstances. Some typefaces are very readable in 9-point type, and others are not. Most of the time, your body text should be set in 10-, 11-, or 12-point type.

Line length

The NORMAL.DOT template sets the left and right margins to 1/4-inch each, which results in a 6-inch line length. That's almost always too wide, especially if you stick with the NORMAL.DOT default 10-point Times New Roman font. You need to reel 'er in a bit.

Unfortunately, there is no hard and fast rule for setting the proper line length. It varies depending on the typeface, point size, and the spacing between lines. All these factors work together. In other words, if you use a larger typeface and a larger point size and increase the amount of space between the lines, you can use a longer line length.

For example, here are two samples of text set in 10-point Times New Roman, with different line lengths:

The Old Grey Donkey, Eeyore, stood by himself in a thistly corner of the forest, his front feet well apart, his head on one side, and thought about things.

The Old Grey Donkey, Eeyore, stood by himself in
a thistly corner of the forest, his front feet well apart,
his head on one side, and thought about things.

The only real test for getting the line length right is to print some samples and read them.

- There are a few rules of thumb that graphics designers follow when setting the line length. One is that the length of the line should average about 50-60 characters; another is that each line should hold about eight to ten words. Yet another rule of thumb is the one-and-a-half-alphabets rule: Type the lowercase alphabet one and a half times, like this:

  abcdefghijklmnopqrstuvwxyzabcdefghijklm

  That should be about the length of one line. Note, however, that these rules of thumb are meant to be applied to two- or three-column layouts. For single-column layouts, these rules usually result in lines that are too short.

- TIP: To adjust the line length, set the page layout margins using the File➪Page Setup command, instead of grabbing the margin doohickeys on the ruler and sliding them. Dragging the ruler's margin doohickeys sets the left and right indents on a paragraph-by-paragraph basis, instead of adjusting the margins for the entire page. If you want to adjust only one paragraph, using the ruler is the way to go.

Line spacing

Line spacing refers to the amount of space added between lines of text. Consider these samples, each set in 10-point Times New Roman but with varying amounts of line spacing:

Line spacing: exactly 10 points

The Old Grey Donkey, Eeyore, stood by himself in a thistly corner of the forest with his front feet well apart and his head on one side, and thought about things. Sometimes he thought sadly to himself, "Why?" and sometimes he thought, "Wherefore?" and sometimes he thought, "Inasmuch as which?"

Line spacing: exactly 12 points

The Old Grey Donkey, Eeyore, stood by himself in a thistly corner of the forest with his front feet well apart and his head on one side, and thought about things. Sometimes he thought sadly to himself, "Why?" and sometimes he thought, "Wherefore?" and sometimes he thought, "Inasmuch as which?"

Line spacing: exactly 14 points

The Old Grey Donkey, Eeyore, stood by himself in a thistly corner of the forest with his front feet well apart and his head on one side, and thought about things. Sometimes he thought sadly to himself, "Why?" and sometimes he thought, "Wherefore?" and sometimes he thought, "Inasmuch as which?"

Increasing the line spacing enables you to run the line longer and use a smaller point size, or use a larger point size on a smaller line. In both cases, the extra line spacing adds definition to each line. To change the line spacing in Word, use the Format➪Paragraph command and adjust the Line Spacing and At settings.

- Extra line spacing beyond the type size is called *leading* (pronounced "ledding"), because back in the old days of lead type, the extra space was added by inserting thin strips of lead between the lines of type.
- If you set the line spacing to *Single,* Word adds a bit of extra leading. How much depends on the size of the type and the typeface you've selected. It usually works out pretty well, but if you want precise control, set the line spacing to *Exactly* instead. (You then also have to set the number of points for the line spacing.)

Alignment

The type of paragraph alignment you use affects the legibility of type, too. Word enables you to use four types of alignment: Left, Centered, Right, and Justified. Body text is either left-aligned or justified. Headings are usually either left-aligned or centered. You can set the text alignment by clicking one of the alignment buttons in the formatting toolbar or by calling up the Format➪Paragraph command and adjusting the Alignment setting.

Justified text gives your document a more formal appearance, but it has another important benefit as well: Justified text usually crams more text onto each line, resulting in fewer lines of text. That's why almost all newspapers set text in justified columns. If you're tight on space, consider using justified text.

Be careful about justified text in narrow columns, though. Word sometimes throws in an excessive amount of space between words to get the line to justify, as shown here:

> Sometimes he thought sadly
> to himself, "Why?" and
> sometimes he
> thought,"Wherefore?" and
> sometimes he thought,
> "Inasmuch as which?"

Notice the humongous gap in the third line. You could throw a Linotype machine through it.

You can fix problems like this usually by throwing in an optional hyphen. To do that, press Ctrl+– where you want the word to be hyphenated. If the word is anywhere near the end of the line, Word hyphenates it. For example:

> Sometimes he thought sadly
> to himself, "Why?" and
> sometimes he thought,
> "Wherefore?" and some-
> times he thought,
> "Inasmuch as which?"

In this example, I hyphenated the word *sometimes.* That solved the problem from the third line, but introduced a new problem in the fifth line. To correct the new problem, hyphenate again:

> Sometimes he thought sadly
> to himself, "Why?" and
> sometimes he thought,
> "Wherefore?" and some-
> times he thought, "In as-
> much as which?"

This is a lot of work, isn't it? That's why I avoid justified type whenever possible.

TIP

You can set up Word to hyphenate your documents automatically. Skip ahead to the next chapter to find out how.

Avoiding Typeface Clash

Faced with a bewildering array of typographical choices, what's a poor Word user to do? Following is some well-intentioned advice on picking fonts to use for body text and display type.

The good news is that you don't have to run out and invest $40 in a font collection to apply the advice contained here. Word 97 comes with a fairly decent collection of fonts right on the CD, so you can break right out of the "Times and Arial Doldrums."

Picking the body text type

The main criterion for selecting a body type is legibility. Unfortunately, legibility is not an either/or proposition. Some typefaces are easy to read in some circumstances and hard to read in others. Several factors work together to make text easy or hard to read. The typeface, the point size, the length of the line, and the amount of space between the lines all work together to create or destroy legibility.

That being said, here are a few rules of thumb for picking a good, legible typeface for body type:

- *Use a serif typeface for body text.* The point of serifs is to make text more legible. You can use sans serif typefaces for body text if you know what you're doing, but the safest way to create legible body text is to stick to a serif typeface.
- *Whatever typeface you use, adjust the point size, line length, and line spacing to improve legibility.* No type looks good when set in 9 point on a 6-inch line with no additional line spacing.
- *Don't bother with Times New Roman.* Times was originally designed for newspapers (the *London Times,* actually). The design goals were something like this: Design a typeface that enables us to cram as much text as possible onto one line and print the newspaper on cruddy presses and cheap paper. Unless you're trying to save paper or you want a newspaper look, you can almost certainly find a better typeface. As an added bonus, you'll stand out from the crowd. *Everybody* has Times New Roman, but not everybody has Vogon Old Style.

Picking the display type

Display type is usually used in short bursts: short headings, captions, titles, and so on. So legibility isn't necessarily the most important consideration when choosing a display type. Other factors, such as how much it contrasts with the body text and what kind of atmosphere is created, are important as well.

The safest way to pick a display type is to opt for a sans serif typeface. That's why Windows includes Arial, a Helvetica look-alike. Arial works with Times New Roman and just about any other serif typeface. Like Times New Roman, though, it's a bit overused. For a more distinctive look, use a different sans serif typeface, such as Century Gothic, Eurostile, or Lucida Sans.

If you want, you can also safely use a variation of the body text typeface for display type. For example, if the body text is 11-point Century Schoolbook, you may set headings as 14-point Century Schoolbook Bold and captions as 10-point Century Schoolbook Italic.

Don't mix different serif typefaces unless you know what you're doing. Some serif typefaces work well together, but others do not, and the subtleties are beyond the reach of most of us. Some designers marvel at your ingenuity in combining Goudy Old Style with Cheltenham, but others turn pale and begin to feel nauseous just thinking about it. Don't risk it.

Chapter 12

Working with Two and Three Column Layouts

In This Chapter

- Creating columns
- Adjusting column width
- Forcing a column break
- Hyphenating your text

If you use Word to create newsletters, brochures, and other stuff for which you really should be using a desktop publishing program like Adobe PageMaker, you'll be happy to know that Word enables you to create beautiful two- or three-column layouts. (Actually, you can create as many as 12 columns on a page, but unless you're using *really* wide paper, that's not such a good idea.)

Word refers to two- and three-column layouts as *newspaper-style columns,* but that's just a bit misleading. To implement a true newspaper-style column feature, Word would have to edit your prose automatically as you type it so that it focused on bad news and added a distinct left-wing slant to your text.

This chapter jumps head-first into setting up newspaper-style columns in Word and tackles a related feature: hyphenation. Hyphenation isn't such a big deal in single-column layouts, but after you add two or three columns to a page, hyphenation can be the key to making the columns look good. Plus, hyphenation didn't really fit anywhere else, and this chapter was kind of short without it.

Creating Columns

Columns are a sectional thing: When you create multiple columns, the column layout is applied to the entire section. If the entire document consists of but one section, the column layout applies to the entire document. If you want part of the document to have one column and another part to have two or three columns, you have to create two or more sections to accommodate the different column layouts.

Creating columns the easy way

Here is the easiest way to create multiple columns in your document:

1. **Click the Columns button (shown in the margin) on the Standard toolbar.**

   The drop-down menu shown in Figure 12-1 appears.

2. **Click and drag the mouse to pick the number of columns you want.**

Figure 12-1: The Columns button.

3. **Let go.**

   Voila! The document is formatted with the number of columns you chose.

Some notes on using multiple columns:

- When you create a multicolumn layout, Word switches you to Page Layout view so that the columns will be visible side-by-side on the screen. If you switch back to Normal view (View➪Normal), the text is formatted according to the width of the column, but the columns are not displayed side by side on-screen.
- For a quick glimpse of how the columns appear when printed, use the File➪Print Preview command. When you've seen enough, click the Close button to return to your document.

- Did you choke when you saw what your document looked like in columns? You can revert to single-column mode by pressing Ctrl+Z (the magic Undo command) or by using the Columns button to set the layout to one column.
- The Columns button enables you to set the number of columns, but it doesn't enable you to control the size of each column or the amount of space between columns. To do these latter actions, you need to use the Format⇨Columns command, described next.

Creating columns the hard way

For more control over the appearance of columns, use the Format⇨Columns command. Grab a cup of coffee and follow these steps:

1. **Move the cursor to the point in the document where you want the columns to begin.**

   If you want to apply columns to the entire document, it doesn't matter where you put the cursor.

2. **Hail the Format⇨Columns command.**

   You are greeted with the Columns dialog box, shown in Figure 12-2.

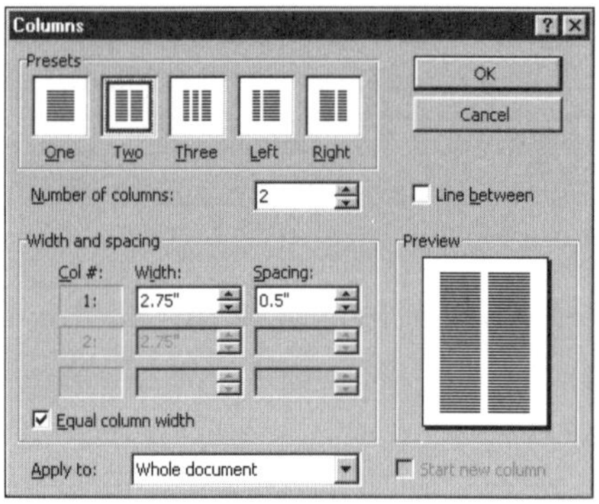

Figure 12-2: The Columns dialog box.

3. **Click one of the five preset column layouts.**

   If you want more than three columns, drop everything. Take a long lunch; clear your head of such nonsense. If you still want four or more columns when you return, use the Number of columns control to set the number of columns you want.

4. **Change the Width or Spacing fields if you must.**

   If you want to change the width of the columns, change the Width field. To change the amount of space between columns, change the Spacing field.

5. **Click the Line between button if you want a line between the columns.**

   This is the line between the stuff you read, not the stuff you read between the lines.

6. **Here's the tricky part: If you want the new column layout to begin at the cursor position, choose This point forward from the Apply to list box.**

   If you choose This point forward, Word adds a section break at the cursor position and applies the column layout to the new section. Thus, text that follows the cursor is formatted in columns, but text that comes before it is not.

7. **Periodically peer at the preview box to see whether you like the column layout.**

8. **Click OK.**

   Excellent!

Here are some things to remember as you twiddle with the Columns dialog box:

- If you check the Equal column width check box, Word balances the columns evenly. If you uncheck this check box, you can create columns of uneven width.
- Using the Apply to: This point forward option is the way to create a headline or title that spans the width of two or three columns. Start by creating the headline, using a large font and centering it. Then use the Format⇨Columns command to create a two- or three-column layout. Set the Apply to field to This point forward to throw the columns into a new section so that the headline remains in a single column.

Adjusting Column Width

If you don't like the width of columns you've created, you can change them at any time. You have two ways to change column width:

- Call up the Format⇨Columns command and play with the Width and Spacing fields.

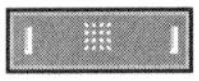

- Click and drag the *column marker,* the box-like separator between columns in the ruler (shown in the margin). If you check the Equal column width check box in the Columns dialog box, all the column markers move in concert so that equal column widths are preserved. Otherwise, you can adjust the column markers individually.

Some things to remember when you adjust column width:

- Even if you use unequal column widths, try to keep the gap between the columns the same widths. Otherwise, you create an unbalanced look.
- When adjusting column width by dragging the column marker, hold down the Alt key before clicking the mouse. Doing so causes Word to display measurements that show the width of each column and the size of the space between columns.
- Remember that any formatting applied to paragraphs in columns is still in effect. If you gave a paragraph a left indent of 1/2-inch, the paragraph is indented 1/2-inch from the left column margin. This reduces the column width.

Forcing a Column Break

Left to its own devices, Word decides when to jump text from the bottom of one column up to the top of the next column. There are times, however, when you want to intervene and insert a column break of your own.

Follow these steps to force a column break:

1. **Place the cursor where you want the new column to begin.**
2. **Press Ctrl+Shift+Enter.**

   Or use the Insert⇨Break command, check the Column Break feature, and click OK.

In Normal view, a column break is indicated in the text by a solid line running all the way across the screen. In Page Layout view, the column break is obvious when you see the text jump to the next column.

Don't try to create two or three columns of equal length by inserting column breaks where you think the bottom of each column should fall. Instead, insert a continuous section break at the end of the last column. A continuous section break balances all the columns in the section so that they're of

equal length and then starts a new section without forcing a page break. To insert a continuous section break, call up the Insert⇨Break command, choose Continuous, and click OK.

Using Linked Textboxes to Create Columns

One of the best new features of Word 97, as far as desktop publishers are concerned, is the linked text box feature. A linked text box is a drawing object that contains text. A series of textboxes can be linked together so that if the first textbox is not large enough to contain all of the text, the text spills over to the second text box. If the second text box isn't large enough to show all the text, a third text box can be added to the link. Check out Chapter 14 for the scoop on linked textboxes.

Hyphenating Your Text

Word has the capability of automatically hyphenating words. You can set it up so that words are hyphenated as you type them, or you can wait until after you've typed your text and then automatically hyphenate the document. Hyphenating as you type can slow Word down, especially if you don't have a blazingly fast computer. Thus, I suggest you type your document first and then hyphenate it.

Here's how:

1. **Type your text.**

   Don't worry about hyphens during this step.

2. **Activate the Tools⇨Language⇨Hyphenation command.**

   The Hyphenation dialog box, shown in Figure 12-3, appears.

3. **Check the Automatically hyphenate document check box.**

4. **Check the Hyphenate words in CAPS check box if you want words made entirely of capital letters to be hyphenated.**

   Uncheck this option if your writing includes specialized jargon that appears in all capitals and should not be hyphenated. For example, if you use terms like TECHNOBABBLE VOCABULATOR, which must not under any circumstances be hyphenated, you'll love this option.

5. **Adjust the Hyphenation zone if you're picky.**

   This zone is the area within which Word tries to end each line. If necessary, Word hyphenates words that cross into this zone.

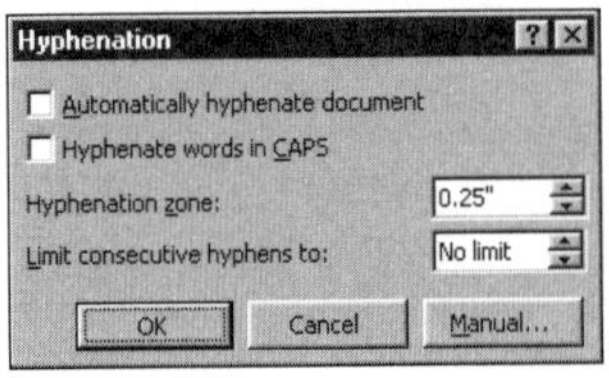

Figure 12-3: The Hyphenation dialog box.

6. **Set the Limit consecutive hyphens to list box to 3 or 4.**

   There's nothing wrong with two hyphens in a row, and three is OK once in awhile. But Word's default setting for this field places no limit to the number of consecutive lines that Word can hyphenate. You don't want to see a column of 20 hyphenated lines, do you?

7. **Click OK.**

   Word hyphenates the document.

8. **Check the results.**

   You may not be happy with Word's hyphenations. You should always check the results and make any necessary corrections.

Here are some hyphenation pointers to keep in mind:

- Word uses its dictionary to determine where to hyphenate words. It probably spells better than you do. (I know it spells better than *I* do!)
- If you want to cause Word to hyphenate a word at a particular spot, place the cursor where you want the word hyphenated and press Ctrl+–. Pressing this creates an *optional hyphen,* which is displayed only when the word falls at the end of a line.
- WARNING! Do *not* hyphenate words simply by typing a hyphen. It may work for the time being, but if you later edit the text so that the hyphenated word no longer falls at the end of a line, the hyphen still appears, now in the middle of the line where it does not belong. Use Ctrl+– instead.
- Sometimes you want to use a hyphen in a compound word, but you don't want the word to be split up at the end of the line because it might look funny. For example, *G-Men.* In that case, you should use Ctrl+Shift+– to create the hyphen rather than the hyphen key alone. Word displays the hyphen but does not break the word at the hyphen.
- TIP If you click the Manual button in the Hyphenation dialog box, Word leads you through the entire document, asking you about each word it wants to hyphenate. This is tiresome beyond belief. Better to just hyphenate the document and then review it and remove any hyphens you don't like.

Chapter 13

Using Clip Art

In This Chapter

- Using free pictures
- Finding a picture you like
- Moving, sizing, and stretching pictures
- Adding a box, shaded background, or shadow to a picture
- Editing a clip art picture
- Letting Word pick the clip art for you

Face it: Most of us are not born with even an ounce of artistic ability. Someday, soon we hope, those genetic researchers combing through the billions and billions of genes strung out on those twisty DNA helixes will discover the Artist Gene. Then in spite of protests from the DaVincis and Monets among us (who fear that their NEA grants will be threatened), doctors will splice the little bugger onto our own DNA strands so that we all can be artists. Of course, this procedure will not be without its side effects: Some will develop an insatiable craving for croissants, and others will inexplicably develop French accents and whack off their ears. But artists we shall be.

Until then, we have to rely on clip art.

The Best Free Pictures Money Can Buy

Whether you buy Word 97 by itself or get it as a part of Microsoft Office 97, you also get a collection of more than 4,000 clip art drawings that you can pop directly into your documents. These drawings were created by high-tech sidewalk artists who work at Microsoft and include subjects ranging from cartoons to pickaxes to stop signs.

The Word clip art pictures are managed by a program called the Clip Gallery. The nifty little Clip Gallery program keeps track of the clip art files spread out all over your hard disk and spares you the unpleasant chore of rummaging through your directories to look for that picture of Elvis you know you have somewhere. Clip Gallery also takes the guesswork out of using clip art: Rather than choosing a filename like ELVISFAT.PCX and hoping that it's the one you remembered, you can see the clip art before you add it to your document.

Clip Gallery organizes your clip art files into categories, such as Architecture, Flags, and Gestures. This organization makes it easy to search through the clip art images that come with Word 97 and find just the right one. (Wouldn't it be great if the Metropolitan Museum of Art used similar categories?)

Clip Gallery works with several other Microsoft applications, including all of the Office 97 applications and also Microsoft Publisher. The clip art that comes with those programs is tossed in with the Word clip art so that you can easily get to it.

You also can add your own pictures to Clip Gallery. You may whip out a detailed replica of the Mona Lisa in Windows Paintbrush, for example, and then toss it into Clip Gallery.

The new version of Clip Gallery that comes with Word 97 can handle digitized pictures, sounds, and videos as well as clip art. In fact, that's precisely why Microsoft has changed the name of this handy little program. It used to be called Clip Art Gallery, but for Word 97, Microsoft changed the name to Clip Gallery to emphasize that the program handles more than just clip art files.

Making a Splash with Clip Art

These steps show you how to drop clip art into your document:

1. **Place the insertion point where you want the clip art to be inserted.**
2. **Choose the Insert⇨Picture⇨Clip Art command.**

   The Clip Gallery appears, as shown in Figure 13-1.
3. **Choose the clip art picture you want.**

   To find the picture you want, first choose the clip art category that contains the picture (if you're not sure, make your best guess). When you first pop up the Clip Gallery, All Categories is the default; this category shows all the clip art pictures in your collection. To narrow your search, scroll through the Categories list until you find the category you want, and then click it.

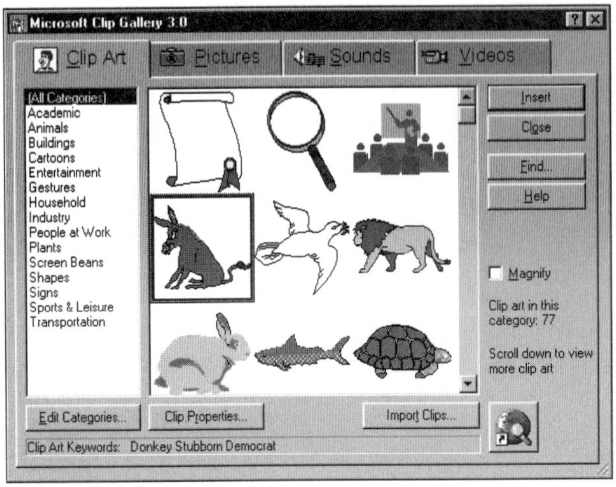

Figure 13-1: The Clip Gallery.

Next, find the specific pictwÊµ you want. Clip Gallery shows nine pictures at a time, but you can display other pictures from the same category by scrolling through the pictures. When you see the picture you want, click it.

4. **Click Insert to insert the picture.**

   Or simply double-click the picture. You're done!

Bammo! Word inserts the clip art picture as an object on the page, as shown in Figure 13-2.

Unfortunately, Word may not stick the picture precisely on the page where you want it, and the picture will probably be too big or too small. You have to wrestle with the picture to get it just the way you want it. See the section "Moving, Sizing, and Stretching Clip Art" later in this chapter for instructions on forcing the picture into compliance.

If you can't find the clip art picture you're looking for, click the Find button in the Clip Gallery dialog box. Clicking the Find button enables you to search for clip art based on a key word. For example, you can look for all pictures that have the word "donkey" in their description.

TIP

Notice the tabs across the top of the Clip Gallery dialog box? These tabs let you insert different types of clips besides clip art: pictures, sounds, and video. What, you ask, is the difference between clip art and pictures? That's a good question. The terms seem almost interchangeable. In Clip Gallery terminology, clip art refers to line drawings, whereas pictures refers to digitized photographs, in which the image is made up of thousands of tiny dots.

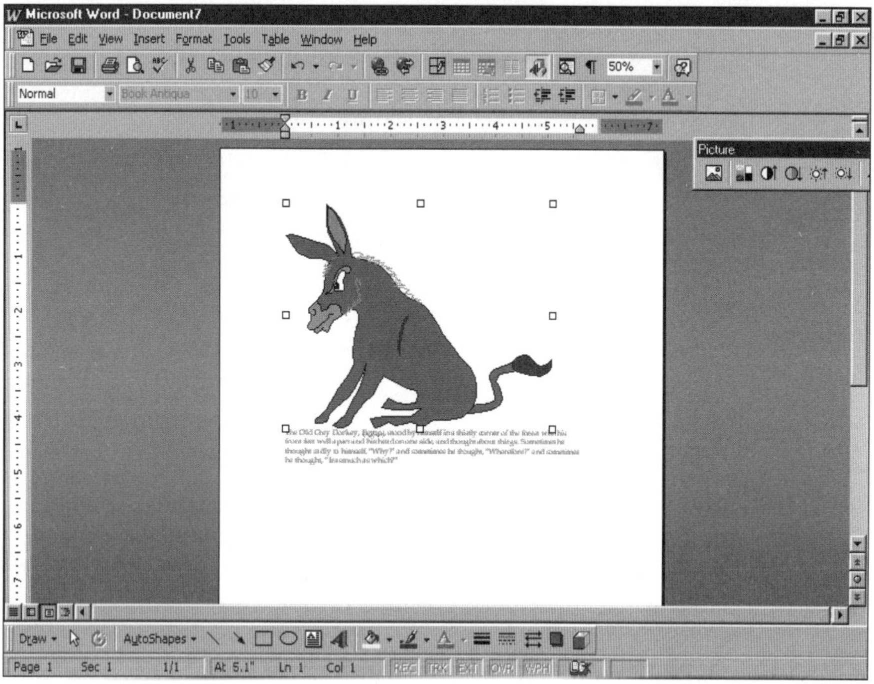

Figure 13-2: A clip art picture is inserted in a document.

Moving, Sizing, and Stretching Clip Art

When Word 97 inserts a clip art picture, the picture probably isn't placed exactly where you want it to appear on the page. So you need to move the clip art to a more convenient location. You probably also want to change its size if it is too big or too small.

Follow these steps to force your inserted clip art into full compliance:

1. **Click the picture and drag it wherever you want.**

   You don't have to worry about clicking exactly the edge of the picture or one of its lines; just click anywhere in the picture and drag it around.

2. **Notice the eight handles. Drag any one of them to resize the picture.**

   In Figure 13-2, notice the eight handles that surround the clip art. You can click and drag any of these handles to adjust the size of the picture. When you click one of the corner handles, the proportion of the picture stays the same as you change its size. When you drag one of the edge handles (top, bottom, left, or right) to change the size of the picture in just one dimension, you distort the picture's outlook as you go.

When you resize a picture, the picture changes its position on the page. As a result, you can count on moving the picture after you resize it. If you hold down the Ctrl key while dragging a handle, however, the picture becomes anchored at its center point as you resize it. Therefore, its position is unchanged, and you probably don't have to move it.

Stretching a clip art picture by dragging one of the edge handles can dramatically change the picture's appearance. To illustrate, Figure 13-3 shows how the same clip art picture can resemble both Arnold Schwarzenegger and Danny DeVito. I just stretched one copy of the picture vertically to make it tall and stretched the other copy horizontally to make it, er, stout.

Playing with Pictures

Word 97 enables you to manipulate clip art pictures in many ways. Whenever you click on a clip art picture to select it, the Picture toolbar appears. This toolbar contains several buttons that you can use to alter the appearance of clip art picture. The function of each of these buttons is listed in Table 13-1.

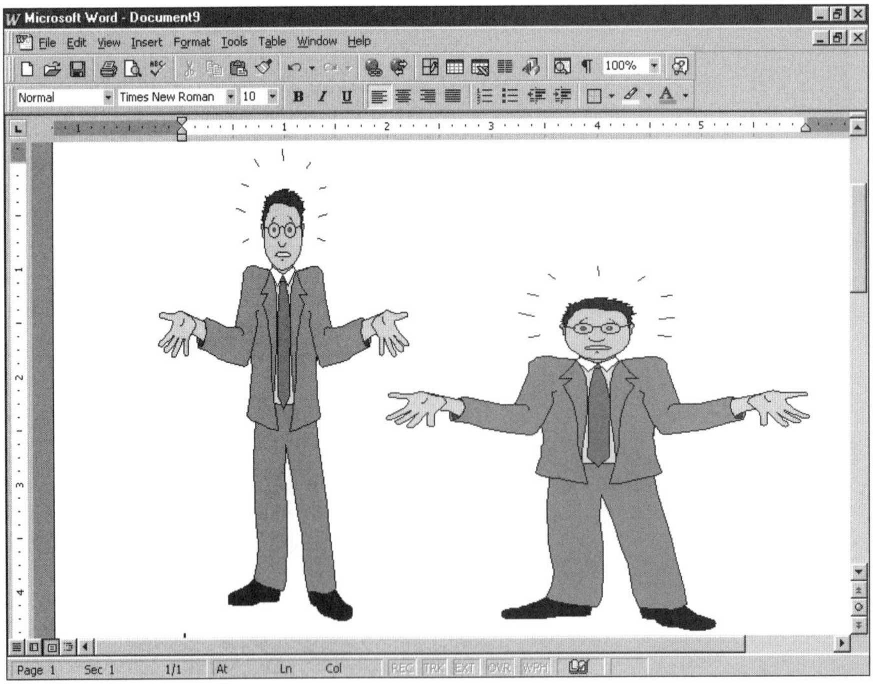

Figure 13-3: Twins.

Table 13-1 Buttons on the Picture Toolbar

Button	*Name*	*What it does*
	Insert picture	Summons the Insert Picture dialog box to insert a different picture.
	Image control	Lets you select one of four color options: Automatic — Displays the image with normal color. Grayscale — Displays the image in shades of gray. Black and White — Displays the image in black and white (with no shades of gray). Watermark — Displays the images in muted tones so that text placed over it can still be read.
	More contrast	Increases the contrast in the picture.
	Less contrast	Decreases the contrast in the picture.
	More brightness	Increases the picture's brightness.
	Less brightness	Decreases the picture's brightness.
	Crop	Allows you to drag a rectangle around the portion of the picture you want visible. Any portion of the picture outside of the rectangle you draw is hidden.
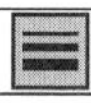	Line style	Lets you add a border around the picture.
	Text wrapping	Lets you indicate how you want text wrapped around the picture. See the section "Wrapping Text around a Picture" later in this chapter.
	Format picture	Calls up the Format Picture dialog box, which allows you to make more-precise settings than the controls on the Picture toolbar permit.
	Set transparent color	Allows you to set one of the colors in a bit-map picture to be transparent — not displayed or printed. This control is not available with clip art pictures.
	Reset picture	Restores the picture settings to their default.

Wrapping Text around a Picture

Suppose that you're rambling along, typing some boring prose about a dull subject, such as using clip art in Word, when it occurs to you that a picture of a Heffalump would be most appreciated right about now. You conjure up the Insert⇨Picture⇨Clip Art command and discover that Word does indeed come with a lovely picture of a Heffalump. But when you insert it, the Heffalump stands there all by itself, on its own line. It's as if all the text in the document is stuffed with fluff, afraid to meet the Heffalump face to face, probably aware that wherever you find a Heffalump, a Woosle is usually not far off.

Well, the text has nothing to fear. Word 97 is quite capable of protecting your precious prose while it snuggles up next to the Heffalump. Have a look at Figure 13-4 to see what I mean.

To wrap text around a picture, just follow these steps:

1. **Insert the picture as you normally would.**

   Use the Insert⇨Picture⇨Clip Art command.

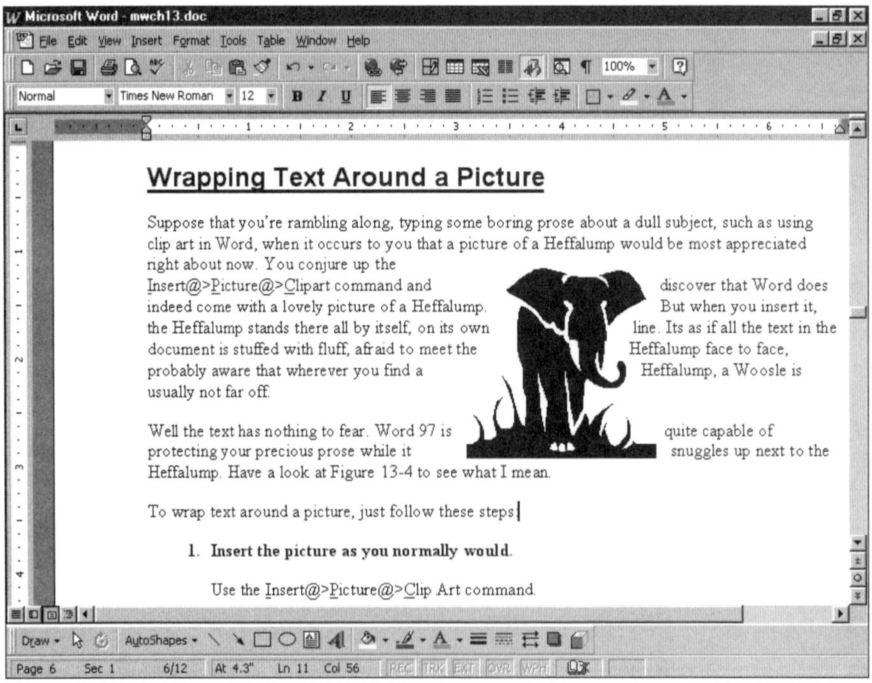

Figure 13-4: This text is not afraid of the Heffalump.

2. **Click the picture to select it.**
3. **Choose the Format⇨Picture command.**

   Or right-click the picture and choose Format Picture from the pop-up menu that appears. Either way, the Format Picture dialog box appears.
4. **Click the Wrapping tab.**

   This brings forth the text wrapping options, as shown in Figure 13-5.

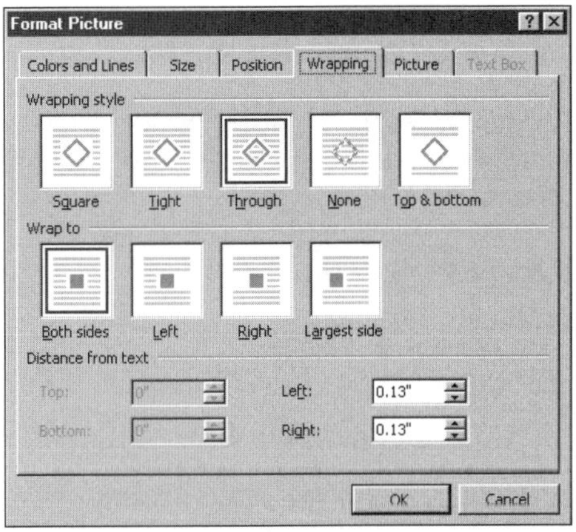

Figure 13-5: The text wrapping options on the Format Picture dialog box.

5. **Choose the wrapping options you want.**

   You can choose a wrapping style (Square, Tight, Through, None, or Top & Bottom) and which side to wrap text to (Both Sides, Left, Right, or Largest Side). You can also adjust the amount of blank space to leave between the text and the picture.
6. **Click OK.**

   Word applies the wrapping options you chose.

Here are some points to ponder about wrapping text around pictures:

- Several common wrapping styles are available directly from the Picture toolbar. Click the Text Wrapping button (shown in the margin) to reveal a menu of text wrapping choices.

- You can choose None for the wrapping style to cause the text to run right through the picture. This option often works well in combination with the Watermark option found under the Image Control button on the Picture toolbar, as the Watermark option softens the colors of the clip art picture so that any text that overlays the picture is more visible.

- If the Tight text wrapping style places text just a bit too close to the picture in places, click the Text Wrapping button in the Picture toolbar, then choose Edit Wrap Points from the pop-up menu that appears. A series of points appears around the clip art picture. Word uses these points to determine how close the text should come to the picture. You can then drag any of these points to fine-tune the exact placement of text around the picture.
- TIP: In previous versions of Word, you had to place a picture in a special frame to get text to wrap around it. Frames are no longer required to get text to wrap around a picture.

Editing a Clip Art Picture

Sometimes one of the clip art pictures supplied with Word 97 is close but not exactly what you want. In that case, you can insert the picture and then edit it to make whatever changes are needed. For example, Figure 13-6 shows two versions of the same clip art picture. The original picture is on the left, and the one on the right has been edited to show what happens after the donkey tells a few more lies.

Figure 13-6: You can edit a picture to change its appearance.

You can't directly edit a clip art picture. Instead you must first convert the picture to the equivalent of a bunch of Word 97 shape objects. Then you can individually select and edit the objects using the shape editing tools described in Chapter 14.

These steps tell how to edit a clip art picture:

1. **Right-click the picture you want to edit and then choose the Grouping⇨Ungroup command.**

   Word converts the picture to it's individual shapes.

   In some cases, you may need to ungroup the picture several times. That's because some of the more complicated clip art pictures are made up of several layers of grouped objects. For more information about grouping, refer to Chapter 14.

2. **Now edit the picture.**

   The clip art picture is converted to an equivalent group of Word 97 drawing objects, so you can use Word's shape editing tools to change their appearance. (See Chapter 14 for the details on editing Word shape objects.) You can drag any of the control handles to reshape an object; you can change colors or even add new stuff to the picture.

After you have ungrouped and edited a picture, you may want to regroup it. You're much less likely to pull the nose off someone's face if the face is a group rather than a bunch of ungrouped ellipse objects.

Getting Clip Art from the Internet

As if the 4,000 or so clip art pictures that come on the Word 97 CD aren't enough, Microsoft also maintains a library of clip art on the Internet that you can access from Clip Gallery. If you have access to the Internet, click the Internet button on the Clip Gallery dialog box (pictured in the margin). This connects you to the Internet, fires up Internet Explorer, Microsoft's software for accessing the World Wide Web, and displays the Microsoft clip art page, called Clip Gallery Live.

Clip Gallery Live lets you browse through clip art pictures by category, or you can search for key words, such as chicken or athlete. Figure 13-7 shows some of the clip art that is available from Clip Gallery Live.

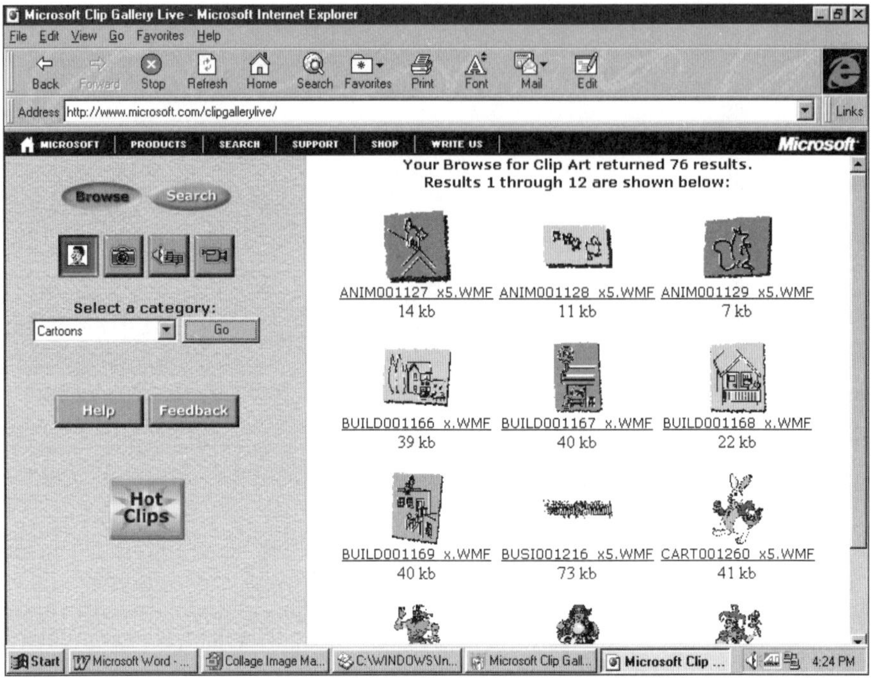

Figure 13-7: Clip Gallery Live lets you get clip art from the Internet.

To download a clip art picture from the Internet, click the filename that appears beneath the picture that you want to download. The picture is copied to your computer and added to Clip Gallery.

Inserting Pictures without Using Clip Gallery

Word 97 also enables you to insert pictures directly into your document without using Clip Gallery. Use this technique to insert pictures that aren't a part of the clip art collection that comes with Word. These steps show you how:

1. **Move the insertion point to the location where you'd like the picture to appear.**
2. **Choose the Insert⇨Picture⇨From File command.**

   Greet the Insert Picture dialog box, shown in Figure 13-8, with a smile.

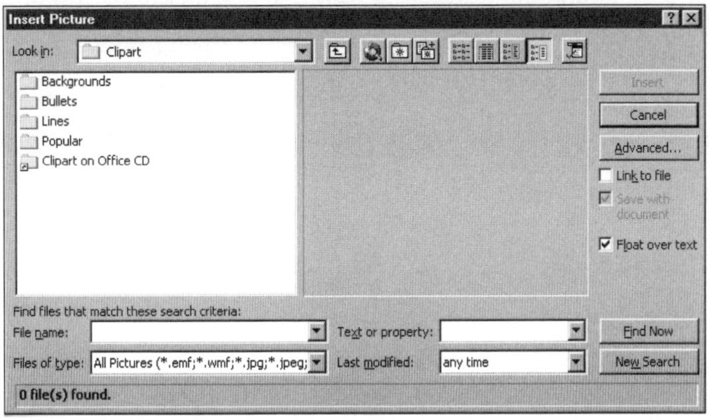

Figure 13-8: The Insert Picture dialog box.

3. **Dig through the bottom of your disk drive until you find the file you want.**

   The picture you want can be anywhere. Fortunately, the Insert Picture dialog box has all the controls you need to search high and low until you find the file. When the Insert Picture dialog box first appears, it is set to look in the folder where Word 97's Setup program installed the clip art files that come with Word.

4. **Click the file and then click Insert.**

   You're done!

You also can paste a picture directly into Word 97 by way of the Clipboard. Anything you can copy to the Clipboard, you can paste into Word. For example, you can doodle a sketch in Paintbrush, copy it, and then zap over to Word and paste it. Voilà — instant picture!

TIP

If you want to narrow your search to files of a particular type, use the Files of type drop-down list box. Word 97 comes with filters that can convert as many as 20 different types of picture files to Word.

If you insert a picture by using the Insert➪Picture➪From File command and then double-click the picture, Word 97 throws you into the program that created the file, where you can edit it any way you want. You also can ungroup the picture by using the Draw➪Ungroup command to convert the picture to Word objects, which you can then edit directly in Word.

TECHNICAL STUFF

If the file type you want doesn't show up in the Files of type drop-down list box, you may not have installed all the graphics filters when you installed Word 97. Run the Word Setup program and see whether the graphics filter you want is available. Better yet, bribe your local computer guru to do this for you. This is definitely Guru Stuff.

Chapter 14

Doodling on Your Documents

In This Chapter

- Drawing straight and curved lines
- Drawing rectangles, squares, and circles
- Drawing polygons and freeform shapes
- Using AutoShapes
- Drawing text boxes and callouts
- Selecting drawing objects
- Setting the fill color and using fill effects
- Creating 3-D objects
- Flipping and rotating objects
- Changing layers
- Aligning objects
- Grouping objects

Art time! Everybody get your crayons and glue and don an old paint shirt. We're going to cut out some simple shapes and paste them on our Word documents so that people either think we are wonderful artists or scoff at us for not using clip art.

This chapter covers Word's drawing features. For Word 97, Microsoft has significantly improved the drawing features that are built in to Word. In fact, Word 97 now sports some drawing capabilities that previously were available only to the lucky folks who owned professional-quality drawing programs, such as CorelDraw! or Micrografx Designer. Word's new drawing features are called OfficeArt, and they work the same in all of the Office 97 applications.

Before You Start Drawing...

Word's drawing tools aren't as powerful as the tools provided with a full-featured drawing program, such as CorelDraw! or Adobe Illustrator, but they are powerful enough to create some fancy pictures. Before I get into the specifics of how to use each tool, this section describes a handful of general tips for drawing pictures.

Zoom in

TIP

When you work with Word's drawing tools, increase the zoom factor so that you can draw more accurately. I usually work at 200 percent when I'm drawing, but sometimes I zoom to 500 percent. To change the zoom factor, click the down arrow next to the Zoom control (near the right side of the Standard toolbar) and choose a zoom factor from the list, or click the zoom factor, type a new zoom percentage, and press Enter.

Before you change the zoom factor to edit an object, select the object you want to edit. That way, Word zooms in on that area of the page. If you don't select an object before you zoom in, you may need to scroll around to find the right location.

Save frequently

Drawing is tedious work. You don't want to spend two hours working on a particularly important drawing, only to lose it all just because some joker on the other side of the world drops a bomb on your backyard. You can prevent catastrophic loss from incidents such as these by pressing Ctrl+S frequently while you work (and working in a hardened bunker located a minimum of 60 feet underground).

Don't forget Ctrl+Z

REMEMBER

Don't forget that you're never more than one keystroke from erasing a boo-boo. If you do something silly — such as forget to group a complex picture before you try to move it — you can always press Ctrl+Z to undo your last action. Ctrl+Z is my favorite and most frequently used Word key.

Introducing the Drawing Toolbar

Word has an entire toolbar devoted to drawing. To make the toolbar visible, use the View➪Toolbars command and then click the Drawing check box. Or just click the Drawing button on the Standard toolbar. Figure 14-1 shows what Word looks like after the Drawing toolbar has been revealed. I explain each buttons drawing functions on both toolbars later in this chapter.

I drew the face shown in Figure 14-1 by using Word's drawing tools.

Word's drawing tools work only in Page Layout view. Word automatically switches to Page Layout view when you activate the Drawing toolbar.

TIP

After you have drawn something on your document, you probably should stick to Page Layout view for the duration. If you switch back to Normal view, Word hides your drawing objects. This is not only disconcerting but also error prone.

Figure 14-1: Word with the Drawing toolbar enabled.

Table 14-1 shows you what each drawing tool does.

Table 14-1 Tools Available on the Drawing Toolbar

Drawing Tool	*What It's Called*	*What It Does*
	Draw menu	Displays a menu of drawing commands.
	Select objects	Not really a drawing tool, but rather the generic mouse pointer used to choose objects.
	Free rotate	When you click here, the Rotate button leaps from the water to make its escape into the open sea while Michael Jackson sings an inspiring song.
	AutoShapes	Pops up the AutoShape menu, which contains a bevy of shapes you can draw, including fancy lines, arrows, crosses, flowchart symbols, stars, and more!
	Line	Draws a line.
	Arrow	Draws an arrow.
	Rectangle	Draws a rectangle. To make a perfect square, hold down the Shift key while you draw.
	Oval	Draws circles and ovals. To create a perfect circle, hold down the Shift key while you draw.
	Text box	Adds a text object.
	Insert WordArt	Summons forth WordArt, which lets you create all sorts of fancy text effects.
	Fill Color	Sets the color used to fill solid objects such as circles and ellipses as well as AutoShapes.
	Line Color	Sets the color used to draw lines, including lines around rectangles, ellipses, and AutoShapes.

Drawing Tool	What It's Called	What It Does
	Font Color	Sets the color used for text.
	Line Style	Sets the style for the selected line.
	Dash style	Sets a dashed line style for the selected line.
	Arrow style	Adds arrowheads to the selected line.
	Shadow	Adds a shadow effect to the selected object.
	3-D	Adds a three-dimensional effect to the selected object.

On the new-fangled toolbars, Microsoft couldn't decide whether toolbars should contain buttons or menus, so they threw in some of both. The Draw and AutoShapes buttons behave just like menus on a normal menu bar: Click them to reveal a menu of choices, or use the Alt-key shortcuts to activate them (Alt+R activates the Draw menu, Alt+U activates the AutoShapes menu).

Drawing Simple Lines and Shapes

You can use several of the buttons on the Drawing toolbar to draw basic shapes. These buttons include:

- **Line:** Draws a straight line. You can always change the attributes of the line later, to create thick lines, dashed lines, or lines with arrowheads.
- **Arrow:** Draws a line with an arrowhead at one end. You can later change the arrowhead style or add an arrowhead to both ends of the line.
- **Rectangle:** Draws rectangles. To make a perfect square, hold down the Shift key while you draw.
- **Oval:** Draws circles and ovals. To create a perfect circle, hold down the Shift key while you draw.

To draw an object, you just click the button that represents the object you want to draw and then use the mouse to draw the object. It's not always as simple as that though. In the following sections, check out detailed instructions for drawing with the more important tools.

Made a mistake? You can delete the object you just drew by pressing the Delete key and then try drawing the object again. You can change its size or stretch it by clicking it and dragging its love handles.

Table 14-2 summarizes some handy shortcuts you can use while you're drawing.

Table 14-2 Drawing Shortcuts

Shortcut	*What It Does*
Shift	Hold down the Shift key to force lines to be horizontal or vertical, to force arcs and ellipses to be true circles, or to force rectangles to be squares.
Ctrl	Hold down the Ctrl key to draw objects from the center, rather than from end to end.
Ctrl+Shift	Draws from center and enforces squareness.
Double-click	Double-click one of the buttons on the toolbar to draw several objects of the same type.

Drawing straight and curved lines

You use the Line button to draw straight lines on your pages. Here's the procedure:

1. **Click the Line button (shown in the margin).**
2. **Point the mouse cursor to where you want the line to start.**
3. **Click and drag the mouse cursor to where you want the line to end.**
4. **Release the mouse button when you reach your destination.**

Previous versions of Word also included an Arc button that you could use to draw curved lines. In Word 97, Microsoft removed the Arc button. In its place, Bill Gates and his minions added a curved line as an AutoShapes type. Thus, you must use the AutoShapes tool to draw a curved line. See the section "Using AutoShapes" later in this chapter for details.

To change the line color and other features (thickness, dashes, and arrowheads) for a line object, use the Line Color, Line Style, Dash Style, and Arrow Style buttons on the Drawing toolbars to change these attributes.

After you draw a line, you can adjust it by clicking it and then dragging the handles that appear on each end of the line.

Remember, you can force a line to be perfectly horizontal or vertical by holding down the Shift key while you draw.

Drawing rectangles, squares, and circles

To draw a rectangle, follow these steps:

1. **Click the Rectangle button (shown in the margin).**
2. **Point the mouse cursor to where you want one corner of the rectangle to be positioned.**
3. **Click the mouse button and drag to where you want the opposite corner of the rectangle to be positioned.**
4. **Release the mouse button.**

The steps for drawing an oval are the same except that you click the Oval button (shown in the margin) rather than the Rectangle button. To draw a square or perfectly round circle, hold down the Shift key while you draw.

You can adjust the size or shape of a rectangle or circle by clicking it and then dragging any of its love handles.

Drawing a text box

A *text box* is a shape that contains text. Unlike text you simply type into your document, you can move a textbox around the page to place the text precisely where you want it.

Drawing a text box is pretty much the same as drawing a rectangle. Follow these steps:

1. **Click the Text Box button.**
2. **Point the mouse cursor to where you want one corner of the text box to be.**
3. **Press the mouse button and drag to where you want the opposite corner of the text box to be.**
4. **Release the mouse button.**
5. **Type some text.**

   The text you type appears inside the box.

6. **If you want to remove the border that surrounds the text box, click the Line Color button and choose the No Line option.**

You can adjust the margins for text that appears within a text box by right-clicking on the border of the text box, choosing the Format Text Box command that appears in the pop-up menu, and then clicking the Text Box tabs. Here, you find the controls that allow you to set the top, bottom, left, and right margins for the text box. (If you don't see a Format Text Box command when you right-click the text box, it's because you didn't click right on the border of the text box. Try again.)

Text boxes also include a linking feature that allows you to create a sequence of text boxes to hold text. Any text that doesn't fit in the first text box spills to the second text box. You can link as many text boxes as you wish in this way. To link two text boxes, first draw both text boxes. Then right-click the first text box and choose the Create Text Box Link command. The mouse pointer changes to a coffee cup. Now all you have to do is click on the second text box.

Using AutoShapes

Rectangles and circles aren't the only two shapes Word can draw automatically. When you click the AutoShapes button on the Drawing toolbar, a whole menu of AutoShapes appears. These AutoShapes make it easy to draw common shapes, such as pentagons, stars, and flowchart symbols.

The AutoShapes menu organizes AutoShapes into the following categories:

- **Lines:** Straight lines, curved lines, lines with arrowheads, scribbly lines, and freeform shapes that can become polygons if you wish.
- **Basic Shapes:** Squares, rectangles, triangles, crosses, happy faces, lightening bolts, and more.
- **Block Arrows:** Fat arrows pointing in various directions.
- **Flowcharts:** Various flowcharting symbols.
- **Stars and Banners:** Shapes that add sparkle to your documents.
- **Callouts:** Text boxes and speech bubbles like those used in comic strips.

These steps show you how to draw an AutoShape:

1. **Click the AutoShapes button on the Drawing toolbar.**

   The AutoShapes menu appears.

2. **Choose the AutoShapes category you want.**

   A toolbar of AutoShapes appears. Figure 14-2 shows all of the toolbars that can be accessed from the AutoShapes menu. Look this figure over to see what kind of AutoShapes are available. (Of course, when you actually use Word, only one of these toolbars is visible at a time.)

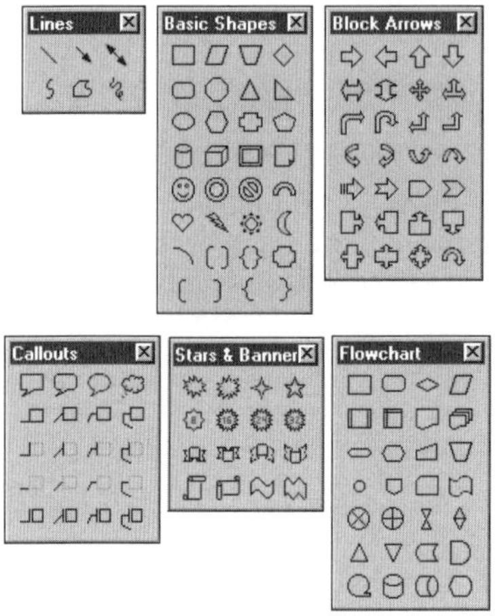

Figure 14-2: All of the shapes available from the AutoShapes menu.

3. **Click the shape you want to draw from the AutoShapes toolbar.**
4. **Click where you want the shape to appear and then drag the shape to the desired size.**

   When you release the mouse button, the object you selected will be filled with the color indicated by the Fill color control on the Drawing toolbar. (To change the fill color, refer to the section "Working with Colors and Fill Effects" later in this chapter.)

5. **Start typing if you want the shape to contain text.**

Hold down the Shift key while drawing the AutoShape to create an undistorted shape.

You can change an object's AutoShape at any time by selecting the object and then choosing the Draw⇨Change AutoShape command from the Drawing toolbar.

TIP

Some of AutoShapes buttons have an extra handle, as shown in Figure 14-3. You can drag this handle to modify the object's shape. For example, the arrow AutoShapes have a handle that lets you increase or decrease the size of the arrowhead.

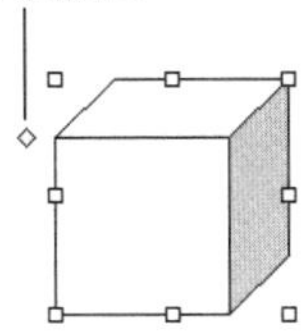

Figure 14-3: The extra handle lets you change the shape of certain AutoShape objects.

Figure 14-4 shows how you can use these extra handles to vary several shapes produced by AutoShapes buttons. For each of the six shapes, there are three different versions. The first version shows how AutoShapes initially draws the shape. The other two demonstrate how you can change the shape by dragging the extra handle.

Drawing a polygon or freeform shape

Mr. Arnold, my seventh grade math teacher, taught me that a *polygon* is a shape that has many sides and has nothing to do with having more than one spouse (one is certainly enough for most of us). Triangles, squares, and rectangles are polygons, but so are hexagons and pentagons, as are any unusual shapes whose sides all consist of straight lines. Politicians frequently invent new polygons when they revise the boundaries of congressional districts.

One of the most useful of AutoShapes buttons is the Freeform tool. It's designed to create polygons, with a twist: Not all the sides have to be straight lines. The Freeform AutoShapes tool lets you build a shape whose sides are a mixture of straight lines and freeform curves. Figure 14-5 shows several examples of shapes that I created with the Freeform AutoShapes tool.

Follow these steps to create a polygon or freeform shape:

1. **Click the AutoShapes button, then choose Lines.**

   The Lines toolbar appears.

2. **Click the Freeform button (shown in the margin).**
3. **Click where you want to position the first corner of the object.**
4. **Click where you want to position the second corner of the object.**

Figure 14-4: Interesting variations are possible by grabbing these AutoShapes' extra handles.

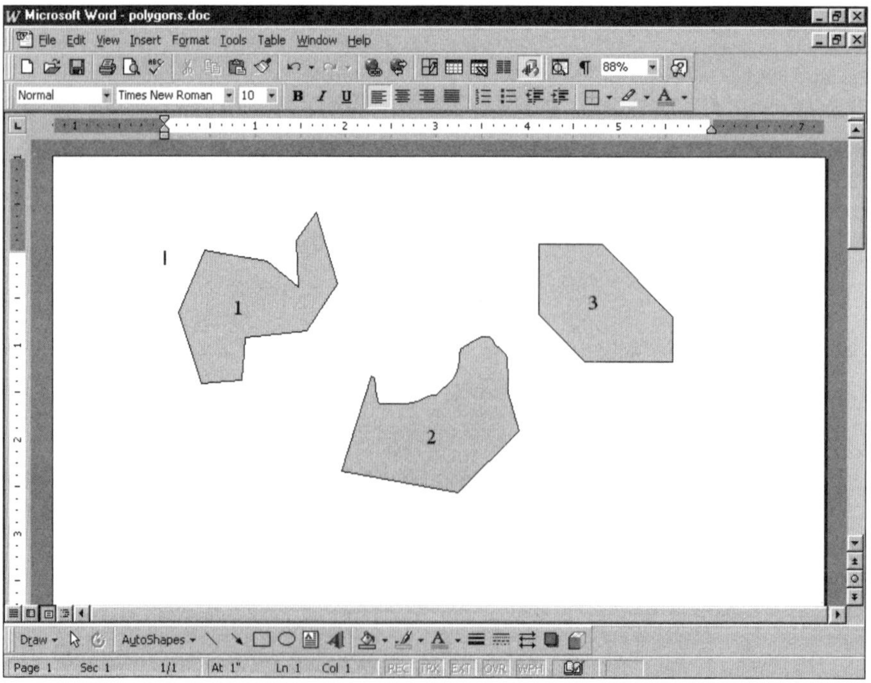

Figure 14-5: Freeform shapes.

5. **Keep clicking wherever you want to position a corner.**
6. **To finish the shape, click near the first corner.**

   You don't have to be exact; if you click anywhere near the first corner you put down, Word assumes that the shape is finished.

   You're finished!

To draw a freeform side on the shape, click and hold the mouse, then drag the mouse to create the freeform side. After you get to the end of the freeform side, release the mouse button. Then you can click again to add more corners. Shape 2 in Figure 14-5 has one freeform side.

You can reshape a polygon or freeform shape by double-clicking it and then dragging any of the love handles that appear on the corners.

If you hold down the Shift key while you draw a polygon, the sides are constrained to 45-degree angles. Shape 3 in Figure 14-5 was drawn in this manner. How about a constitutional amendment requiring Congress to use the Shift key when it redraws congressional boundaries?

You also can use the Freeform AutoShapes tool to draw a multi-segmented line, called an *open shape.* To draw an open shape, you can follow the steps in this section, except that you skip Step 6. Instead, double-click when you get to the last line segment, or press the Esc key when the line is done.

Drawing a curved line or shape

Another useful AutoShape tool is the Curve tool, which lets you draw curved lines or shapes. Figure 14-6 shows several examples of curved lines and shapes drawn with the Curve AutoShape tool.

Here is the procedure for drawing a curved line or shape:

1. **Click the AutoShapes button, then choose Lines.**

   The Lines toolbars appears.

2. **Click the Curve button (shown in the margin).**
3. **Click where you want the curved line or shape to begin.**
4. **Click where you want the first *turn* in the curve to appear.**

   The straight line turns to a curved line, bent around the point where you click. As you move the mouse, the bend of the curve changes.

5. **Click to add additional turns to the curve.**

   Each time you click, Word adds a new bend to the line. Keep clicking until the line is as twisty as you want.

Figure 14-6: Four shapes drawn with the Curve AutoShape tool.

6. **To finish a line, double-click where you want the end of the curved line to appear. To create a closed shape, click the starting point, where you clicked in Step 3.**

Changing the style of your lines

Three buttons in the Drawing toolbar let you change the style of line objects:

- **Line Style:** The thickness of the lines that outline the object.

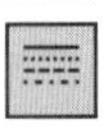

- **Dash Style:** The dashing pattern used for lines that outline an object. The default uses a solid line, but different patterns are available to create dashed lines.

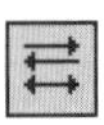

- **Arrow Style:** Lines can have an arrowhead at either or both ends. You use arrowheads mostly on line and arc objects.

To change any of these object attributes, simply select the object or objects you want to change, and then click the appropriate button to change the style. A menu of style options appears.

The Line Style menu includes a More Lines command that summons the dialog box shown in Figure 14-7. From the Format AutoShape dialog box, you can control all aspects of a line's style: its color, width, dash pattern, and end style (various arrowheads can be applied). The Arrow Style command includes a More Arrows command that also summons the same dialog box.

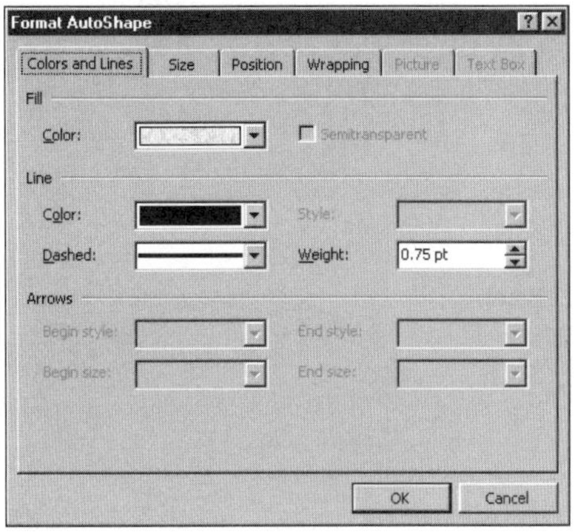

Figure 14-7: Setting the line style.

Drawing a callout

A *callout* is a special type of AutoShape object that is like a text box but has a line or a series of bubbles that connect the callout to some other object, as shown in Figure 14-8. In the figure, I use callouts to illustrate the thoughts of the donkey.

Follow this procedure to create callouts to contain your own thoughts:

1. **Click the AutoShape button, then choose Callouts.**

   A toolbar showing 20 different callout styles appears.

2. **Choose the callout type you want to use.**

3. **Click where you want the upper-left corner of the callout to appear, then drag out the shape of the callout.**

   After you release the mouse, a big one-inch-square callout box appears.

4. **Drag the little yellow dot that appears at the end of the connecting line (or bubbles, if you choose the *thought bubble* type of callout used in Figure 14-8) to the point where you want the callout to indicate.**

   As you drag the little yellow dot around, the shape of the callout changes.

Figure 14-8: The proper use of callouts.

5. **Click in the callout, then type some callout text.**

   Word inserts the text into the callout.

   Presto! You're finished.

Keep the following points in mind when you work with callouts:

- Notice that if you drag a callout around the screen, the callout remains attached to the same point in your document. Cool!
- If the text doesn't fit inside the callout, try dragging the callout by one of its love handles to increase the size. Or select the callout, then choose the Format⇨AutoShape command. Then click the Text Box tab and reduce the margins for the callout. This allows the text to creep closer to the inside boundaries of the callout.

Working with Colors and Fill Effects

The three color controls that appear on the drawing toolbar let you set the fill color (that is, the color used to fill a solid object), the line color, and the color of an object's text. These buttons behave a little strangely, so they merit a bit of explanation.

Each of the color buttons actually consists of two parts: a button and an arrow. Click the button to assign the current fill, line, or text color to the selected object. Click the arrow to apply any color you wish to the selected object.

When you click the arrow, a menu appears. For example, Figure 14-9 shows the Fill Color menu that appears when you click the arrow attached to the Fill Color button. This menu includes a palette of colors you can select. Just click the color you want to use.

Setting the line and text color is similar: Just click the Line Color or Text Color buttons and choose a color.

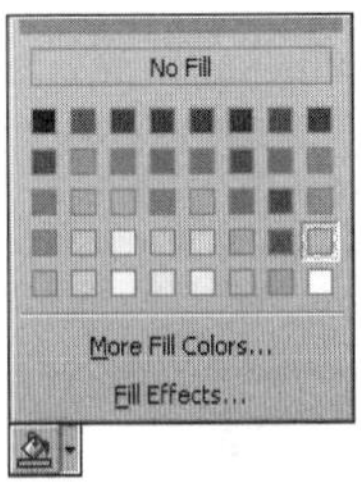

Figure 14-9: The Fill Color menu.

A horse of a different color

If you want to use a color that isn't visible on the menu, select More Fill Colors. Selecting More Fill Colors displays a dialog box that includes a color wheel from which you can select just about any color under the sun, as shown in Figure 14-10. As you can see, the color wheel looks like a tie-dye version of Chinese checkers.

The color choice dialog box in Figure 14-9 shows 127 popular colors, plus black, white, and a few shades of gray. If you want to use a color that doesn't

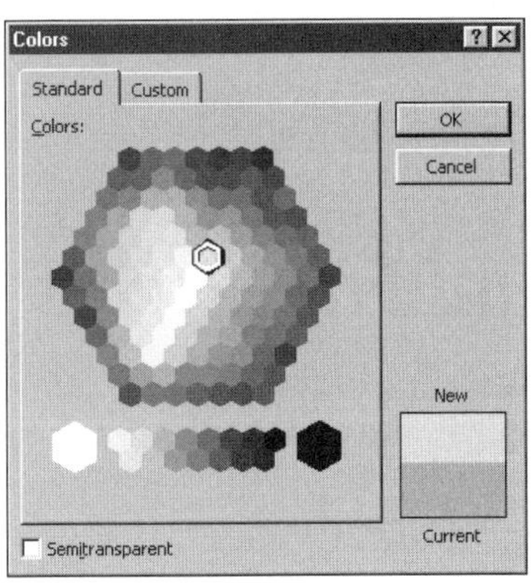

Figure 14-10: Picking another color.

appear in the dialog box, click the Custom tab. This summons the custom color controls shown in Figure 14-11. From this dialog box, you can construct any of the 16 million colors that are theoretically possible with Word 97. You need a Ph.D. in physics to figure out how to adjust the Hue-y, Dewey, and Louie controls, though. Mess around with this stuff if you want, but don't come crying to me for help. You're on your own. (As C3PO put it, "No more adventures!")

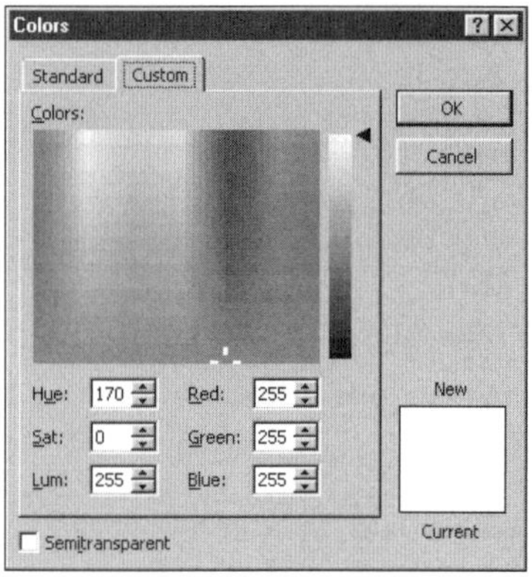

Figure 14-11: Picking another color.

Having your fill

You can apply a fill effect — such as gradient fill or a pattern — to an object by choosing the Fill Effects command from the Fill Color menu. This pops up the Fill Effects dialog box, shown in Figure 14-12.

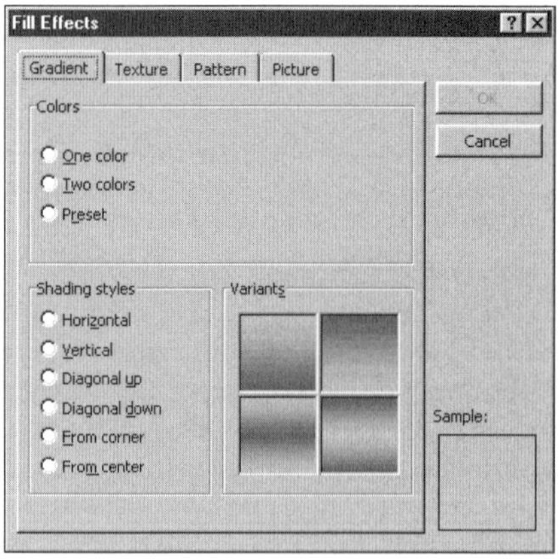

Figure 14-12: The Fill Effects dialog box.

The Fill Effects dialog box allows you to select a gradient fill to use for the object rather than a solid color. Start by selecting a one-color shade, in which a single color fades to white or black, or a two-color shade, in which one color fades into another. Then select the Shade Style — Horizontal, Vertical, Diagonal up, and so on. Finally, select one of the variants in the Variants area of the dialog box.

Alternatively, you can select one of several preset shadings by picking the Preset option. The preset shading options include Early Sunset, Nightfall, Rainbow, and several other interesting effects.

Besides gradient fills, the Fill Effects dialog box provides several other types of interesting fills. You access all of these effects — Texture, Pattern, and Picture — via the tabs in the Fill Effects dialog box.

When you select the Texture tab, shown in Figure 14-13, you can choose one of several textures to give your illustration a polished Formica look.

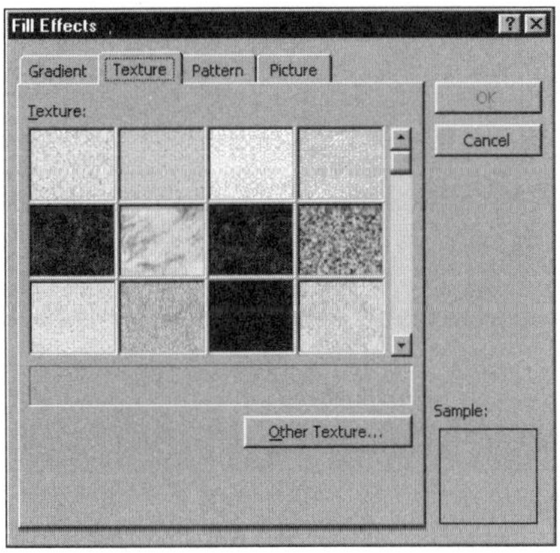

Figure 14-13: The Formica Dialog box (just kidding).

If you select the Pattern tab, you see the dialog box shown in Figure 14-14. Here you can choose from any of 48 different patterns using your choice of foreground and background colors.

If you click the Picture tab and then click the Select Picture button, a dialog box appears (shown in Figure 14-15) that allows you to select a picture to be used as a drawing object's fill. You may have to do some searching to find the image you want. (The Word 97 or Office 97 CD has an assortment of interesting photos; just look on the CD in the \Clipart\Photos folder.)

To give you an idea of the types of fills that are possible using these effects, Figure 14-16 revisits the three odd-shaped polygons that were first pictured back in Figure 14-5. I filled the first polygon with a gradient fill using the From Center shade style. The second polygon has a texture, and the third is filled with a photo ("Ocean" from the Word 97 CD).

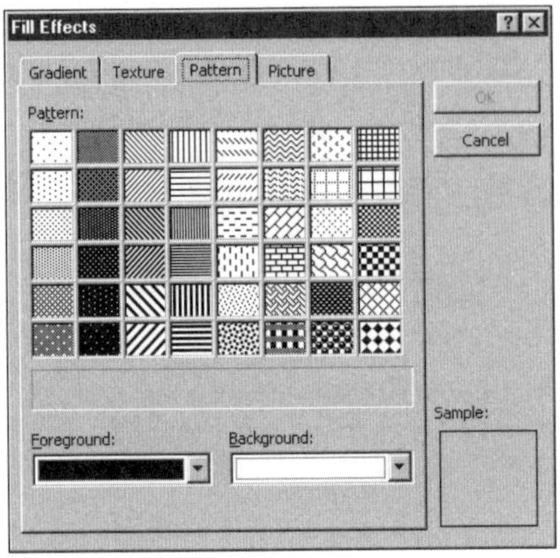

Figure 14-14: Filling an object with a pattern.

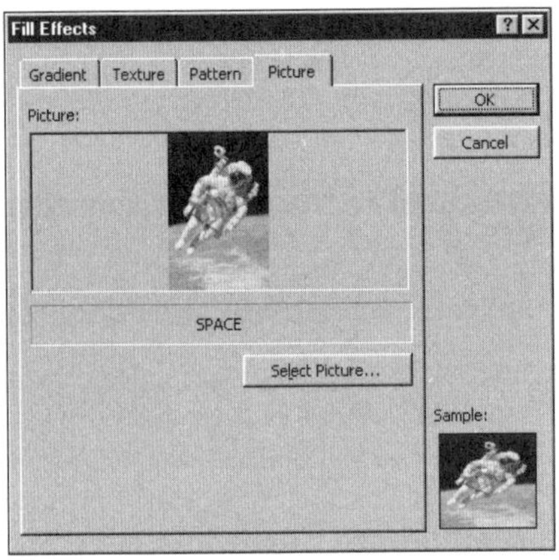

Figure 14-15: The fill Effect dialog box.

The shadow knows

To apply a shadow effect to an object, select the object and click the Shadow button. The Shadow menu, shown in Figure 14-17, appears, offering several shadow styles. Click the shadow style you want the object to assume.

If you select the Shadow Settings command from the Shadow menu, the Shadow Settings toolbar, shown in Figure 14-18, appears. The buttons on this toolbar allow you to nudge the shadow into exactly the right position and change the shadow color to create a custom shadow effect.

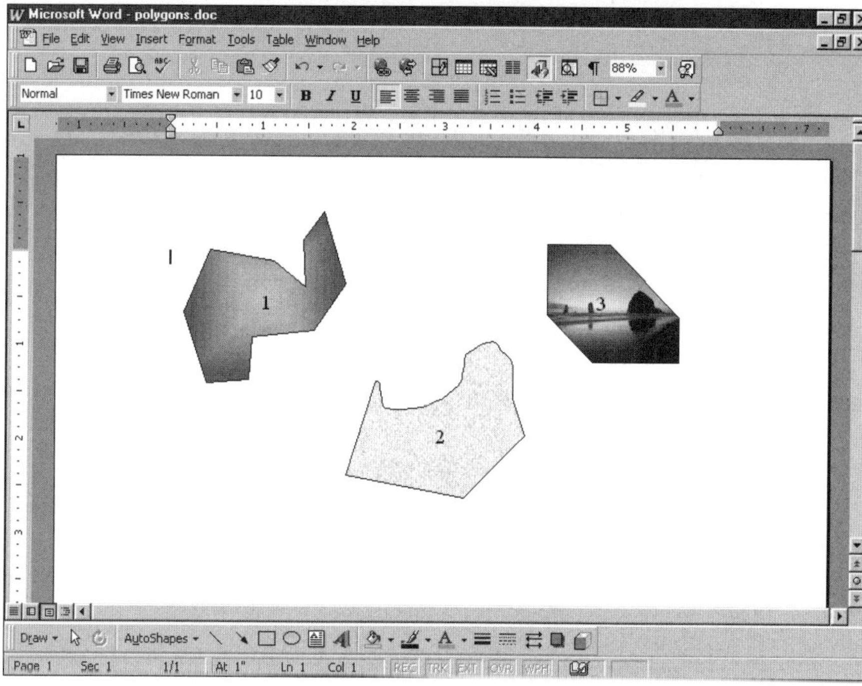

Figure 14-16: Three filled polygons.

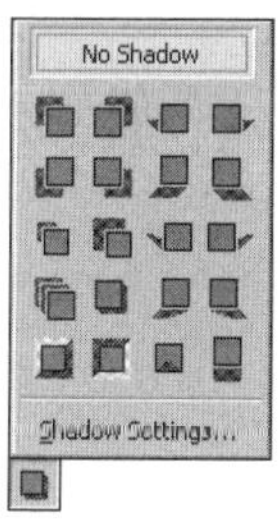

Figure 14-17: The Shadow menu.

Figure 14-18: The Shadow Settings toolbar.

Adding 3-D effects

The 3-D button is one of the coolest buttons on the Drawing toolbar. It lets you transform a dull and lifeless flat object into an exciting, breathtaking three-dimensional object. Figure 14-19 shows how you can use the 3-D

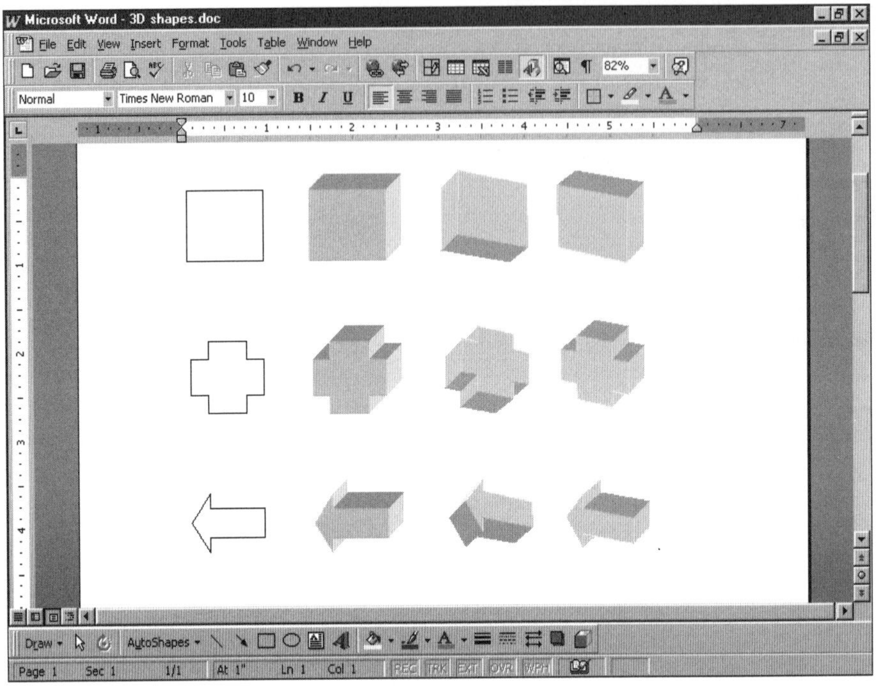

Figure 14-19: The 3-D effects are cool.

button to transform several shapes into 3-D objects. In each case, the object on the left is a simple AutoShape, and the three objects to the right of the simple AutoShape are three dimensional versions of the same shape.

To apply a 3-D effect to a shape, select the shape and click the 3-D button. The 3-D menu shown in Figure 14-20 appears. Click the effect you want to apply.

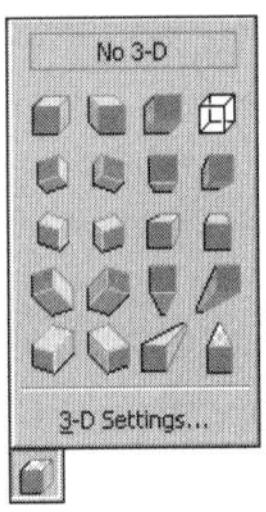

Figure 14-20: The 3-D menu.

If you select 3-D Settings from the 3-D menu, Word displays the toolbar shown in Figure 14-21. You can use the controls on this toolbar to tweak the 3-D settings of the object to obtain just the right effect. You can tilt the object in any direction, set its depth, and apply lighting and surface textures.

Figure 14-21: The 3-D Settings toolbar.

Flipping and Rotating Objects

To *flip* an object means to create a mirror image of it. To *rotate* an object means to turn it about its center. Word enables you to flip objects horizontally or vertically, rotate objects in 90-degree increments, or freely rotate an object to any angle.

Flipping an object

Word enables you to flip an object vertically or horizontally to create a mirror image of the object. To flip an object, follow these steps:

1. **Choose the object that you want to flip.**
2. **Click the Draw button to reveal the Draw menu, choose Rotate or Flip, then choose Flip Horizontal or Flip Vertical.**

Rotating an object 90 degrees

You can rotate an object in 90-degree increments by following these steps:

1. **Choose the object you want to rotate.**
2. **Click the Draw button to reveal the Draw menu, choose Rotate or Flip, then choose Rotate Left or Rotate Right.**
3. **To rotate the object 180 degrees, click the appropriate Rotate button again.**

Using the Free Rotate button

Rotating an object in 90-degree increments is useful sometimes, but if you want to give just a bit of slant to an object, 90-degree rotation doesn't cut it.

That's when the Free Rotate button comes in handy. It enables you to rotate an object to any arbitrary angle just by dragging it with the mouse.

The following steps show you how to use the Free Rotate button:

1. **Choose the object you want to rotate.**
2. **Click the Free Rotate button on the Drawing toolbar (shown in the margin).**
3. **Drag one of the corner rotation handles around the object.**

   As you drag, an outline of the object rotates around. When you get the object's outline to the angle you want, release the mouse button, and the object is redrawn at the new angle.

To restrict the rotation angle to 15-degree increments, hold the Shift key while dragging around the corner handle.

TIP

When you hold down the Ctrl key while dragging a corner handle, the object rotates about the opposite corner handle rather than the center. This feature is strange, but it's occasionally useful.

Remember how all the bad guys' hideouts were slanted in the old Batman TV show? Wasn't that cool?

Drawing a Complicated Picture

When you add more than one drawing object to a page, several problems come up. What happens when the objects overlap? How do you line up objects so that they don't look like they were thrown at the page from a moving car? And how do you keep together objects that belong together?

This section shows you how to use Word features to handle overlapped objects, align objects, and group objects. These features are essential to drawing complicated pictures that involve more than just a few drawing objects.

Changing layers

Whenever you have more than one object on a page, the potential exists for objects to overlap one another. Like most drawing programs, Word handles this problem by layering objects like a stack of plates. The first object you draw is at the bottom of the stack; the second object is on top of the first; the third is atop the second; and so on. If two objects overlap, the one that's at the highest layer wins; objects below it are partially covered.

So far, so good. But what if you don't remember to draw the objects in the correct order? What if you draw a shape that you want to tuck behind a shape you've already drawn, or what if you want to bring an existing shape to the top of the pecking order? No problem. Word enables you to change the stack order by moving objects toward the front or back so that they overlap just the way you want.

The Draw menu on the Drawing toolbar provides four commands for changing the stacking order, all grouped under the Order command:

- **Draw⇨Order⇨Bring to Front:** Brings the chosen object to the top of the stack
- **Draw⇨Order⇨Send to Back:** Sends the chosen object to the back of the stack
- **Draw⇨Order⇨Bring Forward:** Brings the chosen object one step closer to the front of the stack
- **Draw⇨Order⇨Send Backward:** Sends the object one rung down the ladder

The text in a Word document is considered to be a separate layer. Drawing objects can be placed on top of or behind the text. The last two commands on the Draw⇨Order command let you move objects above or below the text layer:

- **Draw⇨Order⇨Bring in Front of Text:** Brings the chosen object above the text. If the object has a fill color, it obscures any text it overlaps.
- **Draw⇨Order⇨Send Behind Text:** Sends the object behind the text layer. Any text that overlaps the object remains visible.

Layering problems are most obvious when objects have a fill color. If an object has no fill color, objects behind it are allowed to show through. In this case, the layering doesn't matter much.

TIP

To bring an object to the top of another, you may have to use the Bring For-ward command several times. The reason is that even though the two ob-jects appear to be adjacent, other objects may occupy the layers between them.

Line 'em up

Nothing looks more amateurish than objects dropped randomly on a page with no apparent concern for how they line up with one another. The Draw menu on the Drawing toolbar provides several alignment commands. To use them, first select the objects you want to align. Then click the Draw button, click Align or Distribute, then choose one of the following commands from the menu that appears:

- Align Left
- Align Center
- Align Right
- Align Top
- Align Middle
- Align Bottom

The first three of these commands align items horizontally; the last three align item vertically.

You can also distribute several items so that they are spaced evenly. Select the items you want to distribute, then click the Draw button, choose Align or Distribute, then choose Distribute Horizontally or Distribute Vertically.

If you want objects to automatically adhere to an invisible grid when you draw them or move them about, click the Draw button, click Snap, then choose To Grid. To turn off the snap-to-grid feature, choose the Draw⇨Snap⇨To Grid command again.

Group therapy

A *group* is a collection of objects that Word treats as though it were one object. Using groups properly is one key to putting simple shapes together to make complex pictures without becoming so frustrated that you have to join a therapy group. ("Hello, my name is Doug, and Word 97 drives me crazy.")

To create a group, follow these steps:

1. **Choose all objects that you want to include in the group.**
2. **Click Draw in the Drawing toolbar, then select the Group command.**

To take a group apart so that Word treats the objects as individuals again, follow these steps:

1. **Choose the object group that you want to break up.**
2. **Invoke the Draw⇨Ungroup command.**

If you create a group and then ungroup it so that you can work on its elements individually, you can easily regroup the objects. These steps show you how:

1. **Select at least one object that was in the original group.**

2. **Choose the Draw⇨Regroup command.**

   Word remembers which objects were in the group and automatically includes them.

Word enables you to create groups of groups. This capability is useful for complex pictures because it allows you to work on one part of the picture, group it, and then work on the next part of the picture without worrying about accidentally disturbing the part you've already grouped. After you have several such groups, select them and group them. You can create groups of groups of groups, and so on, ad nauseam.

Dropping Anchor

Drawing objects — such as AutoShapes, Rectangles, Ovals, and Text Boxes — are said to be *anchored* to a paragraph within the document. When you move an object around the page, Word automatically picks up the anchor and drops it on the nearest paragraph.

Normally, anchors are invisible. However, you can reveal them by choosing the Tools⇨Options command, clicking the View tab, then clicking the Object Anchors option. When you click OK, Word returns you to the document, and the anchors for any visible drawing objects are displayed on the page as an icon that resembles an anchor. If you grab a drawing object and move it to a new location, you see the anchor move to the nearest paragraph.

You can change the behavior of anchors by right-clicking a drawing object and by choosing the Format command that appears at the bottom of the pop-up menu. This summons a Format dialog box that includes a Position tab. Click the Position tab and you find two options that affect anchors:

- **Move object with text:** This option, which is normally on, causes an object to move whenever the paragraph to which the object is anchored moves. If you want a graphic to always be placed near a particular paragraph, leave this option enabled. However, you disable this option if you have placed the object at the precise location on the page where you want it and you want the object to stay at that location, even if edits to the text cause the paragraph to which the object is anchored to move.
- **Lock anchor:** This option, which is normally off, prevents an object's anchor to move to the nearest paragraph whenever you move the object. If you enable the Lock anchor option, the anchor stays on the original paragraph even if you move the object around the page. There's little reason to enable this option, so I suggest you leave it off.

Chapter 15

A Pocket Full of Desktop Publishing Tricks

In This Chapter

- Sidebars
- Pull quotes
- Eyebrows
- Captions
- Icons
- Side heads

This chapter is a compendium of ideas on how to incorporate common graphic design elements into a Word document to make it look like you used a more expensive desktop publishing program like Adobe PageMaker or Corel Ventura.

This chapter is written along the lines of "here's how to use styles, borders, drawing objects, and other stuff you know about to create some really cool effects that only graphic artists used to be able to do." You may come across a feature or two that you're not sure how to use. That's okay; no reason to feel bad. Just hop back to the relevant chapter for a quick refresher and all is well.

On with the show.

Sidebars

A *sidebar* is a short portion of text — usually a paragraph or two — that is incidental to the main flow of text in your document and is given special graphical treatment. This book is filled with sidebars: They're those gray boxes of text usually set off with a Technical Stuff icon.

Sidebars are frequently used in newsletters. If your newsletter has a two- or three-column layout, a sidebar can help you break up the monotony created by column after column of pure text. Figure 15-1 shows what I mean. Here, the sidebar at the bottom of the page spans two columns, breaking up the otherwise long and boring columns.

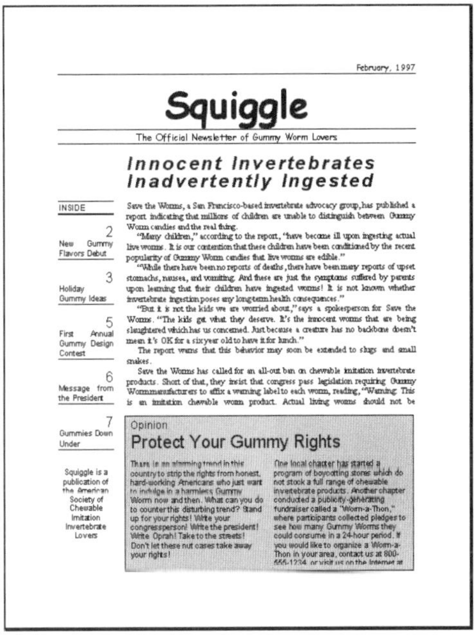

February, 1997

Squiggle

The Official Newsletter of Gummy Worm Lovers

Innocent Invertebrates Inadvertently Ingested

INSIDE

2 New Gummy Flavors Debut

3 Holiday Gummy Ideas

5 First Annual Gummy Design Contest

6 Message from the President

7 Gummies Down Under

Squiggle is a publication of the American Society of Chewable Imitation Invertebrate Lovers

Save the Worms, a San Francisco-based invertebrate advocacy group, has published a report indicating that millions of children are unable to distinguish between Gummy Worm candies and the real thing.

"Many children," according to the report, "have become ill upon ingesting actual live worms. It is our contention that these children have been conditioned by the recent popularity of Gummy Worm candies that live worms are edible."

"While there have been no reports of deaths, there have been many reports of upset stomachs, nausea, and vomiting. And these are just the symptoms suffered by parents upon learning that their children have ingested worms! It is not known whether invertebrate ingestion poses any long-term health consequences."

"But it is not the kids we are worried about," says a spokesperson for Save the Worms. "The kids get what they deserve. It's the innocent worms that are being slaughtered which has us concerned. Just because a creature has no backbone doesn't mean it's OK for a six year old to have it for lunch."

The report warns that this behavior may soon be extended to slugs and small snakes.

Save the Worms has called for an all-out ban on chewable imitation invertebrate products. Short of that, they insist that congress pass legislation requiring Gummy Worm manufacturers to affix a warning label to each worm, reading, "Warning: This is an imitation chewable worm product. Actual living worms should not be

Opinion

Protect Your Gummy Rights

There is an alarming trend in this country to strip the rights from honest, hard-working Americans who just want to indulge in a harmless Gummy Worm now and then. What can you do to counter this disturbing trend? Stand up for your rights! Write your congressperson! Write the president! Write Oprah! Take to the streets! Don't let these nut cases take away your rights!

One local chapter has started a program of boycotting stores which do not stock a full range of chewable invertebrate products. Another chapter conducted a publicity-generating fundraiser called a "Worm-a-Thon," where participants collected pledges to see how many Gummy Worms they could consume in a 24-hour period. If you would like to organize a Worm-a-Thon in your area, contact us at 800-555-1234 or visit us on the Internet at

Figure 15-1: A sidebar can spice up an otherwise dull page.

To create a sidebar like the one in Figure 15-1, follow these steps:

1. **Click the Text Box button in the Drawing toolbar, then draw a text box where you want the sidebar to appear.**
2. **Click in the text box and type the text for the sidebar.**
3. **Apply whatever formatting you want to the sidebar text.**

   The easiest way to do this is to create styles for the sidebar heading and body. Then you simply apply the styles to format the sidebar properly.

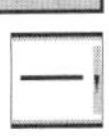

4. **Use the Fill Color and Line Style controls to add shading and an outline to the sidebar.**
5. **You're done.**

   Wasn't that easy?

Here are some random thoughts about creating sidebars:

- Pick a contrasting font for the sidebar. In Figure 15-1, I used a sans-serif font (Arial) for the sidebar's heading and text.
- Unfortunately, Word doesn't let you set up a two-column text box. If you absolutely must have two-column sidebars, it's time to switch to Adobe PageMaker.
- To keep the sidebar from moving around the page after you've found a good spot for it, uncheck the Move with Text under the Position tab of the Format➪Text Box command.
- Don't overuse sidebars. Sidebars lose their impact if they take up more space than the main text.

Pull Quotes

A *pull quote* (also referred to as a *lift-out quote*) is a short quotation pulled out of the article and given special treatment. Its purpose is to pique the reader's interest so that he or she is drawn to read the article.

Pull quotes are usually set in a larger type and are often sandwiched between columns in a two- or three-column layout, as shown in Figure 15-2. To achieve this effect, you create the pull quote in a text box.

Follow these steps to create a pull quote like the one in Figure 15-2:

1. **Draw a Text Box to hold the pull quote.**

   To draw the text box, select the Text Box tool from the Drawing toolbar, position the mouse pointer where you want one of the pull quote's corners to appear, then drag out the Text Box to the size you want.

2. **Click in the text box and type the text that you want to appear in the pull quote.**
3. **Format the pull quote however you want.**

   In Figure 15-2, I use a larger italic version of the body text typeface and center the paragraph.

4. **Right-click the text box border and choose the Format Text Box command from the pop up menu.**

   The Format Text Box dialog box appears. (If it doesn't, you probably didn't click right on the text box border. Try again.)

5. **Click the Text Box tabs and set all margins to zero.**

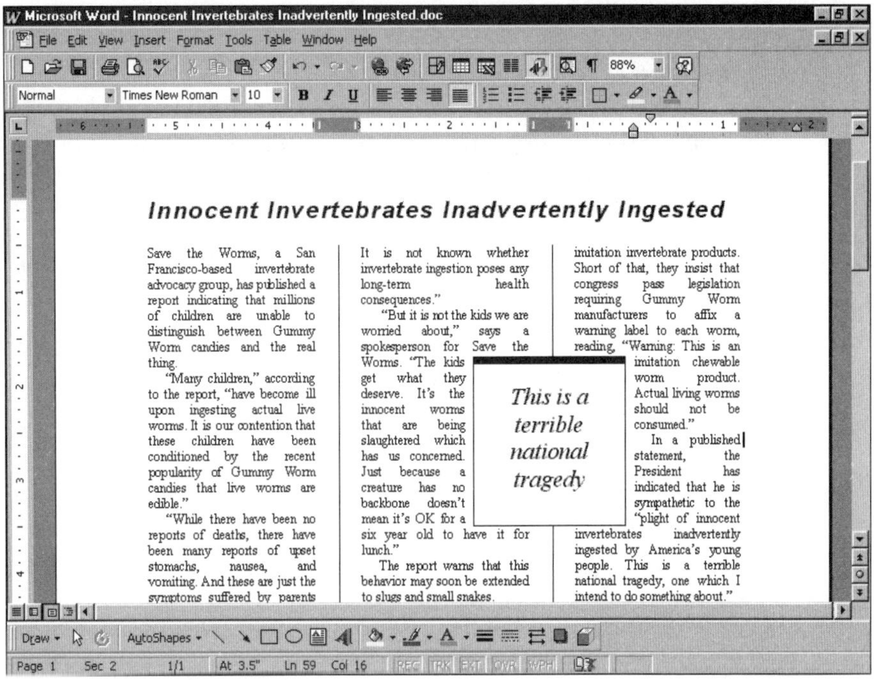

Figure 15-2: A pull quote draws the reader into the text.

6. **Click the Colors and Lines tab and set the Line Color to No Line.**
7. **Click OK to dismiss the Format Text Box dialog box.**
8. **Use the Format⇨Borders and Shading command to add a border to the pull quote.**

   In Figure 15-2, I use a thin border for the left, right, and bottom edge of the paragraph and provide a thicker border at the top. Other border designs can be just as effective.

9. **Adjust the text box position if necessary.**

   Place the pull quote text box in a location that is not too close to the spot where the quote appears in the article. And make sure that you place the text box in the middle of paragraphs, not between them. If you place the pull quote between paragraphs, the reader may think the pull quote is a heading.

Keep these thoughts in mind when you create pull quotes:

- Remember that the purpose of the pull quote is to draw the reader into your text. Pick the most interesting or provocative quotes from the article.
- Pull quotes are typically enclosed in a box border, but sometimes a simple rule above and below does the job of highlighting the quote without imprisoning it.
- Experiment with different column positions for your pull quotes. In Figure 15-2, I sandwich the pull quote between the columns. You can also set a pull quote within a column, or you can create pull quotes that are a full two-columns wide.

Eyebrows

Eyebrows are the short department descriptions that appear over article titles in magazines and newsletters. Eyebrows are a good place to have some typographical fun (if that's possible). Because they're so short (a word or two will do), you don't have to worry much about readability.

Some eyebrows can be created using Word's basic formatting options. For example, you can format your eyebrows with 10-point bold Century Gothic with the letter spacing expanded 6 points, centered over the article title:

E D I T O R I A L

Or use the same typeface, but condense the letter spacing to 1 point:

EDITORIAL

Or add a special symbol from the Wingdings font to characterize the eyebrow and left-align it:

■ EDITORIAL

You can use borders and shading to create interesting effects:

EDITORIAL

In the preceding example, I used two paragraphs for the eyebrow. For the first paragraph, I typed the word EDITORIAL, formatted it with the right font, switched to white characters on a black background, and then played with the paragraph indents until the black shading extended just a bit past each side of the word. For the next paragraph, I added a border line above, with

zero space between the line and the text. Oh, and I made sure the space after the first paragraph and the space before for the second paragraph were both zero.

Some thoughts to think about as you ponder the meaning of eyebrows and other great issues of life:

TIP

- Format your eyebrows consistently. Consistent eyebrows give your publication a more unified look.
- Put the eyebrow formatting information in a style. That's the best way to format them consistently.
- If you really want to get creative with eyebrows, doodle with them by using the WordArt applet. You can find more info about in *Word 97 For Windows For Dummies*.
- For a really dramatic look, try letting your eyebrows run together like Nikita Khrushchev or shaving them off.

Captions

A *caption* is a bit of text that identifies a figure, table, chart, or other visual you've included in a document. Captions usually include a reference number, for example, Figure 58 or Table 293. Figure 15-3 shows a document with a captioned illustration.

If you want, you can create captions simply by typing them in. But Word includes a Caption feature that automatically numbers your captions when you insert them, keeps the numbers in order, and lets you create a table of figures, tables, charts, or whatever when you're all done. You paid for this program, so you may as well know how to use as much of it as possible.

To add a caption to a picture, table, chart, or other graphic goodie, follow these steps:

1. **If you haven't done so already, use the Insert⇨Picture command to insert a picture into your document.**
2. **Select the picture that you want the caption attached to.**
3. **Call up the Insert⇨Caption command.**

   You see the dialog box shown in Figure 15-4.
4. **Type the rest of the caption.**

   Word gives you just the reference number. Type whatever text you want to describe the figure, table, chart, or whatever.

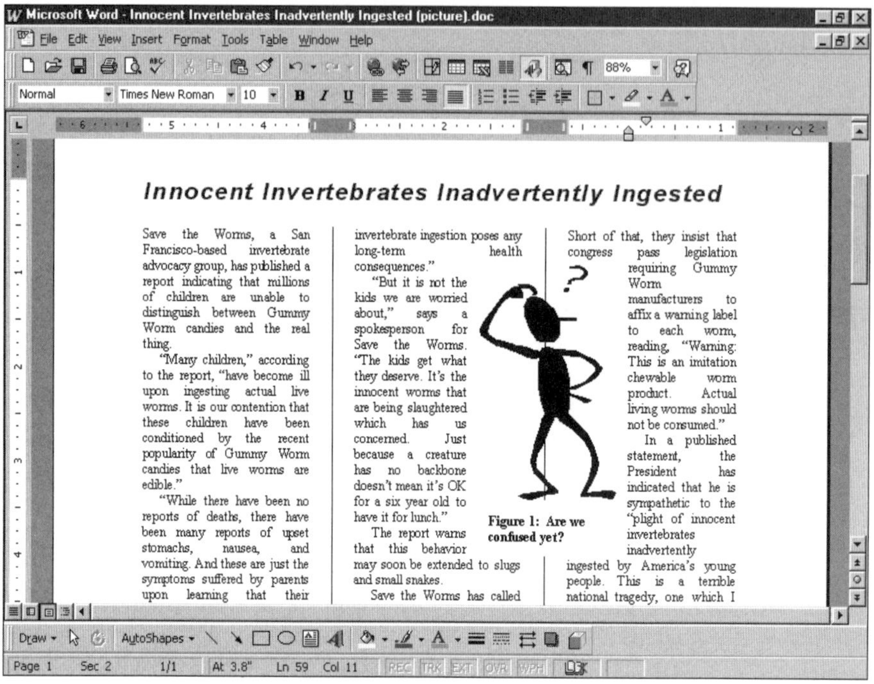

Figure 15-3: A picture with a caption.

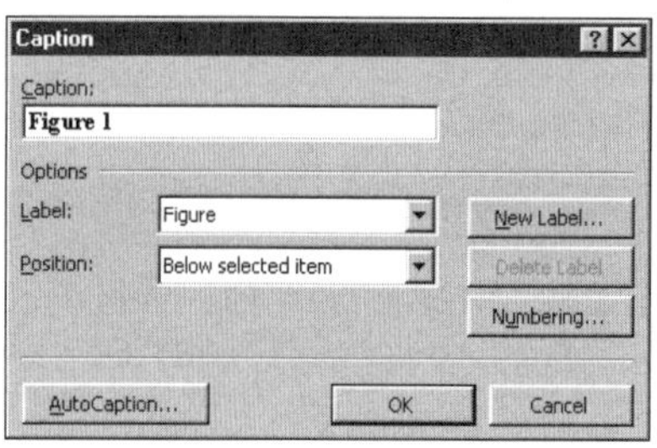

Figure 15-4: The Insert Caption dialog box.

5. **Change the Label field if it is incorrect.**

   Word keeps track of caption numbers for figures, tables, and equations separately. When you insert a caption, make sure the Label field is set to the type of caption you want to create.

6. **Change the Position field if you want to change the positioning.**

   The two options are Above or Below the selected item.

7. **Click OK.**

   Word inserts the caption.

Here are a few rapid-fire thoughts designed to inspire your use of captions:

- If you want to create captions for something other than figures, tables, and equations, click the New Label button and type a label for whatever you want to create captions for; say, for example, a Limerick. Click OK, and from then on, Limerick appears as one of the Label types.
- When you create a caption, Word automatically applies the style named Caption to the caption paragraph. You can control the format of all captions in a document by modifying the Caption style.
- You can create a table of figures, tables, equations, or limericks by using the Insert⇨Index and Tables command. Pick the Table of Figures tab and then choose the type of caption you want to create a table for from the Caption Label field. Click OK and treat yourself to a Snickers bar.
- At various and sundry times, caption numbers get out of sequence. Fear not! Word can put the caption numbers back into sequence when you print the document. If you're tired of looking at out-of-sequence numbers, use the Edit⇨Select All command to select the entire document and then press F9 to recompute the caption numbers.
- If you want Word to always create a caption whenever you insert a particular type of object into your document, click the AutoCaption button in the Caption dialog box. This yields a dialog box that lists all the various types of objects you can insert into a Word document. Check the ones you want to automatically create captions for and then click OK.

Icons

Ever wonder how to insert icons similar to the ones found throughout the margins in this and other *...For Dummies* books using Word? Actually, it's pretty easy. You just insert a picture to use for an icon and line it up where you want it. Figure 15-5 shows an example.

To add icons to a document, follow these steps:

1. **Come up with a really good icon.**

   Use one of the Word clip art files or create your own using Word's drawing tools.

2. **Put the cursor near where you want the icon to be placed.**
3. **Use the Insert⇨Picture command to insert the picture file.**
4. **Resize the picture and drag it to the margin.**

   The picture is probably way too big when you insert it. Cut it down to size, then drag it into the margin next to the paragraph you want to draw attention to.

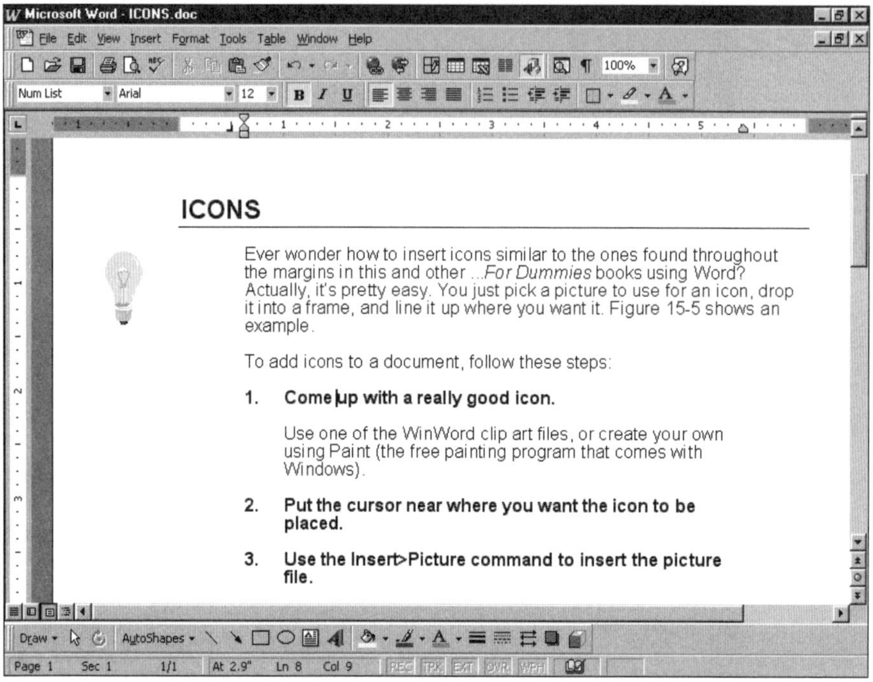

Figure 15-5: Inserting an icon in a Word document.

As you lie awake nights thinking about icons, keep these points in mind:

- Icons work best if you lay out your document so that there is a wide margin at the left side of the page. A wide margin allows room for the icon to be inserted without disrupting the text.
- The purpose of icons is to call attention to text that may be of particular interest. Study the way icons are used in this book and other *...For Dummies* books for the ultimate example of the proper use of icons (but don't share any of this knowledge with other publishers).
- Icons work especially well in procedure manuals. For example, you may design a File Cabinet icon to use whenever you tell the reader to file something away. Or you may create a Computer icon to use whenever the reader is told to do something on a computer.
- The Wingdings font that comes with Windows includes quite a collection of little pictures that may be suitable for icons. To insert a Wingdings character, use the Insert⇨Symbol command, pick the character you want, click Insert, and then click OK. Adjust the point size of the symbol until it is as large as you want.

Side Headings

A *side heading* is a heading that appears in a separate column next to the text it relates to, as in Figure 15-6. You would think that side headings would be easy to do: Just give all your body text paragraphs a generous left indent, and format the heading paragraph with a hanging indent. But this works only when the heading consists of only one line. To create multi-line side headings, such as the ones in Figure 15-6, you have to use a text box.

To create a side head, do the following:

1. **Use the File⇨Page Setup command to lay out your page with a generous left margin.**

   In Figure 15-6, I set the left margin to 3.25 inches.

2. **Type the heading text where you want the heading to appear in your document.**

3. **Assign the appropriate Heading style to the paragraph.**

   For top-level headings, assign Heading 1 to the paragraph. Use Heading 2 or Heading 3 for lower-level headings.

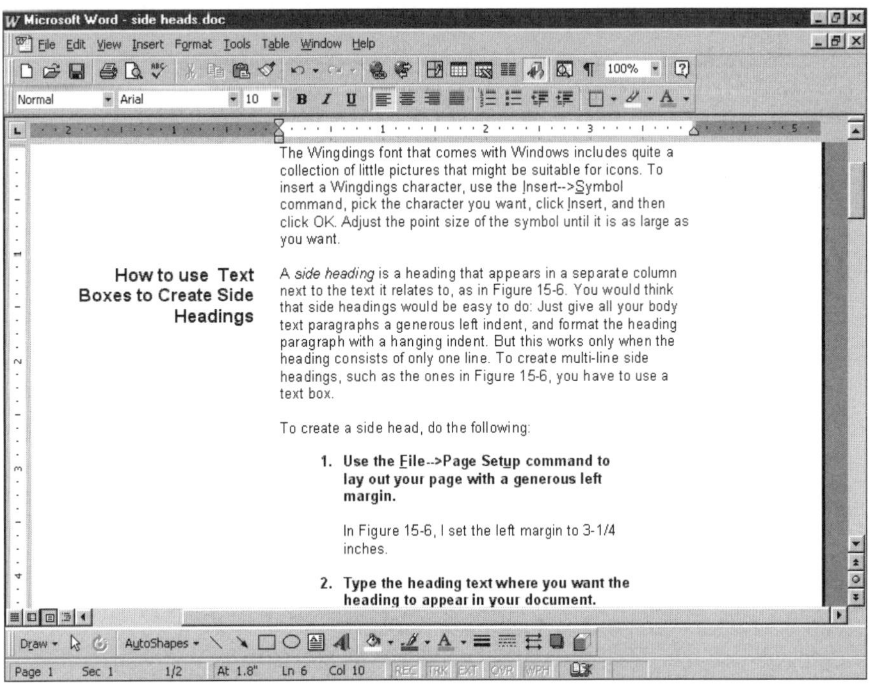

Figure 15-6: Side headings.

4. **Format the characters however you want.**

   In Figure 15-6, the text is 14-point Arial Bold.

5. **Select the entire paragraph and use the Insert➪Text Box to place the heading in a text box.**

   Word converts the paragraph to a text box. It probably doesn't look the way you want just yet, but in a few more steps it will.

6. **Call up the Format➪Text Box command or right-click the text box and choose Format Text Box from the pop-up menu.**

   The Format Text Box dialog box appears.

7. **Adjust the Format Text Box settings.**

   You must adjust settings on several tabs in this dialog box:

   - **Colors and Lines:** Set the Line Color to No Color to remove the border around the text box.
   - **Size:** In the Size tab, set the Width setting to match the width of your heading area. For Figure 15-6, I set the Width to 1.75 inches.
   - **Position:** Use the fields on the Position tab to set the left edge of the heading text box. In Figure 15-6, I set the left edge to 1.25 inches from the edge of the page. Added to the width (1.75 inches), that puts the right-hand edge of the frame at 3 inches, leaving a 0.25-inch empty space between the side head and the left margin of the text (which was set to 3.25 inches in Step 1).

     Make sure you leave the Move with Text option set so that the heading travels with the text.

The hardest part about side headings is planning the layout. The best way to plan the layout is with a blank piece of paper and a ruler. Mark the location of the heading text box and the text column. Set the page margins to accommodate the text column. Set the heading text box's horizontal position and width accordingly.

TIP: If you're not sure that a heading text box is anchored to the text that follows it, select the text box and look for the little anchor. If you can't see the anchor, click the Show/Hide Paragraph button.

If you want to create a style that can format a side heading, one step remains: You must convert the text box to a frame. Frames are an older method of creating text that can be positioned precisely on a page. Microsoft has all but dropped frames in favor of text boxes, but frames still have a few advantages over text boxes, the most important being that a frame can be incorporated into a style.

To convert a text box to a frame, first follow the procedure described in this section to format the heading as a text box. Then call up the Format➪Text Box command, click the Text Box tab, click the Convert to Frame button. Word converts the text box into a frame. (Word is apt to stick a border around the framed paragraph when it makes the conversion. If so, just remove the border with the Format➪Borders and Shading command.)

After you convert the text box to a frame, select the entire heading and reapply the appropriate Heading style. This redefines the Heading using the formatting you've applied, including the frame.

Part III
Webbing With Word

In this part . . .

Two of the hottest new features of Word 97 are its ability to create HTML documents that can be published on the Internet's World Wide Web, and the ability to access the Web directly from within Word. If you're caught up in the hype of the Internet, you'll eat up the chapters in this part.

Chapter 16

Creating Web Pages

In This Chapter

- Using the Web Page Wizard to create a Web page
- Opening an existing Web document with Word
- Converting a Word document to Web format
- Working with Online Layout View
- Creating hyperlinks
- Formatting horizontal lines, scroll bars, and other cool stuff in your Web pages

One of the best new features of Word 97 is that you can display your documents on the Internet's World Wide Web. Unlike normal Word documents, however, which are stored in Word's DOC format, Web pages are stored in HTML — *HyperText Markup Language* — a special format that most World Wide Web pages are written in.

When you work on an HTML document, you find that many of Word's normal formatting features are not available, because the HTML document format doesn't support those features. By the same token, a few new formatting capabilities appear when you edit a Web page.

Note also that this chapter does not show you the details of how you place your web documents on a Web server so that they can be viewed by Internet users. In most cases, you must use a facility called FTP to post your HTML files to your Web site. You have to ask the person who is in charge of the Web server for the name of the FTP directory that has been set up for your Web pages. Then, you can refer to Chapter 17 to learn how to use Word's Save As command to send your HTML file to that FTP directory.

If you can't find the Web authoring features described in this chapter, you may have to re-run the Word 97 or Office 97 setup program to install the Word Web Authoring features.

Creating a Web Page for the First Time

The easiest way to create a Web page in Word 97 is to use the Web Page Wizard. To activate this wizard, follow these steps:

1. **Choose the File⇨New command.**

   The New dialog box appears, offering you several template choices for your new file.

2. **Click the Web Pages tab.**

   Several Web page templates and wizards appear.

3. **Click the Web Page Wizard icon and then click OK.**

   The Web Page Wizard comes to life, as shown in Figure 16-1.

Figure 16-1: The Web Page Wizard offers several choices for the type of Web page you want to create.

4. **Select the type of Web page you want to create.**

   The Web Page Wizard offers several choices for the type of page you want to create, including a personal home page, several types of business forms, a calendar, and some generic layouts with one, two, or three columns.

5. **Click Next.**

   The Web Page Wizard displays a list of visual styles to choose from.

6. **Select the style you want for your page.**

   Each visual style offers its own combination of text formats, backgrounds, and border styles.

7. **Click Finish.**

   Word whirs and spins a minute, then spits out a skeleton Web document such as the one shown in Figure 16-2.

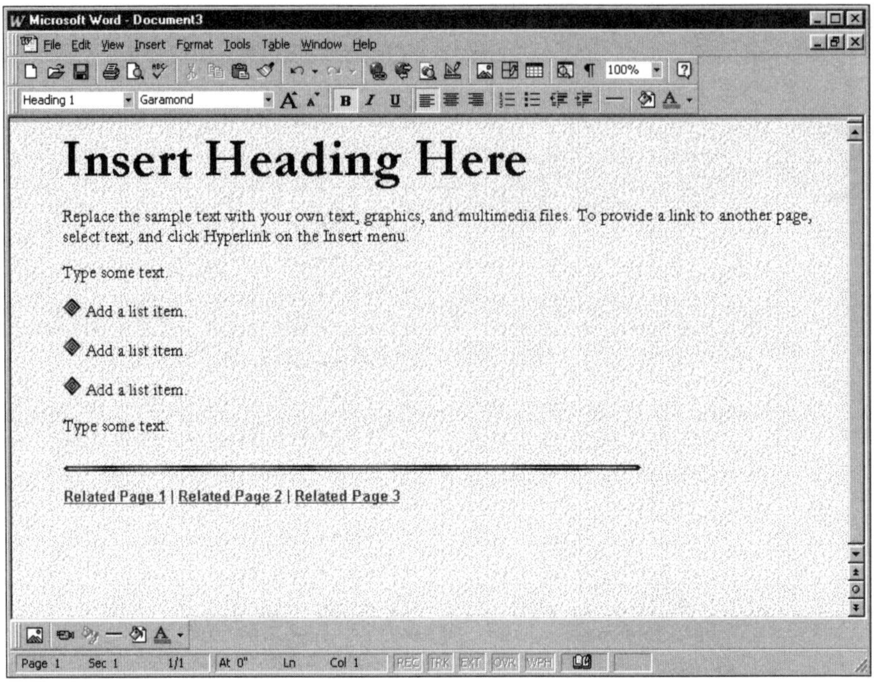

Figure 16-2: A skeleton Web page created by the Web Page Wizard.

8. **Make whatever changes you want to make to the document, filling in the blanks left by the Web Page Wizard.**

   The page created by the Wizard includes text like "Insert Heading Here" and "Type some text." This text serves only as a placeholder for the actual text you want to appear in your Web page. You undoubtedly want to type some more-meaningful text to replace these placeholders, and you want to add paragraphs of your own. Later in this chapter, you can find instructions for applying the most-common types of formatting used in Web pages.

9. **Save the document.**

   Use the File➪Save command to save your work. Word automatically saves the file in HTML format, using .HTML rather than .DOC as the file extension.

TIP: You can also create a Web document from scratch by choosing the File➪New command and selecting the Blank Web Page.

Opening an Existing Web Document

As with any other document, you probably need to edit your HTML documents from time to time. Word 97 allows you to open and edit existing HTML documents as if they were Word documents. You can edit HTML documents you created with Word, or you can open and edit HTML documents created by other programs.

To open and edit an HTML document, call up the File⇨Open command the same way you do to open a normal Word document. In the Open dialog box that appears, change the Files of type list box to "HTML Document," then select the file you want to open and click Open.

There are formatting differences between HTML documents and Word documents. Whenever you open an HTML document, Word 97 automatically switches into HTML gear so that all of the formatting features of HTML are at your disposal.

Converting a Word Document to Web Format

You can convert any existing Word document to HTML format so that it can be published on the Web by following these steps:

1. **Open the document in Word.**

   Use the File⇨Open command just as you normally would.

2. **Choose the File⇨Save As command.**

   The normal Save As dialog box appears.

3. **Select HTML Document (.html) in the Save as type field.**
4. **If desired, choose a new location and name for the file.**
5. **Click the Save button.**

   The file is converted to HTML format and saved.

Keep in mind that there are many differences between Word documents and HTML documents. When you convert a Word document to HTML format, Word does it's best to convert the formatting you have applied to the Word document into HTML formats. However, some Word formatting features have no HTML equivalents. For example, HTML can utilize only certain font sizes. If you have formatted text with a font size that isn't supported by HTML, Word will change the text to the nearest available font size.

Working in Online Layout View

With Word 97, Microsoft adds a new view called Online View, which is designed specifically for working with Web documents. When you're in Online Layout View, the document you see looks similar to how it appears in an Internet Web browser such as Microsoft Internet Explorer or Netscape Navigator.

The most obvious difference between Online Layout View and Word's other views is the appearance of the Document Map, which looks like an outline in its own pane on the left side of the document window. The document map lets you quickly see all of the headings in your document. Plus, you can quickly scroll the document window to any section of your document by clicking on the appropriate heading in the Document Map.

Note that the Document Map is not exclusive to Online Layout View. You can summon it at any time, no matter which view you work in, by clicking the Document Map button (shown in the margin) or by choosing the View➪Document Map command. And you can make the Document Map go away by choosing View➪Document Map or clicking the Document Map button again.

When you open or create an HTML document, Word automatically switches to Online Layout View. You can switch back to one of Word's other views (Normal, Page Layout, or Outline) by using the View commands. You can switch back to Online Layout View at any time by choosing the View➪Online Layout command.

TIP

For some reason, the View buttons that normally appear at the bottom-left corner of the screen disappear when you switch to Online Layout View. Rather than using the buttons, you have to use the View commands to switch out of Online Layout View.

Working with hyperlinks

A *hyperlink* is a bit of text that, when clicked, links users with another page. The link can be to another location in the current document, another page on the World Wide Web (created by you or by someone else), another Word document, or even an Excel or PowerPoint document.

To add a hyperlink to your document, follow these steps:

1. **Type some text or insert a picture that you would like to turn into a link.**

For example, type "click here to go to my home page." Or you can insert a picture of yourself that browsers click in order to get to your home page.

2. **Highlight the text or picture you want to turn into a link.**
3. **Choose the Insert➪Hyperlink command.**

   The Hyperlink dialog box appears, which looks like the one in Figure 16-3.

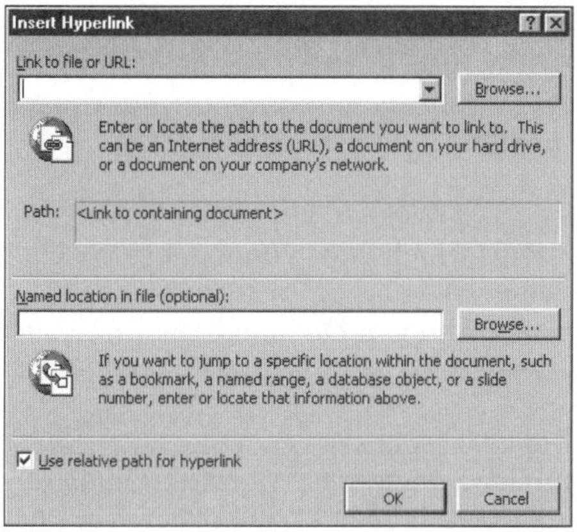

Figure 16-3: Inserting a hyperlink.

4. **In the Link to File or URL field, type the address of the Web page you want to link to.**

   If you want the link to refer to a file on your hard disk instead, click the Browse button and locate the file.

5. **Click OK.**

The text you selected is transformed into a link. To indicate that the text is a link, Word displays it in blue underlined text. (Anyone who views your Web page can change this color. See the section "Changing text colors" later in this chapter to see how.) When Web users view your document on the Web, they can display the page referred to in the link by clicking the highlighted text.

Formatting that you're already used to

HTML formatting is quite different than normal Word document formatting. Many of Word's more advanced formatting features aren't available when working with Web page — HTML — documents. Here is a list of some of the more commonly used Word features that you *can't* use with HTML documents:

- **Font sizes.** HTML documents can only use a limited number of font sizes: 9, 10, 12, 14, 18, 24, and 36.
- **Tabs.**
- **Columns.** HTML does not support column layouts. To create a page that has text in two or more columns, you must create a table.
- **Headers and footers.** Page numbers are not supported either.
- **Footnotes and endnotes.**
- **Tables of contents, tables of authorities, and indexes.**

That's the bad news. The good news is that HTML has a few formatting features of its own that aren't available to normal Word documents. Jump to the next section if you can't wait to hear about these.

Fortunately, many of the formatting techniques that you already know from good-old-Word work the same with HTML documents. Table 16-1 lists some of the more commonly used formatting commands that work the same with Word and HTML documents, along with the Word keyboard shortcut used to apply the format.

Table 16-1 Formatting that works the same for Word and HTML documents

Format	*Button*	*Keyboard shortcut*
Bold		Ctrl+B
Italic		Ctrl+I
Underline		Ctrl+U Left align (left)Ctrl+L
Center		Ctrl+C
Right align		Ctrl+R
Bullet list		
Numbered list		
Heading 1		Ctrl+Alt+1
Heading 2		Ctrl+Alt+2
Heading 3		Ctrl+Alt+3

Formatting options in Online View

Word 97 includes a handful of fancy formatting options — not found with any ordinary Word document — that you can use with Web documents. The following sections describe these features, which are all available from the Format menu.

Adding a horizontal line

One of the commonly used formatting features in HTML documents is the horizontal line, which is drawn across the page to visually separate groups of information. The lines can be simple or ornate, depending on the appearance you want to create on your Web page.

To insert a horizontal line, follow these steps:

1. **Position the insertion point where you want to insert the horizontal line.**
2. **Choose the Insert⇨Horizontal Line command.**

   The Horizontal Line dialog box shown in Figure 16-4 appears.

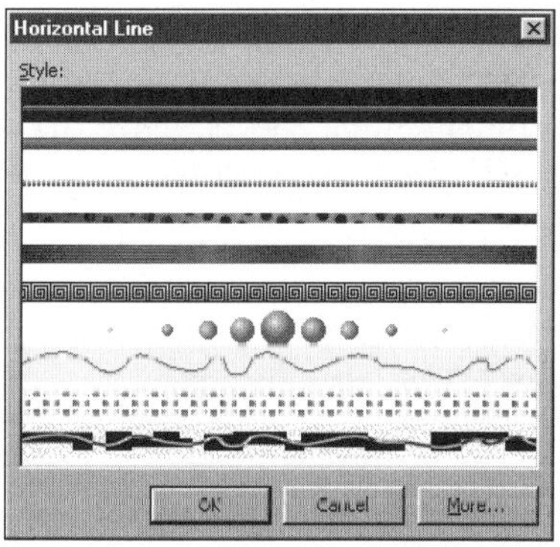

Figure 16-4: Inserting a horizontal line.

3. **Pick the horizontal line style you want to use.**

   Word offers several horizontal line styles to choose from.
4. **Click OK.**

   The line is inserted.

To remove a line later on, select it by clicking anywhere on the line, then press the Delete key.

Inserting a picture

Pictures are one of the most appealing aspects of the Web, and nearly all Web pages have at least a few pictures. In some cases, the pictures are actual scanned photographs, but more often, the pictures are small graphic images created by a drawing program such as Windows Paint (the free drawing program that comes with Windows 95).

Before you can insert a picture on your Web page, of course, you must first obtain the graphic file for the picture you want to insert. Word 97 comes with a collection of useful clip art files, and you can find loads of free artwork on the Web. (Just click your Web browser's Find button and search on the words "clip art.")

To insert a picture into an HTML document, follow these steps:

1. **Move the insertion point to the position where you want the picture inserted.**
2. **Summon the Insert⇨Picture⇨From File command.**

   Or, just click the Insert Picture button in the standard toolbar (shown in the margin.) Either way, an Insert Picture dialog box like the one in Figure 16-5 appears.

Figure 16-5: Inserting a picture.

3. **Locate and select the picture you want to insert.**

   You may have to navigate through the various folders on your hard disk to find the file.

4. **Click Insert.**

   The picture is inserted into your document.

TIP

You can also choose the Insert⇨Picture⇨Browse Web Art Page to access a Microsoft Internet Web page that contains pictures you can download (for free) and use in your Web pages.

WARNING!

Be careful about inserting large graphics in your Web pages. The larger your graphic, the more time it will take to download when a Web user views your page. If the page takes too long to download, the Web user will likely curse under his breath and vow to never visit your page again.

Font formats

Web documents have fewer font formatting options than normal Word documents do. As a result, when you choose the Format➪Font command, you see the abbreviated dialog box shown in Figure 16-6 instead of the normal Font dialog box. This dialog box enables you to set the size, color, and style (bold, italic, underline, strikethrough, superscript, and subscript).

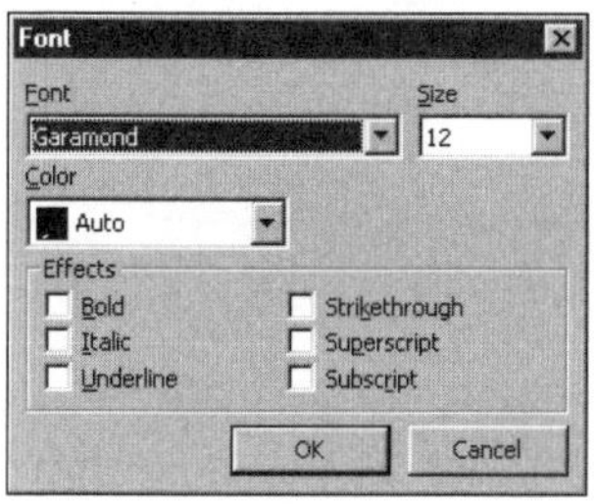

Figure 16-6: The Font dialog box for a Web document.

Bullets and numbers

For HTML documents, simple bullets and numbers work pretty much the same as they do for Word documents. You can click the Bullets or Numbering buttons to create a bullet or numbered list.

In addition, the Bullets and Numbering command for Web pages enables you to customize graphic bullets instead of using plain bullets or numbering styles. Figure 16-7 shows how this dialog box appears. You can select any of several graphic bullets provided by Word 97. Or, you can click More to use any graphic file as a bullet. To apply a numbering style, click the Numbered tab up at the top of the dialog box.

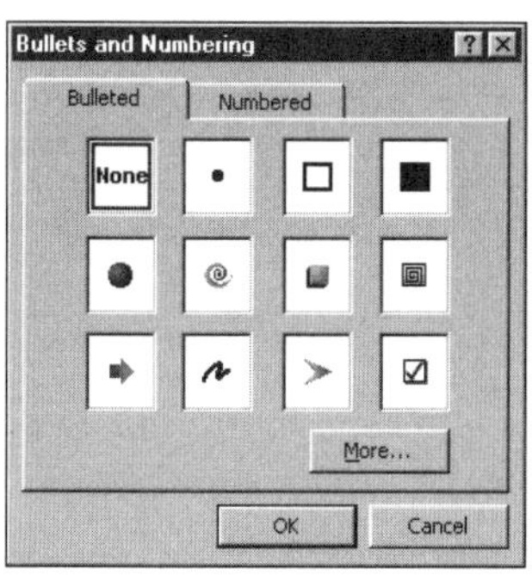

Figure 16-7: The Bullets and Numbering dialog box for a Web document.

Changing text colors

You can change the color used for body text, hyperlinks you haven't visited yet, and hyperlinks that have already been visited by choosing the Format⇨Text colors command (Flip to the section entitled "Working with hyperlinks" in this chapter for the lowdown on linking text and pictures.) This displays the Test Colors dialog box, shown in Figure 16-8, where you select the colors you want to use. Click OK to apply the colors you select.

Note that this changes only the colors displayed on your computer when viewing Web pages. It does not change the colors used when a Web user views your page.

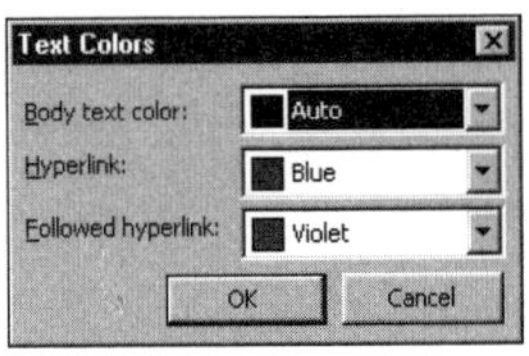

Figure 16-8: Selecting text colors.

Using a graphic background

To apply a graphic texture to your Web page's background, call up the Format⇨Background⇨Fill effects command to display the Fill Effects dialog box, shown in Figure 16-9. Then, select the background effect you want to use and click OK.

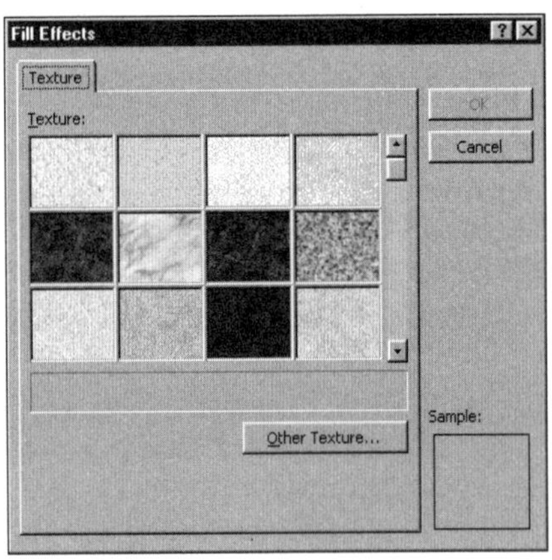

Figure 16-9: Using a background texture.

You can also use the Format⇨Background command to apply a colored background to your web page. Just select the color you want to use from the menu that appears.

TIP

You can apply a background sound that is played whenever a Web user stumbles on to your page by choosing the Insert⇨Background sound command.

Using scrolling text

Choose the Insert⇨Scrolling Text command to create a *marquee* — one of those deals where the text scrolls across the screen from one side to the other. Choosing the Insert⇨Scrolling Text command displays the Scrolling Text dialog box, shown in Figure 16-10. You can play with the various settings in this dialog box to set the text that you want to scroll, the direction you want the text to scroll, and whether you want the text to scroll just once or to repeat in a loop.

You can also click the Size and Speed tab to set the size of the area that you want the text to scroll through, and the speed at which the text scrolls.

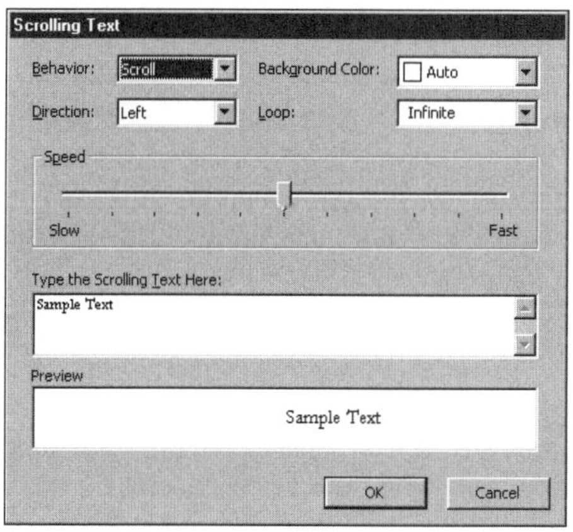

Figure 16-10: Creating a scrolling marquee.

Chapter 17

Surfing the Office Web

In This Chapter

- Opening documents on the Internet
- Accessing FTP sites from Word 97
- Using the Web toolbar

I bet you're thinking that you have to use special Internet software such as Microsoft Internet Explorer or (perish the thought!) Netscape Navigator to access the Internet. Isn't a browser program required to access the World Wide Web?

Until Microsoft released Office 97, it was. But now, all of the Office programs let you access files on the Internet directly, without going through a web browser. Word 97 lets you open Word documents, whether they reside on your computer or on the Internet. And if you try to open some other type of document, such as an Excel spreadsheet or a PowerPoint presentation file, Word automatically launches the appropriate program so that you can view the document.

The Internet features described in this chapter apply not only to the Internet but also to a new type of network that is starting to spring up in companies around the world, called an *intranet*. An intranet is like a local version of the Internet. It looks, feels, and behaves just like the Internet, but it is local to a specific company and cannot be accessed by users from outside the company. If your company has set up a corporate intranet, you can also use Word to open documents that have been stored on it.

This entire chapter assumes that you have access to the Internet. If you do not, you should first pick up a copy of my book, *Internet Explorer 3 For Dummies*, published by IDG Books Worldwide. *Internet Explorer 3 For Dummies* shows you how to get connected to the Internet and, as a bonus, teaches you how to use Internet Explorer 3.0.

Internet Jargon you can't avoid

Unfortunately, there's no way to discuss accessing Internet documents with Word 97 without using some fairly heavy Internet terminology. Here's an overview of some of the more important Internet terms that are used in this chapter:

Internet: The Internet is a huge global network of computers that consists of literally millions of computers.

World Wide Web: The fastest growing segment of the Internet. The Web (as it is usually known) consists of millions of pages of information that a Web browser program (see next definition) displays for you.

Web Browser: A program designed to access the World Wide Web. The two most popular web browsers are Netscape Navigator and Microsoft Internet Explorer.

HTML: The codes used to format a page for the World Wide Web. As a casual Web user, you don't have to concern yourself with HTML. If you want to create Web pages of your own, you do need to know a little HTML.

Web Page: A single page of information on the World Wide Web.

Web Server: A computer that stores Web pages — this allows Internet users such as yourself to retrieve Web pages.

Home Page: A Web page that serves as a starting point for a collection of related web pages (often called a *web site*).

FTP: *File Transfer Protocol*, a way of copying individual files from one Internet computer to another.

FTP Site: A server computer storing files that can be accessed via FTP.

URL: *Uniform Resource Locator*, an Internet address. A URL identifies a web server or FTP server, plus the filename for the document or file to be retrieved.

Opening a Document at a Web Site

Suppose you, or more likely someone else, creates a Word document and decided to make it available to the general public via the Internet. One way to access the Word file is to convert the document to the Internet's popular HTML format — the code used to format web pages. You can then store the document on an Internet World Wide Web server so that anyone with access to the World Wide Web can view your document using their own Internet browser software. In fact, Word 97 makes it easy to do that by including a spiffy new Save as HTML command, which is covered at length in Chapter 16.

But with Word 97, it is also possible to open actual Word documents that have been stored on the Web, without going to the trouble of converting the Word documents to HTML format. To open a Word document that has been placed on a web server, you must know the complete address (called a URL)

of the document you want to open. This address will usually consist of three parts: a *server address,* one or more *directory names,* and the document's filename. For a Web document, the address always begins with `http://` so that Word can distinguish the address from a normal filename. And the other parts of the URL are separated by slashes.

For example, consider this address:

```
http://www.con.com/river/trouble.doc
```

Here, the server name is `www.con.com`, the directory is `river`, and the filename is `trouble.doc`.

When you know the URL, just type the URL in the File name field on the standard Open dialog box, and the document opens. Here's the complete procedure for opening a document at an Internet Web site:

1. **Find out the complete URL of the document you want to open.**
2. **Choose the File➪Open command.**

   Or click the Open button or use the keyboard shortcut Ctrl+O. One way or the other, the Open dialog box, shown in Figure 17-1, appears.

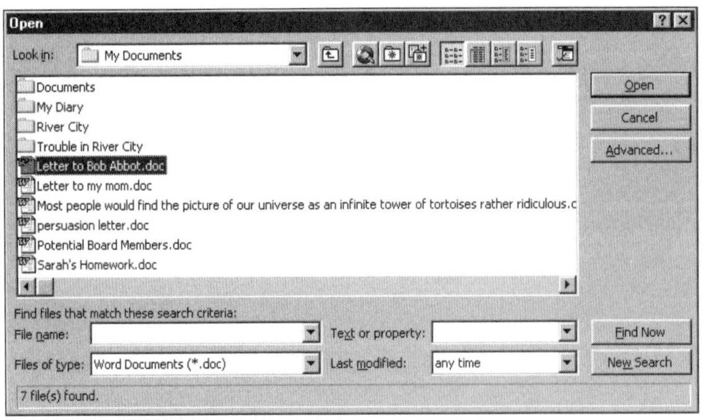

Figure 17-1: The Open dialog box.

3. **Type the URL of the document you want to open in the File name field.**

   For example, type `http://www.con.com/river/trouble.doc`.

4. **Click Open.**

   It will take a few moments — perhaps a few minutes if the document is large — to copy the file from the Internet to your computer. When the transfer is finished, the document is displayed as normal.

Here are some thoughts to ponder concerning retrieving files from the Web:

- It doesn't matter if the file identified by the URL is on a computer halfway around the globe, on a computer two floors up from you, or on your own computer. As long as the URL is valid, Word retrieves the document and displays it.
- Access to a document that is located on the Internet is read-only, which means that Word will let you open the document and view it, but you can't save any changes that you may want to make back to the Internet location. If you make changes to the document, you must save them to your own computer by using the File⇨Save As command.
- The Internet is an inherently slow medium for transferring data — much slower than a local hard disk, and slower than a Local Area Network. Naturally, the larger the document, the longer it will take to transfer the document over the Internet to your computer.

Using an FTP Site

FTP, which stands for *File Transfer Protocol*, is one of the oldest parts of the Internet. FTP is designed to create Internet libraries where files can be stored and retrieved by other Internet users.

FTP uses a directory structure that works much like Windows 95 folders. The main directory of an FTP site is called the *root*. Within the root are other directories, which may contain files, additional directories, or both.

Until Office 97, you had to use separate FTP software to retrieve files that come from an FTP site. With Office 97 (and of course Word 97), you can access FTP sites from the standard Open and Save As dialog boxes. In Word 97, an FTP site looks just like any other folder on your hard drive.

Adding an FTP site to your computer

Before you can access files in an FTP site, you must add the address (URL) of the FTP site to your computer's list of FTP sites. To do that, follow these steps:

1. **In Word, summon the File⇨Open command.**

   This will summon the Open dialog box, illustrated in Figure 17-1.

2. **Click the down arrow for the Look in list box, then scroll down to select "Add/Modify FTP Locations."**

   The dialog box shown in Figure 17-2 appears.

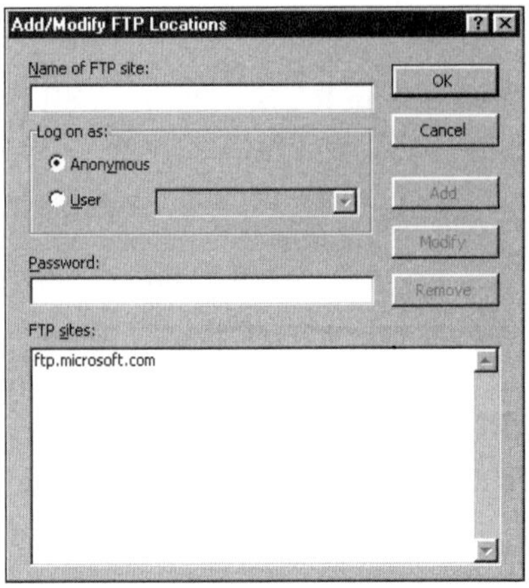

Figure 17-2: Adding an FTP site.

3. **Type the URL of the FTP site in the Name of FTP Site field.**

   Be sure to include `ftp://` at the start of the URL. (This distinguishes the URL from a URL for a Web page.)

4. **If this FTP site requires you to enter a user name and password to gain access, click the User button, then type your user name and password.**

   The administrator of the FTP site you are accessing can tell you what user name and password to use.

   For many FTP sites, you can use "anonymous" as the user ID and your e-mail address as the password.

5. **Click Add.**

   The new FTP site is added.

6. **Click OK.**

   The Add/Modify FTP Locations dialog box vanishes, returning you to the Open dialog box.

7. **Click Cancel to return to Word.**

   Or, if you want to immediately open a document from the FTP site, proceed to the next section.

Opening a document from an FTP site

To open a document from an FTP site, follow these steps:

1. **Choose the File⇨Open command.**

   This summons the Open dialog box.

2. **Click the down arrow for the Look in list box, then scroll down to select the FTP site that contains the document you want to open.**

   Your computer hesitates for a moment as it connects with the FTP site. If you are not already connected to the Internet, Word connects you. Then it displays the Open dialog box, listing the directories that appear at the FTP site's root. See Figure 17-3.

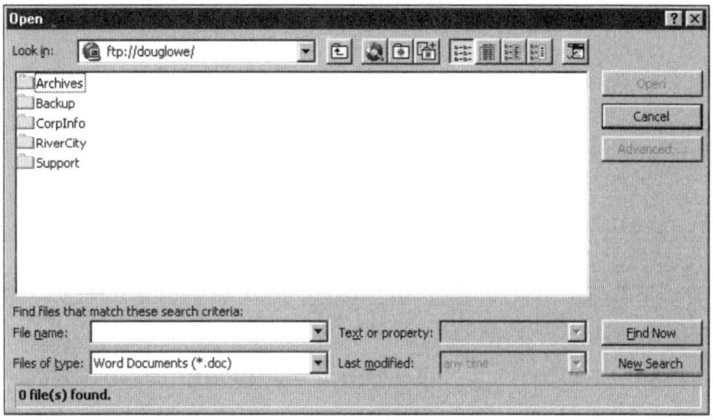

Figure 17-3: Opening a file from an FTP site.

3. **Select the file you want to open.**

   To open a directory, double-click its icon. When you find the file you want, click its icon to select it.

4. **Click Open.**

   Depending on the size of your document, you may have to wait for a few minutes for Word to download the document.

You're done!

Saving a document to an FTP site

You can also save a document directly to an FTP site by choosing the File⇨Save As command to summon the Save As dialog box. In the Save In list, select the FTP server you want to save the file to. Then, browse your way to the directory you want to place your file in, type a name for the file, and click Save.

Using the Web Toolbar

Word 97 sports a new feature called the Web Toolbar. This toolbar is designed to make it easier to view documents that either contain hyperlinks or were retrieved from the World Wide Web. Figure 17-4 shows a document with the Web toolbar active, and Table 17-1 lists the function of each button and control on the Web toolbar.

To summon the Web toolbar, choose the View➪Toolbars➪Web, or click the Web Toolbar button in the standard toolbar.

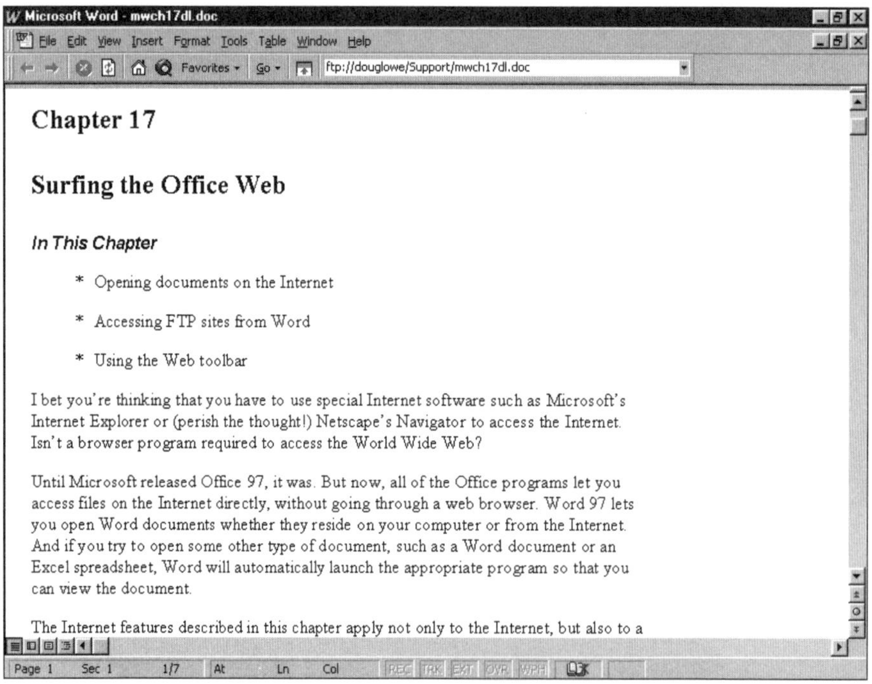

Figure 17-4: The Web Toolbar in action.

Table 17-1 Buttons on the Web Toolbar

Button	*Name*	*What it does*
	Back	Goes to the previously displayed document.
	Forward	Returns to the document you came back from.

(continued)

Table 17-1 (continued)

Button	*Name*	*What it does*
	Stop	Stops a long download.
	Refresh	Reloads the current page.
	Start Page	Displays your designated start page.
	Search	Displays your designated search page.
	Favorites	Displays your favorites list, similar to clicking the Save In Favorites button in an Open or Save dialog box.
	Go	Displays a menu of Web pages you can go to. The Go menu includes Back, Forward, Start, and Search commands that correspond to the Back, Forward, Start, and Search buttons. The Go menu also includes an Open command as well as commands to designate the current page as your start page or search page.
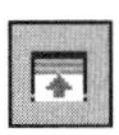	Show Only Web Toolbar	Temporarily hides everything on the screen except the document and the Web toolbar. Click this button again to get the screen back to normal.
	Address	The address of the current page.

Part IV

I've Always Wondered How to Do That

The 5th Wave   By Rich Tennant

"IT'S A MEMO FROM SOFTWARE DOCUMENTATION. IT'S EITHER AN EXPLANATION OF HOW THE NEW SATELLITE COMMUNICATIONS NETWORK FUNCTIONS, OR DIRECTIONS FOR REPLACING BATTERIES IN THE SMOKE DETECTORS."

In this part . . .

Remember the old TV show, *You Asked For It?* People wrote in about things they had always wondered about, and, well, they asked for it, and they got it.

The chapters in this part are like that. All of those Word features you read about on the back of the Word 97 box or in a magazine review but never really learned how they work are here, just waiting for you to ask.

Chapter 18

All the Options You Need to Know

In This Chapter

- What's with all these options?
- View options
- General options
- Edit options
- Print options
- File location options
- Save options

Sometimes I long for the old pre-Windows days, when my favorite word processor was WordPerfect 4.2 and the only real options I had to contend with were to toil a little more with WordPerfect's screen colors or take the afternoon off and catch a quick round of golf. My golf game fell all to pieces after I began using Word. I spend so much of my time trying to figure out what all those options on the Tools⇨Options command are for that I don't have any time left over for such luxuries as golf.

You should read this chapter when you finally decide to give in to the Tools⇨Options command and you want to know what all those options do. This chapter describes the most useful options, but more importantly it tells you which options can be safely ignored so that you (unlike some people I know — me, for example) can catch up on your golf.

I am aware, of course, that for many people, golf is a more frustrating game than playing with Word. And for some, golf is more boring than reading Word's on-line help. If you're one of those poor, unenlightened souls, feel free to substitute your favorite non-golf pastime in the paragraphs above.

What's with All the Options?

When you choose Tools⇨Options, you are presented with one of the most heavily-laden dialog boxes of all time. This dialog box has so many options that it earned Microsoft a Lifetime Achievement Award from the American Society of Windows Programmers.

Like many other dialog boxes in Word, the Options dialog box organizes its settings into tabs. Each tab has its own set of option controls. To switch from one tab to another, just click the tab label at the top of the dialog box.

Most Word dialog boxes that use tabs have two or three tab labels, but the Options dialog box has ten — count 'em, *ten* — tabs:

- **View:** Contains options that control the way your document is displayed on-screen.
- **General:** Contains a hodgepodge of miscellaneous options that the Microsoft programmers couldn't fit on any of the other tabs.
- **Edit:** Contains options that affect the way Word's basic text-editing features work.
- **Print:** Contains options that affect the way the File⇨Print command works.
- **Save:** Has important options that control the way Word saves your documents.
- **Spelling and Grammar:** Turns the spelling and grammar checkers on and off.
- **Track Changes:** Contains options used in conjunction with the Tools⇨Track Changes command, which you can find out about in Chapter 24.
- **User Information:** Stores your name and address and other personal information like your birth date, height, weight, bank account balance, and other information Microsoft might be interested in when Bill Gates finally decides to take over the world. (Just kidding.)
- **Compatibility:** Changes the way Word deals with documents created by other word processors, including older versions of Word.
- **File Locations:** Tells Word where to look for files.

As you fritter away your day playing with these tabs, keep the following points in mind:

- Several of the Options tabs have more than one road that leads to them. You can reach the Print options tab, for example, by choosing File⇨Print and then clicking the Options button.

- To move to a tab, just click the tab label. You can also move from tab to tab by using the keyboard's arrow keys. To move from the General tab to the Edit tab, for example, press the right-arrow key.

Many settings that a normal person would consider *options* are located elsewhere in Word's sinuous menu structure. You use the View⇨Toolbars command, for example, to display or hide toolbars. And you access the AutoCorrect and AutoFormat As You Type features, which control many basic editing options such as automatically capitalizing new sentences and using fancy curly quotes, from the Tools⇨AutoCorrect command.

The following sections describe six of the tabs available on the Options dialog box: View, General, Edit, Print, Save, and File Locations. These tabs contain the options you are most likely to want to change. The other tabs contain options you shouldn't fuss with unless you're really bored on a rainy afternoon.

Control How Word Looks: View Options

The options on the View tab, shown in Figure 18-1, let you customize the appearance of Word's humble display. The View tab options are arranged in three groups: Show, Window, and Nonprinting Characters.

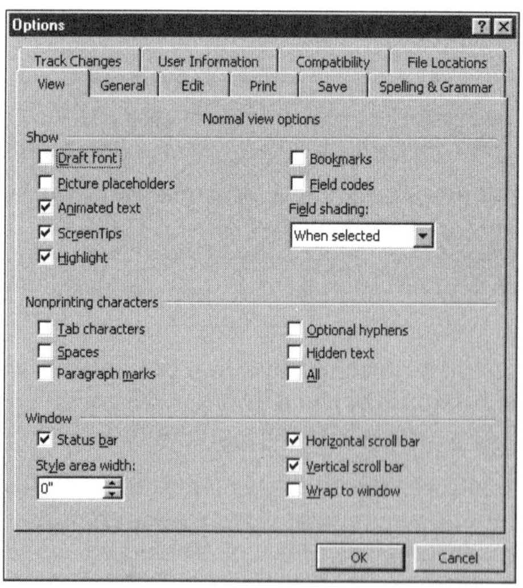

Figure 18-1: The View options.

The Show options

The View options grouped under the Show heading control the amount of detail displayed in the document window.

Some of the Show options appear on the View tab only when you are in Page Layout view. To set those options, you must switch to Page Layout view before choosing Tools⇨Options.

This list gives you the lowdown on each of the options you can set from this tab:

- **Draft Font:** This option displays all text in an ugly sans serif bold typeface and underlines any text that has special formatting, such as boldface or italics. Useful for improving performance when you're running Word on computers that are so slow they have no business running Word. (This option is available only in Normal view.)
- **Picture Placeholders:** If you insert a picture into a document, you notice that Word hesitates a little when you scroll the picture into the document window. If you add 20 pictures to a document, the hesitations may come so often that you want to scream. Checking the Picture Placeholders option causes Word to display a simple rectangle where the picture should go. This step eliminates the hesitation. (The pictures are still printed when you print the document.)
- **Animated Text:** Controls whether text animation effects are shown. (Text animations are set via the Animation tab of the Format⇨Font command.)
- **Screen Tips:** Controls whether reviewers' marks are automatically displayed when you hover the mouse briefly over a comment mark.
- **Highlight:** Turns off the highlighting made by Word's Highlight feature. (See Chapter 24.)
- **Bookmarks**: Takes text referred to in a bookmark and sandwiches it between gray brackets. Chapter 1 has more bookmark information.
- **Field codes:** Shows the codes inserted for each field rather than the results of the field. Use this option when you're struggling with a maniacal mail merge. Chapter 8 is all about mail merge.
- **Field shading:** Shades field results to draw attention to them. This option can be set to Never (which never shades field results), Always (which always shades field results), and When selected (which shades field results only when some or all of the field is selected).
- **Drawings:** Displays a rectangle for each drawing object rather than the object itself. This option is available only in Page Layout view. (That's why it's not shown in Figure 18-1.)
- **Object Anchors:** Displays anchors for frames and drawing objects. Available only in Page Layout view.

- **Text Boundaries:** Displays lines around columns and margins so that you can quickly see the page layout. Available only in Page Layout view.

The Nonprinting characters options

The View options grouped under the Nonprinting characters heading let you control which special characters are displayed in the document window:

- **Tab characters:** Displays tab characters as an arrow. I usually leave this option checked so that I can keep track of tabs.
- **Spaces:** Displays spaces as little dots. I usually leave this option unchecked.
- **Paragraph marks:** Displays paragraph marks. I usually leave this option checked so that I can quickly find extraneous paragraphs.
- **Optional hyphens:** Displays optional hyphens, you use when you want precise control over hyphenation (check out Chapter 12).
- **Hidden text:** Displays hidden text. Hidden text is text that is in your document but isn't printed.
- **All:** Displays all hidden characters. Choosing this option is the same as clicking the Show/Hide Paragraph button on the Standard toolbar.

When the Show/Hide Paragraph button on the Standard toolbar is depressed, all nonprinting characters are displayed. When the button is not depressed, only those nonprinting characters specified on the View options tab are displayed. You should set the options on the View tab so that only those nonprinting characters you *always* want displayed — such as Tab characters and paragraph marks — are checked. You can display the other nonprinting characters at any time simply by clicking the Show/Hide Paragraph tool.

The Window options

The View options grouped under the Window heading let you tweak the appearance of Word document windows. This list shows the details:

- **Status bar:** Word's dashboard. It tells you what page you're on, where you are on the page, whether you pressed the Insert key to switch to Overtype mode, and so on. If all this stuff just takes up space, you can remove it by unchecking the Status bar option. This action leaves more room for your document.
- **Style area width:** If you want to see the names of styles you have assigned to your paragraphs all lined up in a neat row down the left side of the window, increase the setting of this option from 0 inches to about 0.6 inch. To remove the Style area, return this setting to 0.

- **Horizontal scroll bar:** The one at the bottom of the screen. If you discover one day that you have been using Word for two years and didn't know that a horizontal scroll bar was available, uncheck this option to free up more space to display your document. Be aware, though, that in addition to removing the horizontal scroll bar, unchecking this option also removes the view buttons next to it. With these buttons removed, you have to use the View menu commands to switch views.
- **Vertical scroll bar:** At the right edge of the window. If your text is just a wee bit wide for the screen, consider unchecking the Vertical scroll bar option to remove the scroll bar. This action frees up a little space, and you can still press the Page Up and Page Down keys to scroll through your document.
- **Wrap to window:** Keeps text within the document window by breaking lines that are too wide to fit in the window. When you use this option, the line endings you see on-screen are different from the line endings that are printed. (This option is available only in Normal view.)
- **Vertical ruler:** Places a ruler at the left edge of the window. Available only in Page Layout view.
- **Enlarge fonts less than:** Lets you set the minimum size for fonts displayed on the screen. Fonts smaller than the size you set will be automatically enlarged. This option applies only to Online Layout view.

Major General Options

Back in the days of Microsoft Word Version 1.0, the options on the General options tab were lowly Private Options. But they re-upped for Version 2 and eventually decided to become career options. Now they've made it all the way to the rank of General. You had better snap-to whenever you call up these options (see Figure 18-2).

This list gives you the lowdown on what the General options do:

- **Background repagination:** Ever notice that when you take a breather from your sustained typing rate of 90 words per minute, Word sometimes causes page breaks to dance about? This dance is Word's Background repagination feature at work, constantly surveying the length of your document and inserting page breaks where they rightfully belong. If you uncheck this box, Word repaginates the document only when you print it; create a table of contents, index, or other table; or work in Page Layout or Print Preview view.

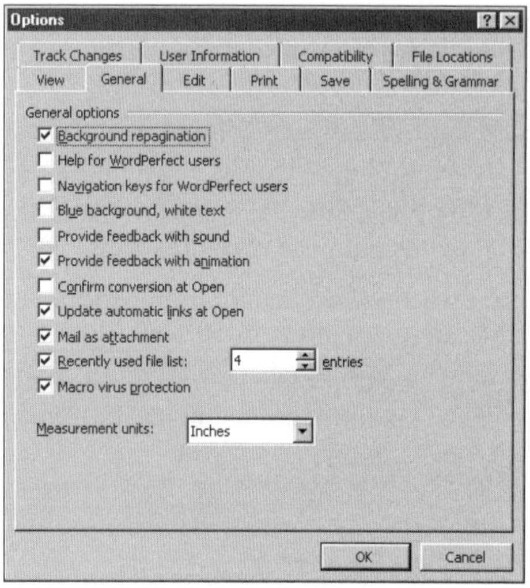

Figure 18-2: The General options.

Turning Background repagination off might make your computer run a little faster, but you'll always be wondering whether you're at the top or bottom of the page. I don't recommend it. (You can't turn off Background repagination when you're in Page Layout view, because Page Layout view requires that page breaks always be up-to-date.)

- **Help for WordPerfect users:** An option that is little more than wishful thinking on behalf of the billions and billions of WordPerfect users who are switching to Word. If you momentarily forget that you're using Word and press a WordPerfect function key, such as Shift-F7, you receive a minor electric shock as a gentle reinforcement to use the correct Word command instead.
- **Navigation keys for WordPerfect users:** Another futile attempt to help WordPerfect users who have been forced at gunpoint to switch to Word, this time by making the Page Up, Page Down, Home, End, and Esc keys behave in the same brain-damaged manner as they do in WordPerfect.
- **Blue background, white text:** Makes Word *really* look like WordPerfect.
- **Provide feedback with sound:** When this option is checked, your neighbors are alerted to the fact that you haven't yet mastered Word.
- **Provide feedback with animation:** Lets Word show off by displaying clever animations when you perform certain actions such as saving files or printing.
- **Confirm conversion at Open:** This is not some kind of option for a religious awakening: Instead, it instructs Word to ask for your consent before opening a non-Word document.

- **Update automatic links at Open:** Automatically updates any files that are linked to a document when you open the document. It's usually best to leave this one on.
- **Mail as attachment:** Relevant only if your computer is attached to a network and you want to zap documents around by using e-mail.
- **Recently used file list:** Tells Word how many files to list at the bottom of the File menu. You can list as many as nine files.
- **Macro virus protection:** Enables Word's built-in but rudimentary protection against viruses that can infect document files.
- **Measurement units:** In case you don't like inches, you can change Word's measurements to centimeters, points, picas, fathoms, leagues, cubits, or parsecs.

Edit Options to Suit Your Fancy

The Edit tab options, shown in Figure 18-3 and in the following list, affect the way Word's basic editing operations work:

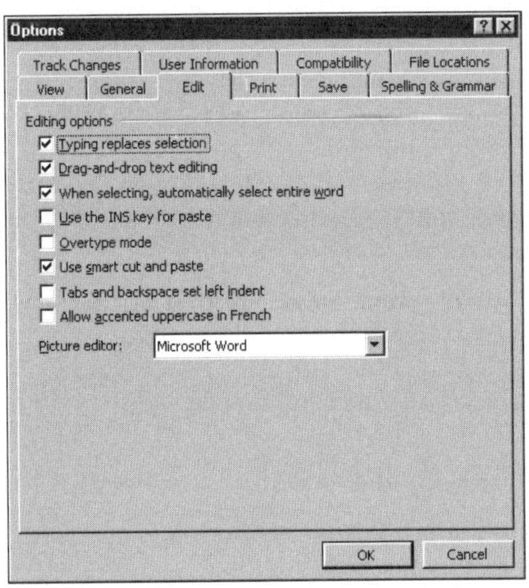

Figure 18-3: The Edit options.

- **Typing replaces selection:** If you highlight text by dragging the mouse over it or by holding down the Shift key while moving the cursor and then type something, the whatever-it-was-you-typed obliterates the whatever-it-was-you-highlighted. If this behavior drives you bonkers, you can turn it off by unchecking the Typing replaces selection box.
- **Drag-and-drop text editing:** More commonly known as dragon dropping; lets you move text by selecting it and then dragging it with the mouse. If it annoys you, turn it off by unchecking this field.
- **When selecting, automatically select entire word:** One of the niftiest features in Word. It causes Word to assume that you meant to select an entire word — when, for example, you place the cursor in the middle of a word and press Ctrl+I, the entire word is italicized. It can be disconcerting at first, though. If it's against your religion, you can turn it off by unchecking the Automatic Word Selection option.
- **Use the INS key for paste:** Makes the Insert key double as a shortcut for the Edit⇨Paste command.
- **Overtype mode:** Puts Word into Overtype mode, in which any text you type obliterates text on-screen. Whether you check this option or not, you can press the Insert key to switch between Insert and Overtype modes (unless you checked the Use the INS key for paste option).
- **Use smart cut and paste:** Adjusts spaces before and after text you cut and paste so that you don't end up with two spaces between some words and no spaces between others. Leave this option checked; it's too good to turn off.
- **Tab and backspace set left indent:** If this option is enabled, the Tab key behaves funny if you use it at the beginning of an existing paragraph: Rather than insert a tab character, it actually increases the paragraph's first line indent setting found in the Format⇨Font command. Similarly, the Backspace key, when used at the beginning of a paragraph, decreases the left indent. This feature drives me crazy, so I usually disable this option.
- **Allow accented uppercase in French:** Lets you put accents on capital letters when text is formatted as French.
- **Picture editor:** Lets you specify which graphics program to use to edit imported graphics. The only two choices are Microsoft Word, which means using Word's built-in graphics features, or Microsoft's Picture Editor, a graphics program which is supplied along with Office 97.

Perfecting the Print Options

Figure 18-4 shows the options that are available from the Print options tab. You can reach this tab by choosing Tools⇨Options, or you can access it from the File⇨Print command by clicking the Options button.

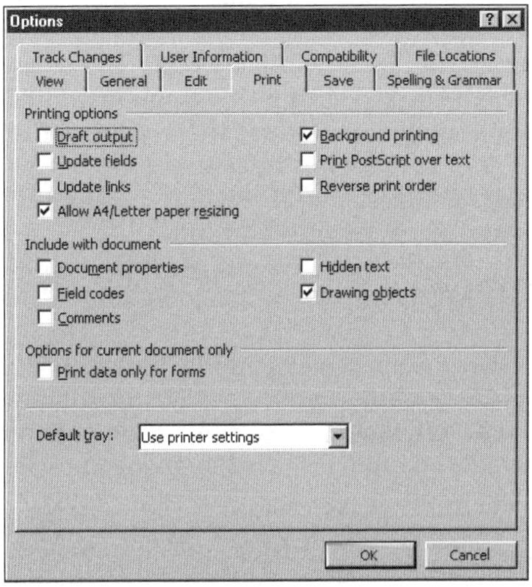

Figure 18-4: The Print options.

The Printing Options group

The Printing Options group includes general printing options:

- **Draft output:** If you check this option, Word may omit complicated formatting to speed printing. Which type of formatting gets axed depends on the printer type.
- **Update fields:** Updates the contents of fields before printing.
- **Update links:** Updates information linked into Word from other files before printing. This option is necessary only if you link files on a network and you want to be abso-posilutely sure that you print the most-current data.
- **Allow A4/Letter paper resizing:** If you normally work with 8.5"x 11" paper but sometimes work with documents formatted for European style A4 paper, or vice-versa, this is the option for you. It automatically adjusts documents to fit your default paper size.

- **Background printing:** With this option checked, you can print a document and continue working while the document is being printed. If you uncheck this option, Word makes you wait, arms folded, while it prints the file. The plus is that printing is faster when this option is unchecked.
- **Print Postscript over text:** Huh? This must have something to do with those fancy Postscript laser printers, which only high-powered desktop publishing people use anymore. I've been ignoring this option for years now with no ill effects.
- **Reverse print order:** Prints pages in reverse order. This option lets you read the end of the document first, sort of like the way I read mystery novels.

The Include with Document options

The next set of Print options tell Word what to print along with the document itself:

- **Document properties:** All that information displayed by the File⇨Properties command is printed on a separate page if you check this option.
- **Field codes:** Check this option if you want to print field codes (such as { SEQ Tables * MERGEFORMAT }) rather than the calculated value of each field.
- **Comments:** If comments have been added to the document, check this option to print them on a separate page. See Chapter 24 for more information about comments.
- **Hidden text:** If the document has any hidden text and you want it printed, check this option.
- **Drawing objects:** Prints stuff you have drawn with Word's drawing tools. See Chapter 14 if you don't know about Word's drawing tools.

Other options

The Print options tab has two other options:

- **Print data only for forms:** If you're one of those who uses the forms feature (you know who you are) to print on preprinted forms (such as invoices and purchase orders), check this box to tell Word to print the data in a form but not print the form itself.
- **Default tray:** Tells Word which paper tray the printer should suck up paper from. Usually the default paper tray set from the Control Panel is used.

Save the Save Options

The Save tab of the Tools⇨Options command contains several options that affect how Word saves document files. These options are shown in Figure 18-5.

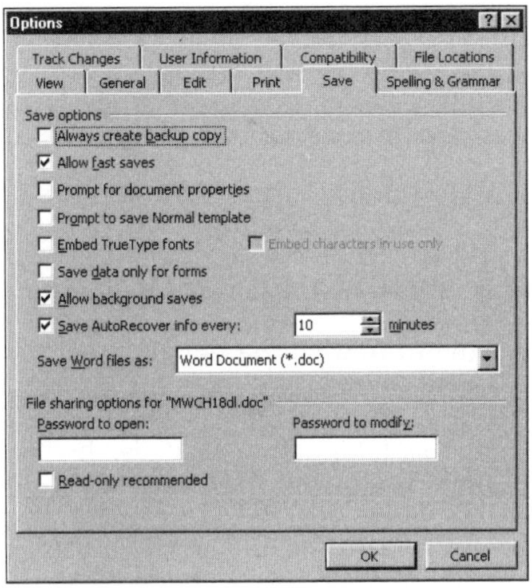

Figure 18-5: The Save options.

Here's what you need to know about the Save options:

- **Always create backup copy:** If this option is selected, Word always saves the previous version of the document as a backup copy each time it saves the document. The backup copy uses the extension *bak*.

  Do not rely on the Always create backup copy option as your only backup of important documents. The backup copy created by this option resides on the same drive and in the same folder as the document itself. As a result, if a disk failure or other problem renders the drive or folder inaccessible, the backup copy will be inaccessible as well. Always back up important documents to a separate disk drive or to tape.

- **Allow fast saves:** If you work with large documents that take a long time to save, you can select the Allow fast saves option to speed things up. This option tells Word to save only those parts of the document that have changed since the last time the document was saved. The changes are written to the end of the document file.

The disadvantages of fast saves are twofold. First, although the fast saves feature makes it faster to save files, it becomes correspondingly slower to open files. Second, the size of the document increases each time you save it with fast saves enabled, as changes to the document are written to the end of the file.

- **Prompt for document properties:** If you want to use document properties such as summary and keyword information, you should enable this option. Then, whenever you save a file for the first time, Word will prompt you for the summary information.
- **Prompt to save Normal template:** This option forces Word to ask for your permission before saving changes to the Normal.dot template. If you're concerned about proliferating changes to this template, enable this option.
- **Embed TrueType fonts:** Saves TrueType fonts in the document file. This option increases the size of the document file but enables you to copy the file to another system without worrying about whether or not the other system has the fonts that are used in the document. If your document uses only the basic Times New Roman and Arial fonts, if you don't plan on using the document on another system, or if you're sure the other system has all the fonts used by the document, don't bother with this option.
- **Save data only for forms:** Saves just the data for a form. This option is useful if you create a new document based on a template that includes a form and then want to save just the data, not the form itself. (If you don't know what a form is, you can safely disregard this option.)
- **Allow background saves:** Allows Word to save a document while you are working on another open document. This option is only applicable when you are working with long documentsthat take more than a split second to save. For small documents, you won't notice any effect from using this option.
- **Save AutoRecover info every:** This option automatically saves your document at regular intervals. The default setting is to save the document every 10 minutes, but you can change the time interval if you wish.
- **Save Word files as:** Lets you set the document format used for saving Word files. The default format is "Word Document (*.doc)," which saves files in Word 97 format. You can select other formats if you wish. Note, however, that if you save a document in any format other than Word Document, any features that are unique to Word 97 — such as Word 97's fancy drawing objects — are lost.

Fidgety File Locations

The File Locations tab of the Tools⇨Options command lets you customize Word by changing the locations of various files that are used. Figure 18-6 shows the File Locations tab.

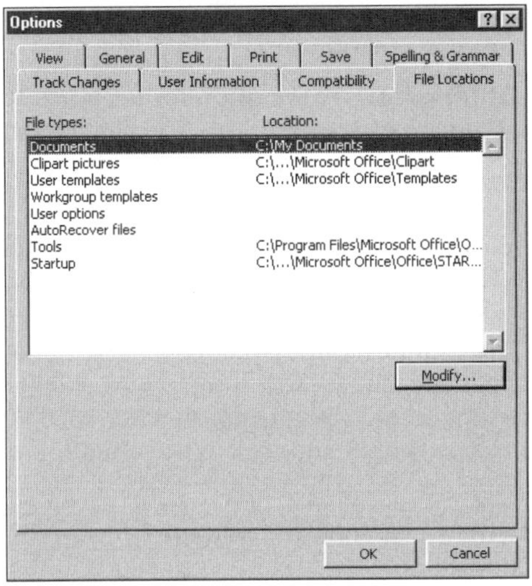

Figure 18-6: The File Locations options.

The File Locations dialog box consists of a list of files used by Word and a Modify button. To change the location of one of these file types, choose it in the File types list and then click Modify. You are greeted with a dialog box you can use to choose the drive and directory in which the files are located.

This list gives you the lowdown on the File types listed in the File Locations dialog box:

- **Documents:** Changes the default folder for the File⇨Open and File⇨Save As commands.
- **Clipart Pictures**: If you have your own collection of clip art, you might want to modify this file type to make your clip art easier to find.
- **User Templates**: You should probably leave this one alone. It tells Word where to create templates.
- **Workgroup Templates**: This option lets you set up a secondary location for template files.
- **All the rest**: Leave the rest of the options alone.

Chapter 19

Creating a Table of Contents or Table of Figures

In This Chapter

- Formatting your document to make a table of contents easy to create
- Creating a table of contents
- Using other styles to create a table of contents
- Creating a table of figures or other similar tables
- Updating tables of contents or tables of figures

In the old days, creating a table of contents for a book, manual, or other long document was a two-step affair. First you created the table of contents, leaving blanks or Xs where the page numbers eventually went. Then after the pages of the document were in their final form, you browsed through the entire document, made a list of the page numbers for each chapter, and added the page numbers to the table of contents.

Now, assuming that you format your document properly, creating a table of contents is a matter of clicking the mouse a few times. Word takes care of the drudgery of counting pages and even adjusts the table of contents for you if you make changes to the document that affect page numbers in the table.

This chapter shows you all the ins and outs of making a table of contents. It also shows you how to create a table of figures or other types of similar tables.

REMEMBER

The term table of contents is a little cumbersome to use over and over again throughout this chapter. Being a bit of a computer nerd myself, I kind of like using TLAs (three-letter acronyms). So I frequently use *TOC* to stand for table of contents in this chapter, if for no other reason than to save paper.

Styles: The Secret to Successful Table of Contents

The Table of Contents feature is one of several Word features that depends on the proper use of styles for trouble-free operation. When you create a table of contents, Word searches through your document and looks for heading paragraphs to include in the table. How on earth does Word know which paragraphs are supposed to be headings? By looking at the style you assigned to each paragraph: The heading paragraphs all should be formatted with heading styles, such as Heading 1, Heading 2, and so on.

If you plan to create a table of contents, make sure that you use heading styles to format your document's headings, especially those headings that you want to appear in the TOC. You should do this anyway, of course: It helps you to format all your headings consistently, and it lets you take advantage of Word's Outline view (see Chapter 7 for more on outlines).

Word provides three shortcut keys for applying heading styles:

Ctrl+Alt+1 Heading 1

Ctrl+Alt+2 Heading 2

Ctrl+Alt+3 Heading 3

If you routinely use additional heading styles for additional heading levels, you can assign those styles to keyboard shortcuts, such as Ctrl+Alt+4, Ctrl+Alt+5, and so on, by using the Tools➪Customize command (Chapter 25) or the Format➪Style command (Chapter 4).

Creating a Table of Contents

If you assign heading styles to your document's headings, creating a table of contents is easy. Just follow these simple steps:

1. **Move the insertion point to the place where you want the table of contents to appear.**

   The TOC generally appears on its own page near the beginning of a document. Press Ctrl+Enter to create a new page if necessary, and click the mouse to position the insertion pointer in the empty page.

You may want to add a heading, such as Contents or Table of Contents, at the top of the page. Format this heading however you want, but don't use one of the heading styles unless you want the TOC to include the page number of the table of contents.

2. **Call up the Insert⇨Index and Tables command and click the Table of Contents tab.**

   The dialog box appears, as shown in Figure 19-1.

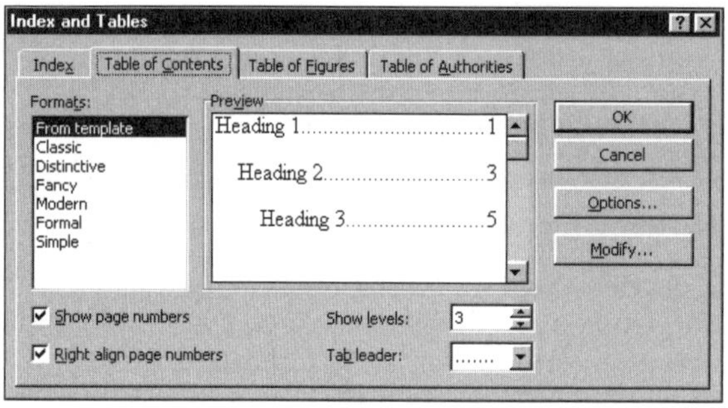

Figure 19-1: The Table of Contents tab of the Index and Tables dialog box.

3. **Choose the Table of Contents style you want from the Formats list.**

   As you click the various formats, the Preview window shows how the resulting TOC will appear.

4. **Play with the other controls to fine-tune the table of contents.**

   - Uncheck the Show page numbers box if you want the TOC to show the document's outline but not page numbers.
   - Uncheck the Right align page numbers if you want the page numbers to be placed right next to the corresponding text rather than at the right margin.
   - Change the Show levels field to include more or less detail in the table.
   - Change the Tab leader field to change or remove the dotted line that connects each TOC entry to its page number.

5. **Click OK.**

   The TOC is inserted into the document.

Here are some things to remember when you compile a TOC:

- If the table of contents looks like {TOC \o 1-3 \p }, call up the Tools⇨Options command, click the View tab, and uncheck the Field Codes check box. Click OK and the table appears as it should.
- You can make changes directly to a TOC by clicking in the table and typing, but that's a bad idea because any changes you make are lost the next time you regenerate the table of contents. See the section "Updating Tables of Contents or Figures" for more information.
- Unfortunately, Word doesn't add Chapter 1 in front of the TOC entry for Chapter 1. If you want chapter numbers to appear in your TOC, you must include them in the paragraphs formatted with a style that is included in the TOC (such as Heading 1).
- To delete a TOC, select the entire table and then press the Delete key. Or press Ctrl+Z immediately after creating the table.
- Word formats entries in a TOC with a set of standard styles named TOC 1, TOC 2, TOC 3, and so on. If you don't like any of the predefined formats listed in the Formats list in the Index and Tables dialog box (see Figure 19-1), choose From Template from the Formats list and click the Modify button. A special version of the Style dialog box appears, in which only the standard TOC styles are shown. You can then change the appearance of your table by modifying the various TOC styles.

Beyond Heading Styles

Using the standard heading styles to create a table of contents is convenient but not always exactly what you want to do. What if you have created a document that consists of several chapters and you have marked the title of each chapter with a style named Chapter Title? Fortunately, Word lets you create a table of contents based on paragraphs formatted with any style you want, not just the standard heading styles.

To create a table of contents by using styles other than the standard heading styles, follow this procedure:

1. **Call up the Insert⇨Index and Tables command and click the Table of Contents tab.**

   The Table of Contents dialog box appears.

2. **Click the Options button.**

   The Table of Contents Options dialog box appears, as shown in Figure 19-2. This dialog box lists all the styles available in the document and lets you assign a Table of Contents level to each style.

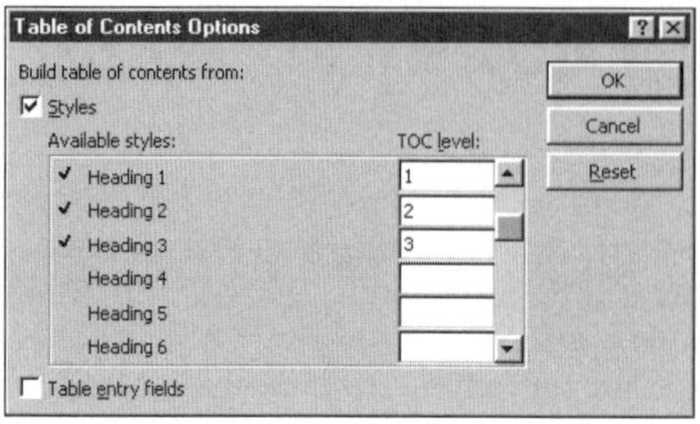

Figure 19-2: The Table of Contents Options dialog box.

3. **Adjust the TOC level fields to reflect the styles you want to include in your table of contents.**

   The TOC level fields initially are set to include standard heading styles, but that's easy to change. To exclude a style from the table of contents, select the style's TOC level field and delete the number in the field. To add a style to the table of contents, choose the style's TOC level field and type a number.

4. **Click OK to return to the Table of Contents dialog box.**
5. **Click OK again to insert the table of contents.**

   Voilà! You're finished.

Keep in mind the following when using styles other than the standard style to create a table of contents:

- The initial settings for the TOC level fields reflect the Show levels setting on the Table of Contents dialog box (see Figure 19-1). If you plan to exclude the standard heading levels from your table of contents, set the Show levels field to 1 before calling up the Table of Contents Options dialog box. Then you only have to clear the TOC level field for the Heading 1 style.
- If you really mess up the Table of Contents options, you can click the Reset button to restore the default settings for the Table of Contents dialog box.
- There's no rule that says that the styles you include in the table of contents all have to appear at different levels. Suppose that you want paragraphs formatted with the Chapter Title, Preface Title, Foreword Title, and Appendix Title styles all included in the table of contents at the top level. No problem. Just type 1 in the TOC level field for each of these styles in the Table of Contents Options dialog box.

Creating a Table of Figures or Other Similar Tables

Tables of contents aren't the only kind of tables you can create with the Insert⇨Index and Tables command. You can also use this command to compile tables of figures, tables, equations, or other similar collectibles. Chapter 20 shows how to use this command to create an index.

These steps show you how to create tables of figures or other similar tables:

1. **Use the Insert⇨Caption command to create a caption for each item you want to include in the table.**

   Figure 19-3 shows the Caption dialog box. Choose the type of caption you want to create (Figure, Table, or Equation) in the Label field. Then type the caption in the Caption field. After you finish, click OK.

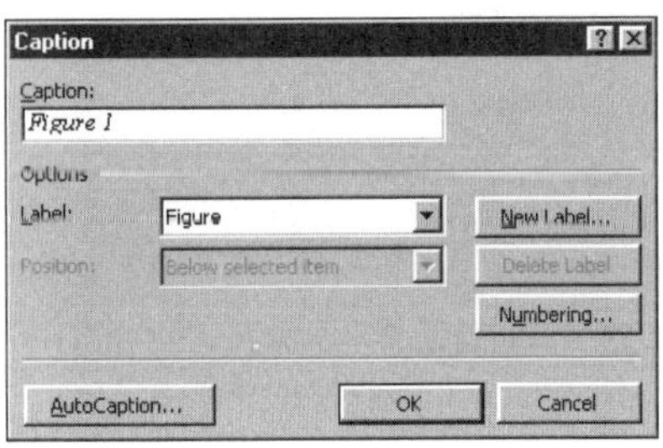

Figure 19-3: The Caption dialog box.

2. **Move the insertion pointer to where you want the table inserted.**
3. **Call up the Insert⇨Index and Tables command and click the Table of Figures tab.**

   Figure 19-4 shows the resulting dialog box.

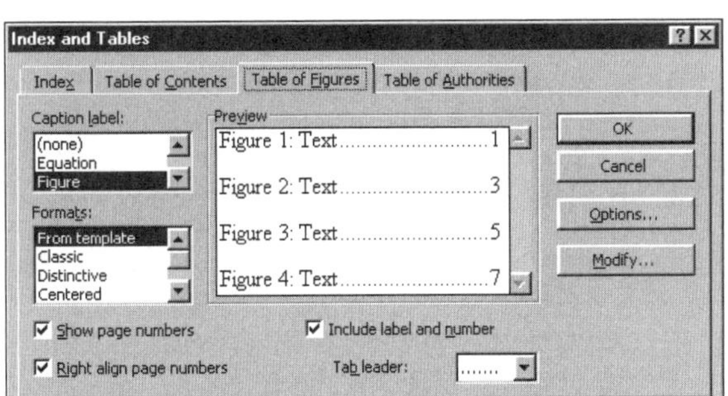

Figure 19-4: The Table of Figures tab of the Index and Tables dialog box.

4. **Choose the type of table you want to create from the Caption label list.**

   The Caption label setting corresponds to the Label setting in the Caption dialog box. To create a table of all figure captions, for example, choose Figure in the Caption label field.

5. **Choose the style you want from the Formats list.**

   As you click the various formats, the Preview window shows how the resulting table appears.

6. **Fiddle with the other controls to fine-tune the table's appearance.**

   • Uncheck the Show page numbers box if you want the table to list the captions but not page numbers.

   • Uncheck the Right align page numbers if you want the page numbers to be placed right next to the corresponding text rather than at the right margin.

   • Uncheck the Include label and number check box if you want the table to include the caption text (for example, "A Heffalump and a Woozle" or "Ratio of Red M&Ms") but not the number (for example, Figure 1 or Table 3).

   • Change the Tab leader field to add or remove the dotted line that connects each table entry with its page number.

7. **Click OK.**

   The table is inserted into the document.

REMEMBER

Here are some things to remember when you compile a table of figures or other similar tables:

- If the table looks like `{ TOC \c  Figure  }`, call up the Tools⇨Options command, click the View button, and uncheck the Field Codes check box. Click OK, and the table appears correctly.
- Word is set up to create captions and tables for equations, figures, and tables. If you want to create other types of captions and tables — for limericks or cartoons, for example — you can add items to the list of labels that appears in the Caption and Table of Figures dialog boxes. Call up the Insert⇨Caption command and click the New Label button. Then type a new label (such as Limerick or Cartoon) and click OK. Type the caption text and click OK to insert the first caption of the new type. Later, when you call up the Insert⇨Index and Tables command and click the Table of Figures tab, the label you created appears in the Caption Label list.
- For more information about captions, see Chapter 15.

If you detest the Insert➪Caption command, type your captions as separate paragraphs and create a style for them. Then call up the Insert➪Index and Tables command, click the Table of Figures tab, and click the Options button. Check the Style check box, and choose the style you used to format the captions.

To delete a table of figures, select the entire table, and press the Delete key. Or press Ctrl+Z immediately after you create the table.

The entries in a table of figures are formatted with a standard style named Table of Figures. If you don't like any of the predefined formats listed in the Formats list in the Index and Tables dialog box, choose From template and click the Modify button. A special version of the Style dialog box appears, showing only the standard Table of Figures style. You can then change the appearance of your table by modifying the Table of Figures style.

Updating Tables of Contents or Figures

As you edit your document, it's likely that a table of contents or table of figures you've created will become out of date. The page numbers may change, you may delete headings or captions, or you may insert headings or captions.

When you print your document, you can make sure that your tables are up-to-date in several ways:

- Call up the Tools➪Options command, click the Print tab, check the Update Fields check box, and then click OK. Then tables (and other fields in the document) are automatically updated every time you print your document.
- To update a table without printing the document, select the table and press F9. A dialog box appears, asking whether you want to just refresh the table's page numbers or completely rebuild the table. Just refreshing the page numbers is faster, but it doesn't account for items you have added or deleted since you created the table.
- If you point to a table and click the right mouse button, the shortcut menu that appears includes an Update Field command. Using this command works the same as pressing F9.
- To update all tables in your document, press Ctrl+A to select the entire document and then press F9.
- Another way to update a table is to select the table and then use the Insert➪Index and Tables command to replace the table.

Don't forget to save your file after you update the table of contents.

Chapter 20

So You Want to Make an Index, Eh?

In This Chapter

- Marking index entries
- Creating an index
- Marking a range of pages
- Building an index from a list of words
- Creating subentries
- Creating cross-references
- Updating an index

If all you ever use Word for is to create one- and two-page memos on mundane subjects, such as how to clean the coffeemaker, you can skip this chapter. After all, you don't need an index for a two-page memo on coffeemaker cleaning unless you work at the Pentagon. If, on the other hand, your memo turns into a 200-page policy manual on appliance maintenance, an index may well be in order.

As luck would have it, Word just happens to have an indexing feature that can help you with the tedious task of indexing. It doesn't create the index for you automatically, but it does help you identify which words to include in the index, and Word compiles and formats the index from the words you mark without too much complaining.

Creating an index is a three-stage affair. First, you must mark (one at a time) all the words and phrases within your document that you want to appear in the index. Second, you call on the Insert⇨Index and Tables command to create the index. This command takes all the words and phrases you marked, sorts them in alphabetical order, and combines identical entries. Third, you carefully review the index, lament that Word didn't do a better job, and fix what you can.

Mark Those Index Entries

The first — and most important — task in creating an index is to mark the words or phrases you want included in the index. The most common way to do that is to insert an index marker in the document at each occurrence of each item you want to appear in the index.

To mark index entries, follow these steps as long as you can stay awake:

1. **Choose File➪Open to open the document you want to index.**
2. **Highlight the word or phrase you want in the index by using the mouse or the keyboard.**

   Start at the beginning of the document and select those items you deem worthy of an entry in the index.
3. **Press the keyboard shortcut Alt+Shift+X.**

   The Alt+Shift+X is one of Word's more memorable keyboard shortcuts, to be sure. It pops up the Mark Index Entry dialog box, shown in Figure 20-1.

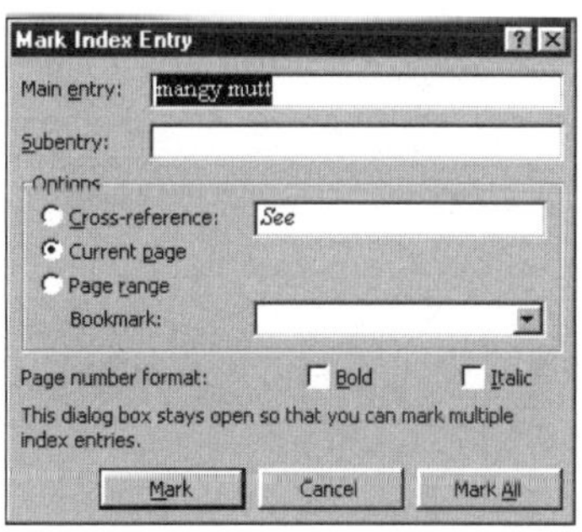

Figure 20-1: The Mark Index Entry dialog box.

4. **Double-check the contents of the Main entry field in the Mark Index Entry dialog box. If correct, click the Mark button. If not, correct it and then click Mark.**

   The text does not have to appear in the index exactly as it appears in the document. You may highlight an abbreviation to include in the index, for example, but then edit the Main entry field so that the full spelling of the word, rather than the abbreviation, appears in the index.
5. **To index an entry under a different word, type the alternative entry in the Main entry field and click the Mark button again.**

   For example, you may want to create an entry for "mutt, mangy" in addition to "mangy mutt."

6. **Mark any additional index entries by highlighting them in the document and clicking the Mark button.**

   The Mark Index Entry dialog box works somewhat like the Spelling dialog box in the way it stays on-screen so that you can efficiently mark additional index entries.

7. **After you mark each of the index entries you want, click the close button.**

The index entries are marked with special codes formatted as hidden text so that you can't normally see them and they don't print. They are there, however, waiting to be counted when you create the index.

TIP

- The most efficient way to create an index is after you've written and edited your document.
- Another way to summon the Mark Index Entry dialog box is to call up the Insert⇨Index and Tables command, click the Index tab, and then click the Mark Entry button.
- If you come across a word or phrase while marking index entries that you know occurs elsewhere in your document, click the Mark All button. By clicking the Mark All button, you create an index entry not only for the selected text, but also for any other occurrence of the selected text within the document.
- Each time you mark an index entry, Word activates the All check box of the Tools⇨Options command's View tab. The All check box then reveals not only the hidden text used to mark index entries, but also other characters normally hidden from view, such as field codes, tab characters, optional hyphens, and so on. This behavior is normal, so don't be surprised when it happens. To return your display to normal, just click the Show/Hide button on the Standard toolbar (shown in the margin).
- Index entries look something like this: `{ XE mangy mutt }`, formatted as hidden text. You can edit the index entry text (the part between quotation marks) if you want to change an index entry after you create it.

Creating an Index

After you mark the index entries, the process of generating the index is relatively easy. Here are the steps:

1. **Move the insertion point to the place where you want the index to appear.**

The index generally begins on a new page near the end of the document. Press Ctrl+Enter to create a new page if necessary, and click the mouse to position the insertion pointer on the empty page.

2. **Call up the Insert⇨Index and Tables command and click the Index tab.**

   The Index and Tables dialog box appears, as shown in Figure 20-2.

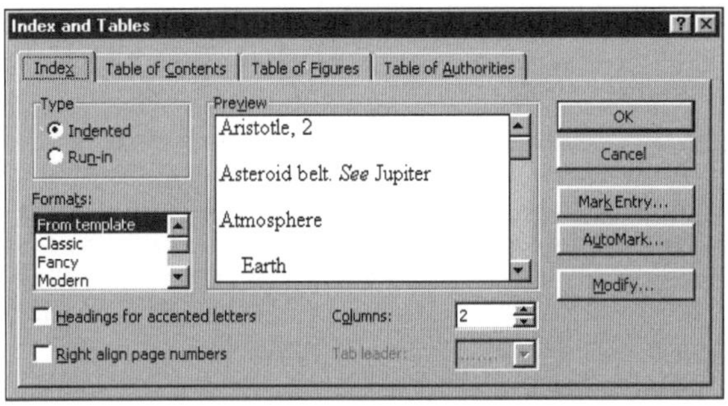

Figure 20-2: The Index tab of the Index and Tables dialog box.

3. **Choose the index style that you want from the Formats list.**

   As you click the various formats, the Preview window shows how the resulting index will appear.

4. **Play with the other controls in the Index tab to fine-tune the index.**

   - The Type option lets you place index subentries on separate indented lines (Indented) or run together (Run-in).
   - Check the Headings for accented letters box if you want the index to have separate sections for accented letters (such as á).
   - Check the Right align page numbers box if you want the page numbers to be placed at the right edge of the index.
   - Set the Columns field to the number of columns you want in the index. Two is the norm.
   - Use the Tab leader field to change or remove the dotted line that connects each index entry to its page number. You can only remove the dotted when the Right align page numbers option is checked.

5. **Click OK.**

   The index is inserted into the document.

If the index looks like `{ INDEX \r \h A \c 2 }`, call up the Tools⇨Options command, click the View button, and uncheck the Field codes check box. Click OK, and the index appears as it should.

To delete an index, select the entire index and then press the Delete key. Or press Ctrl+Z immediately after creating the index.

The entries in an index are formatted with a set of standard styles named Index 1, Index 2, Index 3, and so on. If you don't like any of the predefined formats listed in the Formats list in the Index and Styles dialog box, choose From template and click the Modify button. A special version of the Style dialog box appears listing only the standard Index styles. You can then change the appearance of your index by modifying the various Index styles.

Marking a Range of Pages

If a particular topic is discussed for several pages in your document, you may want to create an index entry that marks a range of pages (for example, 26-29) rather than each page individually (26, 27, 28, 29).

Unfortunately, the procedure for marking page ranges isn't as slick as it could be. You have to mess around with a Word doohickey called a bookmark. A *bookmark* is a name you can assign to a selection of text. To use a bookmark for range of pages, follow these steps. It gets tricky, so hang on to your hat.

1. **Highlight the entire range of text you want included in the index entry's page range.**

   A long discussion of a single topic could go on for pages, so be prepared.

2. **Call up the Insert⇨Bookmark command.**
3. **Type a bookmark name to identify the bookmark.**

   Bookmark names can be as long as 40 characters and can be made up of any combination of letters and numbers. Spaces aren't allowed, but you can use an underscore to double as a space.

4. **Click Add to create the bookmark.**
5. **Position the cursor at the beginning of the bookmark and press Alt+Shift+X.**

   The Mark Index Entry dialog box appears.

6. **Type the text you want to appear in the index in the Main entry text box.**
7. **Click the Current page option button.**
8. **Choose the bookmark you just created from the list of bookmark names in the Bookmark drop-down list box.**
9. **Click the Mark button to create the index entry.**

After you create a bookmark and an index entry naming the bookmark, the index includes the range of page numbers for the entry.

The location of various bookmarks in your document is indicated by large brackets in the text. These brackets appear only if you check the Bookmarks option in the Tools➪Options command (View tab).

Isn't There an Easier Way?

Yet another way to create index entries is to use a word list. You just type a list of words that you want Word to include in the index. Word then creates an index entry for each occurrence of each word in the list. Sounds like a great time-saver, eh? It is, sometimes.

Here's the step-by-step procedure.

1. **Create a new document for the word list.**
2. **Type the list of words you want indexed, each on its own line.**

   For example:

   Kirk

   Spock

   McCoy

   Scotty
3. **If you want the text in the index to be different from the text in the document, press the Tab key and then type the text exactly as you want it to appear in the index.**

   For example:

Kirk	Kirk, James T.
Spock	Spock, Mr.
McCoy	McCoy, Leonard H.
Scotty	Scott, Montgomery

   Note that you can have more than one line referring to the same index entry. For example:

McCoy	McCoy, Leonard H.
Bones	McCoy, Leonard H.
4. **Save the word list document by choosing File➪Save.**
5. **Close the word list document by choosing File➪Close.**
6. **Open the document you want indexed with the File➪Open command.**

7. **Call up the Insert⇨Index and Tables command and click the Index tab.**

   The Index and Tables dialog box pushes its way to the front. If the Index tab isn't on top, click it to bring the indexing options into view.

8. **Click the AutoMark button.**

   A dialog box similar to the File Open dialog box appears.

9. **Find the file you saved in Step 4, choose it, and click Open.**

10. **Hold your breath while Word adds the index entries.**

    If your word list or the document is long, adding the index may take awhile. Be patient.

11. **Now select the index and press F9 to update your index with the marks added in Step 10.**

    It's done.

After the automatic index entries have been created, you probably want to work your way through the document by creating additional index entries.

Unfortunately, the AutoMark option doesn't account for running discussions of a single topic that span several pages. It results in index entries such as "Vogons, 14, 15, 16, 17, 18" that should read "Vogons, 14-18."

TIP

When you use tabs to separate the keywords used to locate the items to be indexed and the actual text you want inserted in the index for those items, keep in mind that the tab-stop positions in the word list document doesn't matter. I usually create a tab stop at about 1/2 inch so that the two columns of information line up, but this step isn't necessary.

If you want, you can use Word's Table feature to create the word list. Create a two-column table and use the first column for the text to find in the document and the second column for the text to include in the index.

TIP

Word refers to the word list as a concordance. Just thought you'd want to know.

Creating Subentries

A subentry is what happens when a word is used for two different meanings or when a word serves as a category organizer for several related words. For example, you may want to create an index entry that looks like the following example:

crew

Kirk, James T., 15

McCoy, Leonard H., 16

Scott, Montgomery, 16

Spock, Mr., 17

Here, the index entries for Kirk, McCoy, Scott, and Spock are all subentries of the main entry, crew.

To create index subentries, you follow the normal procedure for marking index entries. You type text for both the main entry and the subentry, however, in the Mark Index Entry dialog box. Each of the index entries shown above, for example, would have crew for the Main entry field and the individual crew member's name as the subentry.

See Also...

A cross-reference is one of those annoying messages signaling that you're about to embark on a wild-goose chase:

crew, see cast.

To create a cross-reference, begin by marking an index entry as you normally would. On the Mark Index Entry dialog box, check the Cross-reference button and then type some text in the accompanying text box. Word automatically merges the cross-reference with other index entries for the same text.

Updating an Index

Whenever you edit your document, you run the risk of messing up the index. Even a slight change can push text from the bottom of one page to the top of the next and possibly invalidate the index. Fortunately, this section gives you several ways to keep your index up-to-date.

In the Tools⇨Options dialog box, click the Print tab, check the Update Fields check box, and then click OK. Then Word updates the indexes automatically every time you print your document.

TIP

To update an index without printing the document, select the index and press F9. If you point to the index and click the right mouse button, the shortcut menu that appears includes an Update Field command. Using this command works the same as pressing F9.

Chapter 21

Mastering Master Documents

In This Chapter

- Understanding master documents
- Creating a master document from scratch
- Inserting existing files into a master document
- Breaking down an existing document into smaller subdocuments
- Cool things to do after you've made a master document

Suppose a great honor has been bestowed upon you: serving as the moderator of this year's Neat Freaks Convention. As moderator, one of your jobs is assembling a little 1,200-page book titled *Neat Freaks '97: Proceedings of the Annual Neat Freaks Trade Show and Conference.* Notable Neat Freaks from all across the globe will present papers, and your job is to assemble all of these documents into one huge book. Fortunately for you, the International Neat Freak Association (INFA) has adopted Word 97 as its standard word processor, so each neat freak of note will send you a document on disk. All you have to do is combine the files into a single document and print them.

This is definitely a job for Word's Master Document feature. It lets you create long documents by piecing them together from small documents. It's all very confusing and worth figuring out only if you have to do this sort of thing often. If you find yourself needing to read this chapter, I offer my sincerest condolences.

You probably shouldn't tackle master documents until you have a pretty good understanding of Word's Outline view, because the master document feature is sort of an advanced form of outlining. If you haven't yet read Chapter 7, I would read it first if I were you.

What Is a Master Document?

A *master document* contains special links to other documents, which are called *subdocuments*. If you are putting together a book that consists of 30 chapters, for example, you probably don't want to put the entire book into one document. Instead you probably want to create a separate document for each chapter. That's all well and good, but what happens when you want to print the whole thing with page numbers that begin at page one and run through the end of the book rather than restart at page one at the beginning of each chapter? Or what if you want to print a table of contents for the book or create an index?

That's where master documents come in. With a master document, you create each chapter as a separate document. Then you create a master document for the entire book. In this master document, you create links to each of the chapters or subdocuments. Then you can print the entire book, and Word takes care of numbering the pages for you. You can also create a table of contents or index in the master document, and the page numbers are all correct.

Word has a whole separate view for working with master documents, called — drum roll, please — *Master Document view*. Master Document view is a variation of Outline view, except that the portions of the master document that are subdocuments are indicated by little icons. You can double-click one of these icons to open a subdocument in a separate window to edit it.

For the most part, you use Master Document view to create a new master document, to change the order in which individual subdocuments appear in the master document, or to add or remove subdocuments. If all you want to do is edit one of the individual chapters in your book, you just open the chapter document as you normally would, without worrying about its being a subdocument in a master document.

If you open a master document and switch to Normal view or Page Layout view, Word treats the master document and all the subdocuments as though they were a part of one large document. You can scroll through the master document all the way to Chapter 12 and begin typing, for example, or you can use the File⇨Print command to print the entire book, or you can use the Edit⇨Replace command to replace all occurrences of *WordPerfect* with *Word* throughout the entire document.

You can assemble a master document in three ways:

- If you know that you need a master document beforehand, you can create the master document and all the subdocuments from scratch. This technique results in a master document and a collection of empty

subdocuments, which you can then call up and edit as you see fit. See the section "Whipping Up a Master Document" later in this chapter.

- If you get part of the way into a project and realize, "Hey! This document is way too long! I should have used a master document," it's not too late. You can bust a big document into several smaller subdocuments. See the section "Break It Up!" later in this chapter.
- If you already have a bunch of Word documents you want to assemble into a master document, you can create a master document by using the existing documents as the subdocuments. See the section "Putting an Existing File in a Master Document," later in this chapter.

All this stuff about master documents is confusing, I'm sure, but it makes more sense when you begin to use them. (I promise.) Just to muddy the waters a little more, the following list shows you some additional things you need to know about master documents before I jump into the procedures for creating and using them:

- In the master document, each subdocument is contained within its own section. Each subdocument, therefore, can have its own page layout, column arrangement, and any of the other niceties that go along with being in your own section.
- When you work in Master Document view, a small toolbar of specialized master document buttons appears. Table 21-1 summarizes each of these buttons functions.

Table 21-1 Buttons on the Master Document Toolbar

Button	*What It Does*
	Collapses or expands a subdocument
	Breaks the selected text into subdocuments and assigns a filename based on the first heading in the subdocument
	Deletes the selected subdocument
	Inserts an existing file as a subdocument
	Combines two subdocument files into one subdocument file
	Splits a subdocument into two subdocuments
	Locks or unlocks a subdocument

- It's best to base the master document and all the subdocuments on the same templates. Otherwise, it's a nightmare trying to figure out which styles, macros, and other template goodies are available.
- Word 97 uses hyperlinks to indicate subdocuments. Hyperlinks have long been a part of the Internet's World Wide Web but are new to Word 97. Simply put, a hyperlink is a bit of text that refers to another document. The hyperlink is underlined and displayed in blue so that you can recognize it quickly, as shown in Figure 21-1. To open a subdocument, all you have to do is click on the subdocument's hyperlink. (For more information about hyperlinks, refer to Chapter 16.)

You can switch between Outline view and Master Document view by clicking the Master Document View button in the Outlining toolbar.

You can open a subdocument in two ways. The first way is to open the master document. Word displays any subdocuments contained in the master document as hyperlinks. To open a subdocument, all you have to do is click on the subdocument's hyperlink. Alternatively, you can ignore the master document and open the subdocument file the way you would open any other Word document: by using the File⇨Open command or clicking the Open button in the Standard toolbar.

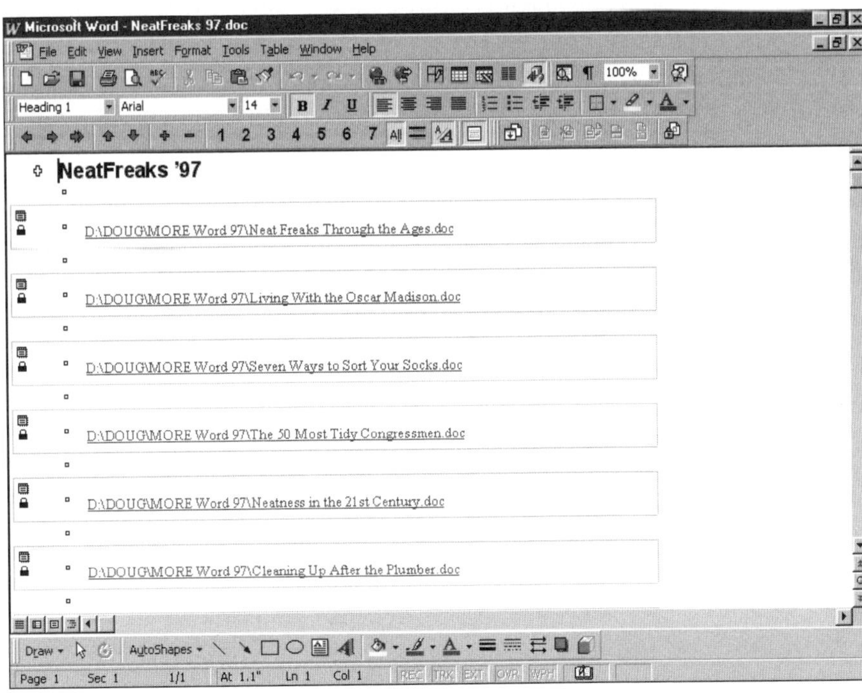

Figure 21-1: A master document with subdocuments shown as hyperlinks.

If you have a network and more than one person is involved with the creation of your documents, Word keeps track of who owns which subdocument, based on the Author Name field of the subdocuments. Before you can edit a subdocument that someone else created, you must unlock it by clicking the Lock/Unlock button in the Master Document toolbar.

TIP

The master document and its subdocuments can be spread out across different directories and can even live on different computers if you have a network. Life is much easier, however, if you create a separate directory for just the master document and all its subdocuments. Trust me.

Whipping Up a Master Document

If none of the documents you want to combine by using a master document has been created yet, the best way to begin is to create the master document and all its subdocuments at the same time. Then you can call up each subdocument individually to fill in the missing chapters of your book.

These steps show you the procedure for creating a master document and its subdocuments from scratch:

1. **Choose the File⇨New command or click the New button.**
2. **Use the View⇨Master Document command.**

   This switches you into Master Document view. Because you're working with a new document, the only immediate change is that the Outlining and Master Document toolbars appear.
3. **Create a Heading 1 paragraph for the title of the master document.**

   If you're creating a book, for example, type the book's title as a Heading 1 paragraph.
4. **Create a Heading 2 paragraph for each subdocument you want to create.**

   If each subdocument represents a chapter, type the chapter titles as Heading 2 paragraphs.

   Figure 21-2 shows an example of a master document with a Heading 1 paragraph for the master document title and a Heading 2 paragraph for each subdocument title.
5. **Select the Heading 2 paragraphs.**

   Drag the mouse or hold down the Shift key while you move the cursor with the arrow keys. Each Heading 2 paragraph you select is converted to a separate subdocument in the next step.

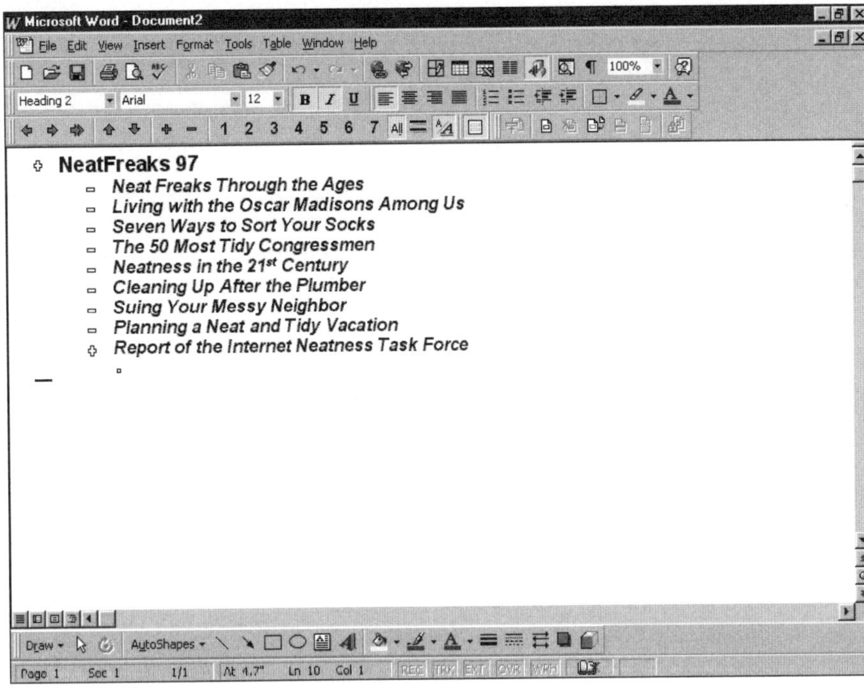

Figure 21-2: A master document, ready to be busted up into subdocuments.

6. **Click the Create Subdocument button in the Master Document toolbar.**

   Clicking this button tells Word to bust up the selected heading paragraphs into smaller subdocuments, sort of like the Justice Department would like to do to Microsoft.

7. **Admire your handiwork.**

   Figure 21-3 shows a document that's been busted up. Notice how Word draws a box around each subdocument and adds a little subdocument icon in the top left corner of the box.

8. **Use the File⇨Save command to save the files.**

   You have to provide the name and location of the master document. Word makes up names for all the subdocuments, using the first eight characters of the heading paragraph if possible.

9. **You're finished.**

   Well, not quite. All you have is the outline of a book with a bunch of empty subdocuments. You still have to write the chapters!

Here are a few thoughts to keep in mind when you're creating a master document from scratch:

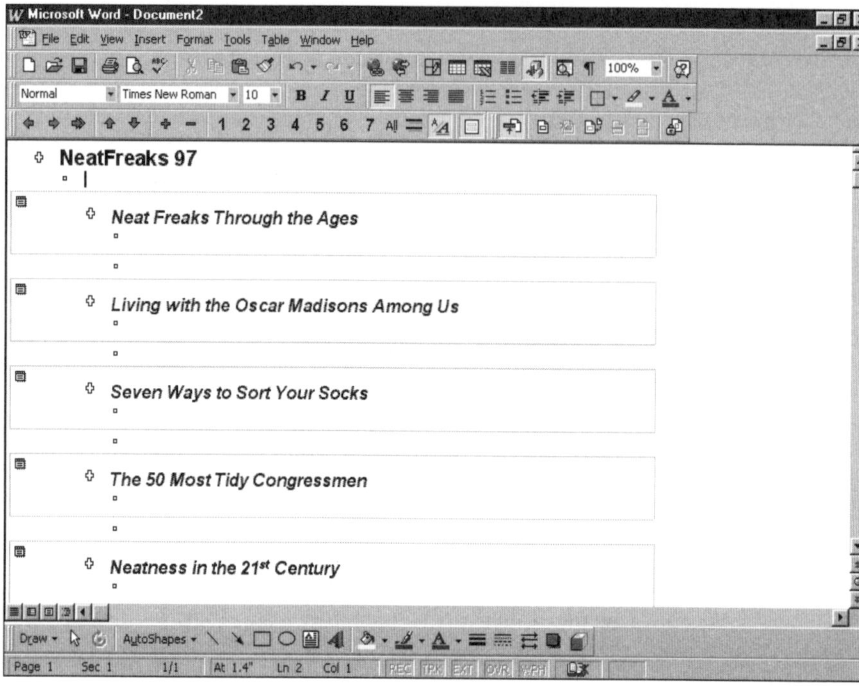

Figure 21-3: You're busted.

REMEMBER

- The subdocuments aren't saved until you use the File➪Save command to save the master document. Then Word automatically saves all the subdocuments in the same directory as the master document.
- After you've created subdocuments, you can edit a subdocument by double-clicking the little subdocument icon next to the subdocument heading. This action opens the subdocument in a separate document window and leaves the master document open in its own window, too. After you finish editing the subdocument, save it and close the window to return to the master document window.

Putting an Existing File in a Master Document

If you (or your buddies) have already created a bunch of smaller files that you want to combine into one larger publication, you can plug each file into a master document as a subdocument. Then you can create a table of contents or an index for the whole publication or print the publication with uninterrupted page numbers.

Follow these steps to create a master document and insert existing documents into it as subdocuments:

1. **Using the My Computer window or Windows Explorer, copy the various files you need into a single folder.**

   This step isn't strictly necessary, because it is acceptable to create a master document from subdocuments spread throughout your hard drive. But life is simpler if the master document and all its subdocuments live together in a single folder.

2. **Run the File➪New command or click the New button.**

3. **Use the View➪Master Document command.**

   Word switches you into Master Document view. Because you're working with a new document, the only immediate change is that the Outlining and Master Document toolbars appear.

4. **Click the Insert Subdocument button in the Master Document toolbar.**

   An Insert Subdocument dialog box appears. This dialog box is identical to the Open dialog box except for its name.

5. **Find the file you want to insert as a subdocument, choose it, and click Open.**

   The file is inserted into the master document as a subdocument. Word creates section breaks before and after it.

6. **Repeat Steps 4 and 5 for any other subdocuments you want to insert.**

7. **Use the File➪Save command to save the master document.**

8. **You're finished.**

Here are a few points to ponder when you insert subdocuments into a master document:

- Inserting a subdocument doesn't change the subdocument file's filename or folder location.
- When you click the Insert Subdocument button, the subdocument is inserted into the master document. Make sure that the insertion point is either at the beginning or end of the master document or between two previously inserted subdocuments. If the insertion point is within a subdocument when you click the Insert Subdocument button, the subdocument you select is inserted *within* the subdocument, not within the master document. If you're not careful, you can end up with subdocuments within subdocuments within subdocuments, kind of like those fancy Russian nesting dolls.

The contents of the subdocument file are not copied into the master document. Instead, a link to the subdocument file is created so that whenever you open the master document, the subdocument file is accessed also. You can still open the subdocument file separately, apart from the master document.

Break It Up!

Sometimes a project just gets out of hand. It starts out as a half-page memo about where to keep spare pencils and ends up being a 300-page office-procedures manual. You obviously wouldn't use a master document for the half-page memo (unless you're really bored), but somewhere around page 100 you may wish that you had. No problem! Just bust up the big document into two or more subdocuments.

Follow these steps to break a large document into smaller subdocuments:

1. **Open the document.**

   Use the good old File⇨Open command.

2. **Choose View⇨Master Document to switch to Master Document view.**
3. **Change the headings to make each section of text you want to become a subdocument begin with a Heading 2 style.**

   The most logical thing is to format the document title as a Heading 1 and each subdocument as a Heading 2

4. **Select the range of text you want converted into subdocuments, beginning with the heading for the first subdocument and ending with the last paragraph of the last subdocument.**
5. **Click the Create Subdocument button.**

   Word breaks up the document into smaller subdocuments based on the heading paragraphs and inserts section breaks before and after each subdocument.

6. **Call up the File⇨Save command to save your work.**

   The master document is saved, as is each of the subdocuments. Word retains the name of the original file for the master document and makes up names for the subdocuments, using the first eight characters of each subdocument's heading, if possible.

7. **You're finished!**

   Celebrate by taking the rest of the day off.

Numbering Subdocument Pages Consecutively

When you use a master document, you can number all the pages of your publication consecutively. In other words, the first page of a subdocument is one greater than the last page of the subdocument that precedes it.

These steps show you the procedure:

1. **Open the master document.**

   You can work in Normal view or Master Document view, but you have to be working with the master document, not with an individual subdocument.

2. **Call up the View➪Header and Footer command.**

   Word temporarily throws you into Page Layout view, confines you to the header area of the page, and throws the Headers and Footers toolbar up on the screen.

   To add a footer rather than a header, click the Switch Between Header and Footer button.

3. **Format the header or footer to include a page number.**

   Type whatever text you want to include in the header or footer. To add a page number, click the Page Number button.

4. **Click the Close button when you're happy with the header or footer.**

   Word returns you to Normal view or Master Document view.

5. **Print the master document and check the page numbers.**

   Pretty cool, eh?

TIP: If you want each subdocument to begin on a new page, add the Page Break Before option to the Heading 2 style's Paragraph format (or whatever style you use for the title of each subdocument). You can find the Page Break Before option on the Text Flow tab of the Format➪Paragraph command.

Chapter 22

Objection, Your Honor (Creating a Table of Authorities)

In This Chapter

- Marking citations
- Creating a table of authorities
- Adding your own categories
- Updating a table of authorities
- Disclaimer of warranties and limit of liability

Inasmuch as you, hereinafter referred to as the *reader,* have deemed it necessary, appropriate, and befitting to create, prepare, and otherwise compile a table, list, or enumeration of various and sundry citations, references, and quotations from legal authorities and other sources, including, but not limited to, cases, statutes, rules, treatises, regulations, constitutional provisions, and other authorities occurring within and among documents, files, and other materials prepared with the word-processing software known as Word 97, hereinafter referred to as *Word,* now therefore and thereupon I, hereinafter referred to as *I,* agree to provide within this chapter a thorough and comprehensive description, discussion, and presentation of the techniques, methods, and procedures required to prepare such aforementioned tables, lists, or enumerations. In consideration hitherto, e pluribus unum, et cetera, et cetera, et cetera.

In other words, this chapter shows you how to use Word's Table of Authorities feature. If you're a lawyer or legal secretary, you already know what a Table of Authorities is. If you aren't, skip ahead to the next chapter before it's too late.

Creating a table of authorities is much like creating an index. First you mark the citations where they appear within the document. Then you use the Insert⇨Index and Tables command to compile the table of authorities based on the citations you marked. If necessary, you can then edit the table or adjust its formatting. You can also update the table to make sure that all the entries are up-to-date.

Marking Citations

The first step in creating a table of authorities is reviewing the entire document and marking any citations you want included in the table. Follow these steps:

1. **Find a citation you want to mark.**

   Start at the beginning of the document and work through the whole thing, marking citations as you go. You can simply read through the document to find citations or you can let Word find the citations for you.

2. **When you find a citation you want to mark, highlight it with the mouse or keyboard and press Alt+Shift+I.**

   The Mark Citation dialog box appears, as shown in Figure 22-1.

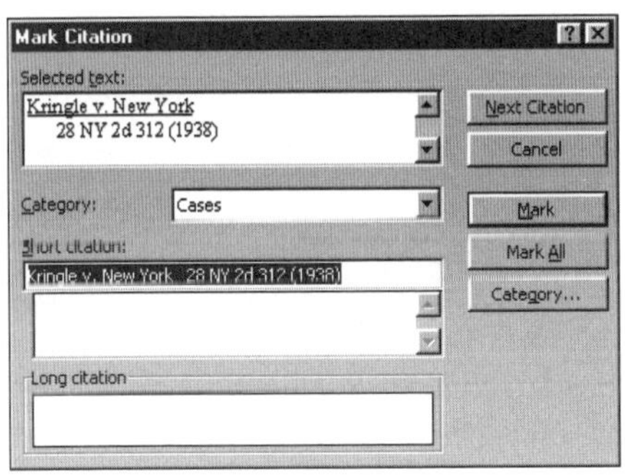

Figure 22-1: The Mark Citation dialog box.

3. **Edit the Selected text field so that it is exactly the way you want the citation to appear in the table of authorities.**

   The Selected text field initially contains the text that was selected when you pressed Alt+Shift+I. If the citation in the document isn't how you want it to appear in the table of authorities, click in the Selected text field and type away. If you want to split the citation into two lines, just position the cursor where you want the line to be split and press Enter.

4. **Edit the Short citation field so that it exactly matches the way the short version of the citation is used in subsequent references throughout the document.**

   The first time you cite an authority, you must provide a complete citation (such as "Kringle v. New York, 28 NY 2d 312 (1938)"), but thereafter you use the short form ("Kringle v. New York"). Edit the Short citation field to match the short form of the citation. That way, Word can automatically locate subsequent citations and mark them.

5. **Choose the type of authority being cited from the Category list box.**

   Word comes equipped with several common categories: Cases, Statutes, Other Authorities, Rules, Treatises, Regulations, and Constitutional Provisions. You can also create your own categories.

6. **Click the Mark button to mark the citation.**

   Word inserts a hidden field code to mark the citation.

7. **The Mark Citation dialog box stays on-screen so that you can mark additional citations. Click the Next Citation button to find the next citation.**

   The Next Citation button searches for the next citation in the document by looking for text that is commonly found in citations, such as v.

8. **Highlight the complete text of the citation found by the Next Citation button.**

   The Next Citation button doesn't highlight the complete citation — only the text it found that convinced it to stop because a citation is probably nearby. Use the mouse to highlight the citation in the document. (The Mark Citation dialog box patiently stays on-screen while you mark the citation.)

9. **Repeat Steps 3 through 8 until you have marked all the citations you can stand.**

10. **After you finish marking citations, click the Close button.**

Word marks citations with field codes formatted as hidden text so that they are normally invisible. They jump to life, however, when you compile a table of authorities. See the next section, "Creating a Table of Authorities," for the procedure.

Another way to summon the Mark Citation dialog box is to call up the Insert⇨Index and Tables command, click the Table of Authorities tab, and then click the Mark Citation button.

If the screen suddenly changes to Print Preview mode when you try to mark a citation, don't panic. You probably pressed Ctrl+Alt+I rather than Alt+Shift+I. Ctrl+Alt+I is the keyboard shortcut for toggling Print Preview on and off. These two keyboard shortcuts are perilously close to one another, but don't worry if you hit the wrong one. Just press Ctrl+Alt+I again to return to Normal view and then start over.

If you stumble on a citation that you know occurs later in your document, click the Mark All button. The Mark All button creates a citation not only for the selected text, but also any subsequent occurrences of the citation.

Each time you mark a citation, Word activates the All check box of the Tools➪Options command's View tab, which reveals not only the hidden text used to mark citations, but also perverts the screen with dots for spaces, paragraph and tab marks, and other obnoxious codes. To return your display to normal, click the Show/Hide button (shown in the margin) on the standard toolbar.

The field codes for citations look like the following example:

```
{ TA \l  Kringle v. New York
28 NY 2d 312 (1938)  \s  Kringle v. New York  \c 1 }
```

The preceding codes are formatted as hidden text, so you don't normally see them. You can edit the long citation text (the part between quotes following \l) or the short citation text (the quoted text that follows \s) if you want to change a citation after you create it.

Creating a Table of Authorities

After you have marked all the citations in your document, follow these steps to create the table of authorities:

1. **Move the insertion point to the place where you want the table of authorities to appear.**

   You can place the table of authorities at the front or back of the document. If you want the table to appear on its own page, press Ctrl+Enter to create a page break. You may also want to type a heading, such as Table of Authorities.

2. **Call up the Insert➪Index and Tables command and click the Table of Authorities tab.**

   The Index and Tables dialog box appears with the Table of Authorities tab in plain view, as shown in Figure 22-2.

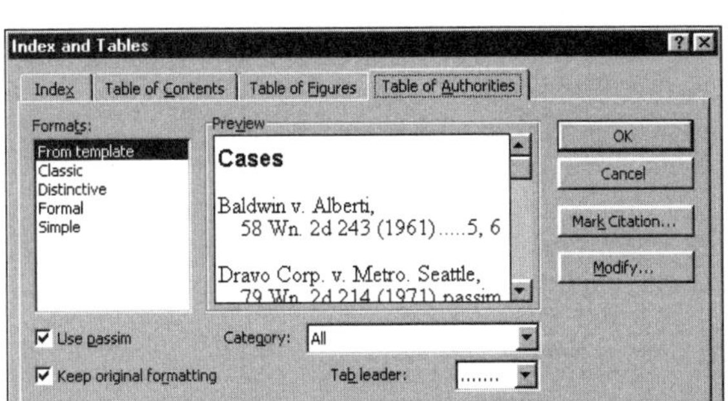

Figure 22-2: The Table of Authorities tab of the Index and Tables dialog box.

3. **Pick the style you want from the Formats list.**

   As you click the various formats, the Preview area shows how the resulting table of authorities appears.

4. **Play with the other controls to fine-tune the table of authorities.**

   - Check the Use passim box if you want Word to use the word passim when a citation occurs on five or more pages. (*Passim* is a Latin word that means "scattered throughout," not an ugly, over grown, rat-like creature that hangs upside down by its tail.)
   - Check the Keep original formatting box if you want the character formatting (such as underline and italics) that Word applies to the document's citation to be carried over into the table of authorities.
   - In the Category list box, choose the citation category you want compiled. Usually you leave the category set to the default, All. If you want to compile a table of one category (cases, rules, regulations, and so on), choose the category from the drop-down list.
   - Change the Tab leader field to change or remove the dotted line that connects each citation to its page number.

5. **Click OK.**

   The table of authorities is created.

Here are some things to remember when you compile a table of authorities:

- If the table of authorities looks like `{ TOA \h \c 1 \p }`, call up the Tools➪Options command, click the View button, and uncheck the Field codes check box. Click OK and the table appears as it should.
- To delete a table of authorities, select the entire table and then press the Delete key. Or press Ctrl+Z immediately after creating the table.
- Word formats the entries in a table of authorities with a standard style name, Table of Authorities, and the headings for categories are formatted by using a style named TOA Heading. If none of the predefined formats listed in the Formats list tickles your fancy, choose From template and click the Modify button. A special version of the Style dialog box appears showing only the standard table of authorities styles. You can customize the appearance of your table by modifying the Table of Authorities and TOA Heading styles.

Updating a Table of Authorities

If you edit a document after creating a table of authorities, the table may become out-of-date. To make sure that the table is up-to-date, use one of these techniques:

TIP

- In the Tools➪Options command, click the Print tab, check the Update fields check box, and then click OK. Then the table of authorities is automatically updated every time you print your document.
- To update a table of authorities without printing the document, select the table and press F9.
- If you point to a table of authorities and click the right mouse button, the shortcut menu that appears includes an Update Field command. Using the Update Field command works the same as pressing F9.

Disclaimer of Warranties and Limit of Liability

The author, Doug Lowe, and IDG Books Worldwide, Inc., make no representations or warranties with respect to the accuracy or completeness of the contents of this chapter and specifically disclaim any implied warranties or merchantability or fitness for any particular purpose and shall in no event be held liable for any loss of profit or any other commercial damage, including, but not limited to, such damages as losing a big case because of a key citation's being omitted from a pleading or a brief; tripping, falling, or stumbling over this book; or the cost of medical treatment and/or hospitalization, pain and suffering, lost wages, or emotional anguish due to stress inflicted or sustained while using or attempting to use the Table of Authorities feature in the Word 97 software program. So let it be written, so let it be done.

Chapter 23

Out Standing in Your Field

In This Chapter

- Understanding fields
- Inserting fields into a document
- Formatting field results with switches
- Updating fields

A field is a special placeholder code that tells Word to insert something — usually text of some sort — into the document. A date field, for example, tells Word to insert the current date into the document. No matter when you edit or print the document, the date field causes the document to contain the current date.

Fields are everywhere in Word. Many of the commands you have come to know and love rely on fields to do their business. Fields let you put the page number in a header or footer, create a table of contents or an index, and print mail-merged letters. These fields get inserted into your document by accident, as a result of your using some other command, such as Insert➪Page Numbers or Tools➪Mail Merge.

This chapter shows you what you need to know to insert fields on purpose, by using the Insert➪Field command. Word provides mass quantities of different types of fields (more than 60). As an act of kindness, I won't go into the boring details of all of them. I do show you how to use ten of the most popular fields.

Be warned that fields can be a source of severe mental anguish. Fortunately, you don't have to read this chapter if you don't want to. This stuff is all very optional.

What Is a Field?

A field is a code that Word translates into text, which is then inserted into the document. When you insert a date field, for example, you're really saying to Word, "Insert the current date right here, and make sure that you get the date right. When I print this document, I want to see today's date. If I print it tomorrow, I want to see tomorrow's date. Next week, I want to see next week's date. A year from now. . . ." You get the idea. A date field is like a placeholder for an actual date, which Word inserts automatically.

Other fields work in the same way. The text Word inserts in place of the field code is called the *result*. For a date field, the result is the current date. For a page-number field, the result is the current page number. Other field types produce more-complicated results, such as a table of contents or an index. For some fields, the result isn't text at all, but a picture or a chart.

When you print a document, there's no way to distinguish between text you typed directly into the document and text that is a field result. Consider, for example, the following text you might use in a letter:

> As of today, Monday, June 16, 1997, you have been banished from Remulak and sentenced to live out the remainder of your existence among the Blunt Skulls of Earth.

You can't tell that "Monday, June 16, 1997" is a field result.

When you edit a document in Word, you must have some way to distinguish between regular text and field results. Word normally displays field results so that the document appears on-screen just as it does when you print it. If the result isn't quite what you expected, however, or if you want to make sure that you used the correct field to produce a result, you can switch the display to show field codes. Word also has an option that displays field results but shades them so that you can distinguish field results from ordinary text.

The preceding letter fragment with field codes displayed looks like this:

> As of today, {TIME \@ "dddd, MMMM dd, yyyy"}, you have been banished from Remulak and sentenced to live out the remainder of your existence among the Blunt Skulls of Earth.

The field is the stuff marked by the curly braces ({ }), which are called *field characters*. Their whole purpose in life is to tell Word that a field lives here. They look just like the curly braces you can type from the keyboard, but they're not. The only way you can create these field characters is by using the Insert⇨Field command or some other Word command that inserts a field.

Trapped between the field characters is the field itself. Each field begins with a field type that tells you what type of field you're dealing with. In the previous example, you're looking at a TIME field, which provides the current date or time in any of about six million formats.

Following the field type are instructions that tell the field what to do. The TIME field in the previous example contains an instruction that tells Word how to format the time: dddd, MMMM dd, yyyy. The hard part about using fields is figuring out what to do with the instructions. Each field type has its own gang of instruction codes.

Inserting a Field

Many Word commands, such as Insert➪Date and Time and Insert➪Index and Tables, quietly insert fields into your document without boasting. But Word provides many other fields you can insert only by using the Insert➪Field command.

Here's how to insert a field in your document:

1. **Move the cursor to the point where you want the field to be inserted.**
2. **Call up the Insert➪Field command.**

   The Field dialog box appears, as shown in Figure 23-1.

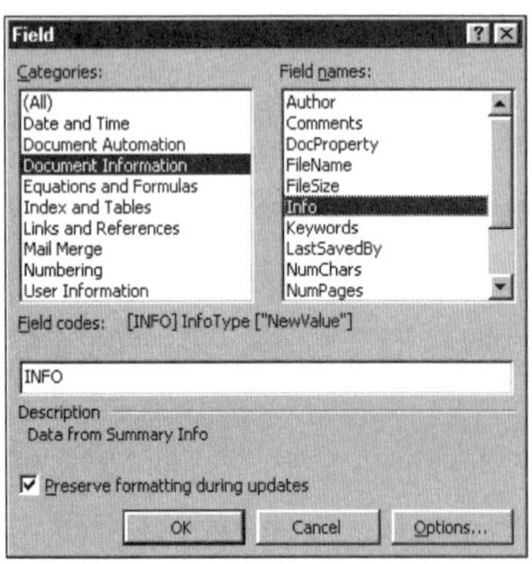

Figure 23-1: The Field dialog box.

3. **Choose the field type you want by scrolling through the Categories and Field names lists.**

   Because mass quantities of field types exist, Word breaks them down into categories to make them easier to find. When you choose a category from the Categories list, the Field names list is updated to list only the field types in the chosen category. If you're not sure which category contains the field you want to insert, choose (All) as the category. Word then lists all the field types in the Field names list.

4. **In the Field codes box, add any additional instructions required by the field.**

   Word automatically adds the field type to the Field codes text box. Then it gives you a hint about how to complete the field code by listing, just above the Field codes box, the instructions that the selected field type accepts. Look back at Figure 23-1. The field type selected in the Field codes box is INFO. Just above that Word shows you that you can include an `InfoType` (whatever that is) and a {“`NewValue` } (huh?). This information is helpful, if you happen to know what an InfoType and NewValue are.

5. **If you're stumped by Step 4, click the Options button.**

   A Field Options dialog box appears, which looks something like Figure 23-2. Now we're getting somewhere.

Figure 23-2: The Field Options dialog box.

6. **Choose the options you want to add from the list of Formatting options and then click Add to Field.**

   The Field Options dialog box sort of resembles a salad bar. You get to peruse the day's offerings (they're different for each field) and add just the ones you want. Every time you click the Add to Field button, the selected option is added to the Field codes box. Also, a concise description of each field option is at the bottom of the Field Options dialog box.

7. **Click OK when you have added all the options you can carry in one trip.**

   You are returned to the Field dialog box.

8. **Click OK to insert the field into the document.**

   The field is inserted into the document.

Here are some deep thoughts to consider as you meditate on the finer points of inserting fields:

- When you insert a field, either the field code or the result is displayed, depending on whether the Field Codes view option is set. You can switch between field codes and field results by pressing Alt+F9.
- A whole bevy of specialized keyboard shortcuts are available for working with fields. They are summarized for your convenience in Table 23-1.

Table 23-1 Keyboard Shortcuts for Fields

Keyboard Shortcut	*What It Does*
F9	Updates the selected field or fields
Shift+F9	Switches the display between field codes and field results for the selected field or fields
Alt+F9	Switches the display between field codes and field results for all fields in the document
Ctrl+F9	Inserts a field into a document
Ctrl+Shift+F9	Converts a field to text (unlinks the field)
F11	Finds the next field in the document
Shift+F11	Finds the previous field in the document
Ctrl+F11	Locks a field so that it cannot be updated
Ctrl+Shift+F11	Unlocks a field

If you get something like `Error!Unknown switch argument` rather than the field result you expected, you made a mistake when you composed the field instructions. You have to edit the field directly by pressing Alt+F9 to reveal the field codes and then you click in the field and type your correction.

Formatting Field Results with Switches

Word provides a gaggle of switches that you can use on most any field to control the formatting applied to the field result. You don't have to use any of these fields if you don't want to. If you omit them, Word makes an educated guess about the format of the field result.

You can use three switches to format a field's result:

- The Format switch, *, tells Word whether to capitalize the results field and, for fields that produce numeric results, which type of numbers to create (Arabic or Roman numerals, for example).
- The Numeric Picture switch, \#, controls the format of numbers.
- The Date-Time Picture switch, \@, sets the format of dates and times.

Each of these switches has numerous options you can mix and match to format the field in just about any way you want. The various uses of these three switches are explained in the following sections.

Preserving formatting when you update fields: the * mergeformat switch

When you update a field, Word usually removes any formatting, such as bold or italics, that you have applied to a field result. If you want Word to keep this type of formatting, include the * mergeformat switch in the field. It's usually a good idea to preserve formatting, so I recommend using this switch.

The nerd way to insert a field

If you have a fetish for typing complicated commands, you can insert a field by typing it directly in your document. Just follow these steps:

1. **Position the cursor where you want the field to be inserted.**
2. **Type the field name and instructions for the field you want to insert. Don't worry about the curly braces for now.**
3. **Select the text you typed in Step 2.**
4. **Press Ctrl+F9.**

Ctrl+F9 converts the selected text to a field by enclosing it in those curly little braces called field codes that look just like the curly braces you type on the keyboard but that aren't the same thing at all. If you prefer, you can reverse these steps: Position the cursor where you want the field to be placed and press Ctrl+F9; an empty field appears, which you can select. Then you can type the field name and instructions within the braces.

You can tell Word to automatically add a * mergeformat switch to a field by checking the Preserve Formatting During Updates check box in the Field dialog box.

If you're not sure what I mean by "updating a field," skip ahead to the section, "Updating a Field."

REMEMBER

I almost always use this switch. You see it in all the field examples in the rest of this chapter, so get used to it.

Capitalizing field results

Use the Format switch (*) options listed in Table 23-2 to control capitalization in a field result. The following field, for example, inserts the name of the current file in lowercase letters:

{ filename * lower * mergeformat }

Table 23-2 Capitalizing Field Results

Switch	*What It Means*
* caps	The First Letter Of Each Word Is Capitalized
* firstcap	The first letter of the first word is capitalized
* lower	all the letters are lowercase
* upper	ALL THE LETTERS ARE UPPERCASE

Using strange number formats

Numbers are usually displayed by using Arabic numerals. You can change the format of numbers in field results, however, by using the switches listed in Table 23-3. Consider the following text, for example:

This is the { page * ordtext * mergeformat } page.

The preceding line produces a result like the following:

This is the thirty-third page.

In this case, the * ordtext switch caused the page number to be spelled out as a number.

Table 23-3 Using Strange Number Formats

Switch	*What It Means*
* alphabetic	Converts numbers to their corresponding letters of the alphabet (1 becomes A, 2 becomes B, and so on)
* arabic	The usual number format (nothing special here)
* cardtext	Spells out the number (for example, 1994 becomes one thousand nine-hundred ninety-four)
* dollartext	Spells out a dollar amount the way you would write it on a check (289.95 becomes two hundred eighty-nine and 95/100)
* hex	A favorite of computer nerds, converts numbers from the normal earth dweller base 10 numbering system to base 16 (for example, 492 becomes 1EC)
* ordinal	Adds st, nd, rd, or whatever is appropriate to the end of the number (for example, 307 becomes 307th)
* ordtext	Spells out the number and adds st, nd, rd, or whatever is appropriate to the end (for example, 307 becomes three hundred seventh)
* roman	Converts the number to Roman numerals; used by film directors to mark copyright dates (for example, 1953 becomes mcmliii)

Creating custom number formats

If you don't like the way Word displays numbers, you can create your own custom number formats by using the Numeric Picture switch (\#). Numeric pictures are created by stringing together a bunch of pound signs, zeros, commas, decimal points, plus or minus signs, dollar signs, and other characters to show how you want numbers to appear. Rather than show you the individual characters you can use, Table 23-4 lists the numeric picture switches you're most likely to use.

TIP

You can automatically add the numeric pictures listed in Table 23-4 to formulas if you use the Table➪Formula command rather than the Insert➪Field command to create the formula. The Table➪Formula command provides a drop-down list box that lists the numeric pictures; just choose the number format you want, and Word inserts the appropriate switch into the field. For more information about the Table➪Formula command, see Chapter 10.

Table 23-4 Sample Numeric Picture Switches

Picture Switch	*Description*
\# #,##0	Prints whole numbers with commas to separate groups of thousands (for example, 1,024 and 1,244,212)
\# #,##0.00	Prints numbers with commas to separate groups of thousands and two decimal positions; both decimal positions are printed even if one or both of them is zero (for example, 1,024.00 and 8.47)
\# $#,##0.00;($#,##0.00)	Prints numbers as money: commas to separate groups of thousands, two decimal positions, and a leading dollar sign; negative numbers are enclosed in parentheses — for example, $1,024.00 and ($97.38)
\# 0	Prints whole numbers without commas (for example, 38 and 124873345)
\# 0%	Prints whole numbers without commas, followed by a percent sign (for example, 98%)
\# 0.00	Prints numbers without commas but with two decimal positions (for example, 1024.00 or 3.14)
\# 0.00%	Prints numbers without commas, with two decimal positions, and followed by a percent sign (for example, 97.99%)

Creating custom date and time formats

When you use the Insert⇨Field command to insert a date field, you can click the Options button and choose from one of 17 different formats. If you don't like any of the 17 formats, you can compose your own custom date format by using the Date-Time Picture switch (\@). You just string together the various components of the date or time by using combinations of characters, such as MMM to stand for the three-letter month abbreviation, and dddd to stand for the day of the week, spelled out.

Frankly, creating custom date and time formats by using the \@ is a bit off the deep end. If none of the 17 date formats listed in the Field Options dialog box for date fields satisfies you, you have to learn to be less picky.

Updating a Field

When you first insert a field, Word calculates the field's result. Thereafter, the field result may become out of date. To recalculate a field result to make sure that it is up to date, follow one of the following procedures:

- Call up the Tools➪Options command and choose the Print tab. Check the Update Fields check box and then click OK. Word then automatically updates all fields every time it prints the document.
- To update a specific field, select the field and press F9. If you select several fields, pressing F9 updates all of them. You can quickly update all the fields in a document by pressing Ctrl+A to select the entire document and then press F9 to update the fields.
- If you point to a field and click the right mouse button, a shortcut menu appears. Choose the Update Field command from the shortcut menu to update the field.

Preventing a Field from Being Updated

If you do not want a field to be updated, you can either lock the field or unlink the field. If you lock the field, Word prevents it from being updated until you unlock the field. If you unlink the field, Word deletes the field code and replaces it with the result text. Locking a field prevents it temporarily from being updated; unlinking the field is permanent.

To lock, unlock, or unlink a field, first select it. Then use the keyboard shortcuts found in Table 23-5.

Table 23-5 Keyboard Shortcuts for Locking, Unlocking, or Unlinking a Field

Keyboard Shortcut	*What It Does*
Ctrl+F11	Locks the field
Ctrl+Shift+F11	Unlocks the field
Ctrl+Shift+F9	Converts the field to results text (unlinks the field)

Chapter 24

Likes People and Works Well with Others (Using Word's Group Editing Features)

In This Chapter

- Tracking revisions as you make them
- Accepting revisions
- Comparing document versions

Rumor has it that Benjamin Franklin was first given the opportunity to write the Declaration of Independence but declined because he refused to write a document that would be edited by others.

Ha!

Old Ben would have hated this chapter. The very thought that Word had features that enabled other people to edit his documents would have sent him out into the storm to fly another kite.

This chapter covers several Word features that are designed for group work. I discuss how to track the changes you and others have made to a document by using revision marks, how to add comments to a document, and how to save different versions of a document in a single file.

All Hail the Honorable Reviewing Toolbar

Word 97's group editing features are handled by a dedicated Reviewing toolbar, which is pictured in Figure 24-1. The Reviewing toolbar contains all of the buttons that you need to track changes to your documents and to add comments that can be read by other reviewers. Table 24-1 lists the function of each of the Reviewing toolbar's buttons.

Figure 24-1: The Reviewing toolbar.

Table 24-1	Buttons on the Reviewing Toolbar	
Button	***Name***	***What it does***
	Insert Comment	Inserts a comment into a document
	Edit Comment	Takes you to a comment window where you can edit the text of a comment
	Previous Comment	Goes to the previous comment in the document
	Next Comment	Goes to the next comment in the document
	Delete Comment	Deletes the selected comment
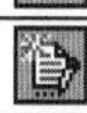	Track Changes	Turns revision marking on or off
	Previous Change	Goes to the previous change
	Next Change	Goes to the next change
	Accept Change	Accepts the current change, making it a permanent part of the document
	Reject Change	Rejects the current change, reverting the text to the way it was before the change was made
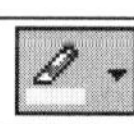	Highlight	Activates the highlighter tool
	Create Outlook Task	Creates a Microsoft Outlook task (useful only if you use and enjoy the Microsoft Outlook task and time scheduling program)
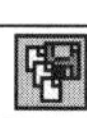	Save Version	Saves a new version of the document
	Send Mail	Sends an e-mail message to another user

Keeping Your Comments To Yourself (Not!)

A comment is a way of adding a note to part of a document without modifying the document. When you insert a comment, Word adds a hidden comment mark to the text at the location of the comment. Word then adds your comments to a separate Comment Pane, which is keyed to the comment marks in much the same way as footnotes are keyed to footnote marks. You can come back later and view each of the comments. (In previous versions of Word, comments were known as *annotations*.)

To insert a comment, follow these steps:

1. **Summon the Reviewing toolbar by choosing View⇨Toolbars⇨Reviewing.**

   The Reviewing toolbar appears.

2. **Select the text you want to comment on.**

   If the text is really long, just move the cursor to the end of the text. If you select the text before creating the comment, Word highlights the text later when you display the comment.

3. **Click the Insert Comment button.**

   Or, if you prefer, use the Insert⇨Comment command. Either way, a comment mark is inserted as hidden text following the text you selected. Then the screen is split in two, revealing the comments in the bottom portion of the screen. Word refers to the screen's bottom portion as the Comment Pane, and Word's right — it is a pain. Figure 24-2 shows a Word screen with the Comment Pane visible.

3. **Type your comments.**

   Word adds your comments to the Comment Pane at the correct position.

4. **Click the Close button to dismiss the Comment Pane and return to the document.**

Here are some things to keep in mind when you insert comments:

- Notice how the comment marks in the document are keyed to comments in the Comment Pane. Word uses your initials (it gets them from the User Info options), followed by a sequence number. For example, the first comment I created in Figure 24-2 is identified as DL1; the second is DL2; and so on. With the user identification feature, several people can add comments to a document, and you can easily determine which comment came from each person.

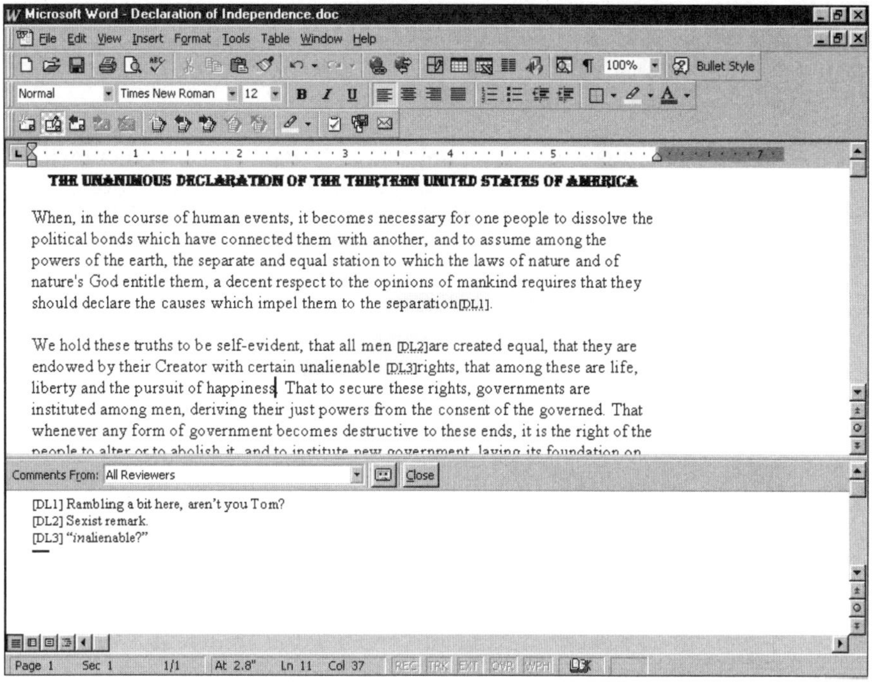

Figure 24-2: A document with comments.

- To insert a bunch of comments, leave the comment pane open. After typing a comment, just click the mouse anywhere in the document. Both the Document Pane and the Comment Pane remain visible. Find the next bit of text you want to comment on, select it, and click the Insert Comment button to insert another comment.
- If you have a sound card, a microphone, and more disk space than you know what to do with, you can add a voice comment by clicking the cassette-tape button in the Comment Pane.
- If you can't say something nice, don't say nothin' at all.

REMEMBER

Viewing Comments

To view comments that have been added to a document, open the Comment Pane by using the View⇨Comments command. You can then scroll through the Document Pane or the Comment Pane to look at comments along with the corresponding document text. Notice that as you scroll through either pane, the other pane scrolls in sync. When you select a comment by clicking it in the Comment Pane, Word scrolls the Document Pane to the text that the comment refers to, and the referenced text is highlighted.

If the document contains comments created by more than one user, you can restrict the Comment Pane so that it shows just that user's comments by choosing that user from the From drop-down list. To display all comments regardless of who inserted them, select All Reviewers.

If you want to copy a comment directly into the document, select the comment text you want to copy. Press Ctrl+C, click in the document at the location where you want the text inserted, and then press Ctrl+I.

If the Comment Pane is too big or too small, you can change its size. Hold the mouse steady over the top edge of the Comment Pane for a moment, and the mouse cursor changes to a double-headed arrow. Hold down the left mouse button and drag the Comment Pane up or down to increase or decrease its size.

You can quickly scroll to the next or previous comment in the document by clicking the Next Comment or Previous Comment buttons found in the Reviewing toolbar.

You can print comments by calling up the Tools⇨Options command, clicking the Print tab, and checking the Comments check box. Then when you print the document, the hidden text that marks the comment locations is printed along with the document, and the comments are printed on a separate page after the document has been printed. In addition, the comments page includes the page number to which each comment refers. (If you want to print just the comments page without printing the document, call up the File⇨Print command and select Comments for the Print What field.)

You can view a comment without calling up the Comment Pane simply by hovering the mouse over text that has been highlighted as a comment. After a moment, the comment appears in a box just above the text. When you move the mouse, the comment disappears.

Removing Comments

To delete a comment, highlight the hidden comment mark in the document text, and press the Delete Comment button, shown in the margin.

Believe it or not, Word doesn't provide a quick way to wipe out all comments in a document. To delete all comments, you have to delete each one individually.

Tracking Changes

Wouldn't it be great if you could quickly see what changes have been made to a document? Such a feature would be great for anyone in charge of maintaining corporate bylaws, legal documents, records about investments in failed savings and loans, congressional testimony, and so on.

With Word's Track Changes feature, you can. Track Changes lets you indicate what changes have been made to a document. Any text that has been deleted is shown with a line running through it (strikethrough). Text that has been inserted is underlined. Any line that contains a change is marked with a vertical line in the margin so that you can quickly scan through a document to find changes. Figure 24-3 shows an example of a document with revision marks. To create revision marks like these, read on.

To track changes to a document while the document is being edited, turn on the Track Changes feature before you begin editing your document. Then Word keeps track of revisions as you make them. You can then print the document with or without the changes, and you can later accept or reject the changes.

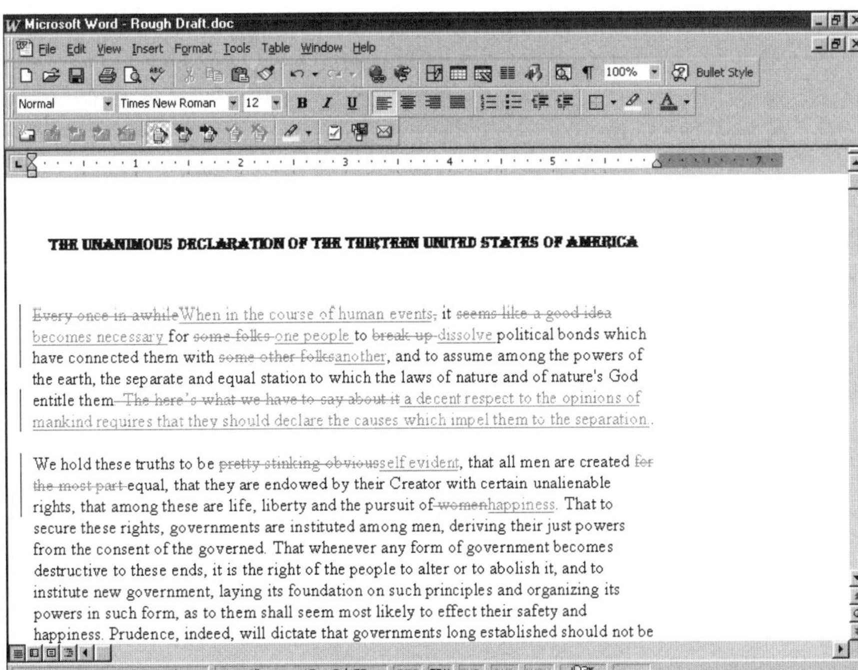

Figure 24-3: This is why Ben Franklin declined the offer to pen the first draft of the Declaration of Independence.

Follow these steps to track changes:

1. **Call up the Tools⇨Track Changes⇨Highlight Changes command.**

   The Highlight Changes dialog box appears, as shown in Figure 24-4.

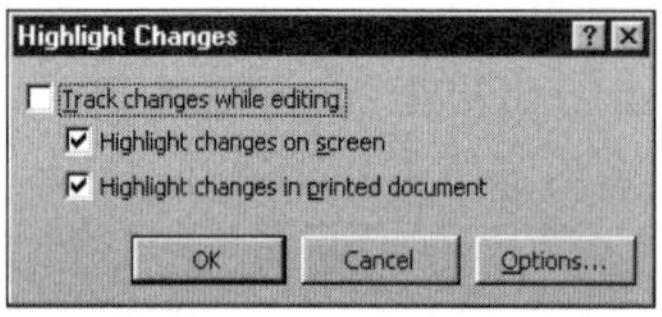

Figure 24-4: The Highlight Changes dialog box.

2. **Check the Track changes while editing check box.**

   Word keeps track of the changes you make while editing the document.

3. **If you do not want the change marks to appear on-screen while you edit the document, uncheck the Highlight changes on screen check box.**

   Normally change marks appear on the screen as you type, which can be annoying, so you may want to uncheck the Highlight changes on screen box. As long as the Track changes while editing box is checked, Word tracks revisions whether or not the revision marks are shown on-screen.

4. **If you do not want the change marks to be printed, uncheck the Highlight changes in printed document check box.**

   Change marks are usually printed when you print the document. Uncheck this box to omit the change marks when the document is printed. You can always check this box later to print the document with revision marks.

5. **Click OK.**

   Word whisks away the Highlight Changes dialog box. The letters TRK are highlighted in the status bar at the bottom of the screen to remind you that changes are being tracked.

To disable revision marking, call up the Tools⇨Track Changes⇨Highlight Changes command again, uncheck the Track changes while editing check box, and click OK. I sometimes do this to correct a simple and obvious typographical error that doesn't need to be highlighted by a revision mark. Then I turn revision marking back on again.

TIP

You can quickly activate Track Changes by double-clicking the letters TRK in the status bar.

Or, you can click the Track Changes button in the Reviewing toolbar to start or stop Track Changes while Editing.

REMEMBER

The three check boxes in the Revisions dialog box work independently of one another. The Track changes while editing box tells Word whether to keep track of changes while you edit your document. The other two boxes control whether change marks are displayed or printed.

If you click the Options button in the Highlight Changes dialog box, Word lets you customize the highlighting and colors used to mark inserted text, deleted text, and changed lines.

Comparing Documents

Word tracks changes only when you activate change tracking as described in the section, "Tracking Changes." If you forget to activate Track Changes, you can still re-create change marks by comparing a document with an earlier version of the same document. Word does its best to mark text that has been inserted or deleted from the older version of the document.

Follow these steps to compare documents:

1. **Open the newer version of the two documents you want to compare.**
2. **Call up the Tools➪Track Changes➪Compare Documents.**

   A dialog box called Select File to Compare with Current Document appears, which is almost identical to a normal File Open dialog box.
3. **Choose the file to which you want to compare the current file.**

   In other words, choose the older version of the file you opened in Step 1.
4. **Click OK.**

Word compares the files and automatically inserts change marks in the newer document.

Don't expect Word to insert change marks perfectly when it compares documents. Word is good at marking minor revisions, but some changes may confuse Word and cause it to insert wacky change marks. You are better off marking revisions as you make them, if possible.

Accepting or Rejecting Changes

When you have accumulated a bunch of change marks, sooner or later you want to accept or reject the revisions. If you accept the changes, the revisions are permanently incorporated into the document, and the change marks are removed. If you reject the changes, the document reverts to its previous state, and the revisions are deleted along with the change marks.

To accept or reject all of the changes to a document in one swift stroke, follow these steps:

1. **Call up the Tools⇨Track Changes⇨Accept or Reject Changes command.**

   The Accept or Reject Changes dialog box appears, as shown in Figure 24-5.

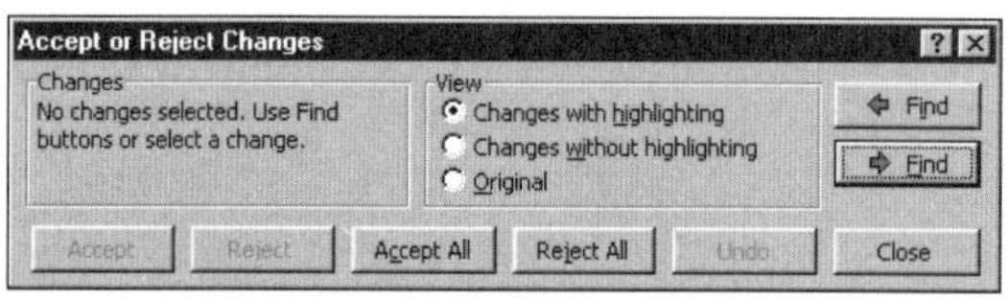

Figure 24-5: The Accept or Reject Changes dialog box.

2. **Click Accept All to accept all changes, or Reject All to reject all changes.**

   Either way, Word asks you a confirming question, such as "Are you nuts?" Click Yes to continue.

3. **Click the Close button.**

   Word returns you to your document.

Skim through your document to confirm that changes have indeed been accepted or rejected as you intended. It should be obvious.

TIP

If you have second thoughts, press Ctrl+Z. The revision marks are restored.

If you prefer to work your way through the changes one at a time, accepting or rejecting each one on its own merits, use the Find buttons in the Accept or Reject Changes dialog box to move to the next or previous change, then click Accept or Reject, depending on what you think of the change. Or use the following four buttons in the Reviewing toolbar:

Find the previous change.

Find the next change.

Accept the change.

Reject the change.

Change marks accumulate in a document until you either accept or reject them. This means that you can collect a set of revision marks over a period of days or weeks and then deal with them all by accepting or rejecting them.

Document Versions

With Word 97, you can now save different versions of a document together in the same document file. Saving several versions of a document in the same file is not only more convenient than saving versions using separate filenames, but it also saves disk space because Word doesn't save the entire text of each document version. Instead, Word saves only the differences between versions.

To save a new version of a document, call up the Reviewing toolbar and click the Save Version button. The Save Version dialog box appears. Type in a complete description of the version, then click OK. Word then saves that version.

Whenever you open a document, Word opens the document's most recent version. However, you can access earlier versions of the document by calling up the File⇨Versions command. The Versions dialog box appears. From the Versions dialog box, you can select any version stored with the document. Click the Open button to open the version as a separate document or the Delete button to delete the version.

Before you send a copy of the document to someone else, make sure the document you send has only the version you want the recipient to see. You have two ways to do that:

- Call up the File⇨Versions command and delete all prior versions of the document.
- Call up the File⇨Versions command and save the version you want to send as a separate file by clicking the Open button.

Part V
Shortcuts and Tips Galore

"I TOLD HIM WE WERE LOOKING FOR SOFTWARE THAT WOULD GIVE US GREATER PRODUCTIVITY, SO HE SOLD ME A WORD PROCESSING PACKAGE THAT CAME WITH THESE SIGNS."

In this part . . .

Ever wondered why there's a shortcut key for Bold and a shortcut key for Italic, but no shortcut key for Bold-Italic? If so, you'll love the chapters in this part. They show you how to customize Word so that it works the way you want it to. You learn how to create your own toolbar buttons, menus, and shortcut keys and how to create simple macros to automate routine chores.

This is definitely pocket-protector stuff, so be prepared to roll up your sleeves.

Chapter 25

Have It Your Way with Toolbars, Menus, and Keyboard Shortcuts

In This Chapter

- Making toolbars appear (and disappear!)
- Adding buttons to a toolbar
- Creating a new toolbar
- Messing with menus
- Adding custom keyboard shortcuts

Hiding down at the bottom of Word's Tools menu is a potent little command called Customize. Lurking within the dialog box that appears when you conjure up this command is the ability to improve the toolbars, menus, and keyboard shortcuts that come with Word. If you routinely apply a style, for example, named Limerick to samples of fine poetry within your documents, you can add a Limerick button to one of Word's templates. Or you can add a Limerick command to the Format menu or define Ctrl+L as a keyboard shortcut for applying the Limerick style. This chapter shows you how.

Please feel free to skip this chapter if you already think that Word is the world's perfect word processor, beyond the need for refinement.

TIP

Customized toolbars, menus, and keyboard shortcuts are stored along with styles, AutoText, and macros in document templates. Unless you specify otherwise, Word stores any customizations you create in the Normal.dot template so that they are available to all documents. If you want, you can store customizations in other templates so that they are available only when you edit documents that have those templates attached. For the complete scoop on templates, see Chapter 5.

Belly Up to the Command Bar

Martin Luther said, "If you must sin, sin boldly!" The people who designed Word's toolbar buttons were apparently students of Luther, because they didn't just throw in a few buttons here and there — they threw in thirteen separate toolbars, with something like 98 buttons. Kind of inspires a song:

> Ninety-eight buttons appear on the screen,
> Ninety-eight buttons appear,
> Tools⇨Customize is one button's demise,
> Ninety-seven buttons appear on the screen.

If 98 buttons aren't enough for you, Word keeps a few unused buttons in reserve. You can add these buttons to any of the existing button bars, or you can create new button bars altogether. And if that's still not enough, you can even design your own buttons!

Toolbars and menu bars in Word are collectively called *command bars*. A command bar can hold several different types of goodies, but the most-common types of command bar controls are buttons, menus, and drop-down lists.

Strictly speaking, the only difference between Word's menu bar and its various toolbars is that the menu bar is a command bar that happens to be filled up with menus, whereas the toolbars are command bars that happen to be filled up with buttons. Note, however, that some of the toolbars actually contain menus. For example, the Drawing toolbar contains two menus: the Draw menu and the AutoShapes menu.

TECHNICAL STUFF

In previous versions of Word, toolbars and menu bars were separate entities. Though Word allowed you to customize toolbars and the menu bar, you couldn't put buttons on the menu bar or menus on toolbars. Although the new combined toolbar/menu bar is officially known as a command bar, the term toolbar is still commonly used — even by Microsoft — to refer to command bars.

Although Word comes configured with just one menu bar and thirteen toolbars that you can access from the View⇨Toolbars command, there are actually a total of 49 toolbars that can be displayed in the Word window. Of course, you wouldn't want to display them all unless you had like a 30" monitor. Just for fun, Figure 25-1 shows how Word appears with about half of the toolbars visible. A bit excessive, eh?

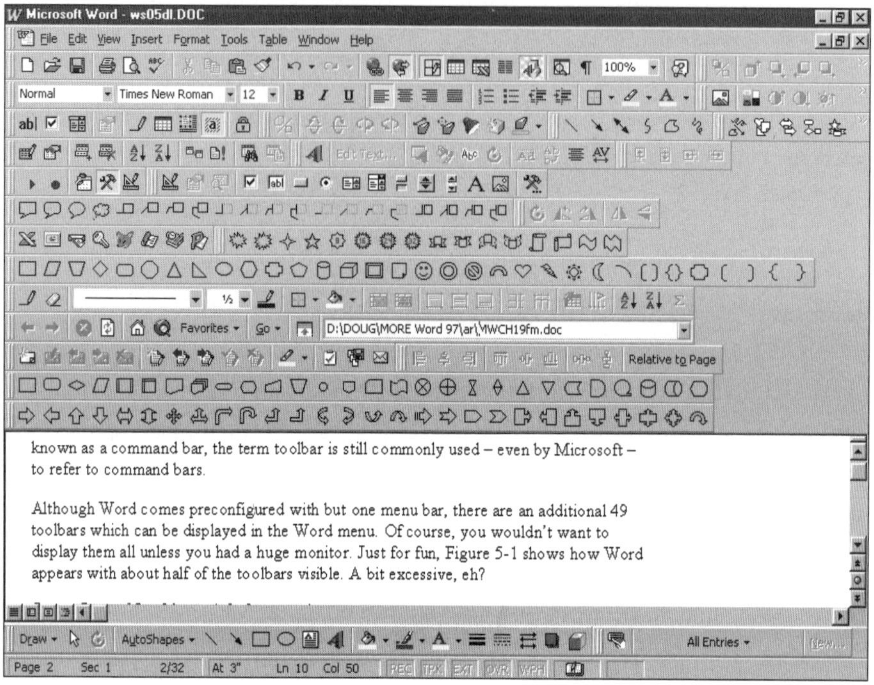

Figure 25-1: If you have a 30-inch monitor, you may be able to work with all of Word's toolbars visible.

The best thing about Word's toolbars is that you can completely customize the toolbars that come with Word, and you can add new command bars of your own. Microsoft did its best to decide which toolbar buttons would be most useful for a wide range of users, and it did a pretty good job, especially with the Standard and Formatting toolbars. Still, you're bound to find several toolbar buttons that you rarely, if ever, use. And if you think for a moment, you can probably come up with a button or two you wish you had.

For example, I almost never use right-justified paragraphs. But I frequently use hanging indents. So I've replaced the Align Right button with a custom Hanging Indent button. I even drew my own design for the button image; it took only a minute or two. Now, Word works and looks the way I want it to, not the way Microsoft thinks I should want it to.

Making toolbars appear (and disappear!)

If your favorite toolbar is missing, you or someone else may have inadvertently sent it to toolbar exile. To get the toolbar back, follow these steps:

1. **Call up the View➪Toolbars command.**

   The Toolbars menu appears, as shown in Figure 25-2.

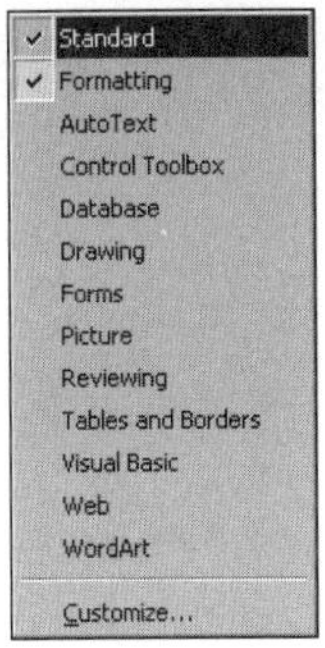

Figure 25-2: The Toolbars menu.

2. **Click the toolbar that you want displayed.**

   A check mark appears in the box, and the toolbar is displayed.

To make a toolbar disappear, repeat the procedure. Choosing a toolbar that is already visible causes that toolbar to vanish.

Here are a few points to ponder when you display toolbars:

- Some toolbars cling to the top of the document window, whereas others are free spirits that wander about the window.
- If you don't like the position of a toolbar on-screen, you can move it. Just point to any part of the toolbar between buttons and drag. You can also change the shape of a floating toolbar by dragging one of its edges or corners.
- If you drag a toolbar to the top of the document window, it clings to the top like the Standard and Formatting toolbars do. If you drag a toolbar far enough away from the top of the window, the toolbar becomes a floater again.
- Another way to summon the Toolbars menu is to right-click on any visible toolbar.

TIP

To make a floating toolbar go away, click the Close button in its top-right corner.

Removing toolbar buttons

In case you don't like the buttons that appear on Word's toolbars, you can remove buttons you don't use. You often have to do this before you add new buttons to a toolbar because the toolbars that come with Word are stuffed to the gills with buttons.

Follow these steps to remove a button:

1. **Summon the Tools⇨Customize command.**

   The Customize dialog box appears, as shown in Figure 25-3.

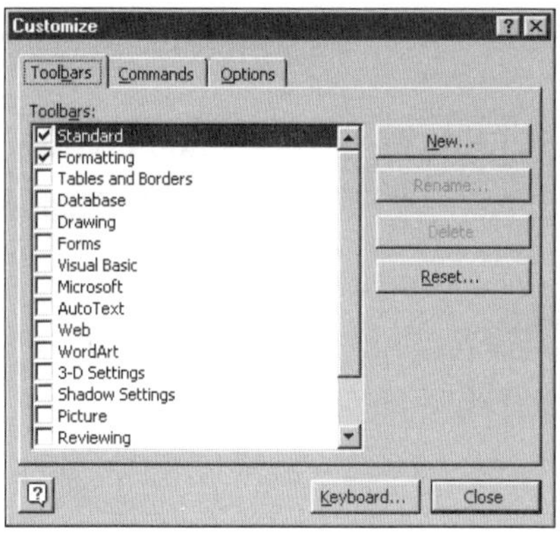

Figure 25-3: The Customize dialog box with the Toolbars tab showing.

2. **Point to the button on the toolbar that you want to remove and then press and hold down the mouse button and drag the button off the toolbar.**

   It doesn't matter where you drag the button; just drag it well clear of the toolbar.

3. **Release the mouse button, and the toolbar button is removed.**

   The other buttons on the toolbar hold a little farewell party and then go on about their business.

Keep these important points in mind when you remove a button:

- The Undo command (Ctrl+Z) doesn't cover modifications you make to a toolbar. If you inadvertently delete a toolbar button, however, you can quickly restore the entire toolbar to its pristine condition by choosing Tools⇨Customize and clicking the Reset button, which appears on the Toolbars tab.
- The Customize command is also available from the View⇨Toolbars menu. You can get to it by right-clicking any toolbar and choosing the Customize command that appears in the pop-up menu.

Adding a new button to a toolbar

Although the View➪Toolbars command lets you access thirteen toolbars capable of showing millions of buttons, that's not enough. If you want to add an extra button to a toolbar, follow these steps:

1. **Call up the Tools➪Customize command.**

   The dialog box, shown in Figure 25-3, appears.

2. **Click the Commands tab to bring up the command buttons.**

   Figure 25-4 shows the Commands tab of the Customize dialog box.

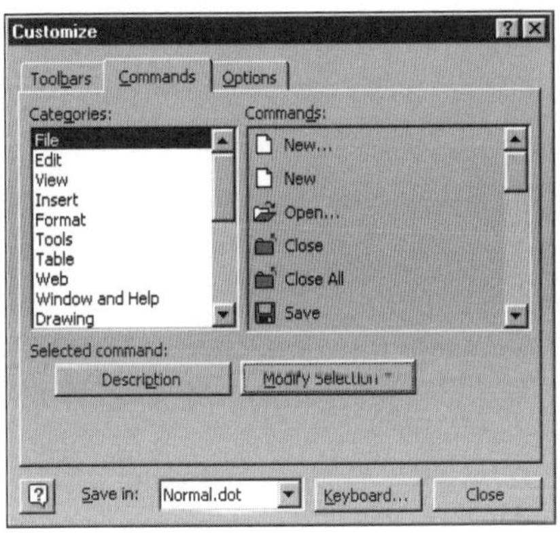

Figure 25-4: The Customize dialog box with the Commands tab showing.

3. **If necessary, make way for the new button by removing a button you don't use.**

   This is the hard part. If there isn't any room on any of the toolbars that are visible, you have to make room by deleting a button or two that you don't use. To delete a button, just drag it off the toolbar. See the preceding section, "Removing toolbar buttons," for more information.

4. **Choose the Category of button you want to add.**

   As you scroll through the Categories list, the buttons shown in the Commands section of the dialog box change to indicate which buttons are available for the category. As you examine the categories, you see familiar buttons, such as the New, Open, and Save buttons, plus unfamiliar buttons, such as binoculars and the padlock.

   If you're patient enough, you can scroll through the entire Categories list and find four interesting categories hiding out at the bottom of the list: Macros, Fonts, AutoText, and Styles. These options don't present a

bunch of predefined buttons you can use. Instead, they let you assign buttons to the specific macros, fonts, AutoText entries, or styles that are available.

Just above the Macros, Fonts, AutoText, and Styles categories is the All Commands category. It lists all the commands available in Word, in alphabetic order.

5. **Choose the button you want to add and drag it to the toolbar at the location where you want the button added.**

   As soon as you release the mouse button, the toolbar button is added to the toolbar right where you clicked.

6. **Click Close to dismiss the Customize Toolbars dialog box.**

   You're finished!

Creating a new toolbar

If you can't find room for a few extra tools in one of the existing toolbars, you can create a new toolbar. Just follow these steps:

1. **Call up the Tools⇨Customize command and click the Toolbars tab.**

   The Toolbars tab of the Customize dialog box appears. If you must look, a picture of it is shown in Figure 25-3

2. **Click New.**

   A dialog box appears, shown in Figure 25-5, asking you to type a name for the new toolbar.

Figure 25-5: The New Toolbar command.

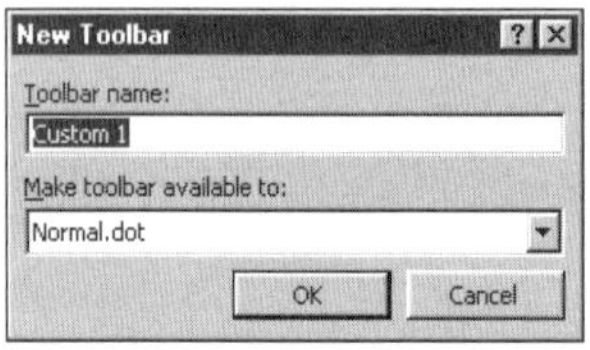

3. **Type a name for the toolbar and then click OK.**

   Use whatever name you want. When you click OK, Word creates a new toolbar. The new toolbar is devoid of buttons, but you take care of that in the next step.

4. **Click the Commands tab in the Customize dialog box and drag whatever buttons you want to the new toolbar.**

   Refer to the section "Adding a new button to a toolbar," earlier in this chapter, for the complete procedure for adding buttons.

5. **Click Close.**

   The Customize dialog box vanishes.

6. **Move the new toolbar to its final resting place.**

   Drag it by the edge to wherever you want it to appear on-screen.

7. **You're finished.**

TIP

To delete a toolbar you created, summon the Toolbars tab of the Tools⇨Customize command. Choose the toolbar you want to delete, and then click the Delete button. Note that Word won't let you delete any of the predefined toolbars that come with Word; you can delete only toolbars you've added yourself.

Messing with Menus

Besides buttons, toolbars can also hold menus. In fact, the standard menu bar is nothing more than a toolbar that contains menus rather than buttons. You can even mix menus and buttons on the same toolbar, as demonstrated by the Drawing toolbar, which has an assortment of buttons for drawing functions in addition to the Draw and AutoShapes menus.

What's with the ampersand (&)?

Before I throw you into the depths of customizing Word's menus, I need to warn you that such work will expose you to a little whiff of programmer-speak, in the form of ampersands intermixed with menu and command names. For example, the File menu is written as &File, and the Format menu is written as F&ormat.

Did the Microsoft programmers who wrote Word suddenly develop a twitch in the index finger of their right hands when it came time to finish the Tools⇨Customize command? Not at all. Instead, they decided to use the ampersand as a symbol to indicate which character will serve as a menu or command's hot key — the key that the user can press in combination with the Alt key to invoke the menu or command. The hot key for the File menu is Alt+F because the ampersand precedes the F. For the Format menu, the hot key is Alt+O because the ampersand precedes the O.

Adding a menu command

When most users begin to probe the depths of Word's customization features, they discover that Word includes many commands that are not available from any of its menus — hundreds of unused commands, in fact. The fact that Microsoft left these commands off the menus should not discourage you from using them. If you find a command that you wish was available via the menus, don't gripe about it, add it to the menu! Here's the procedure:

1. **Choose Tools⇨Customize. When the Customize dialog box appears, click the Commands tab.**
2. **Select the category of the command or other element you want to add to the menu from the Categories list.**

   Don't forget that macros, styles, fonts, and AutoText appear as categories near the bottom of the list.
3. **Select the specific command or other item from the Command list.**

   Note that the title of this box will change if you select the macros, styles, fonts, or AutoText categories.
4. **Drag the command to the menu where you want the command inserted. When the menu appears, continue to drag the command down to the location on the menu where you would like the command to appear.**

   When you finally release the mouse button, the command is inserted in the menu.
5. **If you don't like the name assigned to the new command, change the name by right-clicking the new command and typing a new name into the Name field.**

   Remember to type an ampersand just before the letter that you want to serve as a hot key for the command. (Don't worry, the ampersand itself won't appear in the menu.)

Removing a menu command

The capability to remove commands from menus is just as important as the capability to add commands, not just because it allows you to remove custom commands you've added, but also because it lets you remove built-in commands that you never use. Such commands merely take up space on Word's already-crowded menus.

To remove a menu command, call up the Tools⇨Customize command, right-click the command you want to remove, and choose Delete from the pop-up menu that appears. Poof! The command is banished from the menu.

Rearranging menu commands

Previous versions of Word provided no easy method of rearranging items on a menu; you had to first delete the command and then re-create it in the location you prefer. Now, you can move a menu command to another location simply by summoning the Tools⇨Customize command, and then dragging the menu command you want to move to a new location. You can drag a command to a new location on the same menu, or you can drag the command to an entirely different menu.

Using separators

Word's default menus use spacers to group related commands. For example, pull down the File menu and you'll notice several groups of commands: New/Open/Close, Save/Save As/Save As HTML/Versions, Page Setup/Print Preview/Print, and so on. The groups are separated from one another with a horizontal line called a separator, and you can add or remove separators just as you can in a normal toolbar. Simply right-click the command above which you wish to add a separator and choose Begin a Group from the pop-up menu that appears. To remove a separator, right-click the command and choose Begin a Group again.

Adding a new menu

Besides adding commands to existing Word menus, Word lets you add completely new menus to hold custom commands. Some examples of good reasons for adding a new menu include:

- Creating a menu of commands for features you frequently use that are complicated enough to merit a separate menu. Word includes a Table menu by default because the Table feature is complicated. You can easily create a separate menu for similarly complicated features such as tables of contents, indexes, and so on.
- Creating a menu to apply the styles you use most. I do this for my own writing because it is more efficient than wading through the Style list box that's found on the Formatting toolbar.
- Creating a menu to open commonly accessed documents.

You can add your new menu to the standard menu bar or to any other toolbar. To add a new menu, follow these steps:

1. **Call up the Tools⇨Customize command and select the Commands tab.**
2. **Select the template that you want the custom menu added to in the Save Changes In list box.**

   Pick Normal.dot if you want your menu to always be visible, no matter what document is open.
3. **Scroll all the way to the bottom of the Categories list and click on New Menu.**
4. **Drag New Menu from the Commands list to the location on the menu bar or other toolbar where you want the new menu to be added.**

   A new menu named New Menu will be created.
5. **Right-click the new menu and type a name for the menu in the Name field.**

   Use an ampersand to indicate the hot key for the menu; for example, type **& Styles** to create a Styles menu.
6. **Now drag other commands, styles, AutoText entries, or macros from the Customize dialog box onto the new menu.**

Creating Custom Keyboard Shortcuts

Word lets you assign your own keyboard shortcuts to styles, macros, fonts, AutoText entries, commands, and symbols.

Follow these steps to assign a new keyboard shortcut:

1. **Call up the Tools⇨Customize command.**

   The Customize dialog box appears.
2. **Click the Keyboard button.**

   Figure 25-6 shows the options on its Keyboard tab. If these options aren't visible, click the Keyboard tab to bring them into view.
3. **Choose the command, style, macro, font, or other item for which you want to create a keyboard shortcut by using the Categories and Commands lists.**

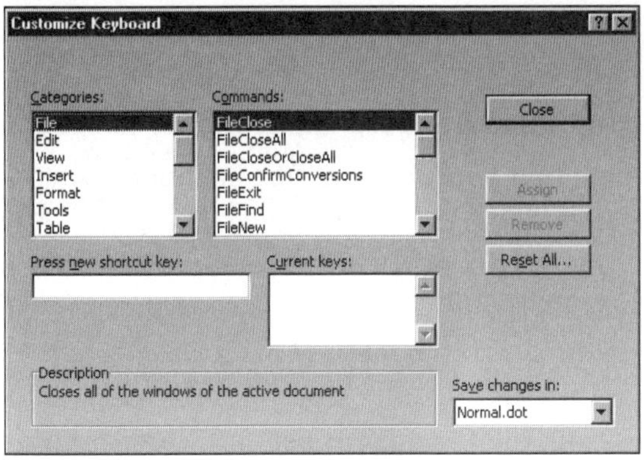

Figure 25-6: Creating custom keyboard shortcuts.

Spend some time exploring these lists. Lots of useful commands are buried amongst a bunch of foreign-looking gobbledygook, such as FileConfirmConversions and TableUpdateAutoFormat.

4. **Click in the Press New Shortcut Key field and then type the new keyboard shortcut.**

   When you type the shortcut, Word lets you know whether the key is already assigned to some other command.

5. **Click Assign to assign the keyboard shortcut. Then choose Close.**

   You're finished! Try the shortcut to see whether it works.

This list presents some key points to remember about keyboard shortcuts:

- You can also assign keyboard shortcuts by choosing Insert⇨Symbol and clicking the Shortcut Key button or choosing Format⇨Style and clicking the Modify button.
- To reset all keyboard shortcuts to their Word defaults, call up the Tools⇨Customize command, choose the Keyboard tab, and click the Reset All button.

Chapter 26

The Magic of Macros

In This Chapter

- Recording a macro
- Running a macro
- Editing a macro

A macro is a sequence of commands or keystrokes that Word records and lets you play back at any time. Macros allow you to create your own customized shortcuts for things you do over and over again. For example, Word comes with built-in keyboard shortcuts to make text bold (Ctrl+B) and to make text italic (Ctrl+I), but no built-in shortcut exists to make text bold and italic all at the same time. To do that, you have to press Ctrl+B and then Ctrl+I. If you do that a million times a day, pretty soon that extra keystroke becomes bothersome. Wouldn't it be nice if you had a shortcut for Bold-Italic? With Word's macro recorder, you can create one.

This chapter shows you how to record and play back simple macros. It doesn't show you how to create complex macros by using Word's macro programming language, Visual Basic for Applications (VBA). That's the subject for an entirely separate, six-pound, 900-page book that comes with a pocket protector and thick glasses stapled to the back cover. I skip that subject entirely.

TECHNICAL STUFF

If your pocket protector is firmly attached, you may want to check out the Microsoft Office Developer Forum at `http//:www.microsoft.com/officedev`. The Microsoft Web site offers tools for assist developers in moving WordPerfect macros to Word 97's new VBA environment.

Where Do All the Macros Go?

In previous versions of Word, macros could only be stored in templates. In Word 97, however, macros can be stored in documents as well as in templates. When you create a macro, you have three choices for where to store the macro:

- The current document
- The template attached to the current document
- The global template called Normal.dot

TIP

When you create a macro, you need to think about when you are going to want to run the macro. If you need to run the macro only from within a specific document, then create the macro in that document. If you want the macro to be available only to documents that are based on a particular template, then create the macro in that template. But if you want the macro to always be available no matter what document you are working on, store the macro in Normal.dot.

Doing the Macro Recorder Dance

Word 97 sports a nifty feature called the *macro recorder,* which is kind of like a videocassette recorder in that after you turn on the macro recorder, it follows you around and makes a precise record of everything you do until you turn the recorder off. Well, not really *everything*. The Word macro recorder records only the stuff you do in Word. It doesn't notice when you dribble coffee down your chin or sneeze on the monitor. But after you turn on the recorder, anything you do in Word — whether it's typing text, applying formatting, calling up a command, or filling out a dialog box — is carefully recorded.

To record a macro, follow these 12 steps:

1. **Try to talk yourself out of it.**

   Fiddling around with macros can be a bit of a time-waster. Ask yourself whether you really will use the macro after you have gone to the trouble of recording it. If not, go directly to Step 12.

2. **Think about what you're going to do.**

   Think through all the steps you have to follow to accomplish whatever task it is you want to automate with a macro. To create a macro that

makes text bold and italic, for example, all you have to do is press Ctrl+B and then press Ctrl+I. That's a pretty simple macro, but other macros can be much more complex, involving dozens of steps. If necessary, rehearse the steps before you record them as a macro.

3. **Call up the Tools➪Macro➪Record New Macro command.**

   The Record Macro dialog box appears, as shown in Figure 26-1.

4. **Type the name of the macro you want to create in the Macro name text box.**

   The name can be anything you want, but it cannot include spaces, commas, or periods. When you first pop up the Record Macro dialog box, the macro name is set to something like Macro1 or Macro2 (or Macro782 if you've been busy). Surely you can come up with a better name than that. (I know, "Yes I can . . . and stop calling me Shirley.")

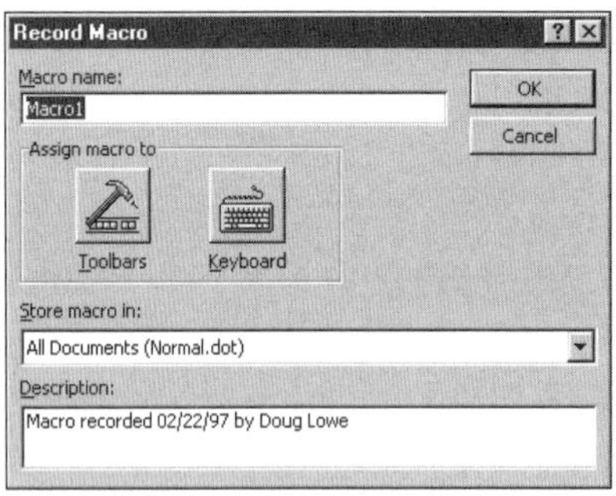

Figure 26-1: The Record Macro dialog box.

5. **Set the Store macro in list box to the location where you want the macro stored.**

   The default setting stores the recorded macro in the Normal.dot template so that it is always available. The other choices available in this drop-down list are storing the macro in the document that you were working on when you called up the macro recorder or storing the macro to the template that document is based on.

6. **To make your macro accessible from a toolbar or the keyboard, click the Toolbars or Keyboard button.**

   This step calls up the Customize dialog box, which is ready to add your macro to a toolbar, menu, or keyboard shortcut. Figure 26-2 shows the Customize Keyboard dialog box that Word displays if you click the Keyboard button. Type the shortcut key combination you want to assign to the macro (in this case, I pressed Ctrl+Shift+B), click the Assign button, and then click the Close button.

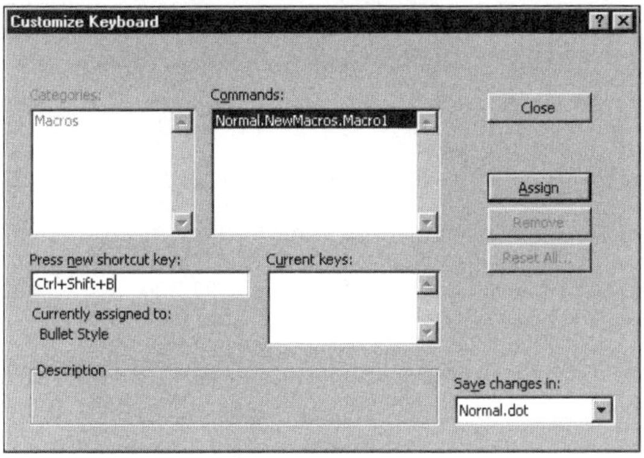

Figure 26-2: The Customize dialog box.

For more information about customizing toolbars, menus, or the keyboard, refer to Chapter 25.

7. **Click OK to begin recording the macro.**

   The Record Macro dialog box disappears, and a little macro recorder toolbar appears, as shown in the margin. You use this toolbar to stop recording the macro.

8. **Type the keystrokes and menu commands you want recorded in the macro.**

   To record the BoldItalic macro, for example, press Ctrl+B and then press Ctrl+I.

   For more-complicated macros, you may have to access menu commands. You can do that by using either the keyboard or the mouse.

9. **If you have to stop recording temporarily, click the Pause button. Click it again to resume recording.**

   You may forget how to do something, for example, especially if you skipped Step 2. If you click the Pause button, you can call up the Word Help command, look up the procedure for whatever it is you forgot, dismiss Help, and click the Pause button again to resume recording.

10. **After you finish recording the macro, click the Stop button.**

    Word adds the macro to the template or document. You're almost done.

11. **Test the macro.**

    If you assigned the macro to a keyboard shortcut, use the shortcut now to see whether the macro works. Otherwise, follow the procedure in the section "Running a macro."

12. You're finished.

Congratulate yourself.

If the function of the macro isn't obvious from the macro name, type a more elaborate description of the macro in the Record Macro dialog box's Description field. You'll thank yourself later when you forget what the macro does.

Macro Recording Tips

Here are some tips to keep in mind as you record macros:

- You can call up the Record Macro dialog box directly by double-clicking the word REC on the status bar at the bottom of the screen. Double-clicking REC saves you from wading through the Tools menu and the Macro dialog box.
- If the macro doesn't work, you may have made a mistake while recording it. If the macro is short enough, the best thing to do is to record the macro again. If the macro is long and you don't have anything important to do, try editing the macro to expunge the problem. See the section "Editing a Macro" later in this chapter.
- Macros are normally stored in the global normal.dot template. To store a macro in the template attached to the current document, change the setting of the Record Macro dialog box's Store macro in.
- Do not make any assumptions about where the insertion point will be when you run the macro. If necessary, begin the macro with a positioning command by moving the insertion point to the beginning of the document, the beginning of the line, or the beginning of a word. (Not all macros require a positioning command. But if your macro depends in any way on the position of the insertion point, this step is a must.)
- Do not use the mouse to select text or navigate through the document. Word does not record these mouse actions. You can use the mouse to select menu commands or to click toolbar buttons.
- Use Ctrl+Home or Ctrl+End to move to the beginning or end of a document. Do not use repeated PageUp or PageDown keys for this purpose. Three PageUps may get you to the top of your document when you record the macro, but when you run the macro, it may not. Similarly, use Home and End, rather than the left or right arrow keys, to move to the start or end of a line.

- If you use the Find or Replace commands, be sure to move to the beginning of the document first.
- Avoid any commands that depend on the contents of document that is active when you record the macro.

Running a Macro

If you assigned a macro to a toolbar, menu, or keyboard shortcut, you can run the macro by clicking the toolbar button, choosing the menu command, or pressing the keyboard shortcut. If you did not, you can run it by following these steps:

1. **Choose the Tools⇨Macro⇨Macros command to summon the Macros dialog box, shown in Figure 26-3. (As a shortcut, you can press Alt+F8.)**
2. **If the macro you want to run isn't already selected, select it now. If the macro you want doesn't appear, try changing the Macros in setting. The macro may be in a different template.**
3. **Click Run.**

I hate to tell you about unexpected side effects

Sometimes a macro has unexpected side effects. Suppose that rather than record the keystrokes Ctrl+B and Ctrl+I for the BoldItalic macro, you decide to record these steps instead:

1. Call up the Format⇨Font command.
2. Choose Bold Italic as the Font Style.
3. Click OK.

The macro seems to work, but sooner or later, you discover that in addition to recording the Bold Italic font style, the macro recorded other character attributes — such as font, size, and effects. If the text to which you applied the Format⇨Font command when you recorded the macro used the Times New Roman font, any text you apply the macro to is switched to Times New Roman.

You can avoid these side effects in two ways:

- Avoid recording dialog boxes in macros whenever a keyboard shortcut or toolbar button can do the trick. Whenever you record a dialog box in a macro, you record all the dialog box's settings.
- Fix the macro later by editing it and removing the extraneous information. See the section "Editing a Macro" later in this chapter.

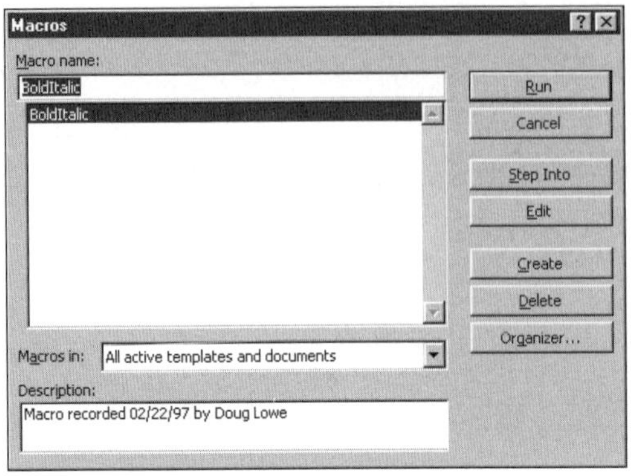

Figure 26-3: The Macros dialog box.

Editing a Macro

If you make a mistake while recording a macro, you can abandon the recording and start over. Or, you can finish the recording and edit the macro to correct the mistake. When you edit the macro, the macro's commands appear in a separate window. You can delete or modify erroneous commands, you can insert new commands if you know how, or you can merely study the macro to try to figure out how it works.

When you edit a macro, you are exposed to Visual Basic for Applications. VBA is not as deadly as the Ebola virus, but it can cause severe headaches and nausea.

Here is the procedure for editing a macro:

1. **Choose the Tools⇨Macro⇨Macros command.**

   The Macro dialog box appears.

2. **Select the macro you want to edit and click the Edit button.**

   Word launches the Visual Basic Editor, with the macro you selected visible in its own window. See Figure 26-4.

3. **Make whatever changes are necessary to the macro.**

   Correct misspelled words, delete extraneous commands, and, if you're brave, add additional commands.

4. **Use the File⇨Save Template command to save your changes.**

5. **Use the File⇨Close command to close the macro window.**

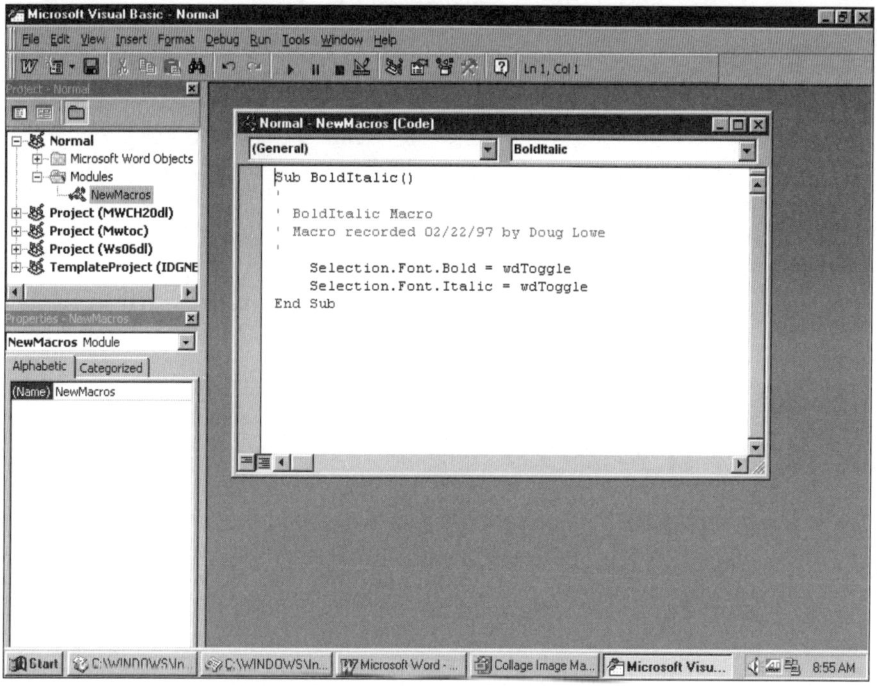

Figure 26-4: Editing a macro.

Simple Macro Edits That Don't Require a Ph.D. in VBA

Before you make massive changes to a macro, you need a pretty good knowledge of VBA. However, you can make certain types of changes without knowing much about VBA at all. Here is a sampling:

- Correct spelling errors. If you inserted text into a document and misspelled it, don't hesitate to edit the macro to correct the misspellings. Text you insert into a document while recording a macro is included in a Selection.TypeText command, like this:

  ```
  Selection.TypeText Text:= This is some simple text.
  ```

  You can correct any spelling mistakes or change the inserted text altogether, provided you take care not to remove either of the quotation marks that appear before and after the text. For example, you could correct the above line to:

  ```
  Selection.TypeText Text:= This is some sample text.
  ```

- Remove extraneous commands. If you inadvertently used a command while recording a macro, you can clean up your macro by removing the unnecessary command.
- Remove unwanted dialog box settings. If you record a dialog box in a macro, Word includes every setting in the dialog box. You can remove the settings that you do not want the macro to change. For example, if you use the Format➪Font command to set the text color to red, Word inserts the following commands into the macro:

```
With Selection.Font
   .Name =  Times New Roman
   .Size = 10
   .Bold = False
   .Italic = False
   .Underline = wdUnderlineNone
   .StrikeThrough = False
   .DoubleStrikeThrough = False
   .Outline = False
   .Emboss = False
   .Shadow = False
   .Hidden = False
   .SmallCaps = False
   .AllCaps = False
   .ColorIndex = wdRed
   .Engrave = False
   .Superscript = False
   .Subscript = False
   .Spacing = 0
   .Scaling = 100
   .Position = 0
   .Kerning = 0
   .Animation = wdAnimationNone
End With
```

  This command looks complicated at first, but if you study it, you see that it is little more than a list of all the dialog box controls that appear on the Format➪Font command's dialog box. The periods look strange appearing in front of each command argument as they do, but they are required. You can safely delete the command arguments that represent dialog box controls you don't want to use so that the resulting command looks like this:

```
With Selection.Font
.ColorIndex = wdRed
End With
```

(Actually, with a little more VBA knowledge, you can also remove the With and End With command, and substitute just the following:

```
Selection.Font.ColorIndex = wdRed
```

Using the Macros That Come with Word

When you install Word for Windows, two templates are installed in the \Program Files\Microsoft Office\Office\Macros folder: Macros8.dot and Support8.dot. These templates contain a collection of useful macros for various functions. To use these macros, use the Tools➪Templates and Add-Ins command to load the template as a global template. Then run the macro via the Tools➪Macro➪Macros command. Alternatively, you can assign a keyboard shortcut, toolbar button, or menu command for the macros you use most.

The following sections describe the macros supplied with each of the templates.

Macros in the Macros8.dot template

The Macros8.dot template contains several macros you may find useful in certain circumstances. In addition to the following macros, Macros8.dot contains a Sample Macros toolbar that you can use to start the macros. After Macro8.dot is loaded as a global template, you can activate the Sample Macros toolbar via the View➪Toolbars command or run the macros directly from the Tools➪Macro➪Macros command.

- **AnsiValue:** The AnsiValue displays the ANSI code value of any selected character. (If you don't know what *ANSI code value* means, don't worry. That's a sure sign you don't need this macro.) To use the AnsiValue macro, first select a character in your document. Then run the AnsiValue macro. A simple dialog box appears, showing you the ANSI value of the selected character.
- **AutoCorrectUtility:** This macro creates a backup copy of the active document's AutoCorrect entries in a file called AutoCorrect Backup.doc. When you run the AutoCorrectUtility macro, the dialog box, shown in Figure 26-5, is displayed. From this dialog box, you can click the Backup button to back up the current document's AutoCorrect entries. Then you can open a different document, run the macro again, and click the Restore button to copy the previously backed-up AutoCorrect entries into the current document.

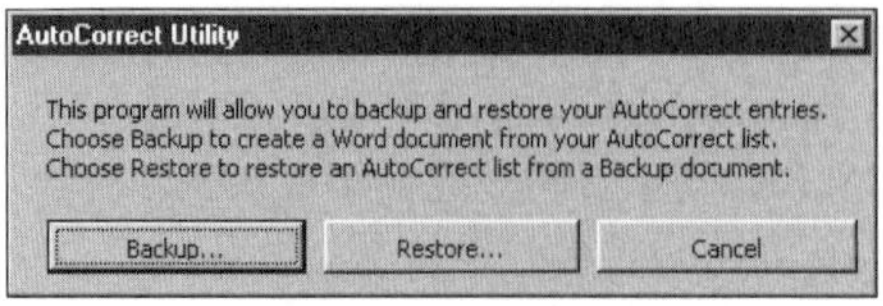

Figure 26-5: The AutoCorrect Utility dialog box.

- **CopySpike:** This macro is actually a series of four related macros that lets you manipulate the contents of the Spike. The Spike is similar to the clipboard except that it allows you to accumulate information that can be later copied or pasted into your document. I describe the Spike in greater detail in Chapter 1.
- **FindSymbol:** FindSymbol allows you to search for and replace symbols that were inserted with the Insert⇨Symbol command. FindSymbol displays the dialog box shown in Figure 26-6. To specify the symbol to find, click the first Symbol button (in the Find What section). This brings up Word's standard Symbol dialog box, the same dialog box that Word displays when you use the Insert⇨Symbol command. To replace one symbol with another, click the second Symbol button (in the Replace With section) and select the replacement symbol. You can use the Entire Document or the Selection options to indicate whether you want the entire document to be searched or just the current selection.

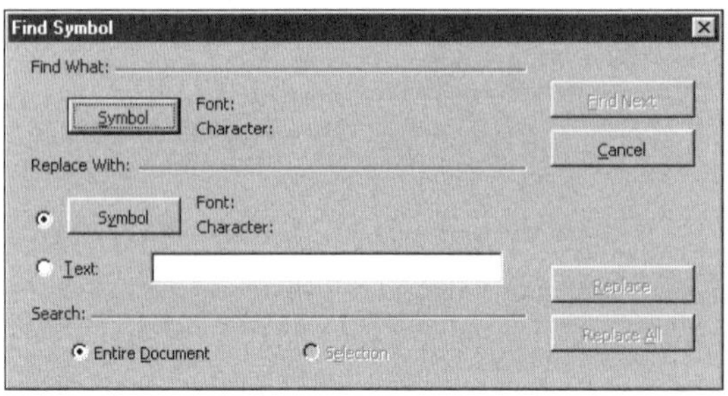

Figure 26-6: The Find Symbol dialog box.

- **InsertFootnote:** This macro is actually the Footnote Wizard, which automatically creates various types of footnotes formatted according to popular style manuals. The wizard asks for pertinent information and inserts a properly formatted footnote. Figure 26-7 shows the Footnote Wizard in action.

Figure 26-7: The Footnote Wizard.

- **NormalViewHeaderFooter:** This macro allows you edit headers and footers similar to the way you could in Word 2, in a separate pane in Normal view. I don't recommend it unless you are thoroughly entrenched in the Word 2 way of dealing with headers and footers.
- **SuperDocStatistics:** This macro displays just about every item of information about a document that you can imagine in a single dialog box, as shown in Figure 26-8. You can click on the various tabs at the top of the dialog box to access different types of information about the document. You can also create a report that lists the document information.

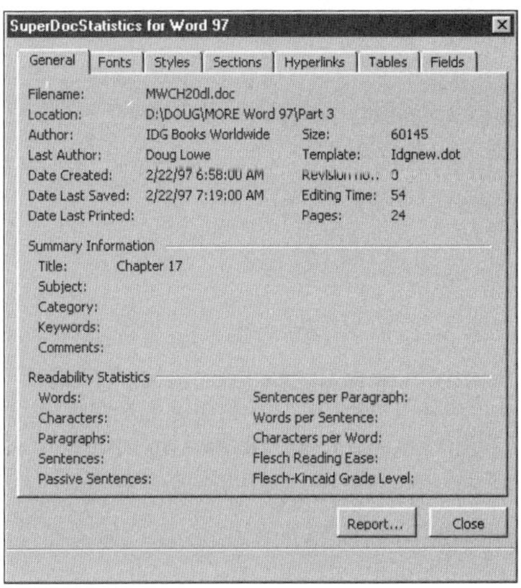

Figure 26-8: The SuperDoc Statistics dialog box.

- **TableCellHelper:** The TableCellHelper displays the table cell column and row for the current cell or range of cells. For example, if you place the insertion point in the first column of the first row of a table, then call up TableCellHelper, Word displays the dialog box, shown in Figure 26-9. As you can see, this dialog box gives you the cell address of the current cell (in this case, A:1) and tells you how many rows and columns are in the table.

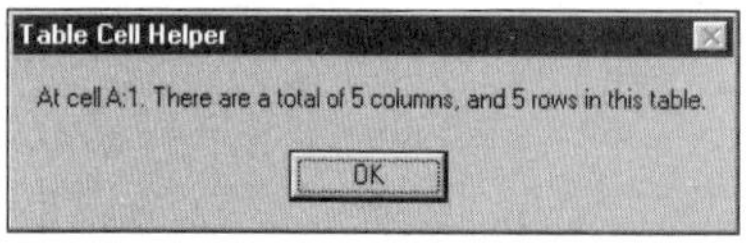

Figure 26-9: The Table Cell Helper dialog box.

Macros in the Support8.dot template

The Support8.dot template contains two macros that can be useful when solving Word problems. If you call up Microsoft for help with a Word problem, don't be surprised if (after waiting on hold for 45 minutes) the technician tells you to run one of these two macros:

- **RegOptions:** This macro provides a convenient way to change Word options. Most of the options that RegOptions lets you change can also be changed from the Tools⇨Options command, but the RegOptions macro gives you access to some options that aren't otherwise available.
- **PrintFlags**: If your printer throws up whenever you try to print a complex document, such as one that has a bunch of graphic objects with peculiar combinations of format settings, this macro may be able to help diagnose the problem.

A Few Easy but Useful Macros

Here are ten (well, five, but who's counting?) moderately easy but often useful macros you can create yourself. Although you can create most of these macros by recording keystrokes, I decided to spice things up a little and let you type the macro commands directly into Visual Basic for Applications. You don't have to invest in a pointy cap or a pocket protector to do this; just follow the bouncing ball, and all should go well.

Follow these steps to create each macro:

1. **Call up the Tools⇨Macro⇨Macros command.**

   The Macros dialog box appears.

2. **Type the name of the macro you want to create.**

   A suggested name is provided for each of the macros, but you can use any name you want.

3. **Click Create.**

   You are sent to the VBA editing window, with a macro containing just a few lines, such as:

```
Sub PrintCurrentPage()

  PrintCurrentPage Macro
  Macro created 02/22/97 by Doug Lowe

End Sub
```

4. **Type the text of the macro between the comments that follow the Sub line and the End Sub line.**

   The four lines that follow the Sub line, which begin with apostrophes, are comments that indicate the name of the macro and when it was created. Type the text for the macro, which is provided along with the macro description in the following sections, immediately after the last of these four commands and before the End Sub line.

5. **Return to Word to run the macro.**

   Many of the macros cannot be run while the VBA window is active. To return to Word, click the Word button in the Task Bar (normally located at the bottom of the screen), or press Alt+Tab.

6. **Run the macro by calling up the Tools⇨Macro⇨Macros command, by choosing the macro, and by clicking Run.**

7. **If you like the macro, use the Tools⇨Customize command to assign a keyboard shortcut to the macro.**

The following sections provide a brief description of each macro along with the text to type between the Sub and End Sub lines. For the macros you can easily record from keystrokes, I include a step-by-step procedure for recording the macro.

PrintCurrentPage

Word places a Print button on the Standard toolbar for printing an entire document, but I frequently want to print just the current page. Rather than go through the Print dialog box, I've created a PrintCurrentPage macro and assigned a toolbar button to it, right next to the Print button on the Standard toolbar. The PrintCurrentPage macro is simple, but I use it all the time.

To create this macro, call up the Tools➪Macro command, click Create, and type the following line between the `Sub MAIN` and `End Sub` lines:

```
Application.PrintOut Range:=wdPrintCurrentPage
```

To create this macro by recording it, double-click the REC indicator on the status bar, type the macro name, and follow these steps:

1. **Call up the File➪Print command.**
2. **Click Current Page.**
3. **Click OK.**
4. **Click the Stop recording button.**

SwapWords

The SwapWords macro provides a quick way to, you guessed it, swap words. It works by selecting the word, cutting it to the Clipboard, moving the cursor one word to the left, and then pasting the Clipboard contents to the new location. To use the macro, first place the cursor in the word you want moved in front of the preceding word. In other words, place the cursor in the second of the two words you want to transpose.

To create the SwapWords macro, call up the Tools➪Macro command, click Create, and type the following lines between the `Sub MAIN` and `End Sub` lines:

```
With Selection
   .Extend
   .Extend
   .Cut
   .MoveLeft Unit:=wdWord, Count:=1
   .Paste
End With
```

If you prefer to record this macro, start recording and then follow these steps:

1. **Press F8.**
2. **Press F8 again to select the current word.**
3. **Press Ctrl+X to cut the selection.**
4. **Press Ctrl+left arrow to move the cursor back one word.**
5. **Press Ctrl+V to paste the Clipboard contents.**

SwapSentences

This macro resembles the SwapWords macro, but it swaps entire sentences. Like SwapWords, it works by selecting an entire sentence, cutting it to the Clipboard, moving the cursor to a point in front of the preceding sentence, and pasting from the Clipboard. To use this macro, first place the cursor somewhere in the second of the two sentences you want to transpose.

To create the SwapSentences macro, call up the Tools➪Macro command, click Create, and type the following lines between the `Sub MAIN` and `End Sub` lines:

```
With Selection
   .Extend
   .Extend
   .Extend
   .Cut
   .MoveLeft Unit:=wdWord, Count:=1
   .Extend
   .Extend
   .Extend
   .EscapeKey
   .MoveLeft Unit:=wdCharacter, Count:=1
   .Paste
End With
```

If you prefer to record this macro, start recording and then follow these steps:

1. **Press F8.**
2. **Press F8 again to select the current word.**

3. **Press F8 a third time to select the entire sentence.**
4. **Press Ctrl+X to cut the selection.**
5. **Press Ctrl+left arrow to move the cursor back one word.**
6. **Press F8 three times to select the sentence.**
7. **Press Escape to deactivate the Extend mode.**
8. **Press the left-arrow key to move the cursor to the left of the sentence.**
9. **Press Ctrl+V to paste the Clipboard contents.**

ShowToolbars

If you want to work with an uncluttered window to see as much text as possible but be able to quickly call up your favorite toolbars, try this macro. It alternately shows and hides the Standard toolbar and the Formatting toolbar. You may want to customize it to show and hide other toolbars also.

To create the ShowToolbars macro, call up the Tools⇨Macro command, click Create, and type the following lines between the `Sub MAIN` and `End Sub` lines:

```
CommandBars( Standard ).Visible = Not
          CommandBars( Standard ).Visible
CommandBars( Formatting ).Visible = Not
          CommandBars( Formatting ).Visible
```

Because this macro involves programming commands, you can't record it from keystrokes. The only way to create it is to type these commands.

UnJumbler

Word's built-in spelling checker has the nifty ability of taking a collection of jumbled-up letters and putting them back in the right order. For example, give it the letters **rmtoucpe**, and it spews forth *computer*. Give it **dnre**, and it emits *nerd* and *rend*.

Unfortunately, Microsoft decided that the people who publish those Jumble puzzles in newspapers may sue them if they made this feature available to just anybody, so they hid it deep within the bowels of Word, where only the high priests of Visual Basic for Applications dwell. To use the Jumble feature, you have to write a macro.

To create the Unjumbler macro, call up the Tools⇨Macro⇨Macros command, type Unjumbler for the macro name, click Create, and type the following lines for the macro:

```
JumbledWord = InputBox( Enter the word to be unjumbled: ,
            Unjumbler )
Set sugList = GetSpellingSuggestions(Word:=JumbledWord, _
  SuggestionMode:=wdAnagram)
If sugList.Count = 0 Then
  MsgBox  No suggestions.
Else
  For Each sug In sugList
    Response = MsgBox(sug.Name, vbOKOnly,  Unjumbler )
  Next sug
End If
```

When you run the UnJumbler macro, a dialog box appears asking you to type in the jumbled word. Then, one or more dialog boxes appear showing the resulting unjumbled word or words.

Note: The UnJumbler can't deal with multiple words. If you type two or more words in the Word to UnJumble field, the UnJumbler ignores them. And you're on your own if the letters represent two or more scrambled-up words.

TIP

Try the UnJumbler on Scrabble puzzles, too. It only works when there is a solution that uses all seven letters, which occurs quite frequently. I tried it on this morning's puzzle, with the following results:

l-e-t-a-y-h-h (second letter double)	healthy (17 points)
b-d-r-e-m-a-l (triple word score)	marbled or rambled (36 points)
g-v-s-n-i-k-i	Vikings or skiving (15 points)
e-a-n-r-d-t-g	granted or dragnet (9 points)

With a 50 point bonus for each seven-letter word, that's a score of 277. Not bad for someone whose editor says he doesn't no how to spel.

You can get the Unjumbler to find six-letter words from a seven-letter Scrabble rack with a little work. Type in just six of the seven letters and click the UnJumble Button. Try it seven times, leaving out a different letter each time, to find the best word.

Chapter 27

Watch Out for Macro Viruses!

In This Chapter

- What a document virus is
- Using the Word 97 Disable Macros feature
- Using better macro-virus protection software

Word allows you to use a special type of macro, called an AutoOpen macro, which is run automatically whenever you open a document that contains the macro. Although AutoOpen macros can be useful in some situations, they can be dangerous in others. In particular, some low-life computer hackers have figured out that AutoOpen macros are a great way to spread computer viruses. All they have to do is create an AutoOpen macro that contains the instructions necessary to *infect* other documents — that is, to copy the AutoOpen macro itself into other documents. In fact, the programming required to create such a virus is pretty trivial. Any competent programmer can create such a virus in a matter of hours. Viruses of this sort are called *macro viruses.*

The first macro virus appears shortly after Microsoft released Word 7 for Windows 95. It was called Concept, because it appeared to be an attempt to prove that macro viruses could be created and spread. Sure enough, it worked. The Concept viruses spread to thousands of computers. In fact, I was working on a book for IDG Books at the time and inadvertently infected IDG's editorial offices when I uploaded an infected document to my editor.

The Concept virus works by infecting your Normal.dot template with a macro that replaces the built-in File⇨Save As command. Then, any document that you subsequently save is infected with the virus — this means that other systems can be infected. As a result, the Concept virus can be spread merely by sharing Word documents. If you save a Word document and then pass the document to a friend, whether over a network or via diskettes, your friend's system is infected when he or she opens the document. The old adage that viruses can only be transmitted via executable programs no longer applies.

Fortunately, the Concept virus is pretty benign. It does manage to convert your document files to template format, which is definitely a major inconvenience. But other than that, it doesn't do any real damage to your computer. Apparently, the Concept virus was created just to prove the point that a virus could be spread in this way.

Unfortunately, in the year and a half since the Concept virus emerged — the first macro virus — hundreds of other macro viruses have been discovered. Some of these macro viruses aren't so benign. One, called MDMA, erases all of the Help files in your Windows folder so that the Help command no longer works. Another, called Nuclear, is a variant of the Concept that attempts to destroy your hard drive's data. The newest macro virus (at the time I wrote this) is called ShareFun. The ShareFun virus has figured out a way to automatically e-mail itself to three names chosen at random from your address book.

Disabling Macros

Unfortunately, Word 97 does not have a built-in virus checking feature. However, it does have a feature that allows you to disable macros in documents that you open. The disabling feature effectively prevents most macro viruses from infecting your computer or spreading to other documents. When you disable macros, *all* macros are disabled — not just the ones that contain viruses.

Whenever you open a document that contains macros, Word 97 displays the Warning dialog box, shown in Figure 27-1. The Warning dialog box gives you three options for dealing with documents that contain macros:

- **Disable Macros:** Click this button to disable any macros contained in the document. If you download a document from the Internet or a buddy sends you a document and the Warning dialog box appears, I suggest that you click the Disable macros. Most documents have no business carrying macros, so when you open a document that contains macros and you get the Warning dialog box, there's a distinct possibility that the document is carrying a macro virus.
- **Enable Macros:** Click this button only if you were expecting the document to contain macros.
- **Do Not Open**: Click this button to cancel the Open command altogether.

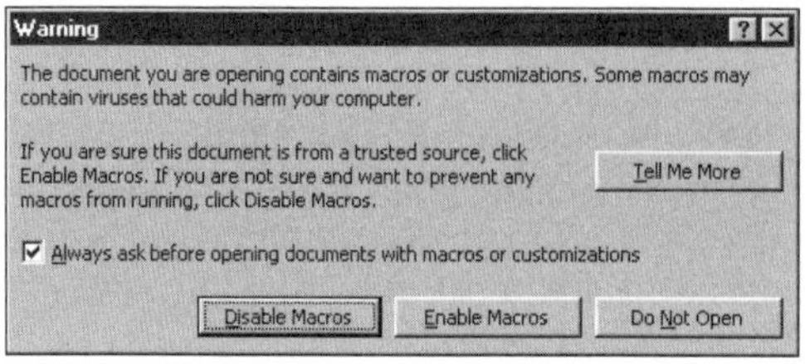

Figure 27-1: The Warning dialog box warns you about possible macro trouble.

The Word 97 macro warning feature is good enough to prevent macro-virus infections for users who never use macros. If you've never used a macro and never intend to, I suggest that you always click the Disable Macros button whenever the Warning dialog box appears.

On the other hand, if you frequently use documents that contain macros, or if you like to play with macros yourself, the macro Warning dialog box quickly becomes an annoyance. Because the Disable Macros feature doesn't discriminate between good macros and bad macros, you have to click the Enable Macros button just about every time the Warning dialog box appears.

WARNING! I cannot stress enough that the macro Warning dialog box is *not* a very effective form of virus protection. If you need to use macros at all, you will probably find yourself clicking the Enable Macros button so often that you'll fall into the habit of clicking it automatically. Sooner or later, you'll click it when you shouldn't have — for a document you weren't expecting to contain macros.

Better Macro-Virus Protection

If you frequently use macros and if you often download documents from the Internet or exchange documents with other computer users, consider purchasing a more effective macro-virus protection utility.

Antivirus software can do more than ban all macros. It can analyze the macros contained in a document to determine if the document has been infected by any of the more than 200 known macro viruses. And, if the antivirus program detects a virus infection, it can remove the virus from the infected documents.

Here are two of the best-known antivirus programs that feature protection from macro viruses in Office 97:

- **Macafee VirusScan95 3.0:** Many computer virus experts consider Macafee to be the best antivirus program available. Its latest version, 3.0, can check for macro viruses in Office 97 documents. For more information about Macafee and to download an evaluation copy of VirusScan95 3.0, check out their Web site on the Internet at `http://www.macafee.com`.
- **Symantec's Norton AntiVirus:** The popular Norton AntiVirus from Symantec recently added support for macro viruses in Office 97 documents. Check out their Web site at `http://www.symantec.com`.

Note that older versions of the preceding antivirus programs, and many other older antivirus programs, cannot detect macro viruses in Office 97 documents. So make sure you get an antivirus program that is specifically designed with Office 97 in mind.

The trick to using antivirus software is to periodically download updates so that the antivirus software can detect and remove the latest viruses. New viruses are discovered every day, so frequently download antivirus updates. Both Macafee and Symantec allow you to download updates free of charge from their Web sites.

Chapter 28

A Bunch of Tips and Shortcuts

In This Chapter

- Having fun with the Assistant
- Setting file properties
- Making Word start all by itself
- Using Word's start-up switches
- Using Word as an e-mail editor
- Using the AutoSummarize feature (or, better yet, *not* using it)
- Using the right mouse button
- Double-clicking in cool places

Like any good mechanic, I always end up with a few parts left over when I finish a project. I thought I was done with this book, but when I swept off my desk, I found a few gems I just couldn't bear to throw away. Thus this chapter was born.

What's with the Paper Clip?

Edison had Watson, Batman had Robin, and Dr. Frankenstein had Igor. Everybody needs an Assistant, and Office users are no exception. That's why Microsoft decided to add a new feature called the *Office Assistant* to Word 97 — and to all the other Office 97 programs.

The Office Assistant is an animated persona who inhabits a small window that periodically comes to view. You can ask the Office Assistant a question when you're not sure what to do, and the Assistant thoroughly searches Word's huge online help database to provide the answer. The Office Assistant will appear whenever you click the Office Assistant button in the Standard toolbar (shown in the margin). The Office Assistant also pops up on its own once in a while, reminding you to save your file before quitting Word or to offer some helpful advice when it thinks you are doing something inefficiently.

When you first start up Word, the Office Assistant appears in its own little Window, as shown in Figure 28-1. The Office Assistant resembles a paper clip. As it turns out, the paper clip — named Clipit — is one of nine Assistants that you can choose from. See the section "Changing Assistants" later in the chapter for instructions on how to switch to a different Assistant.

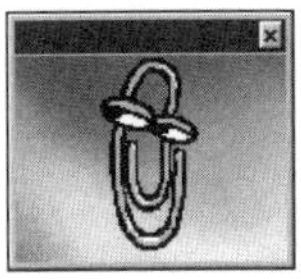

Figure 28-1: Your ever-faithful sidekick, Clipit.

The fun thing about the Assistant is that it's animated. Watch the Assistant on-screen as you work. Every once in a while it blinks, and on occasion it dances or makes a face. The Assistant often responds to commands that you choose in Word. For example, if you call up the Find command (Edit⇨Find or Ctrl+F), the Assistant makes a gesture as if it is searching for something. And when you print your document, the Assistant twists itself into something that looks like a printer.

Microsoft went to a lot of trouble to make sure that the Assistant is entertaining, and the results are sometimes amusing. In fact, you can amuse yourself all day long by forcing the Assistant to perform tricks for you. Just right-click the Assistant window and choose the Animate command that appears in the pop-up menu, and the Assistant performs a different trick.

Summoning the Assistant

You can summon the Assistant in several ways when you need help. In many cases, the Assistant is already on the screen, so all you need to do to get its attention is click in the Assistant window. A balloon dialog box, shown in Figure 28-2, pops up so that you can ask a question.

If the Assistant is not visible on the screen, you can summon it quickly by using one of the following three methods:

- Choose the Help⇨Microsoft Word Help command from the menu.
- Press F1, the magic Help key.
-  Click the Office Assistant button in the Standard toolbar.

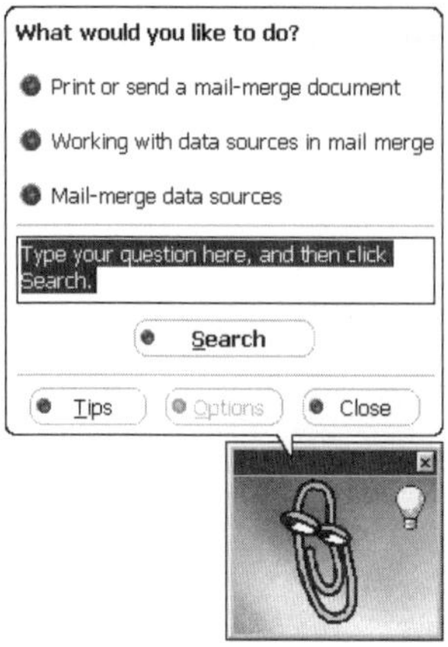

Figure 28-2: Clipit only wants to help.

When you summon the Assistant while working with Word, the Assistant tries to figure out what help you need based on what you were doing at the time you called upon the Assistant. For example, I had just called up the Mail Merge dialog box before I created Figure 28-2. That's why Clipit is suggesting help topics that pertain to mail merge.

If you're lucky enough that one of the topics listed in the Assistant's balloon dialog box is exactly what you're looking for, click the topic and help is displayed. Otherwise, type a question in the balloon dialog box and click Search. The Assistant then displays a list of help topics related to your question.

TIP: You don't really have to type a full question, such as "How do I create a mail merge letter?" Instead, you can just type one or two key words that lead to the information you're interested in. For example, "Mail merge letter" lists the same help topics as "How do I create a mail merge letter?"

Changing Assistants

Clipit, the friendly and helpful paper clip Assistant, is only one of nine Assistants that you can choose from. To select a different Assistant, summon the Assistant by clicking the Office Assistant button or by pressing F1. Then click the Options button to display the Office Assistant dialog box. Click the Gallery tab located at the top of the Assistant dialog box. The Assistant Gallery appears, as shown in Figure 28-3.

To change to a different Assistant, click the Next button. Keep clicking the Next button to work your way through all of the Assistants; when you find the one you want to use, click OK.

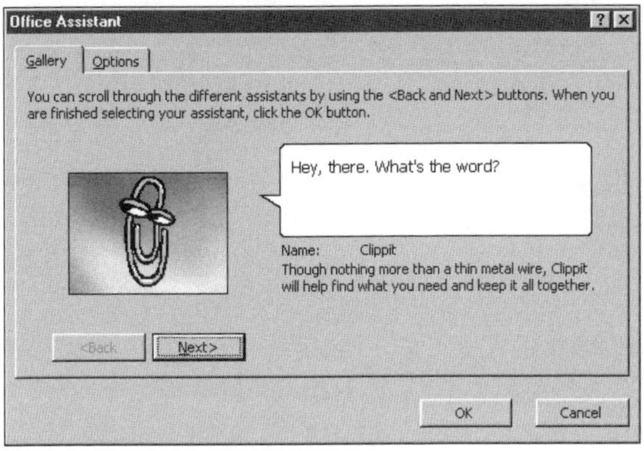

Figure 28-3: Changing Assistants with the Assistant Gallery.

TIP

After you have clicked the Next button once, you can use the Back button to move backwards through the list of Assistants.

In all, you have nine Assistants to choose from. These Assistants differ only in appearance, not in their ability to offer assistance with using Word's features. The nine Assistants are pictured in Table 28-1.

Table 28-1 Assistants That Come with Word 97

Name	*What It Looks Like*	*Description*
Clipit		Clipit is a little twisted metal wire that can contort itself into all sorts of interesting shapes and sizes.
The Dot		The Dot is a little bouncy fellow whose face was invented by Forrest Gump.
The Genius		The Genius can explain everything from the Space Time Continuum to how to add a gradient fill to a drawing object.
Hoverbot		Hoverbot floats in now and then. It reminds me of that *Star Trek* episode where a hovering robot creature named Nomad tried to destroy the Enterprise.

Name	What It Looks Like	Description
Office Logo		Office Logo is the Assistant preferred by three out of four Microsoft marketing vice presidents surveyed.
Mother Nature		Mother Nature is Al Gore's favorite Assistant.
Power Pup		Power Pup has all the qualities of a fine dog, and you don't have to clean up after it.
Scribble		I tawt I taw a putty tat!
Will		Thou didst, thou didst tee a putty tat.

Setting Assistant Options

The Assistant can be configured with several options that alter the way it works. To change these options, summon the Assistant and click the Options button to summon the dialog box shown in Figure 28-4. Change whatever options you want to change, and then click OK.

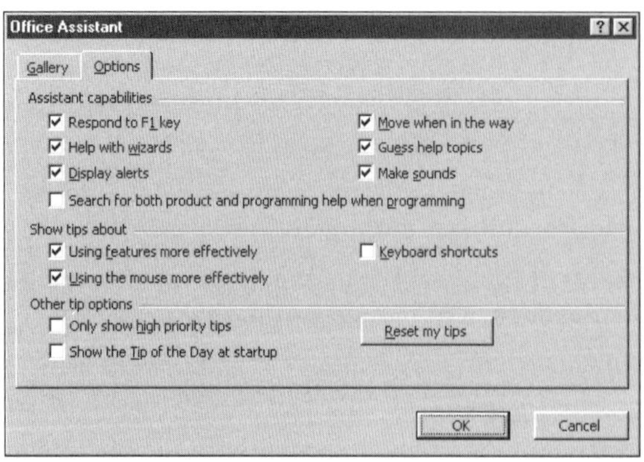

Figure 28-4: Office Assistant's options.

The following paragraphs describe each of the Office Assistant options:

- **Respond to F1 key:** Summons the Office Assistant whenever you press F1.
- **Help with wizards:** Activates the Office Assistant whenever you use a Wizard.
- **Display alerts:** Uses the Assistant to display warnings about saving your file before exiting Word and so on.
- **Move when in the way:** Automatically moves the Assistant dialog box whenever it obscures what you're working on.
- **Guess help topics:** Attempts to guess what topics you need help with.
- **Make sounds:** If you want the Assistant to make noises to get your attention, select this option.
- **Search for both product and programming help when programming:** If you're a programmer, check this option. Otherwise leave it blank.
- **Show tips about:** Offers three categories of tips that Assistant can provide: using features, using the mouse, and using keyboard shortcuts.
- **Other tip options:** Offers two additional options for working with tips: showing only high priority tips, so that minor tips don't appear, and showing a Tip of the Day automatically when you start Word.

Setting File Properties

The File⇨Properties command lets you record information about a document, including the document's title, subject, author, keywords, and comments. Just the type of information that can come in handy down the road when you forget why you created the document.

Figure 28-5 shows the dialog box that appears when you call up the File⇨Properties command. This dialog box groups information about the document under the following tabs:

- **General:** Displays the Windows 95 file properties for the document file (the filename, type, creation date, size in bytes, attributes, and so on).
- **Summary:** Shows summary information about the document, such as the document's title, subject, author, and so on.
- **Statistics:** Includes statistical information, such as the number of characters, words, lines, and paragraphs in the document.
- **Contents**: Displays, as you may expect, the contents of the document.
- **Custom:** Enables you to add any information to the document that you wish.

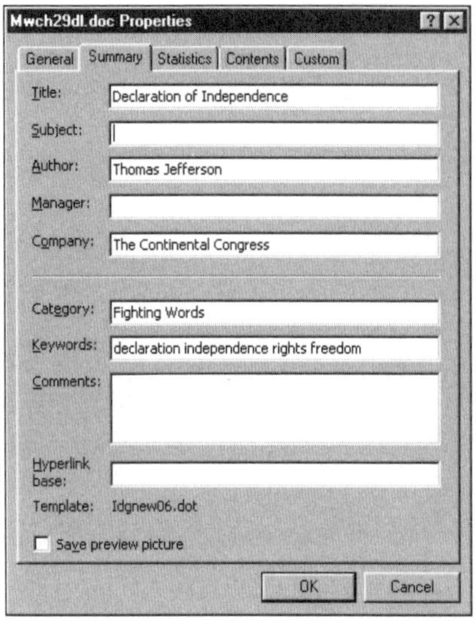

Figure 28-5: The File➪Properties command records useful information about your documents.

Making Word Start All by Itself

If you use Word every day, you're probably bored by now with performing the menial task of clicking on the Start button, pointing to the Program menu, and clicking on the Microsoft Word icon. Wouldn't it be nice if Word would just start all by itself whenever you turn on your computer? Yes, it would, and yes, you can set up Word to do just that. In fact, it's a pretty easy trick. All you have to do is add a shortcut to Word through a special folder called the StartUp folder. (Pocket protectors are not required.)

Follow these easy steps to make Word start automatically whenever you start or restart your computer:

1. **Click on the Start button and point to the Settings command. When the menu appears, click Taskbar.**

   The Taskbar Properties dialog box appears.

2. **Click the Start Menu Programs tab in the Taskbar Properties dialog box.**

   The Taskbar Properties dialog box changes to show controls that let you configure the Start Menu. See Figure 28-6.

3. **Click on the Add button.**

   The Create Shortcut dialog box appears.

4. **Click on Browse.**

   The Browse dialog box appears, which resembles a standard Open dialog box.

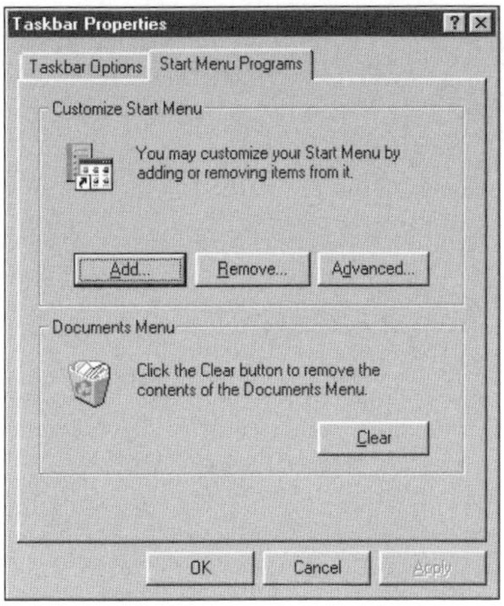

Figure 28-6: Configuring the Start menu.

5. **Locate the Microsoft Word program file in the \Program Files\Microsoft Office folder and double-click it.**
6. **When the Create Shortcut window reappears, click Next.**

   A list of the folders and programs that are already in the Start⇨Programs menu appears.
7. **Double-click the StartUp folder.**

   You may have to scroll down the list to find it. The list is presented in alphabetical order.
8. **Click on Finish and then click on OK to close the Taskbar Properties window.**

You're done! The next time you start your computer, Word will load automatically.

If you decide you no longer want Word to start automatically, you can delete Word from the StartUp folder. Repeat the first two steps of the preceding procedure, but then click Remove instead of Add. A list of programs and folders in the Start⇨Programs menu appears. Double-click on the StartUp folder to reveal the programs in the StartUp folder, and then click on Microsoft Word and click the Remove button. Click Close to return to the Taskbar Properties dialog box, and then click OK.

Playing with Command Line Parameters

Didn't command line parameters vanish 250 million years ago at the end of the Paleo-DOS epoch? I thought so too, until I discovered that command line

parameters are alive and well even with Word 97. These parameters are summarized in Table 28-2.

Table 28-2 Word's Command-Line Parameters

Command	*What It Does*
winword *filename*	Automatically opens a file.
winword /n	Starts Word without loading an initial empty document.
winword /a	Starts Word without loading any templates. Default settings are used for options.
winword /m*macro*	Starts Word and automatically runs a macro.
winword /m	Prevents any AutoExec macro from running.

To use these switches, you must start Word from a shortcut. To create a shortcut that has one of these switches, follow these steps:

1. **Double-click on the My Computer icon on your desktop, then locate the \Program Files\Microsoft Office\Office folder in your C drive.**
2. **Point to the winword.exe icon. Press and hold the right mouse button and drag the winword.exe icon from the My Computer window to your desktop.**
3. **After you release the right mouse button, a pop-up menu appears. Select Create Shortcut Here.**

   A shortcut icon is created on your desktop.
4. **Right-click the new shortcut icon and select the Properties command.**

   The Properties dialog box appears.
5. **Click the Shortcut tab and edit the command that appears in the Target field to include the switch you want to use. Place the switch outside the quotation marks.**

   For example:

   ```
   C:\Program Files\Microsoft Office\Office\ winword.exe
        /m
   ```
6. **Click OK.**

That's it. Now, when you start Word using the desktop icon you just created, the switch is used.

Using Word As Your E-Mail Editor

If you use Microsoft Outlook (which comes with Office 97) for your e-mail, you can set up Word to be your e-mail editor. Having Word as your e-mail editor enables you to use all of Word's formatting capabilities in your electronic mail. Bear in mind that recipients of your mail won't be able to appreciate all of this fancy formatting unless they also use Word as their e-mail editor. But if you frequently exchange e-mail with friends who also use Outlook, you may want to use Word as your e-mail editor.

When you run Outlook for the first time, it offers to set up Word to be its e-mail editor. If you decline the offer, you can easily configure Word as your e-mail editor later on by calling up Outlook's Tools➪Options command, clicking the E-Mail tab, and selecting the Use Microsoft Word as the e-mail editor option.

Figure 28-7 shows a message being edited in Outlook, using Word as the e-mail editor. At first glance, the e-mail window may not look like Word at all. But rest assured, it is. The menu bar has all of Word's familiar menus: File, Edit, View, Insert, Format, Tools, Table, and Help. Note one additional menu — Compose — which appears only when you use Word as an e-mail editor.

Notice also that Word's Formatting toolbar appears in the e-mail window. By calling up the View➪Toolbars, you can summon any of Word's other toolbars as well.

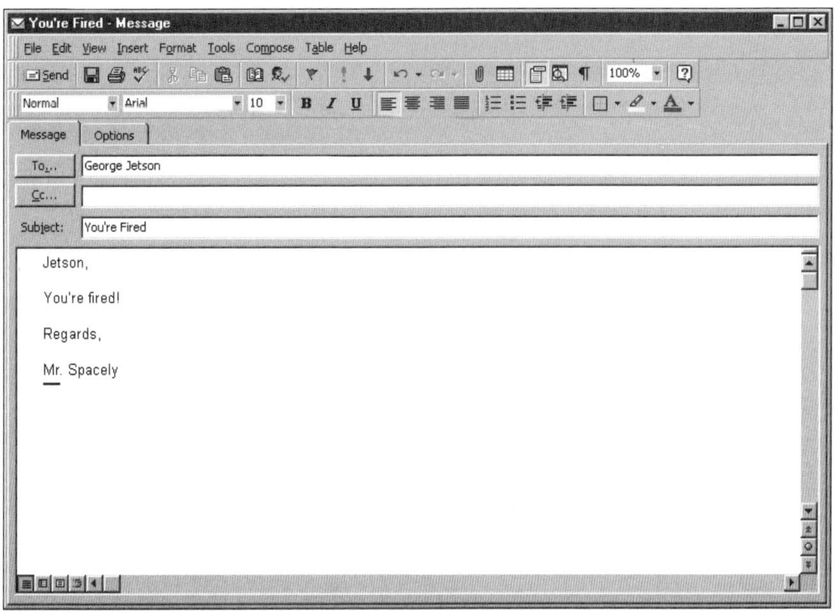

Figure 28-7: Using Word as an e-mail editor.

The AutoSummarize Feature

Word 97 sports a new feature called AutoSummarize, which attempts to analyze a document and highlight the most-important portions of the document so that you don't have to read the whole thing. You summon the AutoSummarize feature by calling up the Tools➪AutoSummarize command. Word then tries to extract the most important 25 percent of the document by analyzing the sentences in the document and trying to figure out which sentences seem to be related to the most recurring themes found in the document.

It sounds like a good idea, and it would be — if it worked. Unfortunately, the AutoSummarize feature doesn't do a particularly good job of picking out which portions of the document are important enough to summarize.

I offer as proof the AutoSummarize feature's attempt at summarizing the Declaration of Independence, shown in Figure 28-8. AutoSummarize skipped over what most of us learned in grade school is the most important sentence in the entire Declaration: "We hold these truths to be self-evident, that all men are created equal, that they are endowed by their Creator with certain unalienable rights, that among these are life, liberty and the pursuit of happiness." If you relied on the Word AutoSummarize feature, you'd miss this sentence entirely.

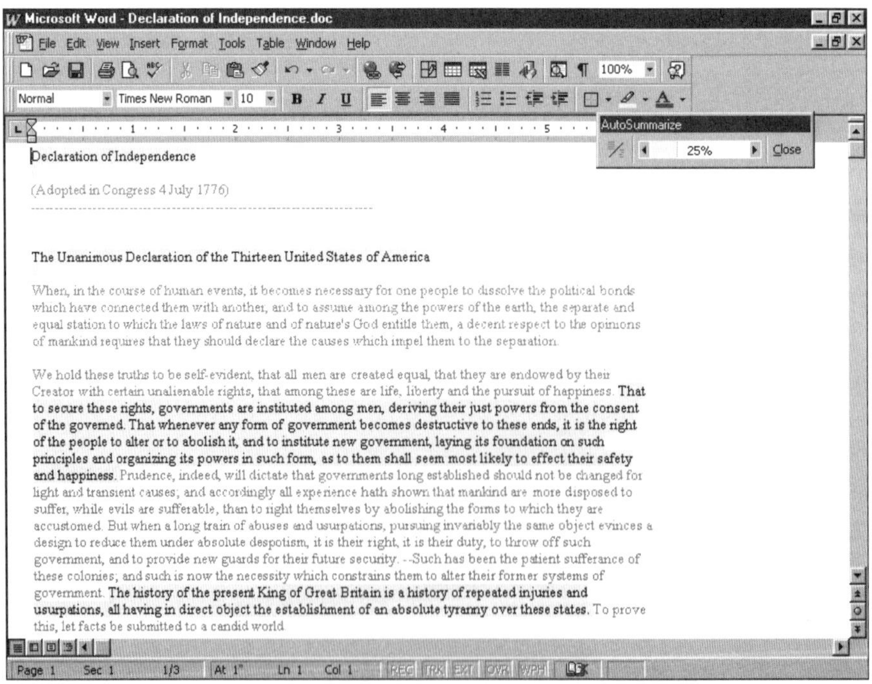

Figure 28-8: AutoSummarize misses the mark when it comes to the Declaration of Independence.

Am I being too critical? Maybe. But the point is that only a human reader can tell what part of a document is truly more important. The AutoSummarize feature is interesting but not reliable enough to use. I sure wouldn't use it when studying for a test or job interview.

Fun with the Right Mouse Button

We Windows users have one stunning advantage over Macintosh users: We have more buttons on our mice than they do. Most of us have two mouse buttons, and some of us even have three. Lowly Macintosh users have but one mouse button.

For years, these extra mouse buttons were fun to brag about at parties but offered few real benefits. With Word though, you can at long last use the right mouse button constructively: Click the right mouse button, and a shortcut menu pops up that's loaded with commands that are relevant to whatever you right-clicked. For example, right-click some plain text and you get the text shortcut menu, shown in Figure 28-9.

Figure 28-9: The shortcut menu for regular text.

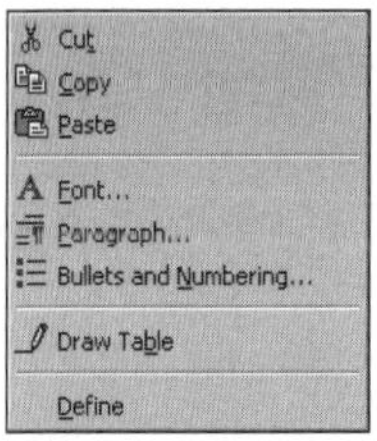

The specific commands that appear in a shortcut menu depend on what text is selected or pointed to when you click the right mouse button.

In all, there are more than 40 different shortcut menus that pop up, depending on where you right-click. There's a special shortcut menu for right-clicking a floating picture, a hyperlink, a table cell, a heading paragraph, a field, a drop cap, and more. There's even a special shortcut menu for right-clicking a toolbar.

- If you're interested, you can see a complete listing of all 40-plus shortcut menus by calling up the Tools➪Customize command, clicking the Toolbars tab, and displaying the Shortcut Menus toolbar. The special Shortcut Menus toolbar contains menus that let you display all of the available shortcut menus.

- If you discover that your favorite command doesn't appear in a shortcut menu, use the Tools➪Customize command to add the command to the shortcut menu. See Chapter 25 for a refresher on creating custom menus.
- Right-clicking plays an important role in the on-the-fly spell and grammar checker. If you right-click a word that has been marked as misspelled, a list of suggested spellings appears in the shortcut menu. Right click a grammar error and you see information about the problem detected by the grammar checker and, in some cases, a list of suggested corrections.

Surprising Places You Can Double-Click

Double-clicking is the art of clicking the mouse button twice, really fast. Depending on what the mouse is pointing at when you double-click, various things happen:

- Double-click a word to select that word. (You can also triple-click to select an entire paragraph.)
- Double-click a toolbar to change the toolbar to a floater. Double-click it again to send it back to its fixed location.
- Double-click an open carton of milk in the refrigerator to remove floaters.

Interesting things can happen when you double-click various parts of the status bar at the bottom of the Word window:

- Double-click the letters REC on the status bar to pop up the Record Macro dialog box and record a macro. See Chapter 26 for more information about macros.
- Double-click the letters TRK in the status bar to track changes. See Chapter 24 for more information.
- Double-click the letters EXT to change Word into Extend mode, where every move causes Word to extend the highlight to select more and more text. The Extend mode will drive you crazy, and you'll want to double-click EXT again to make it stop.
- Double-click the letters OVR to throw Word into overtype mode, in which any text you type clobbers the text already on the screen. Double-click again to revert to regular insert-text-as-you-type mode. (Double-clicking OVR is hardly easier than pressing Insert, which accomplishes the same thing.)

- Double-click the letters WPH to pop up the WordPerfect Help dialog box.
- Double-click the spelling icon to jump to the next misspelled word.
- To cancel printing when you print a document, double-click the dancing printer icon that appears in the status bar.
- Double-click anywhere else on the status bar to pop up the Go To dialog box.

Sometimes it's fun to double-click in the ruler:

- Double-click a tab stop in the ruler to pop up the Tabs dialog box.
- Double-click the indentation sliders in the ruler to pop up the Paragraph (Indents and Spacing) dialog box.
- In a table, double-click the portion of the ruler that appears between cells to pop up the Cell Height and Width dialog box.
- If you have two or more columns, double click the portion of the ruler that appears between the columns to pop up the Columns dialog box.
- Double-click elsewhere on the ruler to pop up the Page Setup dialog box.

Index

NOTE: Page numbers in *italics* refer to illustrations or charts.

• Symbols & Numbers •

• A •

• B •

• C •

• D •

• G •

• H •

• I •

• N •

• Q •

• R •

• S •

• T •

• U •

• V •

• W •

• X •

• Z •

IDG BOOKS WORLDWIDE REGISTRATION CARD

Title of this book: MORE Word 97 For Windows® For Dummies®

My overall rating of this book: ❑ Very good [1] ❑ Good [2] ❑ Satisfactory [3] ❑ Fair [4] ❑ Poor [5]

How I first heard about this book:

❑ Found in bookstore; name: [6] ❑ Book review: [7]

❑ Advertisement: [8] ❑ Catalog: [9]

❑ Word of mouth; heard about book from friend, co-worker, etc.: [10] ❑ Other: [11]

What I liked most about this book:

What I would change, add, delete, etc., in future editions of this book:

Other comments:

Number of computer books I purchase in a year: ❑ 1 [12] ❑ 2-5 [13] ❑ 6-10 [14] ❑ More than 10 [15]

I would characterize my computer skills as: ❑ Beginner [16] ❑ Intermediate [17] ❑ Advanced [18] ❑ Professional [19]

I use ❑ DOS [20] ❑ Windows [21] ❑ OS/2 [22] ❑ Unix [23] ❑ Macintosh [24] ❑ Other: [25]____________________ (please specify)

I would be interested in new books on the following subjects:
(please check all that apply, and use the spaces provided to identify specific software)

❑ Word processing: [26] ❑ Spreadsheets: [27]

❑ Data bases: [28] ❑ Desktop publishing: [29]

❑ File Utilities: [30] ❑ Money management: [31]

❑ Networking: [32] ❑ Programming languages: [33]

❑ Other: [34]

I use a PC at (please check all that apply): ❑ home [35] ❑ work [36] ❑ school [37] ❑ other: [38] ________________

The disks I prefer to use are ❑ 5.25 [39] ❑ 3.5 [40] ❑ other: [41]____________________

I have a CD ROM: ❑ yes [42] ❑ no [43]

I plan to buy or upgrade computer hardware this year: ❑ yes [44] ❑ no [45]

I plan to buy or upgrade computer software this year: ❑ yes [46] ❑ no [47]

Name: Business title: [48] Type of Business: [49]

Address (❑ home [50] ❑ work [51]/Company name:)

Street/Suite#

City [52]/State [53]/Zipcode [54]: Country [55]

❑ **I liked this book!** You may quote me by name in future IDG Books Worldwide promotional materials.

My daytime phone number is ____________________

IDG BOOKS WORLDWIDE
THE WORLD OF COMPUTER KNOWLEDGE®